U.S. STAMP YEARBOOK 2001

A comprehensive record of technical data, design development and stories behind all of the stamps, stamped envelopes, postal cards and souvenir cards issued by the United States Postal Service in 2001.

By
George Amick

Published by *Linn's Stamp News*, the largest and most informative stamp newspaper in the world. *Linn's* is owned by Amos Press, 911 Vandemark Road, Sidney, Ohio 45365. Amos Press also publishes *Scott Stamp Monthly* and the Scott line of catalogs.

ISSN 0748-996X

ACKNOWLEDGMENTS

I am indebted to many people for their help in researching and writing *Linn's U.S. Stamp Yearbook* for 2001.

Foremost among them are Terrence McCaffrey, manager of stamp development for the U.S. Postal Service, and his art directors: Carl Herrman, Phil Jordan, Ethel Kessler, Derry Noyes, Howard Paine and Richard Sheaff. Year after year, their extraordinary generosity with their time and assistance makes the *Yearbook* possible.

Invaluable assistance has been provided by USPS officials Cathy Caggiano, Don Smeraldi, Charles Delaney, Robert Williams, and members of the Citizens' Stamp Advisory Committee. Louis Plummer, Sidney Brown and their associates at PhotoAssist are always available to answer my questions, no matter how trivial.

Thanks also to the artists, designers and photographers who shared their experiences in creating stamp art, including Lisa Catalone, Carr Clifton, John Eastcott, Patricia Fisher, Robert Hautman, Arnold Holeywell, Lawrence Manning, Wendell Minor, Yva Momatiuk, Robert Llewellyn, John Thompson and Mohamed Zakariya.

Others whose help was essential are Cecilia Wertheimer of the Bureau of Engraving and Printing; Joe Sheeran of Ashton-Potter (USA) Ltd.; Terrence Brown of the Society of Illustrators; Alan Cubbage and Monica Metzler of Northwestern University; Pete Dunker, postmaster of Wall, South Dakota; Amy Hooker of the Petroleum Museum; Sally McKay and Thomas Stepp of the University of South Carolina; Ron Menchine, whose postcard collection provided the designs for the Legendary Playing Fields stamps; and Walt Reed of Illustration House,

I'm grateful to many philatelic colleagues, including Robert Dumaine, Stephen Esrati, Kim Johnson, John Larson, Michael Laurence, Michael Schreiber and Charles Snee. I owe special thanks again to Veronica Schreiber, who was responsible for the layout of *Yearbook 2001*.

Finally, as always, I owe my gratitude to the best philatelic book editor in the business, Donna Houseman of *Linn's Stamp News*, and to my wife, Donna Amick, for her tireless research assistance and unfailing encouragement.

George Amick

CONTENTS

Legend for Linn's Yearbook Specification Charts

The following is an explanation of the terminology used in the charts that appear at the beginning of each chapter in this *Yearbook*:

Date of Issue: The official first-day-sale date designated by the Postal Service.

Catalog Number: The number or numbers assigned to the stamp or other postal item by the Scott *Specialized Catalogue of United States Stamps & Covers.*

Colors: The color or colors in which the stamp is printed. A number in parentheses preceded by the letters PMS refers to the color's designation under the Pantone Matching System.

First-Day Cancel: The post office location that is identified in the official first-day cancellations.

FDCs Canceled: This figure represents the total number of first-day covers hand-canceled and machine-canceled for collectors and dealers by Stamp Fulfillment Services in Kansas City, Missouri. It does not include covers canceled at the first-day site on the day of issue.

Format: The number and arrangement of stamps in the panes and printing plates.

Perf: The number of teeth or holes per 2 centimeters, as measured with a perforation gauge, and the type of perforator used.

Selvage Inscriptions: Informational or promotional material printed in the selvage of certain sheet stamps.

Selvage Markings: Standard markings, other than plate numbers, of the kind found on most sheet stamps.

Cover Markings: Material printed on the inside and outside of booklet covers.

Designer: The artist commissioned by USPS to prepare the artwork for the stamp. In 1997, USPS began describing the artist as the "illustrator" and reserved the designation "designer" for the specialist who adapts the illustration to a stamp design.

Art Director: The USPS staff member or private-sector graphic arts specialist assigned to work with the illustrator and designer. Often the art director is also the designer.

Typographer: The specialist who selects and arranges the kind and size of type for the letters and numbers in the stamp design.

Engraver: Person who engraves the die for a stamp with an intaglio component.

Modeler: The specialist who takes the artwork and typography and makes any adaptations that are necessary to meet the requirements of the printing process. After completing this work, the modeler makes a stamp-size, full-color model of the design, which must be approved by USPS before production begins.

Stamp Manufacturing: The agency or company that manufactured the stamp, and the process by which it was made.

Quantity Ordered: The number of stamps or other postal items ordered by USPS.

Plate/Sleeve/Cylinder Number Detail: The number and location of plate, sleeve and/or cylinder numbers on the selvage of sheet stamps, on the peel-off strips, covers or stamps of booklet panes, and on coil stamps at constant intervals along the strip.

Plate/Cylinder Numbers Reported: The numbers or combinations of numbers of plates or cylinders used to print the stamp as reported and compiled by members of the United States Stamp Society.

Tagging: The method used to add phosphor to the stamp in order to activate automated mail-handling equipment in post offices.

INTRODUCTION

Despite two rate changes in 2001 that produced a record number of definitive stamps, the size of the overall United States stamp program took a significant dip, with the U.S. Postal Service issuing 155 stamps and postal stationery items during the year. It was the lowest output since 1997, when 130 stamps and postal cards were released, and it was well below the USPS record of 216 items issued in 2000.

One of the 2001 issues, the 34¢ United We Stand stamp, was planned, designed and printed in near record time in response to the September 11 terrorist attacks on the World Trade Center and the Pentagon. The Citizens' Stamp Advisory Committee met by e-mail to work on the project, and the stamp was issued October 24, exactly six weeks and a day after the deadly aircraft hijackings.

Just 65 commemoratives were issued in 2001, the lowest number in that category since 1991, when 46 were released. Forty of the 2001 commemoratives could be found in three large multiple-stamp panes of 20 or 10.

One pane, in the Classic Collections series, reproduced the art of 20 notable American illustrators, including several whose work previously appeared on U.S. stamps. The Baseball's Legendary Playing Fields 20-stamp pane featured 10 baseball stadiums of the present and past. The third entry in the ongoing Nature of America series depicted a Great Plains prairie scene, with 10 self-adhesive stamps that could be peeled out of the design.

The Postal Service acknowledged philatelic history with a souvenir sheet marking the 100th anniversary of the Pan-American Exposition in Buffalo, New York. Reproduced on the sheet, through use of the original engraved dies, were the three inverted-center errors from the series of bicolor stamps issued in 1901 to commemorate the exposition.

The 2001 program included 42 definitives, an all-time high for the category. These included a Great Seal Official coil stamp and three airmail stamps in the Scenic American Landscapes series, which USPS previously had called Scenic American Landmarks.

With the exception of the United We Stand stamp, each of these definitives was issued in response to the two rate hikes that took place during 2001: an overall set of increases January 7 that included raising the first-class letter rate from 33¢ to 34¢, and a targeted hike July 1 that included increases in the postcard rate from 20¢ to 21¢, the additional-ounce rate from 21¢ to 23¢ and the basic Express Mail rate from $12.25 to $12.45. Because of the second rate increase at mid-year, the stand-alone life of many of the definitives issued in the first half of 2001 was short.

Helping boost the total number of definitives, and complicating life for collectors, was the Postal Service's decision to issue many of its rate-change stamps in different formats. And within single formats for two of them, the 20¢ George Washington and the 21¢ Bison, collectible variations exist in the gauge of the die cuts. It was left to the collecting community to discover these varieties, inasmuch as the Postal Service, far from announcing them, wasn't even aware of them.

There were 22 special stamps released in 2001, including two new additions to the Holiday Celebrations series that USPS said would be the last new designs in the series: one honoring Islamic eids, or festivals, and the other marking Thanksgiving. The postal stationery issues included 22 postal cards and four stamped envelopes.

34¢ YEAR OF THE SNAKE LUNAR NEW YEAR SERIES

Date of Issue: January 20, 2001

Catalog Number: Scott 3500

Colors: black, cyan, magenta, yellow, red (PMS 241)

First-Day Cancel: Oakland, California

First-Day Cancellations: 132,440

Format: pane of 20, horizontal, 4 across, 5 down. Offset printing plates of 180 (12 across, 15 around).

Gum Type: water-activated

Overall Stamp Size: 1.56 by 0.99 inches; 39.624 by 25.171mm

Pane Size: 7.24 by 5.94 inches; 183.896 by 150.876mm

Perforations: 11¼ (Wista stroke perforator)

Selvage Markings: "©2000/USPS." ".34/x20/$6.80." "PLATE/POSITION" and diagram. Universal Product Code (UPC) "450300" in 2 positions.

Designer, Illustrator and Typographer: Clarence Lee of Honolulu, Hawaii

Art Director: Terrence McCaffrey (USPS)

Modeler: Joseph Sheeran of Ashton-Potter (USA) Ltd., Williamsville, New York

Stamp Manufacturing: Stamps printed for Ashton-Potter by Sterling Sommer of Tonawanda, New York, on Akiyama 628 offset press. Stamps finished by Ashton-Potter.

Quantity Ordered: 55,000,000

Plate Number Detail: 5 plate numbers preceded by the letter P in selvage above or below each corner stamp

Plate Number Combination Reporteds: P11111, P22222

Paper Supplier: Tullis Russell

Tagging: phosphored paper

The Stamp

The Postal Service's first commemorative stamp of 2001 marked the Year of the Snake in the modified lunar (lunisolar) calendar that is used in China and other parts of Asia. It was issued January 20 in Oakland, California, and bore a 34¢ denomination to cover the new first-class rate that had taken effect 13 days earlier.

The stamp was the ninth in an annual sequence of stamps that feature the animals for which the lunar years are named. There are 12 animal symbols in the lunisolar calendar. The year 4699 was a Year of the Snake, which is the sixth year of the 12-year cycle, and ran from January 24, 2001, to February 11, 2002.

Many non-Asian countries now issue annual Lunar New Year stamps and souvenir sheets. The first such stamp from the U.S. Postal Service appeared late in 1992 and marked the forthcoming Year of the Rooster. It proved so popular with Asian-Americans and overseas buyers that USPS committed itself to a series. Subsequent stamps commemorated the years of the Dog, Boar, Rat, Ox, Tiger, Hare and Dragon. Future stamps will be for the years of the Horse (2002), Sheep (2003) and, completing the set, Monkey (2004).

Each design is the work of the same illustrator, Clarence Lee, a Chinese-American from Honolulu, Hawaii, who completed all 12 of them in the 1990s. Each bears a stylized image of the creature that gave its name to the year, along with the appropriate Chinese New Year inscription in Kanji characters and the words "HAPPY NEW YEAR!" in English.

The first stamp in the series was printed by American Bank Note Company by a combination of intaglio and offset. The next six were gravure-printed by Stamp Venturers or its successor firm, Sennett Security Products. Then came the Year of the Dragon and Year of the Snake stamps, which were printed by offset lithography by Sterling Sommer for Ashton Potter (USA) Ltd. of Williamsville, New York. Like its predecessors, the Year of the Snake commemorative was issued in panes of 20 and has conventional perforations and water-activated gum.

According to Chinese legend cited by the Postal Service, the order of the 12 signs of the zodiac was determined by Buddha when he invited all the animals in the kingdom to a meeting, and only 12 attended. The first animal was the talkative Rat, the second was the hard-working Ox, and these were followed by the aggressive Tiger and the cautious Hare. The outspoken Dragon, the philosophical Snake, the physically active Horse, the artistic Goat, the spirited Monkey and the showy Rooster joined the others. The last to attend were the watchful Dog and the meticulous Boar. Buddha gave each animal a year of its own, bestowing the nature and characteristics of each upon those born in that animal's year.

The Lunar New Year, a time of celebration, renewal and hope for the future, is one of the most important holidays in the lunar calendar. The snake is a symbol of wisdom and charm, and people born in the Year of the Snake are said to be intelligent, philosophical, elegant and romantic, and have excellent manners.

The Design

Clarence Lee, who has headed his own graphic design firm in Honolulu for more than three decades, depicts the animal on each Lunar New Year stamp in a way that suggests traditional Chinese cut-paper art. He cuts the figure from paper with an Exacto knife, then photographs the cutout and overlays the negative on an airbrushed background so the background color shows through the transparent parts of the figure.

The artist subcontracts the Kanji characters to Lau Bun, a professional calligrapher in Honolulu. Lau Bun is an elderly immigrant from China who comes from a long line of calligraphers. On the Year of the Snake stamp, the character at the upper left signifies "snake" and the character beneath it, which is common to all the stamps, signifies "year." The words "HAPPY NEW YEAR!", in English, are in the upper-right corner.

As with the previous stamps in the series, the featured creature, in this case the snake, is shown in subtle tones of orange, yellow and green. Its coiled body is covered with patterns of concentric arcs, its tongue is extended and it is framed by stylized leaves. It is silhouetted against a solid red-violet background, similar to the background of the third stamp in the series, for the Year of the Pig. In accordance with a plan developed by Lee and Terrence McCaffrey, manager of stamp development for USPS and art director for the Lunar New Year series, the background colors of the first six stamps of the series proceeded through the darker portion of the spectrum, from bright red to blue-green, and the second six are following the same color sequence.

Because the stamp was printed by offset, which USPS considers a less secure printing method than intaglio or gravure, microprinting is included in its design as an extra security device. It consists of the letters "USPS" in one of the arcs on the snake's body (see illustration).

The microprinted "USPS" on the Year of the Snake stamp is printed in reddish purple, the same color as the background of the stamp, and is difficult to see. It is immediately above the bottom-most concentric semicircle in the pattern on the snake's body that is just below the loop in the body.

First-day Facts

Benjamin P. Ocasio, USPS vice president for diversity development, dedicated the stamp in a ceremony at the Asia Pacific Cultural Center on Oakland's Pacific Renaissance Plaza. Jerry Brown, mayor of Oakland and former governor of California, was the speaker, and Oakland Postmaster Lawrence Barnes was master of ceremonies. Other participants included George Ong, national president, Organization of Chinese Americans; Claudine Cheng, the organization's past national president; and Hiroko Kurihara, president of the board of the Asia Pacific Cultural Center.

The earliest-known prerelease use of a Year of the Snake stamp was on a cover machine-canceled in Springfield, Missouri, January 19, one day before the official first day of issue.

34¢ ROY WILKINS
BLACK HERITAGE SERIES

Date of Issue: January 24, 2001

Catalog Number: Scott 3501

Colors: black, blue

First-Day Cancel: Minneapolis, Minnesota

First-Day Cancellations: 111,879

Format: Self-adhesive pane of 20, vertical, 5 across, 4 down. Offset printing plates of 180 (15 across, 12 around).

Gum Type: self-adhesive

Overall Stamp Size: 0.99 by 1.56 inches; 25.146 by 39.624mm

Pane Size: 5.900 by 7.135 inches; 149.860 by 181.229mm

Perforations: 11½ by 11¼ (die-cut simulated perforations) (Arpeco die cutter)

Selvage Markings: "© 2000/USPS." ".34/x20/$6.80." "PLATE/POSITION" and diagram. Universal Product Code (UPC) "450400" in 2 positions.

Photographers: Morgan and Marvin Smith

Designer, Typographer and Art Director: Richard Sheaff of Scottsdale, Arizona

Modeler: Joseph Sheeran of Ashton-Potter (USA) Ltd., Williamsville, New York

Stamp Manufacturing: Stamps printed by Ashton-Potter (USA) Ltd. on offset portion of Stevens Variable Size Security Documents webfed 6-color offset, 3-color intaglio press. Stamps finished by Ashton-Potter.

Quantity Ordered: 200,000,000

Plate Number Detail: 2 plate numbers preceded by the letter P in selvage above or below each corner stamp

13

Plate Number Combinations Reported: P11, P22, P33

Paper Supplier: Fasson/Glatfelter

Tagging: phosphored paper

The Stamp

The 24th annual stamp in the Black Heritage series honored civil rights leader Roy Wilkins in the 100th anniversary year of his birth. Wilkins was an officer of the National Association for the Advancement of Colored People for 46 years, including 12 years as its executive director.

The 34¢ stamp was issued January 24 at Wilkins' alma mater, the University of Minnesota in Minneapolis. A self-adhesive, it was printed by the offset process by Ashton-Potter (USA) Ltd. and sold in panes of 20. Like all the Black Heritage stamps, it is commemorative size, vertically arranged.

USPS ordered 200 million Wilkins stamps, more than any previous individual stamp in the series; the previous leader was the Martin Luther King Jr. stamp of 1979, at 166,435,000 stamps.

In 1998 only 45 million 32¢ Madam C.J. Walker stamps were printed, and the Postal Service found the issue soon was unavailable to customers in many post offices. The print order was increased to 100 million for the 33¢ Malcolm X stamp in 1999, and 150 million for the 33¢ Patricia Roberts Harris stamp in 2000.

The Postal Service unveiled the design of the Wilkins stamp July 9, 2000, more than six months before its issue date, at the opening session of the NAACP's 91st annual national convention in Baltimore, Maryland.

Doing the honors on that occasion were Julian Bond, chairman of the organization's board of directors; Kweisi Mfume, NAACP president and chief executive officer; U.S. Representative Elijah Cummings, D-Maryland; and Roger Wilkins, nephew and only surviving relative of Roy Wilkins. Representing the Postal Service was LeGree S. Daniels, a member of the USPS Board of Governors.

At the unveiling, Bond said: "Roy Wilkins did as much to advance the cause of civil rights as anyone, but his quiet demeanor and selfless personality has made history overlook him. This stamp is an opportunity for all Americans to learn more about this gentle giant."

Wilkins was born in St. Louis, Missouri, August 30, 1901, the grandson of a slave, and was raised in the home of an aunt and uncle living in St. Paul, Minnesota. He graduated from the University of Minnesota in 1923 with a degree in sociology with a minor in journalism.

He worked for several years as a writer and managing editor for *The Kansas City Call*, a prominent black weekly, and joined the NAACP as assistant executive secretary in 1931. In 1934 he succeeded W.E.B. DuBois as the editor of *Crisis*, the organization's official magazine, and held that position for 15 years.

Wilkins was involved in numerous historic civil rights events, including the NAACP Legal Defense Fund lawsuit, *Brown vs. Board of Education*, that resulted in the 1954 U.S. Supreme Court decision that racial segregation in the public schools was unconstitutional. He helped organize and spoke at the 1963 March on Washington for Jobs and Freedom. Under his leadership, the NAACP campaigned for the Civil Rights Act of 1964, the Voting Rights Act of 1965 and the Fair Housing Act of 1968.

As NAACP executive secretary and executive director from 1955 until his retirement in 1977, he conferred with presidents and was widely respected for his dedication to social reform and the principle of non-violence.

Wilkins received the NAACP's Spingarn Medal in 1964 for his civil rights work. In 1969 he received the Presidential Medal of Freedom, the highest civilian award in the United States. The citation for the award reads, in part, "... he has stirred the nation's conscience and mobilized its commitment to make good the century-old promise of emancipation. In so doing, he has helped make our democratic dream a living reality."

He died in New York City September 8, 1981, at the age of 80. A Roy Wilkins memorial was built in St. Paul in 1995.

Shortly after the stamp was issued, the Postal Service repeated earlier official denials that the Black Heritage series would be discontinued. A March 23 press release headed "Rumor about Black Heritage stamp series discontinuing is untrue" read as follows:

"WASHINGTON — Recent media reports and Internet messages saying the U.S. Postal Service is discontinuing its long-standing Black Heritage series of stamps are completely false, but quickly turning into an urban legend! Also untrue is the allegation that the Postal Service has directed that the Black Heritage series stamps be destroyed while still available for sale.

"Here are the facts:

"• The Black Heritage stamp series is one of the most popular of the Postal Service's U.S. commemorative stamp series. As a result of customer demand for the stamps, the Postal Service increased production of this year's Roy Wilkins stamp and last year's Patricia Roberts Harris stamp.

"• It is not the policy of the Postal Service to destroy stamps while they remain available for sale. Post offices with low sales of stamps are advised to return excess stock to their Stamp Distribution Office for subsequent distribution to post offices where stamp sales are high. Generally, commemorative stamps are available for sale for about a year after they are issued.

" 'It is unfortunate that such rumors have spread, and we hope that the Postal Service's ongoing commitment to honoring the historical achievements and contributions of African Americans on stamps will dispel any further concerns,' said Cathy Caggiano, executive director, Stamp Services. 'We have no plans to discontinue the Black Heritage series.' "

The microprinted letters "USPS" can be found on Wilkins' shirt, between the right collar and the right lapel of his jacket.

The Design

The Wilkins stamp is the sixth consecutive stamp in the Black Heritage series with a design based on a monochromatic photograph. The photograph of Wilkins chosen by Richard Sheaff, the designer and art director, was made in the 1940s and shows him in suit and tie. The picture was made by Morgan and Marvin Smith, twin brothers who documented the achievements of black Americans.

The name "ROY WILKINS," in dropout white Futura Medium capitals, is across the bottom of the stamp. The words "BLACK HERITAGE," in block capitals, run up the left side, behind Wilkins' shoulder, and "34/USA" is tucked into the upper-right corner.

Ashton-Potter used only two inks, blue and black, to print the stamp. Because it was produced by offset, USPS required that it include microprinting in the design as a security measure. The letters "USPS" can be found on Wilkins' shirt, between the right collar and the right lapel of his jacket.

First-day Facts

John Sawyer 3d of CSAC dedicated the stamp in a ceremony at the University of Minnesota's Northrop Auditorium. Sawyer was introduced by Wayne D. Rogers, district manager of USPS' Northland District.

Tributes to Roy Wilkins were given by Benjamin Hooks, former NAACP executive director; Lloyd Jordan, international president of the Omega Psi Phi fraternity; Samuel Myers Jr., director of the Wilkins Center at the University of Minnesota; and Tom Mathews, co-author of *Standing Fast, The Autobiography of Roy Wilkins*. Mark G. Yudof, president of the university, gave the welcome, and the ceremony was hosted by Harris Faulkner, anchor of Channel 5/45 Eyewitness News. Honored guests included several local and area officials of USPS and of the NAACP.

The earliest-known prerelease use of a Roy Wilkins stamp was on a cover machine-canceled in Springfield, Missouri, January 19, five days before the official first day of issue.

34¢ AMERICAN ILLUSTRATORS (20 DESIGNS) CLASSIC COLLECTION SERIES

Date of Issue: February 1, 2001

Catalog Numbers: Scott 3502, pane of 20; 3502a-3502t, single stamps

Colors: brown, yellow, magenta, cyan, black; black (back of liner paper)

First-Day Cancel: New York, New York

First-Day Cancellations: 791,269

Format: Panes of 20, vertical, 5 across, 4 down. Gravure printing cylinders of 80 subjects (1 pane across, 4 around) manufactured by Southern Graphics Systems. Also sold in uncut press sheets of 4 panes, 4 across by 1 down

Gum Type: self-adhesive

Overall Stamp Size: 1.225 by 1.560 inches; 31.115 by 39.624mm

Pane Size: 7.25 by 7.75 inches; 184.15 by 196.85mm

Uncut Sheet Size: 28.75 by 7.75 inches

Perforations: 11¼ (die-cut simulated perfs) (Comco Commander rotary die cutter)

Selvage Inscription: "AMERICAN ILLUSTRATORS," "CLASSIC/COLLEC-TION."

Selvage Markings: ".34/x20/$6.80." "©2000/USPS." "PLATE/POSITION" and diagram.

Liner Back Markings: On header: "Advances in printing and publishing made possible by the Industrial Revolution ushered in a new era for Ameri-can/illustrators during the last quarter of the 19th century, allowing their work to be reproduced with increasing fidelity/and attracting some of the country's finest talents to the field. Illustrations originally commissioned for books,/magazines, and advertisements today serve as an invaluable artistic chronicle of American culture —/from fashions and fads to pivotal moments in history." "All stamp images reflect details of original illustra-tions. The header artwork, by illustrator Franklin Booth (1874-1948), appeared on the editorial page of *The Ladies' Home Journal*, February 1918. Maxfield Parrish illustration authorized by The Maxfield/Parrish Family Trust. Rockwell Kent illustration © Plattsburgh State Art Museum, Rockwell Kent Gallery, Plattsburgh, N.Y. Norman Rockwell illustration © 1929 The Curtis Publishing Company. John Held, Jr., illustration courtesy of Judy Held." On selvage: Universal Product Code (UPC) "560400."
On individual stamps:
"Coles Phillips (1880-1927)/consistently demonstrated/his strong sense of design/with his popular 'fadeaway/girl,' who wore colors/and patterns that blended/into the background/of each illustration./His depictions of styl-ish/women graced numerous/advertisements and/magazine covers./Lux-ite hosiery/advertisement, 1918."
"Robert Fawcett/(1903-1967)/brought a superb sense/of composition to his/magazine and advertisement/work; he was also the author/of *On the Art of Drawing*./Fawcett is best remembered/for creating detailed/illustrations to accompany/a series of Sherlock Holmes/stories in *Collier's* maga-zine./Carrier Corporation refrigeration/advertisement, 1949."
"Joseph Christian Leyendecker/(1874-1951)/illustrated more/than 300 covers for/*The Saturday Evening Post*/and was a role model/for Norman Rock-well./Leyendecker also created/the Arrow Collar Man,/an advertising icon who/won the hearts of countless/young women./Arrow Collars and Shirts/advertisement, 1923."
"Maxfield Parrish/(1870-1966) used alternating/layers of paint and varnish to/create the shimmering fantasy/lands in his popular illustrations/for books, advertisements,/magazines, and calendars. The/color of his skies is still known as/'Parrish blue.' In 1925 an/estimated one in four homes/owned a Parrish print./*Interlude* (*The Lute Players*), mural for/the East-man Theatre, Eastman School/of Music, Rochester, New York, 1922."
"James Montgomery Flagg/(1877-1960) was an outspoken/celebrity known as much for/his wit as for his drawings of/glamorous women. He was/his own model for a magazine/cover of Uncle Sam proclaiming/'I Want You,' which became/one of his many military/recruitment posters./First in the Fight, Always Faithful,/U.S. Marine Corps poster, c.1918; Library of Con-gress,/Washington, D.C."
"Dean Cornwell/(1892-1960) was a magazine/illustrator whose dynamic/paintings accompanied stories by/Ernest Hemingway, Pearl S. Buck,/and

18

other prominent writers./He is also remembered for/his murals, including an/ambitious rendering of the/history of California for the/Los Angeles Public Library./cover illustration, *True* magazine,/February 1953; Ohio River Museum,/Marietta, Ohio."

"Rose O'Neill/(1874-1944) was a self-trained/artist who invented the cupid-/like, whimsical Kewpies in 1909/while illustrating for magazines./The popular Kewpies also/appeared in advertisements,/and today Kewpie dolls/are still prized collector's/items. O'Neill was also/a talented sculptor,/novelist, and poet./Kewpie with Kewpie Doodle Dog,/date unknown."

"Howard Pyle (1853-1911)/earned his reputation as the/'father of American illustration'/by training a generation of/influential artists at his highly/selective school. Often/illustrating his own stories, Pyle/inspired readers with vivid/depictions of history and legend./*An Attack on a Galleon*, from the/story 'The Fate of a Treasure-Town' by/Howard Pyle, *Harper's Monthly Magazine*,/December 1905; Delaware Art Museum,/Wilmington, Delaware."

"Arthur Burdett Frost/(1851-1928), who specialized/in humorous drawings, is/best remembered for/illustrating the Uncle Remus/stories of Joel Chandler Harris./He was also a faithful/chronicler of sports and/rural life, especially golfing/and hunting./Br'er Rabbit watercolor,/date unknown; Sterling and Francine/Clark Art Institute, Williamstown,/Massachusetts."

"Al Parker (1906-1985)/delighted the public with/illustrations of mothers and/daughters for the covers of/women's magazines. Parker/demonstrated a wide range of/styles, constantly changing his/own approach while setting/fashion trends in the process./from 'How I Make a Picture,'/correspondence school lesson,/Famous Artists Advanced Program,/Institute of Commercial Art,/Westport, Connecticut, 1949."

"Harvey Dunn/(1884-1952) was a student of/Howard Pyle before becoming/an art teacher himself./He created haunting images/as a military artist during/World War I, and later/he recalled his youth in/a powerful series of paintings/about life on the Dakota prairie./*Something for Supper*, c1940;/Harvey Dunn Collection,/South Dakota Art Museum,/Brookings, South Dakota."

"Jon Whitcomb (1906-1988)/was a prolific magazine illustrator/known for his depictions of/stylish and glamorous women./Whitcomb served as a Navy/artist in the Pacific during/World War II, and also/created a dramatic series of/advertisements anticipating/the postwar homecomings/of American soldiers./*Back Home for Keeps*,/Oneida, Ltd., silverware/advertisement, 1943."

"Neysa McMein/(1888-1949) was a magazine/and advertising illustrator,/a portrait artist, and/a member of the/Algonquin Round Table./One of McMein's significant/contributions to commercial/art was her domestic/design for the original/Betty Crocker character./cover illustration,/*McCall's* magazine,/June 1932."

"Jessie Willcox Smith/(1863-1935) was a student of/Howard Pyle who specialized in/pictures of mothers and children/for magazines. In addition to/creating nearly 200 covers for/*Good Housekeeping*, she is also/remembered for her enchanting/illustrations in children's books/such as Charles Kingsley's/*The Water-Babies*./*The First Lesson*,/from *The Ladies' Home Journal*,/December 1904."

"Edwin Austin Abbey/(1852-1911) began his career as a/magazine illustrator and later/achieved renown as a painter/and muralist. A meticulous/ researcher, Abbey strived for/detail and authenticity in his/depictions of Shakespearean and/other traditionally British subjects./*Galahad's Departure*, from *Harper's/Monthly Magazine*, September 1902;/illustration for *The Quest of the/Holy Grail*, 1895-1902, mural for/the Boston Public Library."

"John Held, Jr./(1889-1958)/was a cartoonist/who chronicled American/culture and college life/during the Jazz Age./He also wrote and/illustrated several books,/designed sets for plays, and/served as artist-in-residence/at Harvard University and/the University of Georgia./*The Girl He Left Behind*, 1920s."

"Norman Rockwell (1894-1978)/charmed the country for/decades with his idealized/depictions of American life/in magazines, calendars, and/advertisements. He painted/more than 300 covers for/*The Saturday Evening Post*/and was awarded the/Presidential Medal of Freedom/in 1977./cover illustration,/*The Saturday Evening Post*,/March 9, 1929."

"Newell Convers Wyeth/(1882-1945) was a student of/Howard Pyle before his prolific/career as a book and magazine/illustrator. Whether painting/ pirates, knights, or scenes from/American history, Wyeth brought/a strong sense of drama to his/work, turning literary masterpieces/into illustrated classics./Captain Bill Bones, 1911,/from *Treasure Island* by Robert Louis/Stevenson; Brandywine River Museum,/Chadds Ford, Pennsylvania."

"Rockwell Kent/(1882-1971) was a versatile/wood engraver, lithographer,/ book illustrator, painter,/and muralist. He designed/a striking edition/of Herman Melville's/*Moby Dick*, and wrote/and illustrated accounts/of his rugged travels/in Alaska, Greenland,/and South America./from *Moby Dick*,/Random House, 1930."

"Frederic Remington/(1861-1909) romanticized/the American cowboy/even as he recorded the end/of the Old West in paintings/and magazine illustrations./He served as an artist and/correspondent in Cuba during/the Spanish-American War,/and was also noted for/his bronze sculptures./*A Dash for the Timber*, 1889;/Amon Carter Museum,/Fort Worth, Texas."

Designer and Art Director: Carl Herrman of Carlsbad, California

Typographer: John Boyd of New York, New York

Stamp Manufacturing: Stamps printed by Avery Dennison Security Printing Division, Clinton, South Carolina, on 8-color Dia Nippon Kiko webfed gravure press. Stamps processed by Avery Dennison.

Quantity Ordered: 125,000,000

Cylinder Number Detail: 1 set of 5 cylinder numbers preceded by the letter V in selvage next to lower left (Frederick Remington) stamp

Cylinder Number Combinations Reported: V11111, V11121, V11131, V11211, V11231, V22112, V22122, V22132, V22212, V22222

Paper Supplier: Fasson Division of Avery Dennison

Tagging: block tagging over stamps

The Stamps

The best of America's illustrators of the late 19th and 20th centuries created a body of brilliantly conceived and crafted artwork for books, magazines, advertisements, posters, prints and murals that entertained and charmed generations of their countrymen. On February 1, the Postal Service issued a pane of stamps in its Classic Collection series honoring 20 of these artists, with each stamp depicting one of their works or a detail thereof.

The first-day ceremony took place in the main floor gallery of the Society of Illustrators, 128 East 62nd Street, New York City, as part of the society's centennial year celebration. Terrence McCaffrey, manager of stamp development for USPS, and all six of his part-time art directors are members of the society.

The set was the tenth in the Classic Collection series, which began with the Legends of the West pane in 1994, and was the second to be self-adhesive. Like the others, it consists of 20 stamps, each with a different design. It was similar in concept to the Four Centuries of American Art pane of 1998, which depicted details from the paintings of 20 distinguished American artists.

The American Illustrators pane was gravure-printed by Avery Dennison Security Printing Division, the first in the series to come from that contractor. It has the standard characteristics of the Classic Collection series: a header, or decorative top selvage; a few lines of descriptive text on the back of each stamp (in this case, on the liner paper); and availability in two formats, individual panes and, through Stamp Fulfillment Services, uncut press sheets. Postal clerks were instructed to sell nothing less than a full pane of 20 — no separate stamps.

The uncut sheets of American Illustrators stamps were unusual for a Classic Collection. With all

Each stamp bears a few lines of descriptive text on the reverse on the liner paper.

21

The American Illustrators uncut press sheet, unlike any previous uncut sheet in the Classic Collection series, consists of four panes laid out side by side horizontally, with all horizontal printers' marks trimmed away.

the previous sets except one, the sheets consisted of six panes, three across by two down. The single exception was the Insects & Spiders pane of 1999, which comprised four panes, two by two. Avery Dennison's American Illustrators sheet, however, was four panes laid out side by side horizontally, with all the horizontal printer's marks trimmed away.

The American Illustrators pane had its origin in 1997 when Terrence Brown, president of the Society of Illustrators, asked for a stamp to mark the society's 100th anniversary. Such a stamp had been suggested by Wendell Minor, a society past president, who had illustrated several U.S. stamps and postal cards. McCaffrey told Brown that the criteria established by the Citizens' Stamp Advisory Committee barred USPS from issuing stamps for organizations as such. "But I said I could take the matter to the committee to discuss whether there's another way, as we did for the PTA," McCaffrey recalled. "There are ways of getting around those criteria and doing something that's worthwhile." The example to which he referred was the 1997 Helping Children Learn stamp, issued in connection with the centennial of the National Congress of Parent and Teacher Associations.

"The CSAC design subcommittee was very interested in the subject, because we had had such success with the Four Centuries of American Art," McCaffrey said. "We felt it was time to honor the more commercial illustrators, who are really unsung heroes. People have seen their work, but they just don't know who they are, with the exception of a few like Norman Rockwell and Howard Pyle. So the subcommittee told us to go ahead and develop the idea."

The Society of Illustrators agreed to create a special panel to recommend the names of illustrators who should be represented on the pane. Its members were: Terrence Brown; Vincent DiFate, a noted science-fiction illustrator and chairman of the society's permanent collection; Christopher Fox Payne and Everett Raymond Kinstler, also contemporary illustrators; Steve Heller, art director for *The New York Times Book Review*; Willis Pyle, chairman emeritus of the society's Hall of Fame Committee; Laurie Norton Moffatt, director of the Norman Rockwell Museum in Stockbridge, Massachusetts; Murray Tinkelman, from the faculty of Syracuse University; and Walt Reed of Illustration House, a commercial gallery in New York City. Reed himself was a former U.S. stamp designer, with the 1976 State Flags pane of 50 stamps to his credit.

The committee submitted a list of 25 illustrators — 20 recommended names, plus five alternates — whose lives collectively spanned a century and three-quarters, from Felix Darley, born in 1822, to Tom Lovell, who died in 1997. The majority flourished during what the society calls "the Golden Age of American illustration," which began in the 1880s and lasted until the collapse of the great magazines in the 1960s. The panel designated a "top four" — Charles Dana Gibson, Maxfield Parrish, Pyle and Rockwell — and made that group into a "top six" by adding the names of J.C. Leyendecker and Jessie Willcox Smith.

The others among the society's favored 20 were Edwin Austin Abbey, Harvey Dunn, James Montgomery Flagg, A.B. Frost, John Held Jr., Rockwell Kent, Neysa McMein, Thomas Nast, Rose O'Neill, Al Parker, Coles Phillips, Frederic Remington, Robert Weaver and N.C. Wyeth. The five alternates it listed were Darley, Lovell, Dean Cornwell, Robert Fawcett

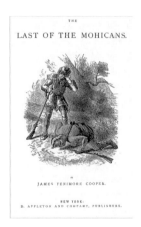

Thomas Nast and Felix Darley, both of whom were on the Society of Illustrators' list, were left off the American Illustrators pane because their delicate pen-and-ink line work wouldn't have reduced successfully to stamp size. Examples of the two men's work, shown here, are Nast's cartoon Let Us Prey, *showing the Tweed ring at bay as a group of vultures, from* Harper's Weekly, *September 23, 1871, and a Darley drawing for the title page of an edition of James Fenimore Cooper's* The Last of the Mohicans.

J.C. LEYENDECKER

ROBERT FAWCETT

COLES PHILLIPS

and Jon Whitcomb.

For various reasons, some of the illustrators on the society's list of 20 recommended names didn't make the Postal Service's final cut and were replaced by alternates (see below). Those honored on the pane as issued were: Abbey, Cornwell, Dunn, Fawcett, Flagg, Frost, Held, Kent, Leyendecker, McMein, O'Neill, Parker, Parrish, Phillips, Pyle, Remington, Rockwell, Smith, Whitcomb and Wyeth. McMein, O'Neill and Smith were the only women represented on the pane — illustration was a field dominated by men during its golden age — but they weren't included because of political correctness. "They belong," Carl Herrman said. "They were great contributors to illustration and their works look great on the pane."

The work of several of the honored 20 previously had appeared on U.S. stamps.

Norman Rockwell led this group. His stamp on the pane, *Doctor and Doll*, from a March 9, 1929, *Saturday Evening Post* cover, was the 10th to reproduce a painting by the popular artist. Rockwell created his first two stamps specifically for the U.S. Post Office Department: the 1960 4¢ Boy Scouts of America (Scott 1145) and the 1963 5¢ City Mail Delivery (Scott 1238). Existing Rockwell illustrations were shown on the 1972 8¢ Tom Sawyer (Scott 1470), the 1994 29¢ Rockwell centennial (Scott 2839), the 1994 Four Freedoms souvenir pane (Scott 2840a-d) and the 1999 33¢

AL PARKER

A.B. FROST

HOWARD PYLE

24

ROSE O'NEILL

DEAN CORNWELL

EDWIN AUSTIN ABBEY

Peace Corps stamp on the 1960s Celebrate the Century pane (Scott 3188f).

Two previous Frederic Remington works appeared on stamps: his painting *The Smoke Signal*, on the 1961 4¢ stamp marking the artist's birth centennial (Scott 1187), and his sculpture *Coming Through the Rye* on an 18¢ American Sculptor stamp of 1981 (Scott 1934). In addition, Remington himself was depicted on the 10¢ Famous Americans/Artists stamp of 1940 (Scott 888).

Six other artists in the American Illustrators set were represented in various ways on earlier stamps. Al Parker designed and illustrated the 1961 4¢ Nursing stamp (Scott 1190). The Scootles doll, designed by Rose O'Neill, is pictured on a 32¢ American Dolls stamp of 1997 (Scott 3151j). James Montgomery Flagg's famous Uncle Sam portrait from an Army recruiting poster is seen on the 32¢ America Enters World War I stamp from the 1910-1919 Celebrate the Century pane of 1998 (Scott 3183i).

John Held Jr.'s art appears on the 32¢ Flappers Do the Charleston stamp of the 1920s Celebrate the Century pane of 1998 (Scott 3184h). The 1940s Celebrate the Century pane of 1999 includes a detail from an N.C. Wyeth poster on its 33¢ World War II stamp (Scott 3186a). And an image from the brush of J.C. Leyendecker showing a celebrating New Year's baby is shown on the 33¢ New Year 2000 stamp issued December 27, 1999 (Scott 3369).

JESSIE WILLCOX SMITH

NEYSA McMEIN

JON WHITCOMB

HARVEY DUNN

FREDERIC REMINGTON

ROCKWELL KENT

Linn's Stamp News noted other stamp connections to the honored illustrators. N.C. Wyeth's grandson, Jamie Wyeth, as a member of CSAC in 1971, designed and illustrated the 8¢ Partridge in a Pear Tree Christmas stamp of that year (Scott 1445). And Robert Fawcett was a member of the Committee of Volunteer Artists, a CSAC precursor created in 1941 to improve U.S. postage-stamp art.

The issuance of the American Illustrators pane was particularly welcomed by a group of admirers of Maxfield Parrish, who had sought a stamp in his honor for at least 10 years. The campaign was led by Kory Darnall of Davenport, Iowa, a collector of Parrish's work, and was centered in Windsor, Vermont, where Parrish lived. In March 1993 the Associated Press reported that more than 10,000 signatures, cards and letters of support had been collected requesting a stamp on July 25, 1995, the 125th anniversary of Parrish's birth. CSAC turned down that request, but Parrish finally got his stamp.

Some of the previous Classic Collections have been accompanied by sets of 20 picture postal cards imprinted with the same stamped images as the stamps. No such cards were produced for American Illustrators, however. "We talked about issuing cards, but we had a severe budget crunch, and we decided not to," Terrence McCaffrey said. "If you don't have the money up front, you don't do it."

N.C. WYETH

NORMAN ROCKWELL

JOHN HELD, JR.

The Designs

CSAC and the Postal Service art directors made no effort to second-guess the Society of Illustrators on its list of 25 names. Because of the expertise of the selection panel, they accepted the list as valid, and Carl Herrman's task then became to review the work of each man or woman and choose subjects that would be appealing as stamp images and would fit comfortably into the designated format: semijumbo size, vertically arranged.

The resources of Illustration House were made available to him. "Walt Reed is the ultimate archivist of American illustration," Herrman said. "He was able to pull out of his file samples of the work of every one of these artists, and between his material and that from the Society of Illustrators I had access to a good selection from each one." In the process, the list of 25 illustrators was whittled to a final 20.

One of the society's "top four," Charles Dana Gibson, was left out because his artistic specialty, the Gibson Girl, had been depicted on a stamp only three years earlier. That 32¢ stamp had been part of the Celebrate the Century pane for the decade of the 1900s; Herrman had served as art director for that pane as well.

Another casualty was Thomas Nast, the 19th-century cartoonist whose memorable creations had included the Democratic donkey and the Republican elephant, as well as the Santa Claus image as we know it today. Nast also created savage caricatures of New York's "Boss" Tweed that helped bring down that corrupt politician. "Nast's line work was just so delicate that it wouldn't work at stamp size," Herrman said. "As for the subject matter, a Santa Claus in black and white wouldn't have been appropriate, and a Boss Tweed cartoon stamp would have shown just a big, rotund man with a snarly face, which I thought wasn't the most delightful image for a stamp."

Felix Darley, listed as an alternate, was, like Nast, an artist whose delicate pen-and-ink work "looked great at full size, but would have turned to mush when you took it down to stamp size," Herrman said.

Tom Lovell was left off the pane for a different reason. Herrman had intended to include him — "His work was just remarkably good, almost

Charles Dana Gibson was left off the pane because a stamp depicting one of his Gibson Girl portraits, such as the essay (near right) developed by Carl Herrman, would have been too similar to the Gibson Girl stamp that was included in the 1900s Celebrate the Century pane of 1998 (far right), also designed by Herrman.

27

Officials were ready to include this design, featuring a detail from Tom Lovell's Comanche Moon, *in the American Illustrators pane until PhotoAssist pointed out the painting's disquieting subject matter: Indian warriors bringing a captive white woman and boy into camp after a raid, while brandishing spears hung with scalps. The woman has been cropped out of the stamp image on the left side. The 35½-inch by 63-inch oil painting is one of four commissioned by oil millionaire George Abell for the Permian Basin Petroleum Museum in Midland, Texas, and completed between 1969 and 1973.*

super-realistic, you would swear you were right there" — and the art director had created a stamp design based on *Comanche Moon*, a dramatic painting of Indian warriors riding into their village. Then PhotoAssist pointed out that the scene depicted the aftermath of a successful raid on a white settlement; the braves were accompanied by a captured woman and boy and brandished spears hung with scalps. As Terrence McCaffrey observed, the image "wasn't politically correct," and Lovell's illustration was replaced on the pane by a piece of advertising art by Robert Fawcett.

Several of the 20 chosen illustrators, such as Maxfield Parrish and Norman Rockwell, left an immense body of work from which to select. Herrman found it a challenge to "choose one particular image out of all the gorgeous things they have done." In some cases he developed alternative designs for the same artist (see illustrations).

"What was fun about the whole thing was that we had a little bit of everything in the way of subject matter on the pane," Herrman said. "Two sophisticated people dancing, a group of young girls with a lyre, a steamboat, a cute illustration of a child and a dog, a pirate, a whale — it was a

This was Carl Herrman's original choice of an illustration by Jessie Willcox Smith, who specialized in painting mothers, babies and children. He replaced it with Smith's The First Lesson, *from* The Ladies' Home Journal *of December 1904.*

This alternative design for the Norman Rockwell stamp used an illustration called The New Television Set *that appeared on the cover of the November 5, 1949,* Saturday Evening Post.

Herrman adapted these two Neysa McMein illustrations as stamp designs before finally selecting for the finished stamp a third McMein painting showing an artist with brush and palette that appeared on the cover of McCall's magazine for June 1932.

Shown here are two unused alternative designs for the N.C. Wyeth stamp, including one (near left) that Wyeth painted for the 1911 edition of Stevenson's Treasure Island.

These are unused alternative designs for the Frederic Remington stamp, showing a lone cowboy, and the J.C. Leyendecker stamp, adapted from a Thanksgiving season Saturday Evening Post cover.

variety that was almost unexpected. We had everything from Peter Rabbit to a U.S. Marine!"

Herrman was pleased with the appearance of most of the 20 stamps, but his favorite is the only black-and-white stamp on the pane, displaying Rockwell Kent's drawing of a climactic episode from Herman Melville's *Moby Dick.* Unlike the art of Thomas Nast and Felix Darley, the lines of Kent's picture were heavy enough to reproduce at stamp size. "There's something about the dynamic of the action, the fact that it's very classy looking in black and white, and the fact that it's right on the very edge of how tiny you can reproduce lines and still make them work, that make it

SAUGUS ICE FOR SURABAYA

This is the 1949 Carrier Corporation refrigeration advertisement illustration by Robert Fawcett from which Carl Herrman cropped the central figure for the Fawcett stamp. Note the additional workmen, buildings and landscape at the sides of the picture. The ad text reads: "Saugus Ice for Surabaya. Fortunes were made in the 1800s shipping ice all the way from New England's ponds to South America, Java and India. Used to cool drinking water and to protect the flavor and goodness of food, it could not compare with modern refrigeration for efficiency and economy!"

outstanding," Herrman said.

The stamp he likes the least is the Howard Pyle *Attack on a Galleon* because the colors deviate from those of the original. "It was not what we intended," he said. "The stamp is much too dark; the water should be a lighter blue. The difficulty in printing it was trying to get the rigging, which is very delicate in the sails, to stand out and not be lost. You do one thing, and then the controls on that take the rest of the colors in another direction.

"Because these images were so different, it was a very difficult job to get what looked like accurate color on all of them. But because of the good work of Dodge Color [the company that makes color separations for USPS], I was extremely pleased, overall, with the way it came out."

Herrman made the most of the space available on each stamp for his illustrations, intruding on the image only with a small "USA 33" in black or dropped-out white Adobe Garamond type tucked discreetly in an upper or lower corner. Borrowing an idea from fellow art director Howard Paine's layout for the Four Centuries of American Art stamps, he placed the name of the illustrator in small black capitals in the center of the lower margin of each stamp, beneath the frameline.

"I could have ruined this pane by having the names of the artists slapped across the art somewhere," Herrman said. "Fortunately, Howard had solved that problem by being extremely delicate with the names, and I did the same thing. It was the perfect solution."

The year date, usually in the lower-left corner, was placed at the right side, just outside the frameline, and in type so small as to be barely noticeable.

Herrman tried several approaches to designing the pane header, including some that displayed only the words "American Illustration" in various typefaces. He also experimented with incorporating drawings by N.C. Wyeth and Herbert Morton Stoops, as well as a full-length painting by Norman Rockwell of the main street of Stockbridge, Massachusetts, in winter. With the latter, however, only limited space was available to include the title of the pane, and as an eye-catching picture it would have competed too strongly for attention with the designs of the stamps themselves.

In the end, Walt Reed of Illustration House solved Herrman's problem by finding a delicate, classic-looking drawing of reclining female figures of the kind that decorated bookplates in the early 20th century. The drawing, by Franklin Booth, had appeared on the editorial page of *The Ladies'*

Shown here are four alternative header designs devised by Carl Herrman. One used words only; another displayed a long painting by Norman Rockwell depicting the main street of Stockbridge, Massachusetts, with the wording penciled in to see whether it would fit satisfactorily (it didn't); the third incorporated an N.C. Wyeth sketch of a farmer plowing; and the fourth reproduced a picture of a cowboy and cattle by Herbert Morton Stoops. The delicate, classical-looking image finally chosen for the header was a drawing by Franklin Booth that appeared on the editorial page of the February 1918 Ladies' Home Journal.

Loretta Knight of Parkersburg, West Virginia, holds the Al Parker illustration of her that is very closely related to the Al Parker stamp from the American Illustrators pane. (Photo courtesy of The Parkersburg News)

Home Journal for February 1918. Herrman chose a dark brown in which to reproduce it.

Besides being a consultant and picture source for the project, Reed also wrote the first draft of the verso text that was printed on the back of the liner paper of each stamp.

After the stamps were issued, a Parkersburg, West Virginia, resident, Loretta Knight, disclosed that she had been the model for the illustration shown on the Al Parker stamp.

According to *The Parkersburg News* of May 14, 2001, the illustration was made from a photograph that Parker had taken of Knight putting up her hair. Knight, whose last name then was Eickhoff, was a student at a junior high school in Westport, Connecticut, at the time. She said several visiting artists had discovered her in the school cafeteria and obtained permission from her parents to use her as a model.

Knight's image appeared in numerous publications, including *The Saturday Evening Post*, *The American Magazine* and the cover of *Redbook*, according to *The News*. The newspaper said Al Parker's illustration of her appeared in the June 1948 issue of *Good Housekeeping*. The text on the back of the pane attributes the image to a "How I Make a Picture" correspondence school lesson from the Famous Artists Advanced Program of the Institute of Commercial Art in Westport, Connecticut, in 1949.

First-day Facts

David L. Solomon, USPS vice president for New York Metro Area operations, dedicated the stamps in a ceremony at the Society of Illustrators, a one-time carriage house that was built in 1875 facing New York's East 63rd Street and occupied by the society since 1939. The event was the society's Founders' Day and launched its centennial activities. Speakers were Terrence McCaffrey of USPS and the society's president, Terrence Brown.

In conjunction with the stamps and the anniversary, the society gallery presented a look at the 20 honored illustrators with personal letters, photos and works from the society's collection from January 10 through February 1. From February 7 to 24 the society staged an exhibition called "The Illustrator in America," displaying more than 120 works by 75 artists.

34¢ DIABETES AWARENESS

Date of Issue: March 16, 2001

Catalog Number: Scott 3503

Colors: black, cyan, magenta, yellow

First-Day Cancel: Boston, Massachusetts. Stamp went on sale nationwide the same day.

First-Day Cancellations: 107,696

Format: Panes of 20, horizontal, 4 across, 5 down. Offset printing plates of 180 subjects, 15 across, 12 around.

Gum Type: self-adhesive

Overall Stamp Size: 1.56 by 0.99 inches; 39.624 by 25.146mm

Pane Size: 7.135 by 5.900 inches; 181.229 by 149.860mm

Perforations: 11¼ by 11½ (die-cut simulated perforations) (Arpeco die cutter)

Selvage Inscription: "For more information/about diabetes visit/www.niddk.nih.gov"

Selvage Markings: "© 2000/USPS." ".34/x20/$6.80." "PLATE/POSITION" and diagram. Universal Product Code (UPC) "450500" in 2 positions.

Illustrator and Typographer: James Steinberg of Amherst, Massachusetts

Designer and Art Director: Richard Sheaff of Scottsdale, Arizona

Modeler: Joseph Sheeran of Ashton-Potter (USA) Ltd., Williamsville, New York

Stamp Manufacturing: Stamps printed by Ashton-Potter on offset portion of Stevens Variable Size Security Documents webfed 6-color offset, 3-color intaglio press. Stamps processed by Ashton-Potter.

Quantity Ordered: 100,000,000

Plate Number Detail: 1 set of 4 plate numbers preceded by the letter P in selvage above or below each corner stamp

Plate Number Combinations Reported: P1111, P2222

Paper Supplier: Fasson/Glatfelter

Tagging: phosphored paper

The Stamp

Since 1957, when the Post Office Department issued a 3¢ stamp commemorating the fight against polio, U.S. stamps periodically have called attention to public health issues. In recent years, the subjects have included AIDS, breast cancer, prostate cancer and organ and tissue donation.

On March 16, USPS added another cause to that list. A 34¢ stamp went on sale nationwide carrying the message "Know More About Diabetes," a disease that kills one American every three minutes. The first-day ceremony was held at the Joslin Diabetes Center in Boston, Massachusetts.

"We believe this stamp will go a long way in helping spread the word about how important it is for everyone to know about this devastating disease," said Postmaster General William J. Henderson in a news release.

The issuance of the Diabetes stamp was part of a year-long diabetes awareness campaign conducted by USPS in cooperation with the Juvenile Diabetes Research Foundation International (JDRF), the American Diabetes Association (ADA), the National Institutes of Health (NIH), the Centers for Disease Control and Prevention (CDC) and the American Association of Diabetes Educators (AADE).

The JDRF spearheaded the drive for a diabetes stamp, soliciting letters from thousands of its volunteers. "They said they were not necessarily after a semipostal [to raise funds]. They wanted to increase awareness," said Terrence McCaffrey, director of stamp development for USPS. "There was congressional pressure, too, for us to support it.

"The [Citizens' Stamp Advisory] Committee felt that since we were doing these social awareness stamps, we should continue, and do diabetes next."

The stamp, a self-adhesive, was printed by Ashton-Potter (USA) Ltd. by the offset process and distributed in panes of 20. Its design was unveiled October 28, 2000, at the Carousel of Hope Ball in Beverly Hills, California, an annual charity event that raises funds for research and care at the Barbara Davis Center for Childhood Diabetes.

Diabetes is a chronic, genetically determined, debilitating disease in which the body fails to produce or properly use insulin, a hormone that is needed to convert sugar, starches and other food into energy needed for daily life. It is a leading cause of blindness, amputation, heart attack, stroke and kidney failure, and accounts for more than $105 billion of the nation's annual health-care bill. One of every four Medicare dollars goes to pay for health care for people with diabetes.

There are two major types of the disease, juvenile (Type 1) and adult onset (Type 2). Anyone can contract diabetes at any age. Although there is no cure — administered insulin provides life support only — researchers hope eventually to find one.

Diabetes symptoms include increased thirst and urination, continuous hunger, weight loss, blurred vision and extreme fatigue. However, the majority of newly diagnosed Type 2 patients never show these overt signs of the disease. Nearly six million Americans are believed to have diabetes and don't know it, which underscores the need to increase the public's awareness.

The Design

Stamps like Diabetes Awareness are among the most difficult to design because they must convey a specific message in eye-catching fashion in a small space. In this instance, CSAC and the project's art director, Richard Sheaff, weren't even certain at the outset exactly what the message should be. Early detection? The need for research to find a cure? The importance of proper diet in controlling the disease? And should they focus on juvenile or adult onset diabetes or diabetes in general?

To help answer these questions and determine a direction, Sheaff prepared a large number of design proposals for CSAC's consideration. Many of them were "lifts" he made from existing art, made for the purpose of obtaining committee reaction. Sheaff call this strategy the "It might not be this photograph, but how about something like this?" method. Other design concepts were commissioned from VSA Partners, a Chicago, Illinois, design firm, and from professional illustrators Tom Suzuki and Robert Northup.

Some of these were quite literal, while others were so abstract as to leave the committee baffled. Some bore only a message in dramatic typography, but "word stamps don't sell," according to Terrence McCaffrey. "They are ugly to look at, no matter how nice the type treatment is." A single red traffic light, conveying the idea of stopping diabetes, was "clever but a little cold," McCaffrey said. Several designs involved children, but in the end CSAC decided against focusing on just one type of diabetes.

"Dick laid everything out on the table, and we went over them and said 'no, no, no, no, no,' " McCaffrey recalled with a smile.

Ultimately, VSA Partners put Sheaff in touch with James Steinberg, an illustrator from Amherst, Massachusetts, who produced a concept that satisfied CSAC. Steinberg, whose clients include corporations and institutions, says his style has evolved from realism to one that is more graphic. His design for the stamp is an example of this style, consisting of a montage of graphic elements.

Two of these elements, a microscope and a test tube containing blood, are associated with diabetes testing and research. Another is the phrase "KNOW MORE ABOUT DIABETES," in hand lettering. A human head is shown in profile with a highlighted eye projecting a beam of vision on the word "DIABETES" and the test tube, to symbolize awareness. "34 USA" is in red on a black block in the lower-right corner.

Steinberg presented the concept in two sketches, one vertical, one horizontal. The vertical "was more of a split view, with the elements separated into top and bottom," Steinberg told *Stamp Collector*'s Kim Frankenhoff. "The head and the vector coming from the eye were at the top, and the vector continued at the bottom with the tube and the microscope. I think CSAC felt that the horizontal layout worked better."

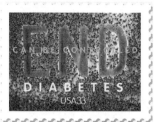

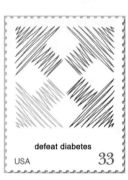

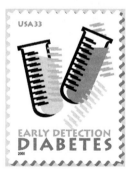

These and the illustrations on the following page were the design concepts prepared by art director Richard Sheaff during the long period when he and CSAC were wrestling with the questions of what should be the message of the diabetes stamp and how best it should be illustrated. They incorporated such elements as typography, symbols (e.g., stethoscopes and hourglasses), children and pure abstraction.

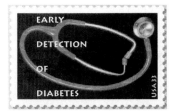

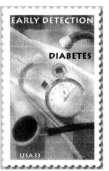

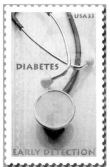

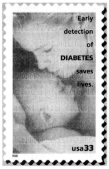

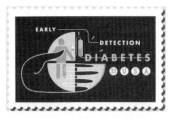

The Chicago design firm of VSA Partners prepared these additional design concepts. Most of them, like Sheaff's designs, stressed the importance of early detection of diabetes.

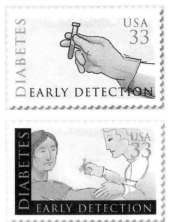

Two freelance illustrators prepared these concept sketches. Robert Northup created the old-fashioned kitchen scene, with potbellied stove and pump. The other three are by Tom Suzuki.

Shown here are John Steinberg's preliminary sketches, one vertical, the other horizontal. Later he would develop the horizontal sketch into the finished design for the stamp.

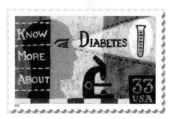

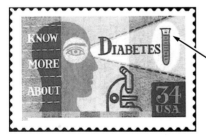

The microprinted letters "USPS" can be found inside the test tube just below the lip of the vessel.

He then made the finished painting, using a combination of gouache, or opaque watercolor, and acrylic. When the denomination change was required, he changed the second 3 of "33¢" to a 4.

Ashton-Potter inserted the letters "USPS," in extremely small microprinting, inside the test tube just below the lip of the vessel.

First-day Facts

Deborah K. Willhite, USPS senior vice president for government relations and public policy, dedicated the stamp in a ceremony at the Joslin Diabetes Center.

Speakers were Massachusetts' two U.S. senators, Democrats Edward M. Kennedy and John Kerry; U.S. Representatives George Nethercutt, Republican of Washington, and Michael Capuano, Democrat of Massachusetts; Dr. C. Ronald Kahn, president of the Joslin center; Dr. Jeffrey P. Koplan, director of the Centers for Disease Control and Prevention; Dr. Lee Sanders, president, health care and education, American Diabetes Association, and author of a book telling the history of diabetes as illustrated on postage stamps; Peter W. Van Etten, president and chief executive officer, Juvenile Diabetes Research Foundation International; and Dr. Allen Spiegel, director of the National Institute of Diabetes and Digestive and Kidney Diseases.

Actor John Ratzenberger, who played letter carrier Cliff Clavin on the television sitcom *Cheers*, presided, and John (Mike) W. Powers 3d, Boston postmaster, directed the opening ceremony. Honored guests included Kathy J. Berkowitz, president-elect of the American Association of Diabetes Education; Dr. Frank Vinicor, director of the Division of Diabetes Translation, Center for Disease Control and Prevention; and James Steinberg, the stamp's illustrator.

In conjunction with the event, free screenings were given for diabetic retinopathy, a major complication of diabetes and the leading cause of new blindness among Americans aged 20 to 74. The condition is treatable, but an estimated one-half of those with it don't have their eyes examined regularly.

The Postal Service approved a pictorial cancellation for use on covers during the nationwide first day of issue by any post office wishing to use it.

The earliest-known use of a Diabetes Awareness stamp was on a cover machine-canceled at the Irving Park Road processing and distribution center in Illinois March 10, six days before the official first-day sale.

ANYTOWN, USA 00000
MAR 16, 2001

The Postal Service approved a pictorial cancellation for use on covers during the nationwide first day of issue by any post office wishing to use it.

34¢ NOBEL PRIZE

Date of Issue: March 22, 2001

Catalog Number: Scott 3504

Colors: brown (PMS 464), gold (PMS 124), (offset); dark brown (intaglio)

First-Day Cancel: Washington, D.C.

First-Day Cancellations: 125,645

Format: Pane of 20, horizontal, 4 across, 5 down. Press sheet consists of six panes (120 stamps). Offset and intaglio printing plates printed 240 stamps in each repeat, 12 across, 20 around.

Gum: water activated

Overall Stamp Size: 1.56 by 0.99 inches; 39.62 by 25.15mm

Pane Size: 7.3745 by 5.9400 inches; 187.20 by 150.88mm

Perforations: 11 (Wista stroke perforator)

Selvage Markings: "©2000/USPS." ".34/x20/$6.80." "Plate/Position" and diagram. Universal Product Code (UPC) "451100" in 2 positions.

Designer and Typographer: Olof Baldursdottir of Sweden Post, Stockholm, Sweden

Art Directors: Terrence McCaffrey, USPS, and Stephan Fransius, Sweden Post

Engraver: Czeslaw Slania, Sweden Post

Modeler: Sandra Lane, Sennett Security Products, Chantilly, Virginia

Stamp Manufacturing: Stamps printed for Sennett Security Products by De La Rue Security Printing, Dulles, Virginia, on Miller offset press and De La Rue intaglio press. Stamps processed by Unique Binders, Fredericksburg, Virginia

Quantity Ordered and Distributed: 35,000,000

Plate Number Detail: 2 offset plate numbers preceded by the letter S and 1 intaglio plate number in selvage above or below each corner stamp

Plate Number Combination Reported: S11-1

Paper Supplier: Ivex/Paper Corporation of the United States

Tagging: phosphored paper

The Stamp

On March 22, the U.S. Postal Service and Sweden Post produced a joint stamp issue depicting Swedish inventor and philanthropist Alfred Nobel and commemorating the 100th anniversary of the Nobel Prizes, which his fortune endowed.

USPS issued a single 34¢ stamp in Washington, D.C., showing a portrait of Nobel and the obverse sides of two Nobel Prize medals. On the same day, in Stockholm, Sweden issued a booklet of four 8-krona stamps, one of which has a design nearly identical to that of the U.S. commemorative.

The stamps for both countries were designed by Olof Baldursdottir of Sweden. She had designed other Swedish stamps, but the U.S. Nobel Prize stamp was her first for USPS.

The engraving for all the stamps was done by Czeslaw Slania, the Polish-born court engraver of Sweden who has achieved worldwide fame as the most prolific stamp engraver in history. The U.S. and Swedish Nobel Prize stamps were his 1,027th and 1,028th, respectively, in a 50-year career.

The U.S. stamp, with water-activated gum and conventional perforations, was printed for Sennett Security Products by De La Rue Security Printing of Dulles, Virginia, using a combination of intaglio and offset. Although Sennett is a long-time stamp supplier for USPS, the London-based De La Rue company had not previously printed a U.S. stamp.

De La Rue, which describes itself as the world's largest commercial printer of stamps, currency and securities, has produced stamps for Great

This is the Swedish Nobel Prize booklet pane, comprising the stamp issued jointly with the United States and three additional stamps depicting the reverses of the medals for physiology/medicine, physics, chemistry and literature.

Britain and the British Commonwealth since 1855. Don Smeraldi, a USPS spokesman, told *Linn's Stamp News* that Sennett selected De La Rue as its subcontractor because of its experience with combination intaglio-offset printing.

The idea for a U.S.-Swedish Nobel Prize joint issue originated in Sweden, where Alfred Nobel was born and where the prizes first were bestowed in 1901. Sweden Post sales director Hans Nyman proposed the project to Rick Arvonio, then-USPS manager of international and direct marketing, during the Italia World Philatelic Exhibition in October 1998.

The initial reaction of the Citizens' Stamp Advisory Committee was to suggest that a U.S. stamp already being planned for 2001 to mark the 100th birth anniversary of Enrico Fermi, the 1938 Nobel laureate in physics, could do double duty as a Nobel Prize centennial issue.

"The committee thought we could kill two birds with one stone," said Terrence McCaffrey, manager of stamp development for USPS. "But Sweden Post said, 'With all due respect, Fermi is one of many Nobel Prize recipients. We'd rather do one on the prize itself and not an individual winner. We don't want to do a joint issue that features one of your people.' "

CSAC agreed to the project on Sweden's terms. In March 2000, McCaffrey and two other USPS officials, James Tolbert, then the director of Stamp Services, and attorney Kelly Spinks, traveled to Stockholm as guests of Nyman and Slania to meet with officials of the Nobel Foundation and work out the details of the joint issue. Negotiations over the design turned out to be unexpectedly difficult (see below), but in the end were successful.

Alfred Nobel was born in Stockholm in 1833, the son of a manufacturer of mines, firearms and other war materiel. At the age of 9, he moved to St. Petersburg, Russia, with his family. As a young man in the 1850s, he experimented with ways to impart more stability to nitroglycerine, a powerful but highly dangerous explosive.

By the time he was 30, Nobel had patented a blasting cap of mercury fulminate that made possible the practical use of nitroglycerine. The cap was one of the most important inventions in explosives since gunpowder. In 1866, he developed his most important invention, dynamite, consisting of nitroglycerine absorbed in a porous material such as silicified earth, that was relatively safe and easy to shape and use. Industrial, mining and military needs created a heavy demand for dynamite, and Nobel became wealthy as a result.

A linguist, poet, lover of literature and the sciences, Nobel included in his will provisions for a foundation for annual philanthropic awards to recognize achievements in physics, chemistry, medicine or physiology, literature and peace. He died in 1896, leaving $9 million to fund the Nobel Prizes.

The Nobel Foundation manages the assets, and the prize winners are selected in accordance with the will, which reads:

"The prizes for physics and chemistry shall be awarded by the Swedish

Academy of Sciences, that for physiology or medical works by the Carolinska Institute in Stockholm, that for literature by the Academy in Stockholm and that for champions of peace by a committee of five persons to be elected by the Norwegian Storting [Parliament]."

In 1968 the Bank of Sweden marked its 300th anniversary by instituting an award in economic sciences "in memory of Alfred Nobel," and placed an annual amount at the disposal of the Nobel Foundation as a basis for a prize to be bestowed by the Academy of Sciences in the same manner as the Nobel Prizes.

A Nobel Prize consists of a gold medal, a diploma and a monetary award. In 1997 the amount for each full prize was about $1 million. Sweden's king presents the awards for the sciences and literature each year on December 10, the anniversary of Nobel's death, at the Stockholm Concert Hall. The Nobel Peace Prize is awarded the same day in Norway at Oslo City Hall, where the Norwegian king oversees the events.

The United States had not previously issued a stamp specific to the Nobel Prizes. However, as of the end of 2001, 38 U.S. stamps had honored 19 individuals, including some non-U.S. citizens, who were Nobel laureates. By category, they are:

Peace: Theodore Roosevelt, Woodrow Wilson, Jane Addams, Dag Hammarskjold, Cordell Hull, George Marshall, Martin Luther King Jr., Ralph Bunche.

Physics: Albert Einstein, Robert Millikan, Enrico Fermi.

Literature: Winston Churchill, Eugene O'Neill, John Steinbeck, Pearl Buck, Sinclair Lewis, T.S. Eliot, William Faulkner, Ernest Hemingway.

Other countries that issued stamps in 2001 to mark the centennial of the Nobel Prizes included Norway and Great Britain. U.S. collectors were able to buy the Swedish stamp booklet from USPS Stamp Fulfillment Services at Kansas City, Missouri, for $3.10.

The Design

When McCaffrey, Tolbert and Spinks arrived at Sweden Post on a cold March day in 2000, they brought with them a proposed design for the joint-issue stamp that had been developed by Howard Paine, one of the Postal Service's part-time art directors. The vertical design, which CSAC had approved late in 1999, depicted the obverse of the Nobel Prize medals given for physics, chemistry, physiology/medicine, literature and economics. Designed by Swedish sculptor and engraver Erik Lindberg, the obverse bears a profile of Alfred Nobel with his years of birth and death in Roman numerals.

The Sweden Post officials liked the design and felt it would work well with the additional three stamps they planned to issue, McCaffrey recalled. That afternoon, the group went to the Nobel Foundation, where complications developed.

"The director, Michael Sohlman, looked at the design and was very nice," McCaffrey said. "Then the information secretary, Kristinia Falle-

This design, developed by art director Howard Paine and depicting the obverse of the Nobel Prize gold medal given for the sciences, literature and economics, was approved by CSAC and taken by USPS officials to Stockholm to show their Swedish counterparts. It was rejected by the Nobel Foundation, however.

nius, arrived. She was very tough. She took one look and said, 'No, no, you cannot do this. You cannot depict the medal itself. We have a policy against that.'

"I said, 'Why?' She said, 'You must tell a story with this.' I said, 'Well, it's [only] a stamp.' The three of us [from USPS] were sitting there with jet lag, barely able to keep our eyes open, and we were told we couldn't use the design.

"All of us, including the Sweden Post people, went away wondering what we were going to do. We had been negotiating for a long time, but now we were on a fast track with the project. We should have made this trip months earlier, but we didn't want to go to Stockholm in December."

The next day, McCaffrey met with Stephan Fransius, a Sweden Post design specialist. Fransius suggested that the Nobel Foundation might consider it "a story" if the design included the peace medal as well as the medal for the sciences, along with a portrait of Nobel himself. "Stephan pulled from his files a print of an existing engraving of Nobel," McCaffrey said. "He said, 'Slania could re-engrave this as the official portrait. We could show the two medals. We could put in words, make it a horizontal instead of a vertical, and see if they'll buy it.'"

Slania agreed that the plan was workable, and Fransius called in an outside designer, Olof Baldursdottir, to assemble the elements into a stamp design. On the last afternoon of the visitors' stay, a few hours before their plane was scheduled to take off, the USPS and Sweden Post teams returned to the Nobel Foundation with their revised design.

"The director said to us, 'This is fine. This tells a story,'" McCaffrey said. "None of us

This photograph of Alfred Nobel, believed to date from the 1890s, was the model for an engraving that later was used as pictorial reference for the designer and the engraver of the Nobel Prize stamps. (Photo courtesy of Sweden Post)

had a clue [as to what that meant], but we weren't about to look a gift horse in the mouth. We drove to the airport and headed back to Washington."

The approved design depicts three overlapping images. At the right is a profile portrait of Nobel. Partially visible behind him is the Lindberg-designed obverse of the medals for literature and the sciences. Partially visible behind that is the obverse of the gold medal awarded for peace, designed by Norwegian sculptor Gustav Vigeland. This obverse also bears Nobel's profile, but differs in typographical details from the other medals.

The engraved elements of the U.S. stamp, all printed in dark brown, are the portrait, the lettering and other details on the medals, the words "The Nobel Prize/1901-2001" at the upper left and the name "ALFRED NOBEL," in small capital letters, arranged vertically at the lower right.

The offset portions are the gold color of the medals; the inscription "USA/34" at the lower left, in light brown; and the tiny year date "2001" at the bottom of the design, also in light brown. Because the increase in the first-class rate from 33¢ to 34¢ was still pending late in 2000, USPS officials decided it would be safer to print the denomination of their stamp in offset, which could be changed quickly if necessary, rather than in intaglio, as originally planned.

Although the designs of the U.S. and Swedish stamps seem to be identical except for the different languages in the inscriptions, the Swedish stamp, and its design, are slightly larger and the engraved lines are darker. Slania created a separate die for each country's stamp. On the Swedish stamp, all the typography as well as the images are engraved, and the names of the designer (O. Baldursdottir) and engraver (Cz. Slania Sc.) are printed in small type beneath the vignettes, a customary practice of Sweden Post.

It wasn't the first time Slania had engraved two dies for a joint issue. For the Grace Kelly stamp of 1993, Slania engraved one version of the portrait of the actress-turned-princess for the 29¢ U.S. version and another one for the matching 5-franc stamp from Monaco.

Other previous Slania engraving assignments for USPS were the 20¢ U.S.-Sweden Treaty of Amity and Commerce commemorative of 1983, which he also designed; the 22¢ World War I Veterans stamp of 1985; the 29¢ Earl Warren Great Americans stamp of 1992; and the 29¢ Dean Acheson commemorative of 1993.

The engraving of Nobel that was used as visual reference by Baldursdottir as she developed the stamp design and by Slania as he engraved it was based on a photograph taken around 1890 by an unknown photographer.

The three additional stamps in the Swedish booklet show the reverse sides of three Nobel medals. The first is for the physiology/medicine prize, the second is the design used for both the physics and chemistry prizes, and the third is for the literature award.

The Postal Service's Terrence McCaffrey, left, stands with world-renowned engraver Czeslaw Slania, holding images of the U.S. and Swedish Nobel Prize stamps. The photograph was made during a January 2001 meeting in Tucson, Arizona.

First-day Facts

John M. Nolan, deputy postmaster general and chief marketing officer for USPS, and Jan Eliasson, Swedish ambassador to the United States, dedicated the U.S. and Swedish Nobel Prize stamps in a ceremony at the Carmichael Auditorium of the Smithsonian Institution's Museum of American History.

Speakers were Arthur Molella, director of the Lemelson Center at the Smithsonian Institution's National Museum of American History; William Phillips, a 1997 Nobel laureate; and Inger Holmstrom, senior vice president and head of public relations for Sweden Post. Gary Stone, manager of Stamp Fulfillment Services for USPS, gave the welcome. Honored guests included Ingegerd Mattsson, Sweden Post's managing director, and stamp engraver Czeslaw Slania.

On the same day, S. David Fineman, vice chairman of the USPS Board of Governors, was the U.S. representative at the dedication of the stamps at the Nobel Foundation in Stockholm.

Postal authorities of the United States and Sweden offered stamps from both countries to their customers, as well as first-day cancels of both countries. Stamp Fulfillment Services offered uncacheted first-day covers bearing both the U.S. and Swedish stamps for $1.33.

The earliest-known use of a Nobel Prize stamp was on a cover bearing a hand-stamped cancellation from the Sandlake branch post office in Orlando, Florida, dated March 15, one week before the official first day of issue. The cancellation also tied to the cover a 34¢ Diabetes Awareness stamp, which was scheduled to be dedicated the following day, March 16. This represented an early use, but not the earliest-known use, for the Diabetes commemorative.

Date of Issue: March 29, 2001

Catalog Numbers: Scott 3505 (sheet of 7); 3505a-c (1¢, 2¢ and 4¢ invert replicas); 3505d (80¢ stamp)

Colors: Intaglio stamp frames: green (PMS 349), 1¢; red (PMS 186), 2¢; brown (PMS 469), 4¢. Intaglio stamp vignettes: black. Offset stamps: special red (PMS 199); special blue (PMS 287), 80¢. Offset selvage image: black, cyan, magenta, yellow.

First-Day Cancel: New York, New York

First-Day Cancellations: 272,995

Format: Souvenir sheet of 7 stamps, vertical, with 3 horizontal stamps in a horizontal row at lower left and 4 diamond-shaped stamps in a vertical row at right. Intaglio and offset printing plates of 4 souvenir sheets, 2 sheets across by 2 sheets around. Souvenir sheets were sold individually or in uncut press sheets of 4 souvenir sheets, 2 across by 2 down.

Gum Type: water-activated

Overall Stamp Size: intaglio stamps, 1.20 by 0.91 inches, 30.50 by 23.20mm; offset stamps, 1.58 by 1.58 inches, 40.00 by 40.00mm.

Souvenir Sheet Size: 6.14 by 6.77 inches; 155.96 by 171.96mm

Uncut Sheet Size: 12.50 by 13.75 inches

Perforations: 12½ by 12 (intaglio stamps), 12 (offset stamps) (Wista BPA 9700 stroke perforator)

Selvage Inscription: "The/Pan-American/Inverts." "PAN-AMERICAN EXPOSITION 1901. BUFFALO, N.Y.U.S.A."

Selvage Markings: "© 2000 USPS."

1901 Designer: R. Ostrander Smith, Bureau of Engraving and Printing

2001 Designer, Art Director and Typographer: Richard Sheaff of Scottsdale, Arizona

1901 Engravers: 1¢: G.F.C. Smillie, vignette; Robert Ponickau, frame; Lyman F. Ellis, lettering and numerals. 2¢ and 4¢: Marcus Baldwin, vignette; Lyman F. Ellis, frame, lettering and numerals. All were employees of the Bureau of Engraving and Printing.

Stamp Manufacturing: Stamps printed by Banknote Corporation of America, Browns Summit, North Carolina, on Epikos 5009 intaglio press and MAN Roland 300 offset press. Stamps processed by BCA.

Quantity Ordered: 1,598,000 sheets (11,186,000 stamps)

Plate Number Detail: none

Paper Supplier: Paper Corporation of the United States/Spinnaker Coatings/Westvaco

Tagging: block tagging over 80¢ stamps; no tagging on 1¢, 2¢ and 4¢ stamps

The Souvenir Sheet

Three of the best-known U.S. stamp errors are the 1¢, 2¢ and 4¢ Pan-American Exposition bicolors of 1901 with their central vignettes inverted in relation to their frames. Although the misprints are commonly called "inverted centers," the black vignettes were printed first as part of a two-stage press operation, so the colored frames are the portions that actually are inverted.

On March 29, 2001, the Postal Service marked the centennial of the great exposition in Buffalo, New York, and of the Pan-American commemorative stamps by issuing a souvenir sheet containing replicas of the three inverts made from the original engraved dies of 100 years ago.

It was only the third time U.S. postal officials had ordered a deliberate printing of stamps with the colors inverted. Coincidentally, the first occasion, in 1901, involved the 4¢ Pan-American commemorative itself. After inverts of the 1¢ and 2¢ stamps reached the public, postal officials mistakenly believed that the same fate had befallen the 4¢ value, and decided to create additional specimens for the postal archives.

The second episode occurred in 1962, when collectors in Ohio and New Jersey bought 4¢ Dag Hammarskjold memorial stamps with their yellow background color inverted. The Post Office Department, embarrassed at the mistake and offended at the thought that individuals might profit from it, destroyed the value of the collectors' stamps by reproducing the error 40 million times for sale to the public.

Any such institutional antipathy to stamp errors on the part of the Postal Service had long since disappeared, however, when John Hotchner, a stamp columnist and a member of the Citizens' Stamp Advisory Committee, proposed to CSAC that USPS celebrate the centennial of the three Pan-American inverts by reprinting them. The committee quickly endorsed the idea.

"The decision up front was not to re-create all six [normal] stamps in the set," said Terrence McCaffrey, USPS manager of stamp development. "We would just reissue the three that exist as inverts, because they are unique and collectible. John pointed out that this would give collectors the opportunity to obtain a group of stamps they normally would not be able to afford. Even though it's a reprint, a second generation, they still are inverts.

"We thought it would also be of interest to the casual collector and to the general public to see these upside-down stamps, and might draw them in to finding out how such things happen and why they are so popular with serious collectors."

In addition to the inverts, the souvenir sheet bears four 80¢ diamond-shaped stamps with a design based on a label used in 1901 to promote the exposition. Inclusion of the extra stamps brought the sheet's face value to $3.27 — high enough, in postal officials' eyes, to justify the expense of producing it.

The tradition of creating new versions of classic U.S. stamps in souvenir-sheet form on their centennials goes back to 1947, when the Post Office Department issued the Centenary International Philatelic Exhibition sheet reproducing the 5¢ and 10¢ stamps of 1847 (Scott 1 and 2). On

that occasion, the Bureau of Engraving and Printing made new dies, working from die proofs of the original 1847 engravings, and printed the stamps in colors different from the red-brown and black of the originals.

In recent years, however, USPS has turned to the original century-old dies to make its reproductions. These recent issues, like the Pan-American Exposition reprints, were designed to appeal to traditional stamp collectors, a cohort that normally doesn't figure prominently in the Postal Service's stamp marketing plans.

The first was in 1992, when the Postal Service re-created the 16 Columbian Exposition commemoratives of 1893 on a set of six souvenir sheets. Two years later, USPS reproduced the $2 Madison definitive of 1894 in a strip of three to mark the 100th anniversary of U.S. stamp production by the Bureau of Engraving and Printing. In both cases, colors similar to those of the original stamps were used. And in 1998 the Trans-Mississippi commemoratives of 1898 were reissued on two souvenir sheets, not as the monochrome stamps they actually had been, but as the bicolors they were meant to be before the Bureau was swamped with heavy new printing demands imposed by the Spanish-American War.

The task of designing the Pan-American sheet was assigned to Richard Sheaff, a USPS art director whose extensive knowledge of vintage U.S. stamps as well as of ephemera (collectible paper artifacts such as greeting cards, postcards and other printed matter from the 19th and early 20th centuries) makes him the natural choice to direct such efforts.

CSAC knew at the outset that the sheet would have to comprise more than simply reproductions of the three Pan-American inverts, with their total face value of only 7¢. Sheaff experimented with making the inverts part of the designs of larger, first-class-rate stamps, but that would have compromised Hotchner's idea of providing collectors with nearly exact replicas of the originals. It also would have raised the total face value of the sheet to only a few pennies more than a dollar, which postal officials felt still would have been too low to enable them to recoup the production costs.

The solution was to add value to the product by including a separate stamp or stamps based on what collectors call a cinderella, which is a stamplike label created for a purpose other than prepaying postage. Sheaff had a candidate in mind from his own collection of ephemera: a diamond-shaped sticker in red and blue, depicting a cavorting buffalo in a circular frame, that had been created by the Pan-American Exposition's promoters in 1901 to advertise their show.

After considering several denominations, including 60¢ and $1, for the

These are three early mockups by Richard Sheaff of small souvenir sheets that would display only the reproductions of the three inverts against a photograph made at the Pan-American Exposition.

Sheaff experimented with making the inverts part of the designs of larger, first-class-rate stamps, as shown here, but that would have compromised the idea of providing collectors with nearly exact replicas of the originals. Also, the total face value it would have produced still would have been too low, in officials' estimation, to enable them to recoup the production costs of the sheet.

extra stamp or stamps, officials decided on 80¢ times four. Each 80¢ stamp would cover the rate for letters weighing up to and including one ounce and addressed to any country other than Canada and Mexico. And, although the officials didn't know it at the time, it also would meet a rate — for a three-ounce domestic letter — that would take effect three months after the sheet was issued.

Banknote Corporation of America, which had acquired useful experience at archival projects like this one when it created the Trans-Mississippi bicolor reprints of 1998 for USPS, was chosen to produce the souvenir sheet. As before, BCA was furnished with the necessary master frame and vignette dies from the vaults of the Bureau of Engraving and Printing.

Rather than chance possible damage to the old dies, BCA printers pressed each of them into a high-emulsion film to create a photographic proof. A matching intaglio proof made from each die was meticulously compared to the photo proof to ensure that every engraved line was reproduced. Once checked and approved, the film was used as the basis to create intaglio plates for the new stamps — separate plates for the vignettes and the frames.

The company printed the inverted-center reproductions in two passes through an Epikos 5009 intaglio press. A MAN Roland 300 offset press was used to print the sheet's four 80¢ add-on stamps and the selvage.

The three inverts are arranged in a se-tenant horizontal row on a white rectangle that is dropped out of the beige background of the selvage. The perforations that surround and separate the stamps don't extend to the edges of the sheet. The reproductions can be distinguished from the century-old originals by the small "2001" year date that appears at the bottom left below the frameline of each stamp and is printed in the same color as the frame.

The four specimens of the 80¢ diamond-shaped add-on stamp are stacked upon a vertical white band at the right side of the sheet. Each stamp has a common perforation with the stamp above and/or below it.

BCA's original plan was to print sheets of nine souvenir sheets each. Three weeks before the scheduled date of issue, the Postal Service announced that the uncut sheets of the new stamps would be made available to collectors "as a four-up sheet," containing four souvenir sheets rather than nine, at the face value of $13.08. The change was attributed to "a minor production problem."

A BCA representative told *Linn's Stamp News* that difficulties in processing the intaglio-printed, gummed stamp paper through the offset printer led to the change. The paper curled, resulting in distortion and creasing of the sheets, *Linn's* was informed. Two production changes were made: first to six-up sheets, which also proved unsuccessful, and finally to four-up sheets.

Collectors often break up uncut press sheets to produce pairs or blocks of stamps that are from adjacent panes and thus could come only from such a sheet. James Kloetzel, editor of the Scott catalogs, pointed out to

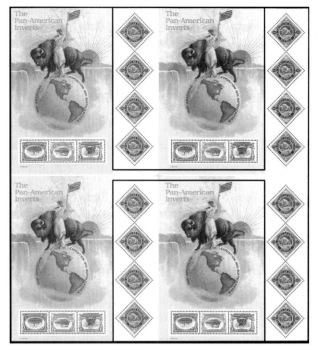

The only logical position piece that can be extracted from a Pan-American inverts press sheet is a souvenir sheet with the four 80¢ stamps in a vertical row on the left side instead of in their normal position on the right. Shown here is a press sheet with the two such obtainable panes outlined in black. Note the registration crosses in the middle of the sheet, which are not visible on single souvenir sheets that are sold as such.

Linn's that the "only logical position piece" that a collector could obtain from a Pan-American press sheet would be a souvenir sheet that is cut from the larger sheet so the 80¢ stamps are on the left side rather than on the right.

Linn's noted that two such souvenir sheets could be extracted from a press sheet. The leftovers would be two sets of three invert stamps (and associated decorative selvage) on the left and two vertical rows of four 80¢ stamps on the right.

At the same time the change in sheet size was announced, the originally announced print quantity of 2 million sheets (14 million stamps) was reduced to 1,598,000 sheets (11,186,000 stamps), a reduction of almost exactly 20 percent. While this is low by normal U.S. commemorative stamp standards, it was not far off the printing figures for the 1992 Columbian Exposition souvenir sheets, which were produced in 2 million sets, with each having a face value of $16.34.

The original six Pan-American Exposition commemoratives were the first bicolored U.S. stamps to be produced by the Bureau of Engraving and Printing (although, as noted above, the Trans-Mississippis originally were intended to be bicolors). Issued May 1, 1901, the opening day of the Pan-American Exposition, the set had a transportation theme and denominations of 1¢, 2¢, 4¢, 5¢, 8¢ and 10¢.

The frame of the 1¢ Fast Lake Navigation is green, the 2¢ Fast Express red and the 4¢ Automobile brown. These three low values exist in invert-

Shown here are the six original 1901 Pan-American Exposition stamps in values ranging from 1¢ to 10¢. The transportation theme of the stamps celebrated the advancements of the just-ended 19th century.

ed-center form. Only the 1¢ and 2¢ inverts were genuine, in that they were printed and distributed by accident, and they were found shortly after the first day of issue.

The 1¢ error (Scott 294a), with the steamer *City of Alpena* cruising on its smokestack, showed up in 10 panes of 100 stamps, and a number of them were used on mail. An estimated 350 specimens exist today, according to philatelic scholar Eliot A. Landau. The error is priced in the 2002 Scott *Specialized Catalogue of U.S. Stamps & Covers* at $15,000 mint never hinged, $10,000 unused and $8,500 used. A footnote reports that the earliest-known use of a used specimen is August 2, 1901, on a cover that sold at auction in 1999 for $121,000.

The 2¢ (Scott 295a), with an upside-down *Empire State Express*, is much scarcer. Landau reports that 200 specimens were printed and issued and an estimated 165 still exist, with 157 actually recorded. The 2002 Scott catalog prices an unused example at $42,500 and a used one at $17,500. A footnote reads: "Almost all unused copies ... have partial or disturbed gum. Values are for examples with full original gum that is slightly disturbed. Value for [a used specimen] is for a well-centered example with faults, as there are no known fault-free examples. Earliest-known use: February 26, (1902?) (dated cancel on off-cover stamp). This is the only used example showing a date of any kind. Sold at auction in 2001 for $66,000."

The 4¢ invert, as mentioned above, was created deliberately. On receiving an erroneous report that such inverts had been sold to the public, the Post Office Department ordered four panes of them printed for its own collection. Roughly half these 400 stamps were then overprinted "Specimen."

Edwin C. Madden, third assistant postmaster general, proceeded to give away more than 100 copies of the manufactured errors to personal friends. This led, predictably, to protests from stamp collectors, and it was followed by an official investigation. (Madden acted "in perfect good faith," the department found, and "certainly did not receive a penny, either directly or indirectly, for the specimens distributed.") One of the panes of 100 did go to the government stamp collection, but was later broken up and most of the copies traded for stamps the collection lacked. The Post Office destroyed another 194 copies.

Eliot Landau estimates that 130 4¢ inverts still exist, including some with the "Specimen" handstamp and others with the handstamp removed. Scott prices an unused copy of the invert without the handstamp at $22,500, and a handstamped copy at $6,500. The catalog notes that almost all unused copies have partial or disturbed gum.

The Pan-American Exposition was held from May 1 through November 2, 1901. Sponsored by the state of New York, the federal government and the Buffalo business community, it was designed to celebrate the accomplishments of the 19th century. Rich with color and electric lighting generated at nearby Niagara Falls, the show featured exhibits demonstrating advances in industry, transportation, music and the arts.

Despite its celebratory mood, the Pan-American Exposition of 1901 will be linked forever to an American tragedy. President William McKinley was shot on September 6 while greeting the public at the exposition's Temple of Music. He died in Buffalo eight days later, and his vice president, Theodore Roosevelt, was sworn to the presidency.

The Design

On the original diamond-shaped cinderella on which the 80¢ stamp is based, the buffalo in the center and the scrollwork in the four corners are in red. A circular blue band around the buffalo image bears the words "PAN-AMERICAN EXPOSITION • BUFFALO" in dropout white capitals. Each of two small blue ovals at the sides contains the year date "1901," also in dropout white.

Because the lithographed original was "kind of fuzzy and wouldn't reproduce very well," Richard Sheaff said, he redrew the entire design on his computer, using Adobe PhotoShop software. In the process, he replaced the "1901" within the

This is the original diamond-shaped cinderella from 1901 on which the 80¢ stamp is based. Sheaff redrew the entire design on his computer, replacing the "1901" in the two side ovals with "USA" and "80," and making the letters inside the circular frame narrower and more uniform.

The 80¢ stamp from the Pan-American Inverts souvenir sheet correctly paid the 80¢ airmail rate to France for this letter, but a postal clerk didn't know what it was and sent it back to the sender marked "Returned for Postage."

two side ovals with "USA" and "80," and made the letters of the inscription narrower and more uniform.

Cases were reported of post office employees refusing to accept the unusual-looking stamps as postage. CSAC member John Hotchner, citing one such instance in his column in *Linn's*, wrote: "In the clerk's defense, it's not very clear that this is really a postage stamp. Specifically, the 'USA' and '80' are minor features in the design, and one might ask the question, 'What does "80" mean?' in this context. It could be a year, or something else. Only if it had a cent sign could anyone be certain of the meaning that the '80' was intended to convey."

For the selvage image, Sheaff gave serious consideration to two different pieces of vintage art. The one chosen, taken from the cover illustration of a 1901 souvenir exposition guide, depicts an allegorical female representing unity among the Americas standing on top of a globe with the Western Hemisphere facing the viewer. In her left hand she holds a flag — half Canadian, half U.S. — and her right arm rests on the back of a buffalo. The words "PAN-AMERICAN EXPOSITION 1901. BUFFALO, N.Y.U.S.A." are on the globe and follow its curved outline. At the rear is the sun rising over Niagara Falls.

In the upper-left corner of the selvage, Sheaff added the words "The/Pan-American/Inverts" in a hollow typeface called Viva.

The alternative picture that he considered was also an illustration from the period. Horizontally arranged, it shows a buffalo atop the globe, while in the background rises the exposition's centerpiece, the 405-foot Electric Tower. CSAC preferred the more compact vertical image with the allegorical female figure.

First-day Facts

The first-day ceremony was held at the Postage Stamp Mega-Event at

This is Sheaff's alternative design for the souvenir sheet, using a different selvage illustration from the period, in which a buffalo stands atop the globe and the background image features the exposition's centerpiece, the 405-foot Electric Tower, topped by the gilded nude Goddess of Light. This layout includes a paragraph of dummy type. Instead of the four 80¢ diamond-shaped stamps that appear on the souvenir sheet as issued, this design contains three $1 stamps for a total face value of $3.07. CSAC preferred a more vertical composition.

Show Pier 92 in New York City, sponsored by the American Philatelic Society, the American Stamp Dealers Association and USPS. The dedicating official was Catherine Caggiano, director of stamp services for USPS. Speakers were Jackson Taylor and Robert E. Lamb, ASDA president and APS executive director, respectively, and Richard Sheaff, the souvenir sheet's designer.

A satellite ceremony was held the same day in Buffalo after the local congressional delegation complained to postal officials that the actual site of the Pan-American Exposition was being snubbed. The event, with speeches by Mayor Anthony M. Masiello and others and first-day cancellations provided by USPS, was held at the Buffalo and Erie County Historical Society, the only surviving building built for the exposition. Douglas Turner of *The Buffalo News* described the ceremony as "a deliberately understated appendage," and reported that USPS "refused to yield to protests from [Rep. Thomas M.] Reynolds' office that the Buffalo ceremony even be mentioned in the ... long news release about the Manhattan event that is posted on the Postal Service's Web site."

Because the stamps on the souvenir sheet included three with denominations below the first-class rate of 34¢, USPS required that all covers submitted to the postmaster in New York City for first-day cancellations must either be part of seven-cover complete sets, with each cover bearing one of the seven stamps from the sheet, or have additional postage affixed to meet the first-class rate. Seven-cover sets had to be accompanied by an addressed stamped envelope for their return.

34¢ GREAT PLAINS PRAIRIE (10 DESIGNS)
NATURE OF AMERICA SERIES

Date of Issue: April 19, 2001

Catalog Number: Scott 3506, pane of 10; 3506a-3506j, stamps

Colors: black, cyan, yellow, magenta

First-Day Cancel: Lincoln, Nebraska

First-Day Cancellations: 801,222

Format: Pane of 10, vertical and horizontal. Offset printing plates of 60 subjects, 2 panes across, 3 panes around. Also sold in uncut sheets of 6 panes, 2 across by 3 down.

Gum Type: self-adhesive

Stamp Size: 1.560 by 1.225 inches; 39.624 by 31.115mm

Pane Size: 9.125 by 6.750 inches; 231.775 by 171.450mm

Uncut Press Sheet Size: 18.25 by 20.50 inches

Perforations: 10 (die-cut simulated perforations) (Arpeco Tracker 2 die cutter)

Selvage Inscription: "GREAT PLAINS PRAIRIE/THIRD IN A SERIES" "NATURE OF AMERICA"

Liner Back Markings: "GREAT PLAINS PRAIRIE/The varied tapestry of the tallgrass, mixed-grass, and/short-grass prairies reaches from the eastern wood-/lands and oak savannas to the foothills of the Rockies./Grasses and wildflowers make good use of limited/rainfall, and fire helps sustain the ecosystem. Prairies/provide habitats for many animals, including the/pronghorn — North America's fastest land animal — /and the prairie dog, one of many burrowing animals/that live on the prairies./Explorers were impressed by the immensity of the/central and western grasslands, the region that came/to be known as the Great Plains. Settlers' steel plows/altered the landscape and transformed life on the/prairies./Native prairie is rare today; remaining patches exist/because of careful management and diligent preser-/vation efforts. But the defining characteristics of the/prairies live on; for instance, cattle, rather than bison,/are now the dominant grazing animals of the plains." Numbered illustration. "1. Purple Prairie Clover/Dalea purpurea/2. Canada Goose/Branta canadensis./3. Pronghorn/Antilocapra americana/4. Badger/Taxidea taxus/5. Buffalo Grass/Buchloe dactyloides/6. Harvester Ant/Pogonomyrmex occidentalis/7. Burrowing Owl/Athene cunicularia/8. Eastern Short-horned/Lizard/ Phrynosoma douglasii brevirostre/9. Plains Pocket Gopher/Geomys bursarius/10. Sharp-tailed Grouse/Tympanuchus phasianellus/11. Bison/ bison bison/12. Wild Alfalfa/Psoralea tenuiflora/13. Black-tailed Prairie Dog/Cynomys ludovicianus/14. Swainson's Hawk/Buteo swainsoni/15. Plains Spadefoot/Spea bombifrons/16. Prairie Rattlesnake/Crotalus viridis viridis/17. Painted Lady Butterfly/Vanessa cardui/18. Prairie Coneflower/Ratibida columnifera/19. Prairie Wild Rose/Rosa arkansana/20. Dung Beetle/Canthon pilularius/21. Little Bluestem/Schizachyrium scoparium/22. Ord's Kangaroo Rat/Dipodomys ordii/23. Two-striped Grasshopper/Melanoplus bivittatus/24. Camel Cricket/Ceuthophilus pallidus/25. Western Meadowlark/Sturnella neglecta." "©2000 USPS/ NATURE OF AMERICA/THIS SERIES OF STAMPS FEATURES THE BEAUTY AND COMPLEXITY OF PLANT AND ANIMAL COMMUNITIES IN NORTH AMERICA."

Illustrator: John Dawson of Hilo, Hawaii

Designer, Typographer and Art Director: Ethel Kessler of Bethesda, Maryland

Modeler: Joseph Sheeran of Ashton-Potter (USA) Ltd., Williamsville, New York

Stamp Manufacturing: Stamps printed by Ashton-Potter (USA) Ltd. on offset portion of Stevens Variable Size Security Documents webfed 6-color offset, 3-color intaglio press. Stamps finished by Ashton-Potter.

Quantity Ordered: 89,600,000 stamps

Plate Number Detail: no plate number

Paper Supplier: Fasson

Tagging: block tagging on individual stamps

The Stamps

On April 19, in Lincoln, Nebraska, the Postal Service issued the third in a planned series of 10-stamp panes called "Nature of America." The pane depicts animal and plant life of the Great Plains prairie.

USPS's original announcement in 1999 said Nature of America would

consist of six "educational stamp panes designed to promote our appreciation of the North American biomes," or major ecological communities. However, in August 2002 Terrence McCaffrey, manager of stamp development for USPS, said the series would be doubled, to a total of 12 panes.

The series prototype appeared in 1999 and featured wildlife of the Sonoran Desert, while the second pane, in 2000, celebrated the flora and fauna of a Pacific Coast rain forest. Like its predecessors, the Great Plains Prairie pane displays a colorful murallike picture, with 10 self-adhesive stamps that form part of the mural and peel off from within it.

The stamps are laid out in a staggered fashion to correspond to the location of their design subjects in the overall illustration. Each stamp has a self-contained design that depicts at least one identifiable plant or animal native to a Great Plains prairie, and each stamp touches at least two others.

The stamps are semijumbo in size. Seven are vertically oriented and three are horizontal. At no point does the die cutting run to the edges of the pane and there are no cuts in the backing paper, which makes it somewhat difficult to extract individual stamps. There are no plate numbers on the pane.

For uniformity, it was decided that all the panes in the series would be created by the same design team: John Dawson of Hilo, Hawaii, illustrator, and Ethel Kessler, a Postal Service art director, designer and typographer. Like the first two panes, the Great Plains Prairie was printed by the offset process, but whereas those panes were printed by Banknote Corporation of America, the contractor for this one was Ashton-Potter (USA) Ltd.

The paper is unphosphored, and the phosphorescent tagging needed to activate post office facer-canceler machines was applied on press, over the printed image. Ashton-Potter coated the stamps with one large, irregularly shaped block of tagging that covers every stamp from edge to edge. The method is similar to that used by BCA for the Sonoran Desert pane, although on that pane the tagging extends somewhat beyond the outer edges of the stamps. For Pacific Rain Forest, BCA tagged each individual stamp with a phosphor block that covers most of the stamp's printed surface, but does not quite extend to its die-cut edges.

As it had done with the first two panes in the series, USPS offered the Great Plains Prairie stamps to collectors in uncut press sheets of six panes at face value ($20.40) through Stamp Fulfillment Services. This time, however, no limit was placed on the number of sheets a collector could buy. With the Sonoran Desert and Pacific Coast Rain Forest, collectors were allowed to purchase no more than five uncut press sheets of each issue.

Frequently, collectors who obtain uncut press sheets of U.S. stamps extract from them blocks and pairs that span the gutters separating individual panes. Such multiples fit in stamp albums, and their gutters are evidence that they came from the larger sheets. The Nature of America sheets, however, don't lend themselves to such a breakdown. The Scott *Specialized Catalogue of U.S. Stamps & Covers*, which normally lists collectible gutter pairs and blocks from uncut sheets, makes no attempt to do so for the Nature of America series.

With Ashton-Potter as the printer, collectors wishing to remove used Great Plains Prairie stamps from envelopes experienced none of the difficulty that they encountered with the first two panes. The stamps on those BCA-printed panes had required hours of soaking in water to release them from their envelopes, and the wet stamps, once free, curled tightly and had to be carefully flattened before drying. The curling, in turn, usually resulted in small cracks in the inked image covering the stamp.

As with the previous panes, the back of the liner displays an outline drawing reproducing the scene on the front, with the plants and animals numbered and keyed to an accompanying list. A total of 25 species are identifiable. (For a list of the species with their scientific names, see the

technical information at the head of this chapter.)

Some of the plants and creatures depicted in Dawson's painting are outside the borders of the 10 stamps. When the stamps are extracted, these species remain behind in the large selvage, which covers a total area of approximately 43 square inches, more than twice the approximately 19 square inches accounted for by the stamps. That ratio has remained constant through the series.

At the time the Sonoran Desert pane was issued, Terrence McCaffrey, manager of stamp development for USPS, acknowledged that there is "waste within the illustration area, but we felt it was a good tradeoff." The alternative, he said, would have been to create five more stamps within the mural for a total of 15. Holding the number of stamps on the pane to 10 keeps a large stamp program from becoming even larger, he said.

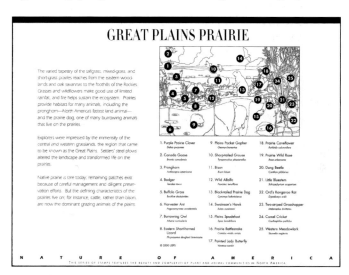

The back of the Great Plains Prairie pane's liner paper contains descriptive text and a key to the plant and animal life shown on the front of the pane.

A large amount of John Dawson's illustration remains after the 10 stamps are removed from the pane.

Officials at first intended that the panes be conventionally gummed and perforated, but this posed a problem. A special perforating die would have to be created to form the stamps within the mural. Once the configuration of the die had been established for the first pane, practical economics would have dictated that it be used for all the subsequent panes, which would have put the illustrator in an artistic straitjacket. He would have had to accommodate his paintings to the perforation pattern, rather than vice versa.

The answer, it turned out, was to make the stamps self-adhesive. The die-cutting mechanism used for self-adhesives could be altered easily to fit any stamp layout and orientation.

The stamps of the Great Plains Prairie pane and the species shown on them are (starting from the upper left and moving down and across): 1. pronghorn antelope, Canada goose. 2. badger, harvester ant, buffalo grass. 3. burrowing owl. 4. Eastern short-horned lizard, plains pocket gopher. 5. bison, wild alfalfa. 6. black-tailed prairie dog. 7. painted lady butterfly, prairie coneflower, prairie wild rose. 8. dung beetle, plains spadefoot. 9. Western meadowlark with a camel cricket in its beak. 10. little bluestem, two-striped grasshopper, Ord's kangaroo rat.

Some of the above-named species appear on more than one stamp and also in the selvage. For example, bison are visible in the distance on five stamps, including the stamp on which a bison is in the foreground and is the dominant subject, and two additional prairie dogs are seen in the cut-

away burrow shown in the selvage at the lower center.

The four identifiable species that appear on the selvage but not on stamps are the sharp-tailed grouse, upper-left center; Swainson's hawk, upper center; prairie coneflower, upper right; and prairie rattlesnake, lower right.

PhotoAssist, the Postal Service's research firm, hired two overall consultants for the 2001 pane who specialize in prairie ecology: James Stubbendieck, a botanist and director of the Center for Great Plains Studies at the University of Nebraska-Lincoln, and Patricia Freeman, curator of zoology for the University of Nebraska State Museum. Stubbendieck compiled the list of characteristic animal and plant species to feature, and Freeman concurred with the selection. Both consultants reviewed and commented on Dawson's artwork as it progressed, paying particular attention to the placement and scale of the animals and the accuracy of the individual depictions.

Additional consultants were called on to review certain species or features of Dawson's art. They were: John L. Hoogland of the University of Maryland's Appalachian Laboratory, an expert on the black-tailed prairie dog; Royce Ballinger of the University of Nebraska, who specializes in reptiles and amphibians; Paul Johnsgard of the University of Nebraska, an ornithologist; and Mike Mogil, an authority on the weather. Brett Ratcliffe, professor and curator of insects at the University of Nebraska State Museum, also was consulted.

David E. Brown and Stanley Faeth of Arizona State University had served with Orie Loucks of Miami University of Ohio as the original consultants for the Nature of America series as a whole. They advised USPS on the concept of the series and the selection of biomes to feature on the panes.

The Designs

John Dawson is a veteran wildlife and nature artist whose previous U.S. stamp credits, besides the Sonoran Desert and Pacific Coast Rain Forest stamps, include the Cats block of four of 1988, the Idaho Statehood commemorative of 1990 and the four Flowering Trees of 1997.

Dawson's assignment for the Nature of America panes called for the crowding of much detail into a relatively small ($8^3/_4$-inch by $5^5/_8$-inch) space. The need to include large animals, such as bison, and small to very small ones, such as birds and insects, required the artist to position the small creatures in the foreground and the large ones in the distance, making their apparent size the same.

The artist's Pacific Coast Rain Forest pane of 2000 had included a cutaway view of a stream that showed the aquatic life therein. His Great Plains Prairie mural also contains a cutaway, but this one is of the teeming life below the grasslands: prairie dogs, a gopher, a rattlesnake and a kangaroo rat, all in their burrows; ants in a network of tunnels and chambers; and the root systems of alfalfa and bluestem.

"We now have this thing down to a rhythm," Ethel Kessler, the art director, said of the design process. "We get a consultants' advance list saying

This is John Dawson's earliest pencil sketch of the scene that would become the Great Plains Prairie pane. The coyote seen peering through the weeds on the right is not to be found on the finished sheet.

'These are the indigenous plants and animals,' PhotoAssist checks it out with several people to make sure the list is a good list, we give the list to John." Dawson makes pencil sketches and color studies. Each version then is reviewed by the consultants and Kessler, who suggest necessary revisions and modifications.

The prairie dogs, for example, required some changes from the way Dawson pictured them in a color study. John Hoogland, the prairie dog expert, found an inconsistency in the position of the sentry prairie dog at the mouth of the burrow. The 'barking' position in which the dog was shown is the animals' "all-clear signal," Hoogland said, and wouldn't be used with two predators, a hawk and badger, so close at hand. He also suggested that the "kissing" dogs in the tunnel be lowered so that the tail of one wasn't protruding, putting the animal in danger.

The ominous weather in the far distance also required some changes. "The consultant, Mike Mogil, was very impressed with your rendition of what he says is a supercell thunderstorm," PhotoAssist informed Dawson. "He thinks it is nearly perfect, but there are two changes that are essential. 1. The cloud formation [on the left] should be in a stairstep pattern. 2. The lightning in storms of this structure comes straight down from the base of the cloud, not the middle at an angle as depicted. It is acceptable to show two or three flashes (the new term for 'bolts') with branches coming out from them." Mogil provided reference photos to illustrate both points.

On the pane, Dawson's mural is surrounded by a narrow white border. All the wording is in capitals. Across the top is a bar of brown and, beneath it, the words "GREAT PLAINS PRAIRIE" in a typeface called Didot. Across the bottom, also in brown, are the words "NATURE OF AMERI-CA" in a font called Eras. The inscription "THIRD IN A SERIES," in small gray Eras lettering, is above the upper-right corner of the illustration. The "USA 34," dropped out of each stamp, is also in Eras type.

This color study by John Dawson differs in numerous respects from his final artwork as it appears on the pane. The changes were made in response to suggestions by the project's consultants and its art director, Ethel Kessler. For example, the barking position of the sentry prairie dog shown here indicates that it is giving the all-clear call, which it would not do with predators — the hawk and the badger — so close at hand. Dawson changed the prairie dog's stance and head position accordingly. He also placed the "kissing" prairie dogs lower in their burrow so that the upper dog's tail isn't sticking out of the burrow, as it is here, which would have put the animal in danger. The painted lady butterfly is on the left side of the picture; Dawson moved it to the right and filled the vacated spot with pronghorn antelopes. For the finished art, he also reduced the size of the badger, changed the flying mallards in the upper left to Canada geese, deleted the bird flying in front of the foremost bison, moved the pocket gopher at lower left somewhat to the right, changed the bobolink in the grass on the right side to a Western meadowlark, and reduced the size of the dung ball that the beetles are pushing and gave it a smoother texture. On the advice of the project's weather consultant, Dawson changed the cumulus cloud formation shown here to a stairstep pattern, and revised the distant lightning flashes so that they come straight down from the base of the cloud, not from the middle at an angle as shown here.

First-day Facts

DeWitt Harris, acting Midwest Area vice president for USPS, dedicated the Great Plains Prairie stamps in a ceremony at the state museum in Morrill Hall at the University of Nebraska at Lincoln. The ceremony opened three days of what USPS described as grassland celebrations and education activities sponsored by the university and several conservation and Great Plains organizations. Partners with USPS for the event were the Nebraska Audubon Society, the Lincoln Stamp Club, the National Wildlife Federation and the university's Centers for Grasslands Studies and Great Plains Studies.

The speakers were Mike Johanns, governor of Nebraska; Harvey Perlman, chancellor, University of Nebraska-Lincoln; James Stubbendieck, director of the Center for Great Plains Studies and one of the project's principal consultants; Mark Van Putten, president and chief executive officer of the National Wildlife Federation; and Ann Marie Downes, president of Little Priest Tribal College, Winnebago, Nebraska.

Doug Emery, Lincoln postmaster, gave the welcome. John Dawson, the stamps' illustrator, was an honored guest.

The Great Plains Prairie stamps were the fifth new issue in seven weeks to have their first-day sale in Lincoln. The 34¢ Apple and Orange stamps, 70¢ Nine-Mile Prairie and the self-adhesive pane version of the 34¢ Flag Over Farm all were released in the Nebraska capital March 6.

The earliest-known prerelease use of a Great Plains Prairie stamp was on a cover machine-canceled in Eureka, California, April 18, one day before the official first day of issue. The stamp was the one depicting pronghorn antelope and Canada geese.

34¢ PEANUTS

Date of Issue: May 17, 2001

Catalog Number: Scott 3507

Colors: black, cyan, magenta, yellow, blue (PMS 542)

First-Day Cancel: Santa Rosa, California

First-Day Cancellations: 263,244

Format: Panes of 20, horizontal, 4 across, 5 down. Offset printing plates of 180 subjects, 15 across, 12 around.

Gum Type: self-adhesive

Overall Stamp Size: 1.56 by 0.99 inches; 39.624 by 25.146mm

Pane Size: 7.135 by 6.292 inches; 181.229 by 159.816mm

Perforations: 11¼ by 11½ (die-cut simulated perforations) (Arpeco die cutter)

Selvage Inscription: "PEANUTS/by/Schulz/PEANUTS ® Characters © UFS, Inc."

Selvage Markings: "© 2000/USPS." ".34/x20/$6.80." "PLATE/POSITION" and diagram. Universal Product Code (UPC) "450600" in 2 positions.

Designer: Paige Braddock, Charles M. Schulz Creative Associates

Art Director and Typographer: Carl Herrman of Carlsbad, California

Modeler: Joseph Sheeran of Ashton-Potter (USA) Ltd., Williamsville, New York

Stamp Manufacturing: Stamps printed by Ashton-Potter on offset portion of Stevens Variable Size Security Documents webfed 6-color offset, 3-color intaglio press. Stamps finished by Ashton-Potter.

Quantity Ordered: 125,000,000

Plate Number Detail: 1 set of 5 plate numbers preceded by the letter P in selvage beside each corner stamp

Plate Number Combinations Reported: P11111, P22222

Paper Supplier: Fasson/Glatfelter

Tagging: block tagging

The Stamp

When the Comic Strip Classics pane of 20 stamps of 1995 was being planned, some Postal Service officials thought it should include not only historic comics but also popular current ones. Carl Herrman, the project's art director, made a mockup of a pane that included such contemporary strips as *Peanuts*, *Calvin and Hobbes*, *The Far Side* and *Garfield*.

However, the Citizens' Stamp Advisory Committee refused to approve any stamps based on strips that still were being drawn by their creators. To include them in Comic Strip Classics, some members said, would amount to free advertising for a commercial enterprise. CSAC adopted an arbitrary rule for the set: Although its purpose was to commemorate the first 100 years of color comics, it could depict only strips that originated in the first half of the century — from 1895 to 1945. Thus *Peanuts*, among others, fell by the wayside.

Six years later, however, CSAC's views on commercial products as stamp subjects had changed. In the interim, it had approved the Looney Tunes stamp series based on Warner Bros. cartoon characters as well as several Celebrate the Century stamps that featured currently marketed consumer products. In March 2001, in a new set of criteria for stamp subject selection, CSAC kept in place the old policy that "stamps or stationery shall not be issued to promote or advertise commercial enterprises or products" but added a wide escape hatch: "Commercial products or enterprises might be used to illustrate more general concepts related to American culture."

And *Peanuts* made it onto a postage stamp.

Peanuts, with an ensemble cast of children and a beagle named Snoopy, "touches something much deeper than the funny bone," Sharon Begley wrote in *Newsweek*. It offers a "sweetly melancholic depiction of the human condition," in which kids "suffer from adult disillusionment, failure and self-doubt," but inhabit a world where "the meaning of life is to go back to sleep and hope that tomorrow will be a better day." At the height of its popularity, *Peanuts* had 355 million readers worldwide; it still appears in some 2,600 newspapers in 75 countries and is translated into 21 languages.

The strip's creator, Charles M. Schulz, died February 12, 2000, only hours before his last original *Peanuts* strip appeared in the Sunday newspapers and a few months short of 50 years after *Peanuts* first appeared in syndication October 2, 1950. Nevertheless, *Peanuts* remains a gold mine for the estate and United Media, which owns the copyright and licenses Snoopy and the other characters for use in a wide variety of products, commercial enterprises and advertising.

Shortly after Schulz's death, United Feature Syndicate, a subsidiary of United Media, began selling its client newspapers classic *Peanuts* strips dating back to 1974. Meanwhile, United Media launched a major lobbying campaign for a *Peanuts* stamp, developing an online form letter that helped generate a large amount of mail to CSAC from *Peanuts* fans.

The campaign succeeded. The stamp was issued May 17, 2001, in Santa Rosa, California, Schulz's hometown, and features a picture of Snoopy in his alter ego of the World War I flying ace in pursuit of his nemesis, the Red Baron.

The decision to issue the stamp was criticized by some. Gary Griffith wrote in *Stamp Collector* that "Snoopy — warm and lovable though he may be — does not belong on a United States postage stamp. ... [H]e's a commercial product. And he's overexposed already on tons of tacky merchandise."

But John M. Hotchner, a CSAC member who was one of the stamp's principal advocates within the committee, defended the decision to issue it. "The subject was right for so many reasons: It is authentic Americana, Schulz blazed new trails in cartooning and the characters are known worldwide and strike a nerve in any language," he wrote in his U.S. Notes column in *Linn's Stamp News*. "That Schulz himself would be honored too by association was just fine with me.

"Here is a man who created beauty in a unique and original way for 50 years and who insisted on doing his own work all that time. I'm only sorry he didn't live to see the stamp issued."

"We felt it was time to honor Charles Schulz because he had made such a great contribution, and the way to honor him was through the comic strip," said Terrence McCaffrey, manager of stamp development. "Carl Herrman was assigned to the project. He had no direction from the committee other than to base the stamp on the strip."

Herrman worked up designs for a set of five se-tenant stamps, each depicting a major *Peanuts* character: Charlie Brown, the strip's angst-ridden protagonist who perseveres despite chronic failure; Snoopy, who

This is Carl Herrman's concept of a five-stamp Peanuts pane depicting the strip's major characters, with a header showing Charlie Brown about to trust Lucy once again not to yank back the football as he is about to kick it. CSAC decided it wanted only one Peanuts stamp and that the stamp should feature Snoopy.

sleeps and fantasizes on top of a pitched-roof doghouse; Lucy Van Pelt, the curbside psychiatrist and fussbudget whose brother Linus once called her "crab grass on the lawn of life"; Schroeder, Beethoven devotee, toy-piano virtuoso and object of Lucy's unrequited love; and Linus, philosopher and owner of the world's most famous security blanket. A header showed Lucy holding a football for Charlie Brown to kick — a recurring incident in the strip, and one that inevitably ended with Lucy yanking the football away at the last minute and Charlie lying supine.

"It was just glorious," Herrman said regretfully. "Each character filled the frame perfectly, it showed a little bit of the story on the top, and it showed the principal characters in the five stamps."

However, CSAC turned down the concept. "The committee deliberated at great length and decided to do just one stamp honoring the strip," McCaffrey said. "We weren't going to do multiple characters or make it into a series.

"The consensus was that the single stamp should show Snoopy. It was pointed out to us that Schulz indicated in an interview that in retrospect, if he had known the way the strip was going to go, he would have named it 'Snoopy,' because Snoopy was his favorite character."

Coincidentally, the earlier *Peanuts* stamp design that Herrman had proposed for the 1995 Comic Strip Classics pane also depicted Snoopy. That one showed him in his persona as novelist, typing away atop his doghouse while his pal, the yellow bird Woodstock, looks on from a perch on the typewriter carriage.

The 2001 *Peanuts* stamp was offset-printed by Ashton-Potter (USA) Ltd. and distributed in panes of 20. Postal clerks were allowed to break the panes and sell stamps individually. USPS ordered a printing of 125 mil-

In an early version of the 20-stamp Comic Strip Classics pane issued in 1995, Carl Herrman included several stamps featuring current strips, including this one for Peanuts. *They were dropped, however, when CSAC decreed that only strips that originated between 1895 and 1945 be depicted.*

lion, and the stamp was sold out at Stamp Fulfillment Services five months after its issuance.

Under USPS and CSAC policy, Charles Schulz won't be eligible to be shown on a stamp until 2010, 10 years after his death. However, officials agreed that his name should appear on the pane, and so the header contains the words "PEANUTS by Schulz," as it had appeared with the Sunday version of the strip each week.

The design was unveiled September 30, 2000, at "Camp Snoopy" at the Mall of America in Bloomington, Minnesota, near Schulz's birthplace of St. Paul, in conjunction with a week-long celebration of the 50th anniversary of *Peanuts*.

The cartoonist was born November 26, 1922. He received his lifelong nickname, Sparky, from an uncle who was fond of Spark Plug, the horse in the *Barney Google* comic strip.

Schulz demonstrated a knack for drawing at an early age. "My ambition from earliest memory was to produce a daily comic strip," he once remarked. During the Depression, he enrolled in a cartooning correspondence course at what is now the Art Instruction Schools in Minneapolis.

After Army service in World War II, Schulz was hired to letter the comics of other artists in a small Roman Catholic magazine. It was his first cartooning job. A second job with Art Instruction Schools helped him develop his skills.

His first comic strip, a single-panel weekly called *Li'l Folks*, appeared in *The St. Paul Pioneer Press*. In time, Schulz signed with United Feature Syndicate. *Li'l Folks* was expanded to four panels and dealt with one event per strip. The syndicate insisted on renaming it *Peanuts*, however, because its name was similar to two other strips, *Little Folks* and *Li'l Abner*. "I was very upset with the [new] title, and still am," Schulz once said.

In all, Schulz drew more than 18,250 strips in nearly 50 years. His characters also starred in animated television specials, feature films and a stage musical, *You're a Good Man, Charlie Brown*.

"As Mr. Schulz got older he began to think about the end of his strip," *The New York Times* said in his obituary. "His hand quavered, but he knew that he did not want anyone else to draw the cartoon. 'Everything has to end,' he once said. 'This is my excuse for existence. No one else will touch it.'

"In November [1999] he was hospitalized for colon cancer and started chemotherapy. On December 14 he announced that his strip would end. But thoughts of death had long since seeped into his strip. 'After you've died, do you get to come back?' Linus once asked Charlie Brown. He replied, 'If they stamp your hand.' "

The Design

The stamp depicts Snoopy sitting on the red roof of his doghouse, a small part of which appears at the bottom of the design. Attired in his leather flight helmet and goggles, yellow scarf streaming behind him, Snoopy extends his front paws to grip the controls of his imaginary Sopwith Camel as he pursues the Red Baron. Carl Herrman allowed the beagle's helmet to extend through the top frameline "to give a little more punch" to the design, he said.

"PEANUTS" is lettered in black in the upper-left corner and "USA 34" in two lines appears in the lower-right corner. The style of lettering suggests that used by Schulz to put words in the mouths of the cartoon characters.

The header depicts Linus, Lucy and Charlie Brown to the left of the "Peanuts by Schulz" pane title, and Snoopy to the right. Snoopy is in a pose similar to that of the stamp, except that he is looking back and to the right rather than straight ahead.

Herrman developed both the stamp and header designs from images furnished by Charles M. Schulz Creative Associates in Santa Rosa. The organization proved difficult to work with.

"They wanted more control than we wanted to give up," recalled Terrence McCaffrey. "It was a little test of wills. They knew they had us over a barrel. They wouldn't approve the design unless they liked it."

The image of Snoopy supplied by the creative group "was kind of a shock, because it had all kinds of strange airbrushed tones," Herrman said. "They were on the leather cap and on Snoopy's face and on the doghouse. There was a background with two airbrushed jet trails of clouds with some strange spots in them unlike anything you had ever seen in the comic strip."

"We came to the conclusion that this wasn't an original Charles Schulz piece of art, but rather the syndicate's version of Schulz," McCaffrey said. "They wanted us to use it, but we wanted Charles Schulz!"

Herrman, by electronic manipulation, "very gently removed about 85 or 90 percent of the halftone, the airbrushing within the Snoopy figure, and put in a flat blue background," he said. "I cleaned it up, because we wanted it to look like a comic strip and not some movie or something."

The art director tried squeezing the art into a vertical commemorative-size format, "but two-thirds of the design was this big, red, wooden doghouse, and there was much less of Snoopy. The image looked much better as a horizontal stamp."

For the header, Herrman said, the Schulz organization "sent me a group of characters that were already grouped together and were in different pro-

Schulz Creative Associates provided this image of Snoopy, an atypical picture with airbrushed clouds and shadows that USPS officials concluded wasn't an original Charles Schulz piece of art, but rather "the syndicate's version of Schulz."

A vertical commemorative-size layout wouldn't work well for the stamp, as these two designs prove; they show too much red doghouse and too little Snoopy.

Schulz Creative Associates supplied this proposed header for the pane, but the proportions of the characters didn't match. Carl Herrman adjusted the sizes on his computer so that all four characters were shown at the same scale.

portions to one another. So I used creative license and readjusted everything so the scale of the characters was the same."

The linework in the images supplied by Schulz Creative Associates was somewhat shaky, coming as it did from Schulz's final years as a cartoonist. "It wasn't representative of what you think of as his style, which was very clean and showed good draftsmanship," Herrman said. "We fought that and finally got something that was better, even though it was not as clean as I would have liked. I wanted to reflect his work at its best. He was such a good artist!"

The Schulz Creative Associates official who provided the graphic material, Paige Braddock, insisted on being credited as the stamp's designer. USPS agreed — "because of contractual agreements, we had to," McCaffrey said — and in the final version of the Peanuts technical details sheet issued by USPS, she is listed as the designer in place of Carl Herrman.

The microprinted black letters "USPS" appear on Snoopy's yellow scarf just behind the portion wrapped around his throat.

Because the stamp was printed by offset, USPS required that the design include microprinting. The tiny black letters "USPS" can be found on Snoopy's yellow scarf just behind the portion wrapped around his throat.

First-day Facts

John Wargo, USPS vice president for strategic marketing, dedicated the Peanuts stamp in a ceremony at the Redwood Empire Ice Arena in Santa Rosa, California. The arena, also known as Snoopy's Home Ice, was built by Charles and Jean Schulz for the Santa Rosa community.

Speakers were Jean Schulz and Monte Schulz, Charles Schulz's son. Peggy Fleming Jenkins, 1968 Olympic gold medalist in figure skating and a long-time friend of the Schulz family, was mistress of ceremonies. Scott Tucker, San Francisco District manager, made the introductions, and Jeffery Lelevich, Santa Rosa postmaster, gave the welcome. Attendees were invited to a free skate after the ceremony.

The only other stamp to have a first-day sale in Santa Rosa was the 3¢ Luther Burbank stamp in the Famous Americans series (Scott 876), issued April 17, 1940.

The earliest-known prerelease use of a Peanuts stamp was on a cover machine-canceled Houston, Texas, May 15, 2001, two days before the official first day of issue.

34¢ HONORING VETERANS

Date of Issue: May 23, 2001

Catalog Number: Scott 3508

Colors: black, cyan, magenta, yellow

First-Day Cancel: Washington, D.C. The stamp was placed on sale nationwide the same day.

First-Day Cancellations: 116,984

Format: Panes of 20, horizontal, 4 across, 5 down. Offset printing plates of 180 subjects, 15 across, 12 around.

Gum Type: self-adhesive

Overall Stamp Size: 1.56 by 0.99 inches; 39.624 by 25.146mm

Pane Size: 7.135 by 5.900 inches; 181.229 by 149.860mm

Perforations: 11¼ by 11½ (die-cut simulated perforations) (Arpeco die cutter)

Selvage Markings: "© 2000/USPS." ".34/x20/$6.80." "PLATE/POSITION" and diagram. Universal Product Code (UPC) "450700" in 2 positions.

Photographer: Harold M. Lambert Studios

Designer, Typographer and Art Director: Carl Herrman of Carlsbad, California

Modeler: Joseph Sheeran of Ashton-Potter (USA) Ltd., Williamsville, New York

Stamp Manufacturing: Stamps printed by Ashton-Potter on offset portion of Stevens Variable Size Security Documents webfed 6-color offset, 3-color intaglio press. Stamps finished by Ashton-Potter.

Quantity Ordered: 200,000,000

Plate Number Detail: 1 set of 4 plate numbers preceded by the letter P in selvage above or below each corner stamp

Plate Number Combinations Reported: P1111, P2222, P3333

Paper Supplier: Fasson/Glatfelter

Tagging: phosphored paper

The Stamp

On May 23, the Postal Service issued nationwide a 34¢ stamp displaying the American flag and honoring veterans of the armed services and their continuing service in their communities.

The stamp represented a second effort in less than two years by the Postal Service to satisfy the demands of veterans' groups for postal recognition.

In 1999 USPS issued a 33¢ commemorative paying tribute to military veterans. But while it was under development, requests came from Congress for a stamp to honor two U.S. Capitol security officers who had been killed by a gun-wielding intruder.

"Other groups had been asking us for stamps to honor firefighters and ... police who had given their lives on the job," said Terrence McCaffrey, manager of stamp development for USPS. "So finally we decided just to put all these requests together under one umbrella and include public safety officers in the group honored by the veterans' stamp.

"Unfortunately in some respects, the initial thrust or purpose behind the stamp was shifted to the two slain policemen and away from the military veterans, and that didn't sit too well with some. The veterans' groups complained, 'Where's our stamp?' 'It's everybody's stamp,' we said. But it had been diluted.

"And, on top of that, the design was lambasted by almost everyone."

The last statement was no exaggeration. The stamp, which depicts a highly stylized American flag comprising 12 wavy red bars and four blue ones, was a runaway winner in the category "worst design" among commemoratives in *Linn's Stamp News*' annual poll, and although the image had some defenders, other writers to the paper used words like "travesty," "abomination" and "bland and uninspiring" to describe it.

"Unfortunately, the majority of people, especially veterans, are literalists," sighed McCaffrey.

The design of the new stamp, accordingly, was made quite literal. It was unveiled in Washington on Veterans' Day, November 11, 2000.

The pressure on USPS to issue such a stamp had been strong. The Veterans of Foreign Wars was one of the principal advocates, and it found supporters within the government in Representative John D. Dingell, Democrat of Michigan, and officials of the Department of Veterans Affairs. McCaffrey and other USPS staffers met at the department with

The stylized design of this 1999 stamp and the fact that veterans had to share it with public safety officials left many veterans' groups dissatisfied and led to their demand for a stamp honoring them and their continuing service.

John Hanson, assistant secretary for public relations and intergovernmental affairs, and Allen "Gummer" Kent, liaison for veterans service organizations, and were told that each of those organizations wanted its own stamp.

"I said, how many groups are there?" McCaffrey recalled. "They pulled out a book and showed me 120 organizations. I said, 'You have to be realistic. We can't do 120 stamps.'

"Then they gave me a list of 37 congressionally recognized organizations, and said that within the 37 95 to 99 percent of all veterans can be found. It's the subgroups that make up the 120. So, could we do 37 stamps? I said, 'No, it's a little better than 120, but we can't do that many. And what would we put on them?'

"They showed us logos for the groups. I said, 'That's the designer's worst nightmare. Some logos are very nice, and others are just plain bad. We can't print 50,000 of one stamp, 2 million of another and 150,000 of another based on the membership of organizations. It's logistically impossible. We have to produce the same quantity for each one. And if we tried to put 37 on one pane, it doesn't work out mathematically for us.' "

During the conversation, McCaffrey said, the department officials assured him that "the organizations understood that they had received many, many stamps already from us honoring their service to their country. What they wanted now were stamps recognizing their continuing commitment to their country, that is, in their communities.

"They brought out published images of veterans working with inner-city youth, things like that. We said, 'That's fine, but how are we going to identify a person on a stamp as a veteran unless we put one of those service caps on them, which they don't wear when they're building a house?' "

However, the community-service angle did offer "a totally different approach" to the concept of veterans' stamps, McCaffrey said. He agreed to return to the Postal Service and consider the matter.

Back at headquarters, "after much deliberation, I said, 'We're not going to change our position. We can't do 37 stamps. It's going to have to be a solution with one stamp. What do veterans like best? They like the American flag. And what do they like about the American flag? They like the whole flag. They don't like it when we crop it and cut it into little pieces and do graphic representations of it.' "

Accordingly, art director Carl Herrman was asked to obtain a patriotic, literal photograph of a flag and develop it into a commemorative-size stamp design. After some discussion of what wording would be appropriate, McCaffrey proposed that a reference to veterans be accompanied by the phrase "Continuing to Serve."

Herrman suggested that he also design a pane header displaying medals awarded to members of the armed forces for service in various wars, but McCaffrey vetoed the idea as inconsistent with the stamp's emphasis on peacetime community activity.

Meanwhile, the officials at the Department of Veterans Affairs had con-

At one point, Carl Herrman suggested that he design a header depicting some of the medals awarded members of the armed forces for service in various wars, but such a header was deemed inconsistent with the concept of peacetime community service that was the theme of the stamp.

cluded that the Postal Service was justified in its decision that the veterans' organizations would have to be satisfied with a single stamp. They arranged a meeting of the organizations' representatives at the department at which McCaffrey, heading a USPS delegation, announced the one-stamp decision and showed the proposed design.

Fortunately, the veterans liked the design. In fact, said McCaffrey, "a number of them were very moved by it." Representative Dingell also approved. "I took it to his office because he had asked to see it before we unveiled it, to make sure this was not a graphic flag," McCaffrey said. "He was sitting in his office with his foot in a cast on the desk — I believe he had broken his ankle — and when we pulled out the image and showed it to him he actually saluted. 'I love this stamp,' he said. He praised it as a great job."

The stamp also proved popular with the public, especially after the September 11, 2001, terrorist attacks, which generated a great demand for all U.S. flag stamps. The Honoring Veterans stamp sold out, despite an initial print order of 200 million, roughly double the run for U.S. commemoratives issued in the past few years. Ashton-Potter (USA) Ltd. produced the stamp by the offset process and distributed it in panes of 20.

The Design

Searching for the ideal flag image, Carl Herrman recalled that many years earlier, when he was art director for Doubleday Inc., he had used a striking stock photograph of a U.S. flag on the cover of an issue of the Literary Guild magazine. The issue featured one of the *Guild*'s monthly selections, *The Glory and the Dream*, William Manchester's two-volume

narrative history of America from 1932 to 1972, and Herrman set out in search of it.

"By some extraordinary bit of luck, although I had changed residences about eight times since I worked for Doubleday, I had a box containing all my Literary Guild magazines, and this one was right on top," Herrman said.

The magazine was the December 1974 issue, and Herrman sent it to PhotoAssist, the Postal Service's research firm. PhotoAssist was able to obtain a transparency of the cover photograph from Harold M. Lambert Studios, the source credited in the magazine.

The flag, attached to a flagpole, waves in a stiff breeze against a deep blue sky. Portions of wispy clouds are visible at lower left and lower right. "In photographing a flag, it's hard to get it blowing but not twisted," Herrman said. "It seems a simple thing, but it's hard to do."

Because this particular flag was so big — some 40 feet in width — "you have this incredible resolution that you normally wouldn't get on a flag photo," Herrman said. "That helped make this probably the nicest and most crisp photograph you could ever imagine. You could actually see the stitching and the texture of the cloth in the transparency.

"It's a very straightforward picture, but I think it suited this job perfectly."

Herrman placed the words "HONORING VETERANS" in dropout white Goudy type across the top of the stamp. "34 USA," in two lines of black Goudy, is in the upper right. "Continuing to Serve," in black Garamond italic, appears beneath the flag. The microprinting on the Honoring Veterans stamp consists of the tiny letters "USA" printed vertically on the flagpole just below the top.

The design recalls that of several definitive-size flag stamps issued in recent years, particularly the 25¢ Flag With Clouds sheet and booklet stamps of 1988.

The microprinting on the Honoring Veterans stamp consists of the tiny letters "USA" printed vertically on the flagpole near the top.

The design of the Honoring Veterans stamp is reminiscent of several definitive-size U.S. flag stamps issued in recent years, particularly the 25¢ Flag With Clouds sheet and booklet stamps of 1988.

First-day Facts

John F. Walsh, a member of the Postal Service Board of Governors, dedicated the stamp in a ceremony at the Capitol in Washington, D.C.

Speakers were two U.S. senators, Susan M. Collins, Republican of Maine, and Max Cleland, Democrat of Georgia; three U.S. representatives, Christopher Smith, Republican of New Jersey and chairman of the House Veterans' Affairs Committee, Lane Evans, Democrat of Illinois, and John D. Dingell; and Anthony J. Principi, secretary of Veterans Affairs.

Lance Hatten, site manager, mall operations, National Parks-Central, gave the welcome. Deborah K. Willhite, the Postal Service's senior vice president for government relations and public policy, presided.

The earliest-known prerelease use of an Honoring Veterans stamp was on a cover machine-canceled in Portland, Maine, May 15, eight days before the official first day of issue.

34¢ FRIDA KAHLO

Date of Issue: June 21, 2001

Catalog Number: Scott 3509

Colors: black, cyan, magenta, yellow

First-Day Cancel: Phoenix, Arizona

First-Day Cancellations: 105,362

Format: Pane of 20, vertical, 5 across, 4 down. Offset printing plates of 80 subjects (10 across, 8 around).

Gum Type: water-activated

Overall Stamp Size: 0.99 by 1.56 inches; 25.146 by 39.624mm

Pane Size: 9.000 by 7.375 inches; 228.600 by 197.326mm

Perforations: 11¼ (Wista stroke perforator)

Selvage Inscription: "FRIDA/KAHLO/'I paint self-/portraits/because I am/so often alone,/because I am the/person I know/best.' " "© 2001 Banco de Mexico Diego Rivera & Frida Kahlo Museums Trust./Reproduction authorized by the National Institute of Fine Arts and Literature."

Selvage Markings: "©2000 USPS." "20 x .34 = $6.80." "PLATE/POSITION" and diagram.

Designer, Art Director and Typographer: Richard Sheaff of Scottsdale, Arizona

Modeler: Joseph Sheeran, Ashton-Potter (USA) Ltd., Williamsville, New York

Stamp Manufacturing: Stamps printed for Ashton-Potter by Sterling Sommer, Tonawanda, New York, on Akiyama 628 offset press. Stamps finished by Ashton-Potter.

Quantity Ordered: 55,000,000

Plate Number Detail: 1 set of 4 plate numbers preceded by the letter P in selvage next to each corner stamp

Plate Number Combinations Reported: P1111, P2222

Paper Supplier: Tullis Russell

Tagging: block tagging on stamps

The Stamp

As part of its continuing quest for diversity in the people it depicts on stamps, the U.S. Postal Service honored a Hispanic woman of the Americas for the first time by issuing a commemorative for Mexican painter Frida Kahlo. The stamp, dedicated June 21 in Phoenix, Arizona, turned out to be one of the most controversial in years.

Kahlo (1907-1954) has been called by her admirers "probably the most idolized woman artist of her time" and "one of the major figures of 20th-century Western painting." But she and her husband, Mexican muralist Diego Rivera, also were dedicated communists. Although two recent U.S. stamps depicting W.E.B. DuBois, who had communist ties, had produced little adverse reaction, Kahlo's stamp drew heavy critical fire.

The first prominent dissenter to weigh in was John J. Miller, a writer for *National Review*, in a *Wall Street Journal* column July 6 headlined "The Stalinist and the Stamp." Miller began by agreeing with the Postal Service that Kahlo represented diversity, "if by diverse one means membership in a certified victim group." "Not only was Kahlo Hispanic and female — she was bisexual and handicapped, too," he wrote. More troublesome, though, in Miller's eyes, was Kahlo's devotion to Stalinist communism. He concluded:

"By honoring Kahlo, the Postal Service demeans the millions of Latin American immigrants who have come here in search of freedom and opportunity. It also says that not a single Hispanic-American woman, going back to the days of the first Spanish settlers arriving in what is now New Mexico, deserves a spot on a stamp before this communist foreigner whose art wasn't especially good.

"If ever a stamp cried out for cancellation, it is this one."

Then Senator Jesse Helms, R-North Carolina, was heard from. Helms, ranking Republican on the Senate Foreign Relations Committee and one of the leading conservatives in Congress, wrote to Postmaster General John E. Potter July 11, urging him not to release the stamp, which at that time had been on sale for nearly three weeks.

"She preached Moscow's line throughout her adult life," Helms informed Potter. "She embraced Marxism enthusiastically in her personal affairs and in her work. She and her husband Diego Rivera sheltered Leon Trotsky in 1937. She was known for her fawning portrayals of dictator Joseph Stalin and for her damning portraits of life in the United States. ...

"I find it personally offensive to learn that the U.S. Postal Service has enshrined her likeness on a U.S. postage stamp."

Stamp collectors also jumped into the controversy, on both sides. Over the course of several weeks, *Linn's Stamp News* published letters both attacking and supporting the choice of Kahlo as a stamp subject. Meanwhile, postal officials, described by *Linn's* Washington correspondent Bill McAllister as surprised by the intensity of the criticism, defended their decision to issue the stamp.

USPS "honors Frida Kahlo's artistic contributions, not her political beliefs," it said in a statement. "The Postal Service realizes that Frida Kahlo was a communist; however, she was a very influential Mexican artist whose work is displayed, and owned, within the United States, as well as other countries."

The statement continued, "In an effort to provide more stamps reflecting Hispanic themes, as well as women, her work was chosen. Her popularity among the various Hispanic groups is legendary. Therefore, we felt our choice was appropriate. ...

"While it is true that our general policy is to feature Americans or American-related subjects on U.S. postage stamps and stationery, our stamp program also honors individuals who have had an influence on American culture, which Frida Kahlo has."

"We [USPS staff and the Citizens' Stamp Advisory Committee] knew everything about her going in," Terrence McCaffrey, director of stamp development for USPS, told *The Yearbook*. "The feeling was that we were honoring her for her artwork, not for her communist affiliation, just as we didn't honor Elvis Presley for his prescription drug abuse, or W.E.B. DuBois for joining the Communist Party and renouncing his U.S. citizenship. Yes, she wasn't an American, but honoring a non-American isn't unprecedented. She and her husband had a great influence on Hispanic-American culture."

Words of approval for the stamp came from the National Association of Hispanic Journalists, which was meeting in Phoenix when the stamp was issued. "As Latinos, we are pleased by the U.S. Postal Service's recognition of the artistic genius of Frida Kahlo," said Cecilia Alvear, president of the association. "This stamp, honoring a Mexican artist who has transcended 'la frontera' and has become an icon to Hispanics, feminists and art lovers, will be a further reminder of the continuous cultural contributions of Latinos to the United States."

The first public speculation that a Kahlo stamp might be in the works came from Lloyd de Vries, who manages the Delphi Stamp Collecting Forum on the Internet's World Wide Web. On November 30, 1999, de Vries posted a message to the forum saying the stamp might be issued in 2000. In May 2000, USPS spokesman Don Smeraldi said plans to issue the stamp had been put "on hold" but that it might appear in the future. When USPS announced its 2001 commemorative stamp program November 13, 2000, the Kahlo stamp was part of it.

The stamp was the fourth in an informal series of stamps with similar formats that feature the works of artists and sculptors: Georgia O'Keeffe in 1996, Alexander Calder in 1998 and Louise Nevelson in 2000. The stamps depict one or more of the paintings or sculptures, while a wide selvage on one side of the pane bears a photograph of the individual being honored.

The Frida Kahlo pane consists of 20 stamps of a single design, offset-printed by Ashton-Potter (USA) Ltd. with water-activated gum and conventional perforations. The horizontal rows of perforations extend to the left edge of the selvage to facilitate the stamps' removal from the pane. Although the background color of the selvage is olive green, the 20 stamps are framed by a white border that contains the plate numbers, one in each corner. The block tagging covers the stamps to the edges of the perforations.

Originally, USPS had intended that the stamp be part of a joint issue with the Mexican Postal Service, which had expressed interest in future projects after the two countries jointly issued Cinco de Mayo stamps with the same basic design in 1998. McCaffrey and Kelly Spinks, a Postal Service attorney, discussed the possibility of a Frida Kahlo joint issue with Mexican officials at a meeting of international stamp agents in Kansas City, Missouri, and showed them the proposed U.S. design.

"They were thrilled with the idea, and said, yes, we want to do this," McCaffrey recalled.

However, the proposal then disappeared in Mexico's postal bureaucracy, a slow-moving entity made even slower at the time by the prospect of reorganization under newly elected president Vicente Fox Quesada. U.S. inquiries went unanswered, confirmation never came, and finally, McCaffrey said, "We were going to have to issue our stamp whether they did or not. We couldn't wait for them any longer. We had to send the stamp to printing. We said, 'Here's where and when we're going to issue it. We'll see you there.'

"It wasn't until maybe a week before our issuance that we got an e-mail from them saying that the Mexican Postal Service will be issuing a Frida Kahlo stamp but will not consider it a joint issue with USPS. There was

This is Mexico's Frida Kahlo stamp. Although it was issued at the suggestion of USPS, on the same day and with the same portrait as the U.S. stamp, the Mexico Postal Service didn't consider it a joint issue.

no explanation. We replied, asking what the problem was, but got no response.

"To this day, we have no idea why they chose not to make it a joint issue."

Mexico's Frida Kahlo stamp, also issued on June 21, with a denomination of 4.20 pesos, featured the same portrait as the U.S. stamp.

Kahlo was born Magdalena Carmen Frida Kahlo y Calderon in Coyoacan, Mexico, July 6, 1907. She later changed her declared date of birth to honor the beginning of the Mexican revolution.

At the age of 7, she was stricken with polio, which left her with a limp. A promising student, she was one of 35 girls enrolled at the National Preparatory School with 2,000 boys in 1925 when she was severely injured in a bus-trolley collision that impaled her on a handrail and shattered her body from her legs to her collarbone. She suffered from its effects for the rest of her life.

Kahlo began to draw and paint during her convalescence, adopting themes of pain and suffering, with primitive brushwork and often extravagant foliage that would mark her style thereafter. Frequently bedridden, she turned inward for subject matter, and approximately one-third of her output consists of self-portraits. One of her more famous paintings depicts her head attached to the arrow-riddled body of a fleeing deer. She rejected the label of surrealism that often was bestowed on her canvases, which were full of tears, blood and viscera.

Kahlo's marriage to Rivera in 1929 was both tender and tumultuous, marked by infidelities and jealous rages. "I suffered two grave accidents in my life," she once said. "One in which a streetcar knocked me down ... The other accident is Diego."

Wounded Deer, *a 1946 painting by Kahlo, won the admiration of surrealists. Her head grows from the deer, whose body is pierced with arrows, symbolizing Kahlo's suffering.*

Her marriage took her to the United States, where Rivera was commissioned to do murals in San Francisco, Detroit and New York. As Kahlo's own artistic reputation spread, her work was exhibited in prominent U.S. museums. In time, her health deteriorated, she lost a leg to gangrene and amputation, and she died July 13, 1954, at the age of 47.

One *Linn's* reader took issue with the Postal Service's claim that Kahlo was "the first Hispanic woman to be honored with a U.S. postage stamp." Because the word Hispanic means pertaining to Spain, wrote Ken Scherzer of Lake Worth, Florida, "Queen Isabella could qualify as the first Hispanic woman to appear on a U.S. postage stamp, specifically on six stamps in the ... Columbian Exposition set of 1893."

Frida, a motion picture based on the lives of Kahlo and Diego Rivera and starring Mexican actress Salma Hayek and Alfred Molina, was scheduled for an October 2002 release by Miramax Films. Miramax informed the Postal Service of plans to purchase a large number of the Kahlo stamps and use them on promotional mail, even though extra postage would be required after June 30, 2002, when the first-class rate rose to 37¢.

The Design

Richard Sheaff, the stamp's art director, adapted several of Kahlo's self-portraits as stamp designs, in commemorative size and vertically arranged. Some of these had elaborate backgrounds, however, which CSAC members found distracting or otherwise unsatisfactory.

The committee selected a simple image, the oil-on-metal *Self-Portrait with Necklace*. Kahlo painted it in 1933 in Detroit, Michigan, where Rivera had been commissioned to create murals celebrating the city's industry. It shows her dressed in a white blouse with lace trim around the scoop neckline and a string of pre-Columbian jade beads. The color of jade is repeated in the wool that holds back her braids and in the painting's

Shown here are three alternative Frida Kahlo self-portraits that Richard Sheaff adapted as stamp designs for CSAC's consideration. From left to right, they were painted in 1930, 1938 (with monkey) and 1941 (with parrot).

The stamp design depicted this 1933 oil-on-metal painting by Kahlo, Self-Portrait with Necklace.

pale green background.

The painting is part of the collection of Jacques and Natasha Gelman, which has been called the world's most significant private holding of 20th-century Mexican art. To reproduce it, USPS had to obtain permission from both the Bank of Mexico, which administers Kahlo's estate, and Mexico's National Institute of Fine Arts.

To *New York Times* writer Holland Cotter, Kahlo's self-portraits "are like nothing else, by anyone else, anywhere." The one chosen for the stamp, Cotter wrote, "sets the template: the grave, mistrustful, haughty sidelong stare, the Indian blouse and the chunky pre-Columbian jewelry, the facial fuzz and merging eyebrows, rendered hair by hair. It seems to say: I'm strange, and I like me. Bizarre is beautiful."

Kahlo signed the painting "Frieda Kahlo"; although her name is spelled Frida on her birth certificate, until the late 1930s, she spelled it with an "e," in the German manner.

The color photograph used in the selvage was made by portrait photographer Nickolas Muray and is credited to George Eastman House in Rochester, New York. Although Muray didn't date his photos, this one was probably taken in the late 1930s, according to PhotoAssist, the Postal Service's research firm. It is a carbro print, described as a photographic print made by pressing a specially sensitized carbon tissue against a wet bromide print and then developing the tissue.

Sheaff included in the selvage design Kahlo's frequently quoted comment, "I paint self-portraits because I am so often alone, because I am the person I know best." The name "FRIDA KAHLO" on the stamp and selvage, and the "USA 34" on the stamp, are in a typeface called Anna.

Because the stamp was offset-printed, the microprinted letters "USPS" were included in its design. They can be seen with a magnifying glass on Kahlo's throat just above the seventh bead visible from the right on her necklace.

The microprinted letters "USPS" can be found on Kahlo's throat just above the seventh bead visible from the right on her necklace.

89

First-day Facts

Benjamin P. Ocasio, vice president, diversity development, for USPS, dedicated the Kahlo stamp in a ceremony at the Phoenix Art Museum.

Skip Rimsza, mayor of Phoenix, was the speaker. James K. Ballinger, director of the museum, gave the welcome, and Charles M. Davis, USPS district manager, was master of ceremonies.

Special guests were Anna Kolokotsas, described in the program as a family member; Ruben Beltran, consul general of Mexico; stamp designer Richard Sheaff; and Johnray Egelhoff and Alvaro A. Alvarez, postmasters of Phoenix and Tucson, Arizona, respectively.

At the time, the museum was featuring the exhibit "Frida Kahlo, Diego Rivera and Twentieth-Century Mexican Art: The Jacques and Natasha Gelman Collection," which included the painting reproduced on the stamp.

33¢ BASEBALL'S LEGENDARY PLAYING FIELDS (10 DESIGNS)

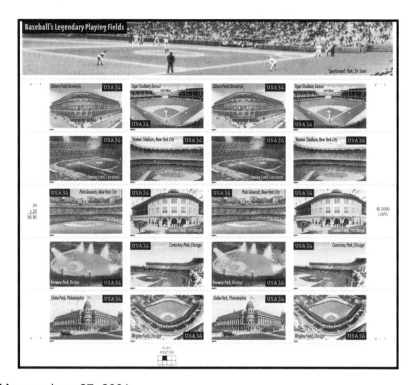

Date of Issue: June 27, 2001

Catalog Numbers: Scott 3510-3519, single stamps; 3519a, block of 10

Colors: yellow, magenta, cyan, black; black (back of liner paper)

First-Day Cancels: New York, New York; Boston, Massachusetts; Chicago, Illinois; Detroit, Michigan

First-Day Cancellations: 1,219,195

Format: Panes of 20, horizontal, 4 across, 5 down. Gravure printing cylinders of 160 subjects (2 panes across, 4 around) manufactured by Southern Graphics System. Also sold in uncut press sheets of 8 panes, 4 across by 2 down.

Gum Type: self-adhesive

Overall Stamp Size: 1.56 by 0.99 inches; 39.62 by 25.15mm

Pane Size: 7.25 by 6.50 inches; 184.15 by 165.10mm

Uncut Sheet Size: 41.00 by 13.25 inches

Perforations: 11¼ by 11½ (die-cut simulated perfs) (Comco Commander rotary die cutter)

Selvage Inscription: "Baseball's Legendary Playing Fields," "Sportsman's Park, St. Louis."

Selvage Markings: ".34/x20/$6.80." "©2000/USPS." "PLATE/POSITION" and diagram.

Liner Back Markings: On header: "Baseball's Legendary Playing Fields/Featuring vintage postcards, this stamp pane commemorates eleven/of the Major League Baseball® legendary playing fields./Built during a time when their dimensions were shaped by their/urban surroundings, these ballparks had quirks and irregularities that/made them unique and endearing." "Sportsman's Park, St. Louis/This St. Louis landmark had joint/occupants — the Browns and the Cardinals — /for 33 years. It hosted the high/jinks of the Cardinals' Gas House/Gang. The Browns' flamboyant owner/once put a 65-pound, 3-foot-7-inch/player up to bat." Cooperstown Collection logo. On selvage: "Major League Baseball trademarks and/copyrights are used with permission of/Major League Baseball Properties, Inc." Universal Product Code (UPC) "450800."

On stamps (each paragraph repeated twice):

"Tiger Stadium, Detroit/Opened in 1912 as Navin Field,/Tiger Stadium was home to the/Detroit Tigers for 88 seasons. It put/fans very close to the field/and featured a right field upper/deck that jutted out/ten feet farther than the lower deck."

"Ebbets Field, Brooklyn/Home to the game's most colorful/fans, this Brooklyn park had quirks/galore, including an angled right/field wall and a sign that when hit/won the batter a new suit. The/Major League Baseball TV debut/occurred at Ebbets Field in 1939."

"Yankee Stadium, New York City/Yankee Stadium has hosted more/World Series games than any other/ballpark. Deep to the power alleys/but short down the lines,/beyond its left-center field fence/lie monuments and plaques/honoring Yankee greats."

"Crosley Field, Cincinnati/Major League Baseball night games/debuted at this Cincinnati park in/1935, with FDR switching on/the lights from the White House./One of the game's smallest, most/intimate stadiums, players had to/run uphill to the outfield fence."

"Forbes Field, Pittsburgh/With expansive foul territory and/deep outfield dimensions, this park/was a pitcher's friend./Ironically, in the 61 years that the/Pittsburgh Pirates called Forbes Field/home, no one ever pitched/a no-hitter there."

"Polo Grounds, New York City/This storied ballpark — onetime home/to the Giants, the Yankees, and,/briefly, the Mets — was the site of the/entire 1921 and 1922 World Series./The horseshoe-shaped field hosted/one of the most famous home/runs: the 1951 'Shot Heard/'Round the World.' "

"Comiskey Park, Chicago/A symmetrical park that favored/pitchers over hitters, this South Side/Chicago landmark featured/graceful arched windows. In 1933/it hosted the first All-Star Game./A fan of gimmicks, the owner/installed the first exploding/scoreboard in 1960."

"Fenway Park, Boston/Boston's intimate Fenway Park has/the Green Monster, a 37-foot-high/left field wall. Red Sox fielders/who mastered its unpredictable/caroms became legends./The home run that ended game six/of the 1975 World Series made/history there."

92

"Wrigley Field, Chicago/Ivy-covered outfield walls, a/hand-operated score-board, and more/day than night games are just a few/of the reasons fans everywhere love/Chicago's Wrigley Field. When/the wind blows out, scores can/enter double digits; when it blows/in, Wrigley is a pitcher's delight."

"Shibe Park, Philadelphia/The first Major League Baseball/concrete-and-steel stadium,/Philadelphia's Shibe Park featured/a 34-foot-high right field wall, as/well as a facade with stately/columns and a French/Renaissance cupola."

Designer, Typographer and Art Director: Phil Jordan of Falls Church, Virginia

Stamp Manufacturing: Stamps printed by Avery Dennison Security Printing Division, Clinton, South Carolina, on 8-color Dia Nippon Kiko webfed gravure press. Stamps processed by Avery Dennison.

Quantity Ordered: 125,000,000

Cylinder Number Detail: 1 set of 4 plate numbers preceded by the letter V in selvage next to each corner stamp

Cylinder Number Combination Reported: V1111

Paper Supplier: Fasson Division of Avery Dennison

Tagging: block tagging over stamps

The Stamps

On June 27, the Postal Service issued 10 self-adhesive stamps depicting classic National League and American League baseball stadiums, with the images taken from vintage picture postcards. Two of each variety of stamp are contained in a pane of 20.

Titled "Baseball's Legendary Playing Fields," the set features Chicago's original Comiskey Park, Cincinnati's Crosley Field, Brooklyn's Ebbets Field, Boston's Fenway Park, Pittsburgh's Forbes Field, New York's Polo Grounds, Philadelphia's Shibe Park, Detroit's Tiger Stadium, Chicago's Wrigley Field and New York's Yankee Stadium. An 11th stadium, St. Louis' Sportsman's Park, is shown on the header of the pane.

Only four of these playing fields still stand: Tiger Stadium, Fenway Park, Wrigley Field and Yankee Stadium. The last three still are in use by their respective teams. USPS held first-day ceremonies at all four stadiums on June 27, with the ceremonies at Fenway, Wrigley and Yankee Stadium taking place before baseball games scheduled for that date.

The pane grew out of a proposal a few years earlier from Richard "Digger" Phelps, a television sports commentator and former college basketball coach who sits on the Citizens' Stamp Advisory Committee. Phelps urged that a series of stamps be developed cele-

brating great sports venues: baseball parks, football stadiums, hockey rinks, basketball arenas, golf courses, even automobile racetracks. CSAC members and the Postal Service's art directors foresaw design problems, but Phelps pushed so strongly for his idea that they agreed to give it a try.

"I had a great deal of difficulty figuring out how we were going to do this with any kind of consistency from one set to the next," said Phil Jordan, one of the art directors. Old baseball stadiums were photogenic and had enough idiosyncrasies to make them interesting, he said, but arenas like Boston Garden and New York's Madison Square Garden were in tight urban settings and architecturally "were about as distinctive as a cinder block." Seen from the inside, hockey rinks or basketball floors look very similar, with a handful of exceptions like Boston Garden's parquet playing surface. As for football stadiums, "You might have a distinctive one here and there, but basically they all look pretty much the same; they lack the history and interest of baseball."

Golf courses were problematic, as well. A few holes on famous courses have a distinctive look, like the 16th at Cypress Point, California, which sits on a peninsula jutting out into the Pacific Ocean, and the 18th at the Augusta National Golf Club, where the clubhouse lies behind the green. "But, basically, one hole looks pretty much like another," Jordan said. "I could not, in my mind, see a continuous visual theme." To add to the difficulty, he said, "The officials of one of the most famous golf courses in the world, which I won't name, told me, 'No thanks, we're not interested.' They absolutely would not give us permission to use in any way any part of their golf course."

Ethel Kessler, another USPS art director, laid out a pane of sports-venue stamps using photographs supplied by PhotoAssist, the Postal Service's research firm in Washington, D.C. Labeled "Legendary Sports Sites" in the header, it presented 20 interior or exterior views of locations for baseball, football, basketball, automobile racing, horse racing, boxing, golf, tennis and bowling. Kessler also developed layouts for a pane called "Legendary Baseball Sites" containing smaller units of stamps that showed only baseball stadiums.

Kessler's layouts combined beautiful contemporary color photographs — one showed Dodger Stadium at dusk with palm trees silhouetted against a mauve sky — and historical pictures, such as an old black-and-white photo of a long-gone Ebbets Field. This apples-and-oranges mix left

CSAC and the art directors dissatisfied, and the project was placed on hold.

Eventually, Phelps' idea was revived, but limited to baseball stadiums. Two developments made it possible to create such a pane and provide sufficient variety of images and consistency of theme to satisfy CSAC and its design specialists.

This ambitious layout by art director Ethel Kessler for a proposed "Legendary Sports Sites" pane comprised 20 stamps with photographs of a variety of sports venues. From upper left to lower right, they are: Dodger Stadium, Fenway Park, Yankee Stadium, Wrigley Field, Ebbets Field, Notre Dame Stadium, Lambeau Field, Rose Bowl (two stamps), Soldier Field, Boston Garden (two stamps), Great Western Forum, Indianapolis Speedway, Daytona Speedway, Churchill Downs, Madison Square Garden, Pebble Beach, Forest Hills, National Bowling Stadium.

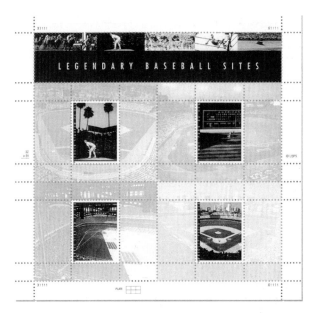

Ethel Kessler developed these early design concepts for panes of stamps depicting baseball stadiums. The panes have elaborate selvage designs, one of which consists of a montage of baseball images.

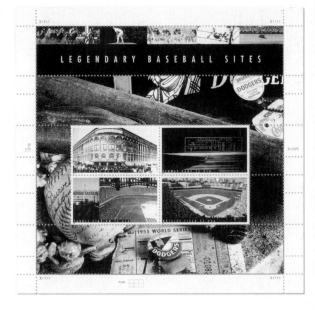

One was Phil Jordan's discovery, in the book *Baseball Treasures: Memorabilia from the National Pastime* by Douglas Congdon-Martin and John Kashmanian, of a replica of an old picture postcard depicting "Shibe Baseball Stadium," circa 1915. Serendipitously, the dimensions of the card were almost exactly those of a horizontally arranged commemorative stamp. "It struck me that maybe we could do the stamps by showing old postcards," Jordan said.

The other development was the Postal Service's successful collaboration with Major League Baseball on a pane of stamps, issued in 2000, that honored 20 famous players from the past. Under that arrangement, linked to a promotion called the All-Century Team, USPS was allowed to use images and titles covered by Major League Baseball Properties copyrights and trademarks without having to pay royalties or obtain permission from numerous individual rights holders. The experience opened the way to a similar cooperative effort involving stadiums.

With the direction now clear, McCaffrey instructed Jordan to develop designs for a set of stamps numbering no more than 10 varieties, and PhotoAssist was called on to secure the necessary resources.

The company hired two prominent baseball writers, Lawrence Ritter and Jonathan Kronstadt, to suggest which ball parks, former and existing, were the most historic and appropriate for depiction in the set. To obtain the necessary postcard images, PhotoAssist's Louis Plummer turned to Ron Menchine of Long Green, Maryland, a retired play-by-play announcer for the old Washington Senators, who has written three books on baseball cards and memorabilia and another on propaganda postcards of World War II.

Menchine visited PhotoAssist's office with cards from his collection to be photographed for reference and scanned for Jordan to use in preparing stamp designs. In the final stages of the pane's development, PhotoAssist sent the chosen cards to Dodge Color, the Bethesda, Maryland, company that does prepress work for USPS, for high-resolution scans.

"I took the top 10 on the consultants' list and selected the best of the postcard photos," Jordan said. "I was able to do what I did with the Classic American Aircraft pane [of 1997]: insert an additional subject in the header. I chose Sportsman's Park, which is a really neat venue. Its post-card was the only one that I could suitably crop into that long, narrow horizontal header format."

The oldest park of the 11 shown on the pane was the Polo Grounds, dedicated April 22, 1891. Sportsman's Park dated to 1902; Shibe Park and Forbes Field, 1909; Comiskey Park, 1910; Tiger Stadium, Fenway Park and

Crosley Field, 1912; Ebbets Field, 1913; and Wrigley Field, 1914. The newest of the 11 is Yankee Stadium, dedicated April 18, 1923.

Besides Sportsman's Park, the "also-rans" on the consultants' list were Hilltop Park in New York City; League Park and Municipal Stadium in Cleveland, Ohio; Braves Field in Boston; and Griffith Park in Washington, D.C.

The stamps were printed by the gravure process by Avery Dennison Security Products Division. Descriptive text is printed on the back of the backing paper of each stamp and the pane header. This verso material includes the logo for "Cooperstown Collection," a reference to the Baseball Hall of Fame at Cooperstown, New York, in accordance with the Postal Service's agreement with Major League Baseball Properties Inc.

The verso text includes at least one dangling modifier ("One of the game's smallest, most intimate stadiums, players had to run uphill to the outfield fence" in the paragraph on Crosley Field), and describes as irony a fact that actually is merely a curiosity ("Ironically, in the 61 years that the Pittsburgh Pirates called Forbes Field home, no one ever pitched a no-hitter there").

Besides being sold in panes of 20, the stamps were offered to collectors in uncut press sheets of eight panes for their face value, $54.40. Because of an unusual arrangement of the panes on the press, a collector who bought an uncut press sheet was able to extract from it items that were new to U.S. philately, namely, position pieces containing stamps that are oriented tete-beche, or head-to-tail. That is because the bottom row of four panes on a press sheet is inverted in relation to the top row of four panes.

The 2002 Scott *Specialized Catalogue of United States Stamps & Covers* lists the following position pieces from the uncut press sheet: cross-gutter block of 12 (gutter refers to the selvage that separates individual panes on a sheet), horizontal block of 10 with vertical gutter, block of four with horizontal gutter, vertical pair with horizontal gutter and horizontal pair with vertical gutter. An example of the first four of these is outlined in black on the sheet illustrated nearby.

Of the Scott-listed position pieces, only the cross-gutter block of 12 contains at least one specimen of each of the 10 stamp varieties and also displays the tete-beche effect. Horizontal blocks and pairs with vertical gutters are not tete-beche, because all the stamps are oriented right-side up.

Other position pieces, such as a cross-gutter block of four containing a single corner stamp from four panes, weren't listed by Scott. James Kloetzel, Scott catalog editor, told *Linn's Stamp News* that the company originally considered listing a cross-gutter block of 20, "but it would be too big for a standard Scott album page, so we opted to list the smaller cross-gutter block of 12."

According to USPS, the printer arranged the eight Playing Fields panes on the press in this manner for "production accuracy."

The scene from Sportsman's Park on the pane header "bleeds" off the top edge of the pane, and Avery Dennison wanted to avoid "a white border appearing above the header selvage of individual panes cut from the printed roll of paper," USPS spokesman Don Smeraldi told *Linn's*. "Rather than printing sheets with all eight panes right side up, Avery chose this arrangement."

Charles Snee, writing in *Linn's*, pointed out "a rather odd quirk of this tete-beche arrangement on the Playing Fields press sheet [relating] to the pane-position diagrams that appear in the horizontal selvage between the two rows of panes."

"If the sheet is viewed as shown here [in the illustration], the position of the black square in the diagram below the second vertical row of stamps in each pane matches the physical location of that pane in the sheet," Snee wrote. "So far, so good.

"But now look at the sheet by turning the [illustration] upside down. When the sheet is viewed this way, the pane-position diagrams for the top row of panes apparently do not match the locations of the panes. For example, pane one (when the sheet shown here is viewed upside down)

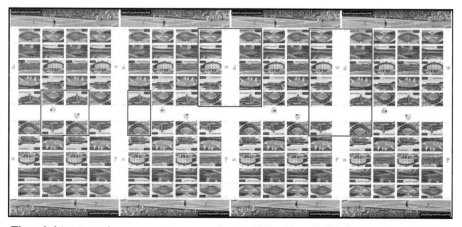

The eight panes in an uncut press sheet of the Baseball's Legendary Playing Fields stamps are so arranged that the top row of four panes is inverted in relation to the bottom row. This means that some of the position pieces that can be extracted from the sheet will contain stamps that are tete-beche (head-to-tail). Three of these pieces are outlined in black in this illustration; a fourth outlined block contains all 10 varieties, but the stamps are all oriented the same way.

has a position diagram with a black square in position eight.

"Now turn the [illustration] right side up again and perform a few mental gymnastics with me. If you mentally flip any of the panes in the bottom row 180 degrees, so that the header selvage is now at the top, you'll see that the pane position for that pane is correct.

"Of course, this bizarre artifact of the printing process disappears once the panes are cut from a given sheet."

A companion set of 10 21¢ picture postal cards was issued at the same time as the stamps. The cards reproduce the stamp images in their imprinted stamps and bear enlarged replicas of the same images, minus the printing, on their picture sides. (See separate chapter.)

The Designs

Of the images from Ron Menchine's vintage postcards that Phil Jordan chose for his stamp designs, three — Ebbets Field, Forbes Field and Shibe Park — depict the stadium exteriors. The remaining seven, plus the header, show the playing fields rimmed by crowded stands.

Two of the postcard photographs, of Wrigley Field and Fenway Park, were taken from the air. In the case of the former, Jordan said, the combination of distance and the small size of a postage stamp make it difficult to see Wrigley's most famous feature, its ivy-covered outfield walls. The Fenway and Crosley Field stamps show night games, with beams of light that obviously were enhanced by the postcard manufacturers.

Some of the images were touched up or cropped slightly for adaptation to stamp designs, but essentially the designs reflect the originals, Phil Jordan said. In the case of Tiger Stadium, he said, "we never could quite figure out what that white item was in center field," but it was left unaltered.

The title of the pane, as it ultimately appeared on the header, is "Baseball's Legendary Playing Fields." "Originally, I wanted another headline title, with 'Legendary Playing Fields' as a subhead," Jordan said. "CSAC nixed this, to my disappointment."

One of Jordan's earlier suggested titles was "Grand Stands of Green." Many old reference works give the word "grandstand" as two words, he explained, and by dividing it in the title he could play on the dual meaning of the word "stand": a growth of grass, and a structure on which spectators could sit.

100

Another proposed alternative was "The Green Fields of Home," a title that evokes the thought of home plate. Still another was "The Thrill of the Grass," a phrase coined by baseball novelist W.P. Kinsella to describe what a fan first sees upon emerging from a stadium runway. "It worked well," Terrence McCaffrey said of the latter title, "but it could be misread as referring to marijuana, so we thought it wouldn't be appropriate."

Jordan placed a green "USA 34" on a small black panel in one corner of each design. The serif typeface is called Officina. The name and location of the ballpark, e.g. "Yankee Stadium, New York City," are in black or dropout white letters in another corner, in an italic sans-serif font called Futura Condensed. "Baseball's Legendary Playing Fields," in green Triplex font letters on a black background, is in the upper-left corner of the header.

Stamp designer Phil Jordan turned down this postcard view of Comiskey Park in Chicago because the postcard's printer had tampered with the image and superimposed a derby-hatted spectator, identified as Charles Comiskey, owner of the White Sox, onto the picture. Instead, Jordan used another postcard identical to this one except that Comiskey isn't in it. (Photograph courtesy of Ron Menchine)

This postcard picture of Sportsman's Park was cropped tightly at the top and bottom to create the header image for the Baseball's Legendary Playing Fields pane. (Photograph courtesy of Ron Menchine)

Forbes Field, Champion Pirates' Base Ball Park, Pittsburgh, Pa.

Shown here are three of the postcard pictures that were adapted for use on the Baseball's Legendary Playing Fields stamps: Forbes Field in Pittsburgh (some of its flags were cropped out of the stamp design), New York's Polo Grounds, and Shibe Park in Philadelphia. (Photographs courtesy of Ron Menchine)

157   Polo Grounds, New York City

152:—Exterior Shibe Baseball Stadium, Philadelphia, Pa.

First-day Facts

Of the four first-day ceremonies June 27, the one most resembling a traditional first-day was held at Tiger Stadium, where John H. Talick, a USPS district manager, dedicated the stamps. The speakers were U.S. Senator Carl Levin, Democrat of Michigan; Detroit Mayor Dennis Archer; and historian Thomas Stanton. Mark H. Anderson, Detroit's acting postmaster, gave the welcome.

"Grand Stands of Green" and "The Thrill of the Grass" were two additional titles for the pane suggested by art director and designer Phil Jordan. In its final version, the pane was titled simply "Baseball's Legendary Playing Fields."

The other ceremonies were held before large crowds prior to ball games.

Participants at Fenway Park were S. David Fineman, vice chairman of the USPS Board of Governors; Lou Gorman, former general manager of the Boston Red Sox; Jon Steele, USPS Northeast Area vice president for operations; Charles Lynch, plant manager and acting Boston District manager for USPS; and Mike Powers, Boston postmaster.

At Wrigley Field, the participants were CSAC's "Digger" Phelps; former Chicago Cubs manager Don Baylor; Danny Jackson, Great Lakes Area vice president of USPS; and Alan C. Kessler, a member of the USPS Board of Governors.

The Postal Service could provide no information on the Yankee Stadium event.

The stamps were available June 27 at the four stadiums and at post offices in Detroit, Boston, Chicago and New York. They were placed on sale nationwide the following day.

Stamp Fulfillment Services of the Postal Service offered sets of 10 uncacheted first-day covers for $7.40 and a full-pane first-day cover for $8.80. The individual covers bore New York first-day cancellations on the Yankee Stadium, Polo Grounds, Ebbets Field, Shibe Park and Forbes Field stamps; Chicago cancellations on the Wrigley Field and Comiskey Park stamps; Detroit cancellations on the Tiger Stadium and Crosley Field stamps; and a Boston cancellation on the Fenway Park stamp. The full-pane cover was postmarked with cancellations for all four first-day cities.

34¢ LEONARD BERNSTEIN

Date of Issue: July 10, 2001

Catalog Number: Scott 3521

Colors: black, cyan, magenta, yellow

First-Day Cancel: New York, New York

First-Day Cancellations: 112,244

Format: Panes of 20, vertical, 5 across, 4 down. Offset printing plates of 180 subjects, 12 across, 15 around.

Gum Type: water-activated

Overall Stamp Size: 0.99 by 1.56 inches; 25.171 by 39.624mm

Pane Size: 5.94 by 7.24 inches; 150.876 by 183.896mm

Perforations: 11¼ (Wista stroke perforator)

Selvage Inscription: "The name, likeness and signature of Leonard Bernstein ® are registered trademarks of Amberson Holdings, LLC."

Selvage Markings: "© 2000/USPS." ".34/x20/$6.80." "PLATE/POSITION" and diagram. Universal Product Code (UPC) "451600" in 2 positions.

Photographer: Don Hunstein

Designer and Art Director: Howard Paine of Delaplane, Virginia

Typographer: Thomas Mann of Vancouver, Washington

Modeler: Joseph Sheeran of Ashton-Potter (USA) Ltd., Williamsville, New York

Stamp Manufacturing: Stamps printed for Ashton-Potter by Sterling Sommer, Tonawanda, New York, on Heidelberg 840 offset press. Stamps finished by Ashton-Potter.

Quantity Ordered: 55,000,000

Plate Number Detail: 1 set of 4 plate numbers preceded by the letter P in selvage above or below each corner stamp

Plate Number Combinations Reported: P1111, P2222

Paper Supplier: Tullis Russell

Tagging: phosphored paper

The Stamp

Leonard Bernstein was the most prominent figure in American classical music in the second half of the 20th century. As conductor of the New York Philharmonic, composer for the concert hall and the theater, piano virtuoso, author, teacher and lecturer, he was in the public eye and ear for decades before his death in 1990.

But when the Postal Service issued its Legends of Music series, consisting of 93 stamps between 1993 and 1999 honoring creators and performers in 14 musical categories, Bernstein wasn't eligible for inclusion. A rule of the Citizens' Stamp Advisory Committee prohibits stamps for anyone other than a former president until he or she has been dead for 10 years.

By 2001, Bernstein had met the 10-year requirement, and on July 10, USPS issued a 34¢ commemorative stamp depicting him in his conductor's role, a baton in his hand.

Before the Legends of Music series was inaugurated, the Postal Service had a long-running series called "Performing Arts" that included such musical achievers as George M. Cohan, John McCormack, Jerome Kern, Duke Ellington, Enrico Caruso, Arturo Toscanini and Cole Porter. However, the Bernstein stamp wasn't part of it.

The stamp was issued in New York, Bernstein's home city, in a ceremony that preceded the opening of the New York Philharmonic's 37th season of Concerts in the Parks in Central Park. It was placed on sale nationwide the following day.

Earlier, the Postal Service unveiled the design during the October 15, 2000, telecast of *CBS Sunday Morning with Charles Osgood*. Preliminary artwork had been shown to journalists during a USPS-sponsored meeting in August 2000.

The Bernstein stamp has water-activated gum and conventional perforations. It was offset-printed by Sterling Sommer for Ashton-Potter (USA) Ltd. and issued in panes of 20.

Leonard Bernstein — known as "Lenny" to his friends — was born August 25, 1918, in Lawrence, Massachusetts. He took piano lessons as a boy and developed a talent that led him to Harvard, where he earned a degree in music in 1939. In 1941 he received a diploma in conducting from the Curtis Institute of Music in Philadelphia. He also trained at the Berkshire Music Center at Tanglewood, Massachusetts.

In August 1943, Bernstein was named assistant conductor of the New York Philharmonic. On November 14, 1943, at 25, he substituted for the ailing guest conductor, Bruno Walter, and, without rehearsal, led the orchestra in a Carnegie Hall concert that was nationally aired on CBS radio. The reviews, including front-page coverage in *The New York Times*, were enthusiastic, and Bernstein's name suddenly was known throughout the country.

From 1945 to 1957, Bernstein was the music director of the New York City Symphony orchestra. In 1958, he became music director of the New York Philharmonic, the first conductor to hold that position who had been born and trained in the United States. He retired in 1969 to become the orchestra's laureate conductor, and continued to appear often with the Philharmonic and other great orchestras around the world.

He conveyed to players and audiences the excitement he felt in the music with a conducting style that was exuberant, emotional, animated and unique. "He was something to watch," recalled Howard Paine, art director and designer for the Bernstein stamp, "swinging his hips and shoulders, knifing and chopping the air with his arms, virtually pouncing on the orchestra!"

Bernstein composed symphonies, chamber music and vocal music as well as music for ballet, opera, film and the Broadway musical stage. Several compositions celebrate his Jewish heritage, including the symphonies *Jeremiah* and *Kaddish*. Among his other works are the symphony *The Age of Anxiety*, the ballet *Fancy Free*, the operas *Trouble in Tahiti* and *A Quiet Place*, and *Mass*, written for the opening of the Kennedy Center in Washington. His contributions to musical theater include scores for *On the Town*, *Wonderful Town*, *Candide* and *West Side Story*, which was made into an Academy Award-winning film. His score for the film *On the Waterfront* was nominated for an Academy Award.

Bernstein's televised lecture-demonstrations on *Omnibus* and in his *Young People's Concerts* series made the mysteries of musical theory, structure and performance comprehensible and appealing to millions of viewers. His books, such as *The Joy of Music* (1959), and his lectures, in particular the 1973 Norton lectures at Harvard ("The Unanswered Question"), enhanced his reputation as a great teacher.

He died in New York City October 14, 1990, a few days after announcing his retirement from public performances.

The Design

Howard Paine had been art director and designer of the Legends of Music series, and his initial thought was to use the same design approach for the Bernstein stamp that he had used for the Legends: semijumbo size, horizontally arranged, with a portrait done by an illustrator and the subject's name on a black panel suggestive of a torn ticket stub.

"I had hoped that any new stamp that came along for a music hero would reflect the format of the Legends series," Paine said. "I believe stamp collectors love continuity. Whether it's a ship or a lighthouse or a musician, they like to see it in an ongoing series.

"But Terry [Terrence McCaffrey, manager of stamp development] told me firmly, 'No, we're not going to continue the Legends of Music series. That's it. It's like the Transportation coils or Great Americans; it's done, dead, over with.' "

At least, Paine thought, he could order a Bernstein stamp portrait from the same artist, Burt Silverman, who had painted the classical composers and conductors for the 1997 Legends of American Music set in that category. Silverman is one of Paine's favorites. "Burt's work is 'painterly,' " Paine once said. "He works in oil, and you see dabs of color and you see brush strokes and you see the human touch."

But Silverman declined the job on grounds it was "work for hire," a reference to the Postal Service's policy of keeping the artwork it commissions and not returning it to the artist. Rather than consider another artist for the Bernstein assignment, Paine decided instead to find a suitable photograph of the musician and use it on the stamp.

PhotoAssist, the Postal Service's research firm, sent him a large selection of Bernstein photographs. From these, Paine chose two dramatically different images to adapt as stamp designs.

One of these depicts the conductor in action, eyes closed, head thrown back, white hair flying, hands upraised and clutching at the air. The picture was taken late in Bernstein's career as he rehearsed the orchestra for an 11-part public television series featuring the music of Beethoven. Paine worked up the photo in both square and horizontal commemorative-size formats.

The other photograph was a dignified frontal portrait of the conductor in formal wear, holding a baton in his right hand. It was taken in June 1968, when Bernstein was 50, by Don Hunstein, a photographer for CBS Records whose specialty was portraits of musicians. This image, which Paine arranged as a commemorative-size vertical, was chosen by CSAC for the stamp.

"It shows him as handsome and reflective," Paine said. "I started with

As an alternative design, Paine adapted a photograph of Bernstein in action on the podium for two formats, square and commemorative-size horizontal. The photo was taken late in Bernstein's career as he rehearsed the orchestra for a public television series featuring the music of Beethoven.

107

The photograph of Bernstein shown on the stamp was taken in June 1968 by Don Hunstein, a photographer for CBS Records. The print used by USPS was autographed by the musician. After the image was scanned, the autograph was removed electronically from the copy.

The letters "USPS" appear in microtype on the shirt cuff covering Bernstein's right wrist.

a great subject, got a good photo, cropped it and placed the type and sent it off. It was the easiest stamp ever to do."

The name "Leonard Bernstein," in uppercase and lowercase Galliard type, is dropped out of the background along the left side of the design. "34 USA," also in Galliard, is in the upper-right corner.

The stamp is single-color black, as Paine intended it to be from the beginning. However, in printing it Sterling Sommer used not only black but also the other three process colors, cyan, magenta and yellow, which imparted a richer look to the finished stamp.

Because an offset press was used, the Postal Service required microprinting in the design. The tiny letters "USPS" can be found on the shirt cuff covering Bernstein's right wrist.

First-day Facts

The first-day ceremony was held outdoors on the Great Lawn in Central Park. Zarin Mehta, executive director of the New York Philharmonic, gave the welcome and introduced the orchestra, and John F. Walsh, a member of the USPS Board of Governors, dedicated the stamp. "The ceremony was nearly over," *The New York Times* reported pointedly, "before anyone thought to tell the representative from the Postal Service's Board of Governors how to pronounce Bernstein's name. (It rhymes with fine.)"

The speakers were Paul B. Guenther, chairman of the board of the New York Philharmonic; Gerald M. Levin, chief executive officer of AOL Time Warner, a sponsor of the Concerts in the Parks series; Henry J. Stern, com-

108

missioner of parks and recreation for New York City; Schuyler G. Chapin, the city's commissioner of cultural affairs; and C. Virginia Fields, Manhattan borough president.

The first half of the concert that followed was devoted to Bernstein's music. Selections by the orchestra under guest conductor William Eddins, violinist Joshua Bell and soprano Kristin Chenoweth included the *Candide* overture, the aria *Glitter and Be Gay* from the same show, and dances and other themes from *West Side Story*.

The earliest-known prerelease use of a Leonard Bernstein stamp was on an envelope machine-canceled in Santa Clarita, California, July 5, five days before the official first day of issue.

34¢ LUCILLE BALL
LEGENDS OF HOLLYWOOD SERIES

Date of Issue: August 6, 2001

Catalog Number: Scott 3523

Colors: black, cyan, magenta, yellow

First-Day Cancel: Los Angeles, California

First-Day Cancellations: 144,398

Format: Panes of 20, vertical, 5 across, 4 down. Offset printing plates of 180 subjects (15 stamps across, 12 around). Also sold in uncut sheets of 9 panes, 3 across by 3 down.

Gum Type: self-adhesive

Overall Stamp Size: 0.99 inch by 1.56 inches; 25.15 by 39.62mm

Pane Size: 8.48 by 7.17 inches; 215.39 by 182.12mm

Uncut Press Sheet Size: 25.50 by 21.75 inches

Perforations: 11 (die-cut simulated perforations) (Speedmaster 102 rotary die cutter)

Selvage Inscription: "LEGENDS OF HOLLYWOOD/America's 'Queen of Comedy,' Lucille Ball,/is best loved for her portrayal of that wacky/redhead Lucy Ricardo in the 1950s TV series/*I Love Lucy*. Her wit, charm, and amazing/ability for physical comedy have endeared/this star of radio, stage, television, and film/to generations of fans worldwide." "Image of Lucille Ball is used/with permission of Desilu, too, LLC." " 'I Love Lucy' is a registered trademark/of CBS Worldwide Inc."

Selvage Markings: "© 2000 USPS." "20 x .34 = $6.80." "PLATE/POSITION" and diagram.

Illustrator: Drew Struzan of Pasadena, California

Designer, Typographer and Art Director: Derry Noyes of Washington, D.C.

Stamp Manufacturing: Stamps printed by Banknote Corporation of America (BCA), Browns Summit, North Carolina, on MAN Roland 300 offset press. Stamps finished by BCA.

Quantity Ordered: 110,000,000

Plate Number Detail: 1 set of 4 plate numbers preceded by the letter B in selvage beside each corner stamp

Plate Number Combination Reported: B1111

Paper Supplier: Paper Corporation of the United States/Glatfelter/Consolidated/Spinnaker Coating

Tagging: block tagging on stamps

The Stamp

The seventh stamp in the Postal Service's Legends of Hollywood series, and the first to be a self-adhesive, honored actress Lucille Ball, star of film, stage, radio and the memorable 1950s television situation comedy *I Love Lucy*. It was issued in Hollywood, California, August 6, which would have been Ball's 90th birthday.

The stamp was the second in a little more than two years to depict the actress. A stamp on the Celebrate the Century pane for the decade of the 1950s, issued May 26, 1999, featured a black-and-white photograph of Ball and her husband, Desi Arnaz, in their TV personas as Lucy and Ricky Ricardo.

Ball's Legends of Hollywood stamp displays a portrait painted by Drew Struzan showing the subject as herself. However, the image on the wide selvage on the right side — a standard feature of the series — is a photograph that again shows Ball in her *I Love Lucy* role.

The previous stamps in the annual series honored Marilyn Monroe (1995), James Dean, Humphrey Bogart, Alfred Hitchcock, James Cagney and Edward G. Robinson. Like them, the Lucille Ball stamp is vertically arranged and was

111

The 33¢ I Love Lucy stamp, from the 1950s Celebrate the Century pane (Scott 3187l) issued in 1999, pictures both Ball and Desi Arnaz.

issued in panes of 20. It also was made available to collectors in uncut press sheets of nine panes at face value ($61.20).

The pattern of its die-cut simulated perfs is similar to the pattern of the conventional perfs on the previous Legends of Hollywood stamps. A second row of die-cuts around the outer edges of the block of 20 stamps creates a narrow inner selvage, which is blank except for a set of plate numbers in each corner. The seven horizontal rows of die cuts extend to the edge of the pane on the left side and penetrate the liner paper, enabling postal clerks to detach and sell single or multiple stamps.

However, because it is die-cut, the Ball stamp lacks the star-shaped perfs at the corners that had become a consistent feature of the Legends of Hollywood series. In addition, it was the first stamp in the series to be printed by a company other than Sennett Security Products or its predecessor, Stamp Venturers. Sennett produced the first six Legends stamps by the gravure process; this one was offset-printed by Banknote Corporation of America.

The tagging pattern also differs from those of the previous panes of the series. On the first three, for Monroe, Dean and Bogart, a large block of taggant was applied over all 20 stamps but stopped short of the outer margins of the 14 outside stamps, leaving those margins untagged (and making single stamps from the outside distinguishable from each other and from the six singles from the interior of the pane). On the next three panes, the block of taggant was extended to the outer perforations of the 20 stamps but not beyond. On the Lucille Ball pane, however, the taggant extends beyond the stamps and slightly into the selvage.

Ball was the first entertainer to be honored in the series who is primarily remembered for her television work. Although she appeared in 87 movies, she is closely identified in the public's mind with the *I Love Lucy* sitcom.

Her selection as the subject of the 2001 Legends stamp was announced and the design was unveiled July 21, 2000, more than a year before the stamp's issuance. The unveiling took place at the Hilton Burbank Airport Convention Center in Burbank, California, to open Loving Lucy 2000, the international Lucille Ball fan club's fifth annual convention.

Lucille Desiree Ball was born August 6, 1911, in Celeron, New York, near Jamestown. Although she was one of the world's most famous redheads, she was a natural brunette.

She was raised by her grandparents. Show business attracted Ball at an early age, and she became a Ziegfield Girl while still in her teens. She made her movie debut in 1933 as a slave girl in the Eddie Cantor vehicle *Roman Scandals*, and worked in bit parts through the 1930s, graduating to starring roles in 1940s "B" movies. One of her best-remembered big screen roles was as Groucho Marx's girlfriend in *Room Service*.

A part in *Too Many Girls*, the 1940 film version of the Rodgers and Hart musical, changed Ball's life and entertainment history. She and fellow cast member Desiderato (Desi) Arnaz fell in love and were married later that year.

Ball starred in the radio comedy *My Favorite Husband* from 1948 to 1950. When TV executives asked her to re-create the role for the new medium, she persuaded them to include her real-life husband in the program. The executives reportedly were apprehensive about whether American viewers would accept an Anglo-Hispanic mixed marriage in a TV comedy. They need not have worried.

I Love Lucy, which ran from 1951 to 1957, was one of the most popular series in TV history. The January 19, 1953, episode in which Lucy Ricardo gave birth to "Little Ricky" was watched by more people than any other show of its time. The 50-year-old episodes still are aired in syndication in more than 80 countries. Ball and Arnaz are credited with numerous television production innovations, including the use of three cameras in filming episodes before a live audience.

The show's popularity led to a new format, *The Lucy-Desi Comedy Hour*, which ran from 1957 until Ball and Arnaz divorced in 1960. The couple founded their own studio, Desilu Productions. Ball bought out her ex-husband in 1962 to become sole owner of Desilu and the first woman to head a major Hollywood production company.

From 1962 until 1974, she was featured in two other network TV shows, *The Lucy Show* and *Here's Lucy*. Her final venture into TV sitcoms, *Life With Lucy* in 1986, lasted only a single season. She made eight TV specials and many guest appearances on other programs, starred in the Broadway musical *Wildcat* in 1960, and returned to films in later life, receiving a Golden Globe nomination for her title role in the 1974 movie musical *Mame*.

Ball's last TV appearance, a year before her death on April 26, 1989, was on *America's Tribute to Bob Hope*. She was posthumously awarded the Presidential Medal of Freedom.

The Design

To create the portrait for the Lucille Ball stamp, art director Derry Noyes called on Drew Struzan, a well-known artist in the entertainment field whose most recent stamp credits were the Edward G. Robinson stamp in the Legends of Hollywood series and the 15 Celebrate the Century stamps for the decade of the 1990s.

Ball's children, Luci Arnaz and Desi Arnaz Jr., made it clear that they wanted their mother depicted on a stamp not as Lucy Ricardo, a comedienne or clown. "They said their mother was much bigger than that; she

An early pencil sketch by Drew Struzan showed Ball in clown costume and makeup. Her children, however, wanted her shown as a glamorous woman.

This circa 1955 black-and-white photograph of the actress was the source of Drew Struzan's stamp portrait.

was a movie star," said Terrence McCaffrey, manager of stamp development for USPS. "We had done a stamp for Celebrate the Century that featured *I Love Lucy*, so we told them, 'Sure, we'll do a portrait of your mother.'

"They provided the photograph they wanted us to work from. It was very striking."

The photo, made circa 1955 by an unknown professional, showed Ball in a glamorous pose, wearing a black beaded gown and diamond earrings. Struzan used it as the model for his acrylic-and-colored pencil portrait of the actress. Because the photo was black and white, he had to provide the color, including an appropriate shade of red for the hair and a blue for the eyes that the artist echoed in her earrings and their shadow on her neck. As he had done with his Celebrate the Century stamps, Struzan gave his artwork a "soft edge" instead of the hard frameline that has characterized previous Legends of Hollywood designs.

Luci and Desi Jr. were dissatisfied with the first version of the portrait. "They said, 'There are too many speckles on her face,' " McCaffrey recalled. "But that was Drew's style; they were looking at paint flecks, which looked like freckles to them. They said her nose was too long, her chin was too long, her cheek was too pronounced, one eye was larger than the other — there were a number of things they were concerned about. We all sat there and just stared at the art and at the photograph and said, 'We don't see it. This is a perfect likeness.'

"I took the black-and-white photo and I made a film positive on our copier, a good halftone positive, and made it the exact same size as Drew's art, and I laid it right over the top and it fit perfectly. Her chin was perfect, her nose was perfect, her eyes were the same size — everything was perfect.

"We toned down the speckles on her face, and softened the line in her cheek, all on the computer. We sent it back to the family without mentioning that we had made no other changes, and they loved it."

Derry Noyes' typography consisted of a small "33 usa" in blue Frutiger type, tucked into the space between Ball's shoulder and hair, and the name "Lucille Ball" across the top, in a white scriptlike typeface called Snell. "I wanted to make the typography as subtle as possible," Noyes said. "I think we managed to make it readable without blasting you with it."

Having met the children's wishes insofar as the stamp portrait was concerned, postal officials felt no constraint against using a scene from *I Love Lucy* in the stamp selvage. Struzan provided a painted version, showing Lucy talking on the telephone, but Noyes and the Citizens' Stamp Advisory Committee decided that a black-and-white photo would more accurately represent the television show and would offer an attractive contrast to the colorful painted portrait on the stamp.

"It was fun to go back and look at all the old *I Love Lucy* images," Noyes said. "Everyone on the committee had opinions about what they wanted to see there. But it had to work in a vertical space, and once again the family didn't want her looking too outrageous."

The contenders included scenes from the "candy factory" episode, in which Lucy and her friend Ethel Mertz take jobs on a candy assembly line; the "grape stomping" episode, featuring Lucy working in a vineyard; and the show in which the star is hired to do a TV commercial for "Vitameatavegamin" health tonic. The photo that finally was chosen shows Lucy in a state of openmouthed surprise and is from Episode 175, "Housewarming," that first aired April 1, 1957.

"It had that expression on her face that we're all so used to, and the gesture," Noyes said. "It allowed room for type in the selvage, and it worked as a vertical, even though the overall picture is a horizontal."

The stamp design includes the microprinted letters "USPS." These can be found on Ball's shoulder, in one of the see-through portions of her bodice.

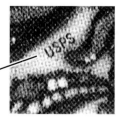

The microprinted letters "USPS" can be found on Ball's shoulder, in one of the see-through portions of her bodice.

These are three alternative selvage images showing episodes from I Love Lucy that were considered by Derry Noyes and CSAC, including one in color that was painted by stamp illustrator Drew Struzan and two black-and-white stills.

Varieties

Soon after the stamp was issued, panes lacking their die-cut simulated perforations were purchased at post offices in California and Iowa.

First-day Facts

Alan C. Kessler, a member of the USPS Board of Governors, dedicated the stamp in a ceremony in the lobby of the Hollywood History Museum at the old Max Factor Building. The site was appropriate, in that Ball's promotional arrangement with Max Factor began in 1935 and lasted longer than that of any other star.

Speakers were Jean Picker Firstenberg, director and chief executive officer of the American Film Institute; actress Virginia Mayo; and Fred Ball, Lucille Ball's brother, the only family member present.

Johnny Grant, chairman of the Walk of Fame and honorary mayor of Hollywood, was master of ceremonies. He reminded the audience that it was he who pushed Lucy into the wet cement outside the Chinese Theater in a classic episode of *I Love Lucy*.

The welcome was given by Donelle Dadigan, founder and president of the Hollywood History Museum. Stamp illustrator Drew Struzan was on hand to autograph covers for collectors.

"The Max Factor Building was an integral part of Ball's career, but it was a poor choice for a first-day ceremony of such magnitude," John E. Peterson, secretary-treasurer of the American Ceremony Program Society, wrote in *Linn's Stamp News*.

"Fewer than 20 of the more than 100 people lined up to enter the ceremony actually got in to see it. The lobby ... was simply too small to accommodate everyone who wished to witness the ceremony. By the time the press, celebrities, USPS employees and personal guests of the venue's owner came in, there was little room left for the public, many of whom had invitations.

"The fire marshal was on hand to make sure that the venue was not overcrowded. Chairs had to be removed, and it was standing room only in one part of the lobby ...

"Local postal officials in Los Angeles warned the promotions staff at USPS headquarters that the venue was inadequate for the number of people expected to attend. The promotions staff thought that the ceremony would be held in a larger room upstairs. ... Although the agreement over which room the ceremony was to be in was apparently broken, the decision was made to stay with the venue since the USPS had already publicized it."

The Postal Service's decision to issue the stamp in Hollywood rather than in or near Ball's hometown was criticized by Michael Calleri, a columnist in the Buffalo, New York, alternative newspaper *Blue Dog*. "The fabled Lucy's [90th] birthday anniversary is being celebrated at the Lucy-Desi Museum in Jamestown with a three-day party, to be held

August 3-5," he wrote. "In town that weekend will be Lucy and Desi Arnaz's children. So where is the vaunted USPS issuing the Lucy stamp? ... [A]lthough issuing it in Jamestown would make sense to even the most dimwitted dim bulb, the stamp is first being released in some seedy post office in Los Angeles."

The earliest-known prerelease use of a Lucille Ball stamp was on a cover hand-canceled Fresno, California, August 4, two days before the official first day of issue.

34¢ AMISH QUILTS (4 DESIGNS)
AMERICAN TREASURES SERIES

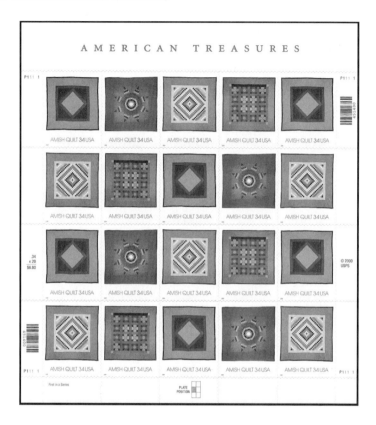

Date of Issue: August 9, 2001

Catalog Numbers: Scott 3524-3527, single stamps; 3527a, block or strip of 4

Colors: black, cyan, magenta, yellow, red (PMS 187)

First-Day Cancel: Nappanee, Indiana

First-Day Cancellations: 320,195

Format: Panes of 20, vertical, 5 across, 4 down. Offset printing plates of 120 subjects (8 across, 15 around).

Gum Type: self-adhesive

Overall Stamp Size: 1.225 by 1.560 inches; 31.115 by 39.624mm

Pane Size: 7.063 by 7.750 inches; 179.40 by 196.85mm

Perforations: 11¼ by 11½ (die-cut simulated perfs)

Selvage Inscription: "AMERICAN TREASURES." "First in a Series."

Selvage Markings: ".34/x20/$6.80." "©USPS/2000." "PLATE/POSITION" and diagram. Universal Product Code (UPC) "451400" in 2 locations.

Designer, Art Director and Typographer: Derry Noyes of Washington, D.C.

Modeler: Joseph Sheeran of Ashton-Potter (USA) Ltd., Williamsville, New York

Stamp Manufacturing: Stamps printed by Ashton-Potter (USA) Ltd. on offset portion of Stevens Variable Size Security Documents webfed 6-color offset, 3-color intaglio press. Stamps finished by Ashton-Potter.

Quantity Ordered: 96,000,000

Plate Number Detail: 1 set of 5 plate numbers preceded by the letter P in selvage next to each corner stamp

Plate Number Combinations Reported: P11111, P22222

Paper Supplier: Fasson/Tullis Russell

Tagging: block tagging over stamps

The Stamps

On August 9, the Postal Service inaugurated a new series it called "American Treasures" with a set of four stamps depicting colorful Amish quilts. The first-day sale was held in Nappanee, Indiana, a state with the second largest Amish population in the United States, after Ohio and ahead of Pennsylvania.

According to USPS, "The Amish quilt is a uniquely American folk-art form. Distinctive in its simplicity, symmetry, deft needlework and broad fields of deep color, the Amish quilt is one of the most expressive in American design. Amish quilting traditions vary from region to region, yet all are influenced by the religious and social values of Amish daily life: humility, simplicity, modesty and serviceability.

"The four quilts repeated on this pane of stamps display the saturated colors, bold geometric patterns and central design motifs characteristic of quilts made in Lancaster County, Pennsylvania, in the first half of the 20th century. The quilts belong to the Foundation for Deep Ecology in San Francisco, and are curated by The Quilt Complex, located in Albion, California.

"Unknown Amish quilt makers in Lancaster County ... created each quilt in pieced wools. From left to right in the top row, the four quilts are: Diamond in the Square, circa 1920, 78 by 78 inches; Lone Star, circa 1920, 88 by 89 inches; Sunshine and Shadow, circa 1910, 80 by 80 inches; and Double Ninepatch (variation), 79 by 79 inches."

Diamond in the Square, also called Center Diamond, is one of the oldest and plainest of

  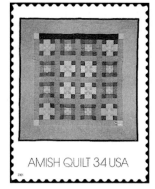

Amish quilt patterns. Lone Star features a large star that appears to burst from the center of the design. Sunshine and Shadow received its name from the light and dark effects achieved by the positioning of squares of color to form a series of concentric diamonds. The Double Ninepatch variation, circa 1940, has 16 double nine patches, with each double nine patch resembling a small tick-tack-toe board inside a larger one.

Ashton-Potter (USA) produced the semi-jumbo self-adhesive stamps by the offset process and distributed them in panes of 20. The stamps are arranged on the pane in what USPS described as "a repeating, rhythmic, quiltlike pattern," with each block of four containing all four varieties.

Most 20-stamp panes with four designs contain five specimens of each design. The Amish Quilts pane, however, achieves its quiltlike look by combining six each of two varieties — Diamond in the Square and Sunshine and Shadow, arranged in symmetrical patterns — and four each of the other two varieties, laid out in zigzag patterns.

The pane header displays the inscription "AMERICAN TREASURES," in a font called Minion, which will be used to identify future stamps and sets in the series.

Terrence McCaffrey, USPS manager of stamp development, explained in an interview with *Stamp Collector*'s Fred Baumann why the Postal Service was launching a new series when a seemingly similar series, American Folk Art, had produced several sets of

A previous set of U.S. quilt stamps was this 1978 se-tenant block of 13¢ American Folk Art commemoratives depicting basket designs (Scott 1745-48) designed by Christopher Pullman after an 1875 quilt made in New York City.

se-tenant commemoratives in quartets — including one (Scott 1745-1748), in 1978, that featured quilts.

"The American Folk Art series seemed to die of its own volition," McCaffrey said. "There was no concentrated effort to kill the series. We just moved on to other projects. We also try to not let series go on for great lengths of time. So, in retrospect, having a series run from between 1977 and 1995 [American Folk Art's span], we felt that was plenty of time.

"The new American Treasures series was established by the Citizens' Stamp Advisory Committee as a way of using existing art masterpieces — fine art, crafts or whatever. CSAC wanted to showcase the various types of art within a format that would get more use on mail. The [1996 32¢] Georgia O'Keeffe Poppy spurred them to do it. They found that the Poppy was used more on mail than other commemoratives, so they wanted to develop a series of attractive, colorful images that people would be prone to use on their mail.

"Other distinguishing features that set American Treasures apart from American Folk Art are the commemorative header at the top of each pane and being a series in a self-adhesive format. So what really sets the two series apart is the fact that in this new series we will be using fine art paintings, not just blankets, bowls and crafts."

A USPS press release further explained that the American Treasures series was created to showcase subjects that might otherwise not have been selected for stamps because they lacked a date-specific anniversary or some other logical reason to be honored.

"The idea behind the series was to create stamps using beautiful, artistic images that highlighted American art treasures, whether they are painting, crafts, photography or other mediums of artistic expression," the release said. "The name was chosen because USPS wanted to identify these ... as 'treasures' worthy of commemoration."

Derry Noyes, one of the Postal Service's part-time art directors, was assigned the job of deciding "what belongs in this category; what does one think of as truly an American Treasure," she said. "The idea of Amish quilts jumped right out at me.

"I've always loved textiles, and I particularly loved quilts. I had been toying with the idea of doing quilts on stamps as a way to reflect our diversity as a country; there are so many different kinds.

"Amish quilts are colorful and beautiful and graphic — they hold up beautifully at stamp size — so it seemed obvious to me that they should be part of this series. When I started playing around with the designs, they held up so well that they filled the bill for the first one."

It had been CSAC's intention that stamps in the American Treasures series be available continuously at post offices. Unfortunately, Noyes said, after the Amish Quilts set was issued, "the stamps turned out to be very much like other commemoratives, in that once the post offices ran out of them they weren't reordered. It was too bad not to see them around longer."

The Designs

Derry Noyes previously had served as art director for the two American Folk Art sets that featured fabrics: Navajo Art (1986), which she also designed, and Lacemaking (1987).

For the inaugural set in the American Treasures series, she experimented with various configurations of panes and convertible booklets, including some in which the stamps were of the special size used for holiday and Love stamps and some that included a fifth Amish quilt design. CSAC decided to limit the set to four varieties, semijumbo in size and arranged vertically, in a 20-stamp pane format.

In her design, common to each stamp, the square quilt floats against a white background. The inscription "AMISH QUILT 34 USA" is contained in a single line of Avant-Garde Extra Light type beneath the quilt. The letters are gray — actually, a screened black — and the numbers are red (PMS 187), a color also used for the words on the header.

The quilts Noyes selected are illustrated in *Amish: The Art of the Quilt*, text by Robert Hughes, published by

This early layout of a 20-stamp pane includes a fifth Amish quilt design (upper-right corner) and contains four specimens of each design variety.

Among the formats tried by Derry Noyes during the development of the Amish Quilts stamps was this double-sided booklet.

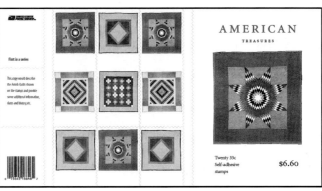

123

Alfred A. Knopf Inc. "It was just a matter of finding four — not unlike the Navajo rugs — that are compatible, yet different enough that you feel as if you are getting variety," she said.

"I could have done four that were all like the first one, the red diamond, but in different colors, but I would have had to leave out the stars and the little checks. I could have done 20 different quilts, which would have been gorgeous, but that would have inflated the stamp program, and we wouldn't do it."

In designing the individual stamps, Noyes had to decide whether to commit herself and CSAC to a common design style that would continue in future American Treasures issues. "Am I going to go with squares forever, with one little line of type at the bottom, or will there be variety within the series?" she asked herself. "What's going to make it hold together as a series?

"I decided that the header would be the same on all of them — the colors might be different, but the type would remain the same — and that would tie them together. It would allow me, as I got into the series, to change the typography on the stamps, because some would be commemorative size and shape and some would be semijumbo, and sometimes the type could be integrated into the art and not apart from it, as it had to be with the Amish quilts."

The words "First in a Series" are printed in the selvage beneath the lower-left corner stamp. It was the first time USPS had launched a stamp series with such an explicit promise of more to come.

First-day Facts

Danny Jackson, vice president for Great Lakes Area operations for USPS, dedicated the stamps in a ceremony at the Round Barn Theatre at Amish Acres Historic Farm in the small town of Nappanee, which has an Amish community numbering more than 2,500. The event was part of opening day of the 39th annual Amish Acres Arts and Crafts Festival.

The principal speaker was Richard Pletcher, founder and chief executive officer of Amish Acres. Kenneth J. Brown, USPS Greater Indiana District manager, was master of ceremonies, and Nappanee Mayor Larry Thompson gave the welcome. Honored guests included LaVern and Lenore Pletcher, co-founders of Amish Acres; Wilma George, an Amish Acres docent; and Joy Johnson, a quilter.

A special pictorial first-day cancellation depicting the Round Barn Theatre was designed by Nappanee artist Jeff Stillson, creative director for Amish Acres.

This pictorial first-day cancellation depicting the Round Barn Theatre was designed by Jeff Stillson, creative director for Amish Acres.

First Day of Issue
August 9, 2001

34¢ CARNIVOROUS PLANTS (4 DESIGNS)

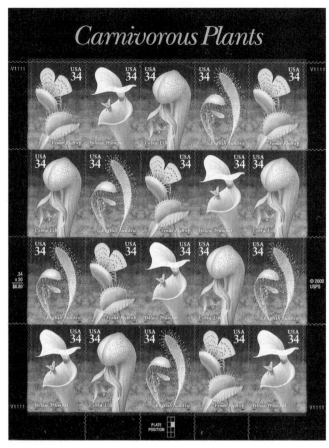

Date of Issue: August 23, 2001

Catalog Numbers: Scott 3528-3531, single stamps; 3531a, block or strip of 4

Colors: yellow, magenta, cyan, black

First-Day Cancel: Des Plaines, Illinois

First-Day Cancellations: 301,922

Format: Panes of 20, vertical, 5 across, 4 down. Gravure printing cylinders of 160 subjects, 10 across, 16 around, manufactured by Armotek Industries.

Gum Type: self-adhesive

Overall Stamp Size: 0.990 by 1.560 inches; 25.146 by 39.624mm

Pane Size: 5.85 by 7.75 inches; 148.59 by 196.85mm

Perforations: 11½ (die-cut simulated perforations) (Comco Commander rotary die cutter)

Selvage Inscription: "Carnivorous Plants"

Selvage Markings: "© 2000/USPS." ".34 x 20/=$6.80." "PLATE/POSITION" and diagram.

Illustrator, Designer and Typographer: Steve Buchanan of Winsted, Connecticut

Art Director: Phil Jordan of Falls Church, Virginia

Stamp Manufacturing: Stamps printed by Avery Dennison Security Printing Division, Clinton, South Carolina, on 8-color Dia Nippon Kiko webfed gravure press. Stamps processed by Avery Dennison.

Quantity Ordered: 100,000,000

Plate Number Detail: 1 set of 4 plate numbers preceded by the letter V in selvage next to each corner stamp

Plate Number Combination Reported: V1111

Paper Supplier: Fasson Division of Avery Dennison

Tagging: block tagging on stamps

The Stamps

Because botanical items are among the most frequent U.S. stamp subjects, the Citizens' Stamp Advisory Committee is challenged to come up with variations that haven't been used before. It found one in the form of carnivorous plants. On August 23 USPS issued a block of stamps depicting four flesh-eating flora native to the United States.

The stamps were dedicated at the American Philatelic Society Stampshow 2001 in Rosemont, Illinois, a suburb of Chicago, although the official first-day city was nearby Des Plaines. They were placed on sale nationwide the following day.

The self-adhesive stamps were gravure-printed by Avery Dennison Security Products Division and issued in panes of 20, so arranged that any block of four or vertical strip of four contains all four varieties and any horizontal strip of five contains all four plus one duplicate. USPS announced that postal clerks would be allowed to separate single stamps from the pane to be sold individually, an option not often given for multiple-image issues in sheet form.

Carnivorous plants have structures suited for attracting, trapping and digesting insects. Some 500 species are known worldwide, many of them found in swamps and marshlands. The four shown on the stamps are the Venus flytrap, yellow trumpet, cobra lily and English sundew.

The Venus flytrap (dionaea muscipula), which is common in the coastal areas of the Carolinas, is shown with a metalmark butterfly caught in one of its traps. The other trap is open, revealing the bright pink-red interior that serves as a lure.

The trap is a modified leaf, consisting of two lobes. Each lobe is lined with a row of spikes that interlock when the lobes are closed. A small number of bristles, called trigger hairs, are found on the inside of each lobe. If a hapless insect bumps one of these hairs, the lobes rapidly close on it.

The plant secretes enzymes, which dissolve the insect's tissues. The resulting fluids are absorbed by the plant. After several days, the trap opens and the insect's chitinous remains fall out or are carried away by the wind.

The yellow trumpet (sarracenia flava) is also known as the trumpet, yellow pitcher plant or huntsman's horn. Found in the southeastern United States, the plant can reach four feet in height.

Its trap, also a modified leaf, is long and tubular. It flares at the end, like a trumpet. Scented nectar ringing the flared end entices an insect, such as the fly shown on the stamp, to alight and investigate. A narcoticlike substance in the nectar dulls the insect's awareness as it feeds.

While moving around to find more nectar, the creature encounters a slippery surface just below the rim of the pitcher and falls into a pool of water and digestive enzymes at the bottom. The narrowness of the space hampers the insect's wings, and downward-pointing hairs that line the tube assist its descent but prevent it from climbing out.

The cobra lily (darlingtonia californica) is native to the Pacific coast and is sometimes called the California pitcher plant. It has an upright pitcher like the yellow trumpet, but the top folds over, forming a chamber that resembles the spread hood of an agitated cobra.

Translucent patches cover the top of the chamber. A brightly colored ribbonlike structure near the mouth lures an insect, like the unwary wasp shown on the stamp, toward the opening. Once inside, the prey flies toward the light entering the top of the chamber. Unable to escape because of a collar around the entrance, the creature eventually falls to the bottom of the pitcher, where it is digested.

Yellow Trumpet

Cobra Lily

English Sundew

The English sundew (drosera anglica) is a small plant found in mossy bogs across the northern United States and on the Pacific coast as far south as California. Its beauty belies its deadly nature.

Its modified leaves are covered with slender tentacles, the tips of which secrete clear drops of sticky mucous that glisten in the sunlight, giving the plant its name. Insects like the syrphid fly shown on the stamp are attracted, but when they alight they are trapped. During digestion by enzymes in the mucous, the leaf often bends around its prey.

The Designs

The designs represent Steve Buchanan's third creative effort for USPS. He illustrated the four 33¢ Tropical Flowers stamps and the 20 33¢ Insects and Spiders stamps, both issued in 1999.

Buchanan creates his artwork on a computer, using a digitizing tablet and stylus as a painting tool and viewing the results in progress on his monitor. He describes the digitizing tablet as a pressure-sensitive flat plastic pad with a working area about a foot square on which he sketches, using the stylus and tablet like a pencil, brush or charcoal on paper. Pressing down harder with the stylus creates a broader stroke, just as it would if he were using more conventional art implements.

The four plants, illuminated from the upper left, are shown against a background of a grassy field that shades into black in the top one-third of the stamp. Each design bleeds off all four sides of the stamp and into adjacent designs. The designs of the stamps on the outside of the block of 20 extend slightly beyond the die-cut simulated perfs into the selvage, which is solid black.

Care was required on the part of the printer to line up each horizontal row of die cuts with the edge where the grassy bottom of a horizontal strip of stamps meets the black top of the strip beneath it. The slight encroachment that can be found on some singles isn't readily apparent because of the subtlety of Buchanan's shading and the overall darkness of the background.

PhotoAssist, the Postal Service's research firm, hired a quartet of consultants for the project. They were: William B. McLaughlin of the U.S. Botanic Garden; Jay Lechtman, president of the International Carnivorous Plant Society and the National Capital Carnivorous Plant Society; Donald E. Schnell, author of *Carnivorous Plants of the United States and Canada*; and C. Ritchie Bell, professor emeritus of the Department of Botany at the University of North Carolina, Chapel Hill. They provided a list of recommended plants for the project, and Buchanan set to work, using books from the New York Botanical Garden library and his own collection as visual reference sources.

Two of the four plants on the consultants' list, the Venus flytrap and cobra lily, are on the issued stamps. However, the list also included intermediate sundew (drosera intermedia) and an alternative, the sundew (drosera roundifolia). These eventually were replaced by the English sundew (drosera anglica). The white-topped pitcher plant (sarracenia leuco-phylla) also was listed, along with an alternative, the purple pitcher plant (sarracenia purpurea); they were replaced by a close relative, the yellow trumpet (sarracenia flava).

In an e-mail message to art director Phil Jordan in August 1998, accompanying a group of early sketches, Buchanan described the problem with the consultants' list as he saw it.

"As a botanical selection they're completely sensible, but as graphic subjects it seems to me they have some limitations," the artist wrote. "The colors of all four of them are predominately yellow-green with maroon markings. Even the flowers of the cobra lily and white pitcher plant are maroon.

"Also, the sundews are so much smaller than the others that it will be impossible to do anything that suggests the relative sizes of the four plants, and their habit as a flat rosette of leaves is hard to cast into the vertical format that the taller plants seem to require."

Substituting the yellow trumpet, on the other hand, "provides some yellow both in leaves and flowers," Buchanan noted, and another variety of sundew "is larger and has a more useful vertical habit."

In a message accompanying additional sketches in October 1998, Buchanan offered another idea. "We could take advantage of the fact that Venus flytraps can actually catch small moths and butterflies to expand our color range," he wrote. "We'll choose a butterfly with some useful color."

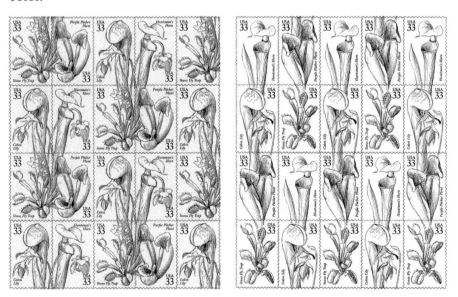

In these early pencil-sketch layouts by Steve Buchanan, the designs flow into each other horizontally and vertically in one example, and vertically in the other. The purple pitcher plant in these sketches ultimately was replaced by the English sundew.

This colored pencil sketch depicts the four plants and their prey approximately as they are seen on the finished stamps, only with a white background at the top instead of a black one. On the consultant's recommendation, the name "huntsman's horn" was changed to "yellow trumpet," "sundew" became "English sundew" and "fly trap" was made one word.

Inclusion of the butterfly prompted some discussion among the consultants. One said he never had seen a Venus flytrap devour a butterfly or moth, but another had personally witnessed such an event. In the end, the experts agreed that the little orange metalmark would be an appropriate prey for the plant shown on the stamp.

The English names of the plants are in white Baskerville type in a lower corner of each design. "USA 34" is in an upper corner, dropped out of the black background.

Similarly, all marginal markings on the pane are dropped out of the black selvage. The header bears the words "Carnivorous Plants," in green type, also Baskerville. The four gravure cylinder numbers preceded by the letter V in each corner of the selvage are printed in the appropriate colors. The number for the black cylinder and the V are screened (gray) to make them visible.

First-day Facts

Einar V. Dyhrkopp, a member of the USPS Board of Governors, dedicated the stamps in a ceremony held in the Donald E. Stephens Convention Center in Rosemont on the first day of the four-day stamp exhibition.

Stamp artist Steve Buchanan was the speaker. Danny Jackson, USPS vice president for the Great Lakes area, was master of ceremonies, and Peter McCann, president of the American Philatelic Society, gave the welcome. Honored guests included John M. Hotchner and Ronald A. Robinson of CSAC.

34¢ ENRICO FERMI

Date of Issue: September 29, 2001

Catalog Number: Scott 3533

Colors: black, cyan, magenta, yellow

First-Day Cancel: Chicago, Illinois

First-Day Cancellations: 107,498

Format: Panes of 20, vertical, 5 across, 4 down. Offset printing plates of 180 subjects, 12 across, 15 around.

Gum Type: water-activated

Overall Stamp Size: 0.99 by 1.56 inches; 25.171 by 39.624mm

Pane Size: 5.940 by 7.135 inches; 150.876 by 181.229mm

Perforations: 11 (Wista stroke perforator)

Selvage Markings: "© 2000/USPS." ".34/x20/$6.80." "PLATE/POSITION" and diagram. Universal Product Code (UPC) "451500" in 2 positions.

Photo Source: American Institute of Physics Emilio Segre Visual Archives

Designer, Art Director and Typographer: Richard Sheaff of Scottsdale, Arizona

Modeler: Joseph Sheeran of Ashton-Potter (USA) Ltd., Williamsville, New York

Stamp Manufacturing: Stamps printed for Ashton-Potter by Sterling Sommer, Tonawanda, New York, on Akiyama 628 offset press. Stamps finished by Ashton-Potter.

Quantity Ordered: 30,000,000

Plate Number Detail: 1 set of 4 plate numbers preceded by the letter P in selvage above or below each corner stamp

Plate Number Combination Reported: P1111

Paper Supplier: Tullis Russell Coatings

Tagging: phosphored paper

The Stamp

On September 29, the Postal Service issued a stamp in honor of Enrico Fermi, one of the leading physicists of the atomic age. The date was the 100th anniversary of Fermi's birth.

The stamp was dedicated at the University of Chicago in Chicago, Illinois. Here, during World War II, Fermi supervised the design and assembly of the first nuclear reactor as part of the secret Manhattan Project, the coordinated U.S. effort to produce an atomic bomb.

Italy, where Fermi was born, also issued a stamp September 29 to mark his centennial. However, it was not a joint issue with the United States. The Italian stamp was designed by Christian Bruscaglia and is denominated 800 lira/0.41 euros.

The Citizens' Stamp Advisory Committee approved a commemorative for Fermi in keeping with a desire to include more scientists in the stamp program, according to Terrence McCaffrey, manager of stamp development for USPS. Later, CSAC and Postal Service officials thought their Fermi stamp might do double duty as a joint issue with Sweden to commemorate the 100th anniversary of the Nobel Prize, of which Fermi was a recipient, but Sweden turned down the idea (see chapter on the Nobel Prize stamp).

The Fermi stamp was offset-printed by Sterling Sommer for Ashton-Potter (USA) Ltd. It has water-activated gum and conventional perforations and was issued in panes of 20. Only 30 million were ordered, a low printing for a modern U.S. commemorative.

Enrico Fermi was the son of a high-ranking Italian civil servant. He received a doctorate in physics from the University of Pisa in 1922, later studied in Germany, and from 1927 to 1938 was professor of theoretical physics at the University of Rome in his home city. He was made a Nobel laureate in physics in 1938 for his work with slow or thermal neutrons, which are of paramount importance for a controlled chain reaction.

Shortly after receiving the prize in Stockholm, Fermi fled Italy with his wife, Laura Capon — who was Jewish — and their two children to escape anti-Semitic persecution under Mussolini. In 1939, he began teaching physics at Columbia University.

The Fermis were part of a growing stream of refugees from totalitarianism and anti-Semitism who would enhance America's scientific prowess and help win the war. The core members of the group that would build the atomic

This is Italy's 800-lira/0.41-euro stamp marking the 100th anniversary of the birth of Enrico Fermi. Although issued on the same day, September 29, it was not a joint issue with the United States.

bomb were all European emigres: Eugene Wigner, Edward Teller, Leo Szilard, Hans Bethe, John von Neumann and Fermi himself.

It was Fermi, along with Teller and Szilard, who persuaded Albert Einstein, another refugee, to write his famous letter to President Franklin D. Roosevelt warning of German research into atomic weapons and urging that the United States enter the race. The letter led directly to the Manhattan Project and the world's first functional nuclear reactor, designed and built by Fermi and Szilard.

The reactor, consisting of uranium rods and a graphite core, was built on a doubles squash court beneath the stands of the University of Chicago's Amos Alonzo Stagg Field. Fermi and his team made history December 2, 1942, when they achieved the first controlled and self-sustaining man-made nuclear chain reaction. Their success was fundamental to the production of plutonium; thereafter, the actual construction of the atomic bomb became the primary focus of the Manhattan Project.

In September 1944, Fermi moved to Los Alamos, New Mexico, to help direct the project's scientific team there. He was present when the first atomic bomb was tested in the desert near Alamogordo July 16, 1945.

After the war, he joined the faculty of the new Institute for Nuclear Studies at the University of Chicago. There he turned his attention to high-energy physics and helped develop the synchrocyclotron, which at the time was the largest particle accelerator, or atom smasher, in the world.

On November 16, 1954, President Dwight D. Eisenhower and the Atomic Energy Commission gave Fermi an award for his "lifetime of accomplishments in physics and, in particular, for the development of atomic energy." He died of cancer 12 days later, November 28, 1954, at the age of 53.

In 1955 the Institute for Nuclear Studies was renamed the Enrico Fermi Institute for Nuclear Studies in his memory. The name was shortened to the Enrico Fermi Institute in 1968. The element fermium also bears his name.

The Design

The Fermi stamp is commemorative-size and arranged vertically. For the central image, Richard Sheaff, the art director and designer, chose a photograph of Fermi taken March 26, 1948, when Fermi was a professor at the University of Chicago's Institute for Nuclear Studies.

The photo is credited to the American Institute of Physics Emilio Segre Visual Archives. It shows the smiling physicist, dressed in a three-piece tweed suit, standing in front of a classroom and pointing to a chalkboard on which he has drawn a diagram and written equations. The photo is black and white, but Sheaff gave it a subtle colorization on his computer, using Adobe PhotoShop software.

A small panel in the design bears the inscription "USA 34 Enrico Fermi" in Helvetica type. In the lower-left corner is a model of a carbon atom, with six electrons orbiting a nucleus, symbolic of Fermi's work in

Richard Sheaff proposed these alternative symbolic images for the lower-left corner of the Fermi stamp: the mushroom-shaped cloud of a nuclear test explosion at Bikini atoll, and the obverse of a Nobel Prize medal. The device finally chosen for the space was a model of a carbon atom.

The microprinted letters "USPS" can be found in the atomic diagram, inside a line tracing the orbit of one of the electrons around the nucleus.

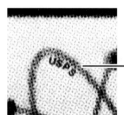

nuclear physics.

Before settling on a device for that lower corner, Sheaff had tried at least two other images in the space. One, showing the mushroom cloud of a nuclear test explosion at Bikini atoll, was quickly vetoed by CSAC and postal officials. They well remembered the international uproar in 1995 that caused USPS to scrap a mushroom-cloud design for a World War II series stamp to mark the 50th anniversary of the destruction of Hiroshima and Nagasaki by U.S. atomic bombs. Another proposed image was a Nobel Prize medal, a reminder that Fermi had won a Nobel in physics.

In the drawing of an atom that ultimately was chosen, inside one of the orbital lines, are the microprinted letters "USPS." The Postal Service requires microprinting for added security on all single-design offset-printed issues.

After the stamp design was made public, a member of the physics faculty at the University of Massachusetts, Greg Huber, turned his attention to one of the equations on the chalkboard shown in the photograph and found that Fermi, in his words, "completely screwed it up."

"Enrico Fermi was well-known for giving his students outrageous problems that could be tackled with insightful back-of-the envelope estimates, but it seems that the stamp just issued by the U.S. Postal Service ... presents its own problems," Huber wrote in a letter to *Science* magazine published October 5, 2001. "The problem has to do with what Fermi wrote on

134

the board, and you don't have to be a nuclear physicist to figure it out ...

"In an online search, my friend Chris Bergevin found the picture [used on the stamp] at the American Institute of Physics Emilio Segre Visual Archives. The Segre Archives has designated the original photo 'Fermi A16.' In the upper left-hand corner of the stamp is part of a formula neatly written on the board, the full expression being out of the frame ...

"A little digging with the marvelous staff at the Segre Archives turned up another photograph, 'Fermi A15,' taken on the same day, at the same photo shoot, probably within a minute or two of Fermi A16 (the postage stamp photo). And, there it is — Fermi has written the definition of *alpha*, the fine-structure constant. Well — sort of."

The fine-structure constant is the measure of strength of electromagnetic force that governs how electrically charged elementary particles and light interact. But Fermi botched the equation, Huber wrote, by interchanging the role of h and e. The expression should have read *alpha* = e squared over hc, he wrote, instead of h squared over ec, as it appears in the source photographs.

"At first, I was reluctant to believe that Fermi, author of the 4-vertex model, maestro of the neutron, the atomic pile, and other great ideas, could have committed a blunder of this magnitude," Huber continued. "I considered other explanations: (i) Fermi didn't write the equations on the board. Nope, it's his handwriting. I compared it with characters from his handwritten notes. (ii) His *alpha* is another quantity. Highly unlikely. If you work out the units — mass times length to the 3/2 power — they make no sense. Or (iii) Fermi was a prankster. Perhaps, but what is the joke, or is it funny?

"While pondering this last alternative, I ran into a friend, a distinguished professor at the University of Chicago, and he pointed out the obvious: 'Fermi was just having a bad day. Trotted out in front of the camera, his memory playing tricks on him, he simply misregurgitated *alpha*. End of story. It could happen to anyone.' I think my friend is right ..."

First-day Facts

Einar V. Dyhrkopp, a member of the USPS Board of Governors, dedicated the stamp in a ceremony at the Cloister Club inside Ida Noyes Hall at the University of Chicago.

Speakers were Roger H. Hildebrand, Samuel K. Allison Distinguished Service Professor Emeritus of the Department of Physics, Astronomy and Astrophysics at the Enrico Fermi Institute, and Danny Jackson, Great Lakes Area vice president for USPS. Don Michael Randel, president of the University of Chicago, gave the welcome, and Akinyinka O. Akinyele, lead executive district manager for the Chicago District of USPS, was master of ceremonies.

The earliest-known prerelease use of an Enrico Fermi stamp was on an envelope machine-canceled in Youngstown, Ohio, September 27, two days before the official first day of issue.

34¢ PORKY PIG "THAT'S ALL FOLKS" LOONEY TUNES SERIES

Date of Issue: October 1, 2001

Catalog Number: Scott 3534 (pane of 10); 3534a (single stamp); 3534b (half pane of 9); 3534c (half pane of 1)

Colors: black, cyan, magenta, yellow

First-Day Cancel: Beverly Hills, California

First-Day Cancellations: 151,009 (includes special printing version and picture postal cards)

Format: Pane of 10, vertical, 3 across, 3 down, with 10th stamp set apart in selvage portion, all on backing paper. Gravure printing cylinders of 120 stamps (2 panes across, 6 around). Also sold in uncut half press sheets of 6 panes, 2 panes across, 3 panes down.

Gum Type: self-adhesive

Stamp Size: 0.99 by 1.56 inches; 25.146 by 39.624mm

Pane Size: 6.830 by 5.125 inches; 173.480 by 130.175mm

Uncut Half Press Sheet Size: 15.000 inches by 15.375 inches

Perforations: 11 (die-cut simulated perforations) (Comco Commander rotary die cutter). Die cutting does not extend through the backing paper. On each pane, backing paper is microperfed vertically so selvage portion with 10th stamp can be separated from remaining 9 stamps.

Selvage Inscription: "That's all Folks!"

Back Markings: On portion containing 9 stamps: "$3.40/Ten/Self-adhesive/Stamps/1 800 STAMP-24/For information about additional stamps/ available from the U.S. Postal Service, call/the toll-free number or visit www.usps.com." Universal Product Code (UPC) "560200." On portion containing 1 stamp and selvage: "Bugs Bunny, who appeared on one of/the most popular stamps ever, is back to/introduce one of his old friends: Porky Pig./Cute, wide-eyed Porky Pig has played the/straight man in many silly situations, ranging/from hunting the uncatchable Daffy Duck to/traveling with him to outer space. Porky Pig's/innocence and wry wit contrast with Daffy/Duck's zaniness./Porky Pig, already a famous star, was/guaranteed immortality when he was chosen/to deliver his famous phrase 'That's all Folks!'/at the end of the Looney Tunes cartoons. Even/though Porky Pig ends the Looney Tunes/stamp series with this trademark expression,/that's no reason to stop collecting stamps."/USPS logo/"© 2000 USPS"/"LOONEY TUNES, characters, names and all related indicia are trademarks of Warner Bros. © 2000./For more information on Looney Tunes, visit www.warnerbros.com."

Liner Markings (under stamps): "That's all Folks!" in a repeat pattern

Illustrator and Designer: Ed Wleczyk, Warner Bros., Los Angeles, California

Character Art: Frank Espinosa, Warner Bros.

Concept: Brenda Guttman, Warner Bros.

Art Director: Terrence McCaffrey (USPS)

Stamp Manufacturing: Stamps printed by Avery Dennison Security Printing Division, Clinton, South Carolina, on 8-color Dia Nippon Kiko webfed gravure press. Stamps processed by Avery Dennison.

Quantity Ordered: 275,000,000 stamps, including 140,000 sold in press sheet halves; 7,000 top halves, 7,000 bottom halves.

Cylinder Number Detail: 4 sets of cylinder numbers on each side of selvage of half sheets from lower half of printing sheet. Each set consists of 3 digits preceded by the letter V.

Cylinder Number Combinations Reported: VA048-VA047-VA046-VA054, VA048-VA047-VA046-VA045, VA057-VA056-VA046-VA054, stamp side; VA049-VA050-VA051-VA052, VA058-VA059-VA060-VA061, cover side.

Paper Supplier: Fasson Division of Avery Dennison

Tagging: phosphored paper, with phosphor blocker applied over selvage area.

34¢ PORKY PIG "THAT'S ALL FOLKS"
SPECIAL PRINTING
LOONEY TUNES SERIES

Date of Issue: October 1, 2001

Catalog Number: Scott 3535 (pane of 10); 3535a (single with die-cut simulated perforations); 3535b (half pane of 9 with die-cut simulated perforations); 3535c (half pane containing 1 imperforate stamp and selvage)

Colors: black, cyan, magenta, yellow

First-Day Cancel: Beverly Hills, California

First-Day Cancellations: 151,009 (includes regular version and picture postal card)

Format: Pane of 10, vertical, 3 across, 3 down, with 10th stamp, imperforate, set apart in selvage portion, all on backing paper. Gravure printing cylinders of 120 stamps (2 panes across, 6 around).

Gum Type: self-adhesive

Stamp Size: 0.99 by 1.56 inches; 25.146 by 39.624mm

Pane Size: 6.830 by 5.125 inches

Perforations: 11 (die-cut simulated perforations) (Comco Commander rotary die cutter) for 9 stamps on left. Die cutting extends through the backing paper. Imperforate 10th stamp on right. On each pane, backing paper is microperfed vertically so selvage portion with 10th stamp can be separated from remaining 9 stamps.

Selvage Inscription: "That's all Folks!"

Back Markings: On portion containing 9 stamps: "$3.40/Ten/Self-adhesive/Stamps/1 800 STAMP-24/For information about additional stamps/ available from the U.S. Postal Service, call/the toll-free number or visit www.usps.com." Universal Product Code (UPC) "560200." On portion containing 1 stamp and selvage: "Bugs Bunny, who appeared on one of/the most popular stamps ever, is back to/introduce one of his old friends: Porky Pig./Cute, wide-eyed Porky Pig has played the/straight man in many silly situations, ranging/from hunting the uncatchable Daffy Duck to/traveling with him to outer space. Porky Pig's/innocence and wry wit contrast with Daffy/Duck's zaniness./Porky Pig, already a famous star, was/guaranteed immortality when he was chosen/to deliver his famous phrase 'That's all Folks!'/at the end of the Looney Tunes cartoons. Even/though Porky Pig ends the Looney Tunes/stamp series with this trademark expression,/that's no reason to stop collecting stamps."/USPS logo/"© 2000 USPS"/"LOONEY TUNES, characters, names and all related indicia are trademarks of Warner Bros. © 2000./For more information on Looney Tunes, visit www.warnerbros.com."

Liner Markings (under stamps): "That's all Folks!" in a repeat pattern

Illustrator and Designer: Ed Wleczyk, Warner Bros., Los Angeles, California

Character Art: Frank Espinosa, Warner Bros.

Concept: Brenda Guttman, Warner Bros.

Art Director: Terrence McCaffrey (USPS)

Stamp Manufacturing: Stamps printed by Avery Dennison Security Printing Division, Clinton, South Carolina, on 8-color Dia Nippon Kiko webfed gravure press. Stamps processed by Avery Dennison.

Quantity Ordered: 236,000 panes each containing 1 imperforate stamp

Cylinder Number Detail: no cylinder numbers

Paper Supplier: Fasson Division of Avery Dennison

Tagging: phosphored paper, with phosphor blocker applied over selvage area

The Stamps

Although Porky Pig was Warner Bros.' earliest successful animated cartoon character, he was the last to be honored in the Postal Service commemorative stamp series depicting members of the studio's Looney Tunes film ensemble. Porky's stamp, the fifth and final one in the set, was issued October 1.

Porky was chosen to wind up the series because it was his assignment, during the heyday of Looney Tunes cartoon shorts, to signal the end of each episode by appearing on the screen to stammer "That's all Folks!" Appropriately, the stamp bearing his picture carried that same message.

The stamp dedication ceremony, in Beverly Hills, California, marked the start of the Postal Service's National Stamp Collecting Month, which takes place in October each year. The theme of National Stamp Collecting Month 2001 was "Stamp Collecting: Your Passport to the World."

The Looney Tunes series began with Bugs Bunny in 1997 and continued annually with Sylvester/Tweety, Daffy Duck and Wile E. Coyote/Road Runner. Like those stamps, the Porky Pig is a self-adhesive and was sold in several formats: standard post office pane of 10 with die-cut simulated perforations around all 10 stamps, special-die-cut pane of 10 on which the 10th stamp has no die cuts, and top and bottom press-sheet halves of 60 stamps (six panes) each.

Each Porky Pig pane consists of nine stamps in a block on the left side and a single stamp near the lower-right corner of the right side, set within a larger selvage picture. It is the single stamp that is the imperforate one on the special-die-cut panes.

On all previous Looney Tunes panes, the larger selvage image duplicates the image on the stamp, minus the typography. On the Porky Pig pane, however, the picture on the right side shows Porky along with the six characters that appear on the earlier panes.

Like the previous stamps in the series, the Porky Pig stamp was accompanied by a picture postal card reproducing the stamp image on the imprinted stamp and the selvage image on the picture side (see separate chapter).

Standard panes of 10 stamps were available at post offices and postal stores throughout the country beginning October 2. The special die-cut pane and press-sheet halves were available only through the Stamp Fulfillment Services mail-order center in Kansas City, Missouri. Orders for press-sheet halves were limited to a maximum of five for each press-sheet half per customer.

A total of 275 million Porky Pig stamps were ordered, down from 300 million for 2000's Coyote/Road Runner stamp. The order for special-die-cut panes was 236,000, the same as for Coyote/Road Runner. There were

7,000 each of the Porky Pig top and bottom press-sheet halves, representing a 30 percent decrease from the 10,000 each Coyote/Road Runner press-sheet halves.

As with the four previous Looney Tunes panes, the inside of the liner paper on the Porky Pig pane, revealed when a stamp is peeled from it, features a saying, in a repeat pattern, identified with the character depicted. In this case, the words are "That's all Folks!"

To print the Porky Pig stamp, USPS turned again to the gravure presses of Avery Dennison Security Printing Division, which had produced the Bugs Bunny, Sylvester/Tweety and Daffy Duck stamps. The Coyote/Road Runner stamp had been printed on the offset press of Banknote Corporation of America.

Postal Service spokesman Don Smeraldi told *Linn's Stamp News* the decision to return to Avery Dennison for Porky Pig was purely a financial one. "Avery was the low bidder for this issue," Smeraldi said.

All die-cut simulated perforations on the Porky Pig stamp measure 11 on a perforation gauge, but specialists have identified at least three different varieties of die cuts, two from the standard post office pane and a third from the special pane.

The varieties are distinguishable by examining the peaks and valleys of the die cuts in the top left corner of a given stamp. Charles Snee of *Linn's Stamp News* designates these varieties peak/peak (P/P for short), so called because the horizontal die cutting begins with a peak and the vertical die cutting begins with a peak; peak/valley (P/V); and valley/peak (V/P), the latter found only on the special pane (see illustration).

As with previous Looney Tunes stamps printed by Avery Dennison, cylinder numbers are found only on the bottom press-sheet halves. They consist of four sets of numbers printed vertically in sequence in the left selvage of the bottom-left pane. Each set consists of three digits preceded by the letter V (for Avery Dennison) and represents one of the four process colors used to print the stamps: black, cyan, magenta and yellow.

Similar numbers also are found on the reverse, or cover, side of the bottom press-sheet halves. These represent the gravure cylinders used to print the picture and type on the covers.

The stamp was printed on phosphored paper to activate post office

Shown here are three die-cut varieties of the Porky Pig stamp, peak/peak (left), peak/valley (center) and valley/peak (right), the latter found only on the special die-cut pane.

Bottom left pane of a Porky Pig bottom-half press sheet, cropped to show the four cylinder numbers in the left selvage. A spray-on, nine-digit printer's control number is seen just below the cylinder numbers.

facer-canceler machines. Avery Dennison applied a coat of clear varnish to the large area of selvage on the right side of the regular and special die-cut panes to block the phosphoresence so no part of it could be used as a stamp. This was done with a separate cylinder on the Dia Nippon Kiko gravure press.

Porky Pig made his first appearance in 1935 in Warner Bros. director Fritz Freleng's animated short *I Haven't Got a Hat*, which depicted a pageant in Miss Cud's elementary school class. Porky appears as a chubby, stuttering schoolboy trying to recite *The Midnight Ride of Paul Revere*. The following year, Porky turned up again, this time as a monstrously fat adult caught up in the California gold rush, in a cartoon called *The Golddiggers of '49*.

"We repeated Porky because he stood out," Freleng told Charles Solomon, author of *Enchanted Drawings: The History of Animation* (Knopf, 1989). "We didn't really have any star characters at the time — we were just kind of floundering."

In 1937, Porky Pig was a frequent title character, in such shorts as *Porky's Romance, Picador Porky, Porky and Gabby, Porky's Super Service* and *Porky's Duck Hunt* (1937), in which Daffy Duck, the second famous Warner Bros. cartoon personality, made his debut.

From those films onward, Porky's endearing stutter was the work of vocal virtuoso Mel Blanc, who provided the voices of most of the classic Warner Bros. characters from 1937 until his death in 1989.

The Design

When the Looney Tunes series was in the planning stage, Warner Bros. submitted several proposed stamp designs featuring various animated cartoon characters, including Porky Pig. Some of these were tight close-ups, presented in a style that Brenda Guttman, creative director for the studio's publishing group in Los Angeles, called "in your face." Others showed the characters as letter carriers.

"There were multiple designs for multiple characters," recalled Ter-

Shown here are two early design proposals for the Porky Pig stamp, offered to the Postal Service by Warner Bros. before the design style for the series was established with the Bugs Bunny stamp.

rence McCaffrey, manager of stamp development for USPS and the art director for the Looney Tunes series. "Warner Bros. tried to inundate us with images of characters so we would do a whole big series, and at one point we were talking about doing as many as 12 stamps, but we began retrenching and cut it down to five."

Later, when USPS officials chose a design for the Bugs Bunny stamp, they also established a design style for subsequent stamps in the series. A wooden rural mailbox was the unifying illustrative element, and clouds in the sky formed the denomination and "USA" on the Bugs, Sylvester/Tweety, Daffy Duck and Coyote/Road Runner stamps.

For the fifth and last stamp in the series, however, McCaffrey and the Citizens' Stamp Advisory Committee wanted to alter the formula slightly. "We wanted to finalize things by adding 'That's all Folks!' and having Porky burst out of the Merry Melodies concentric circles the way he does in the cartoons," McCaffrey said.

"Warner Bros. originally rejected the idea of doing the circles in blue. They said they didn't use that particular color scheme any more; it was orange. But when we laid the orange design next to the other four stamps in the series, all of which had strong blue areas, this one stood out like a sore thumb.

"So we showed it to them in context and asked if they would reconsider, and they agreed to let us [do the circles] in blue."

In the finished design, a beaming Porky stands halfway out of the center circle, the mailbox beside him. He is attired in a dark blue jacket and trousers and a red bow tie, with a "U.S. Mail" bag hanging at his side, the strap across his shoulder. The pants could be interpreted as an example of Postal Service prudery; Porky didn't wear them during his 60-plus years on the movie screen, and none of the other Looney Tunes characters in the stamp series wore anything but their natural fur and feathers.

Porky holds up a letter in his left hand. The only element on the letter that can be made out, even with a good magnifying glass, is the address: "ACME ACRES/U.S.A." However, an enlargement of the original design

This is the original version of the finished design of the Porky Pig stamp, prepared by Warner Bros. illustrators and annotated with instructions by Terrence McCaffrey after consulting with the Citizens' Stamp Advisory Committee. The concentric circles are orange in color. Warner Bros. ultimately changed them to blue at the Postal Service's request. Also on the final version, the stamp on the envelope was changed from a Daffy Duck to a Wile E. Coyote/Roadrunner, the shape of Porky's eyes was altered and his features were revised in other subtle ways.

On the Porky Pig stamp itself, the stamp on the letter Porky is holding can't be clearly seen, nor can the return address. An enlargement of the original artwork shows that the stamp is a Wile E. Coyote/Road Runner commemorative and the return address is made up of nonsense words.

shows that the envelope is franked with a Coyote/Road Runner stamp and the return address is a nonsense one: "Wosbio Prus/2035 Trohun fr./Munegre MY 02356."

(Charles Snee, writing in *Linn's Stamp News*, pointed out that the design "incorporates an innovative stamps-on-stamp-on-stamp-on-stamp theme." This is intellectually — albeit not visually — the case. The actual Coyote/Road Runner stamp depicts a letter franked with a canceled Daffy Duck stamp. In the Daffy Duck stamp's design, in turn, two letters are in the mailbox, one franked with a Bugs Bunny stamp, the other with a Sylvester and Tweety stamp.)

At the top of the Porky Pig stamp, in a line of curved script, is "That's all Folks!" with quotation marks and a dropped shadow. At the bottom is "USA 33" in white, but instead of the cloud typography used on the first four stamps in the series, the letters and numbers are in a conventional block type.

This image isn't duplicated in enlarged form in the pane selvage, however. For series finale, McCaffrey and CSAC decided to vary the established pattern by using a different picture, one based on a concept sketch that Warner Bros. had created for a proposed brochure cover. The sketch included additional characters, such as Marvin the Martian, but at McCaffrey's request the selvage depicted only the seven that were shown on stamps.

"I was very pleased that we were able to use a different piece of art in the selvage," McCaffrey said. "It finalized the series, summed everything up, brought back all the characters one more time — and also locked the door and made it clear we weren't going to do any more!"

First-day Facts

Tirso del Junco, a member of the USPS Board of Governors, was scheduled to dedicate the stamp at the Museum of Television and Radio in Beverly Hills. However, the ceremony was canceled. "The Postal Service felt it was inappropriate to hold such an event so soon after 9/11," said Don Smeraldi, a USPS spokesman.

The earliest-known prerelease use of a Porky Pig stamp was on a cover machine-canceled in Manchester, New Hampshire, September 27, four days before the stamp was dedicated.

34¢ JAMES MADISON

Date of Issue: October 18, 2001

Catalog Number: Scott 3545

Colors: black (offset); green (modified PMS 560) (intaglio)

First-Day Cancel: New York, New York

First-Day Cancellations: 102,630

Format: Pane of 20, horizontal, 4 across, 5 down. Offset and intaglio printing plates of 120 subjects, 8 across, 15 around. Also sold in uncut sheets of 6 panes, 2 across by 3 down.

Gum: water activated

Overall Stamp Size: 1.56 by 0.99 inches; 39.62 by 25.15mm

Pane Size: 7.26 by 5.94 inches; 184.40 by 150.88mm

Uncut Press Sheet Size: 17.80 by 15.06 inches; 452.120 by 382.524mm

Perforations: 11 by 11¼ (Wista BPA 9070 stroke perforator)

Selvage Markings: "©/USPS/2001." ".34/x20/$6.80." "PLATE/POSITION" and diagram. Universal Product Code (UPC) "451700" in 2 positions.

Illustrator and Designer: John Thompson of Waterloo, Iowa

Art Director and Typographer: Carl Herrman of Carlsbad, California

Engraver: Photoengraved by Banknote Corporation of America, Browns Summit, North Carolina

Stamp Manufacturing: Stamps printed by BCA on Goebel 670 offset press and Epikos 5009 intaglio press. Stamps processed by BCA.

Quantity Ordered and Distributed: 32,000,000

Plate Number Detail: 1 offset plate number preceded by the letter B and 1 intaglio plate number in selvage above or below each corner stamp

Plate Number Combination Reported: B11

Paper Supplier: Tullis Russell Coatings

Tagging: phosphored paper

The Stamp

In 1995, the Postal Service issued a 32¢ commemorative stamp in definitive size and with old-fashioned decorative embellishments in the design to mark the 200th anniversary of the birth of James K. Polk, the nation's 11th president. The stamp had been sought by prominent Tennessee residents and personally endorsed by then-Postmaster General Marvin T. Runyon, a Tennesseean himself.

At the time, Robin Wright, a spokesman for USPS, told *Linn's Stamp News* that the Polk stamp would be the first in a series commemorating the bicentennials of the births of former U.S. presidents. Consistent with that plan, John Thompson, the designer of the Polk stamp, in 1998 made preliminary sketches of similar designs for the presidents who next would be eligible: Millard Fillmore, the 13th chief executive, whose 200th birth anniversary would fall in 2000, and James Madison, the fourth, whose 250th anniversary would come in 2001.

Then USPS staffers and the Citizens' Stamp Advisory Committee "decided that we didn't want to get caught in the trap of doing a whole new series," said Terrence McCaffrey, manager of stamp development for USPS. "We've done so many presidential stamps, we thought: 'Let's not do this.'"

Fillmore's 200th came and went with little notice, no stamp and no complaint from the philatelic community or from the obscure president's relatively few present-day admirers. And as Madison's 250th birth year neared, the Postal Service made no plans to honor him, either.

Enter Philip B. Meggs, a professor of graphic design and member of CSAC. Early in 2000, Meggs read a newspaper article about upcoming plans to mark the 250th anniversary of Madison's birth, and concluded, he said, "that this is a man who needed to be commemorated with a stamp."

In a presentation to CSAC's subject subcommittee, Meggs convinced the members that it would be an oversight not to mark so important an anniversary for Madison, who has been called "the father of the U.S. Constitution," authored its first 10 amendments that are known collectively as the Bill of Rights, and was president during the War of 1812. The subcommittee unanimously recommended approval.

The full committee discussed the issue — some members were concerned because Madison had been a slaveholder, although the same was

In 1998, when a presidential commemorative series still was a possibility, John Thompson made this pencil sketch for a Millard Fillmore stamp that would be issued in his 200th anniversary year of 2000. The series idea was quickly abandoned, and no Fillmore stamp was approved by CSAC.

148

Shown here are two of John Thompson's 1998 pencil sketches for a James Madison 250th anniversary stamp, in definitive stamp size and with old-fashioned frames and embellishments.

true of his fellow Virginians and frequent stamp subjects George Washington and Thomas Jefferson — and then voted to accept the subcommittee's recommendation.

The 34¢ Madison commemorative was issued October 18, 2001, at the Postage Stamp Mega-Event show in New York City. Conventionally perforated and with water-activated gum, it was printed by a combination of intaglio and offset by Banknote Corporation of America (BCA) and issued in panes of 20. The print order of 32 million was low even when compared to the smaller printings of many commemoratives in recent years, but it reflected the declining public appeal of old-fashioned "lick-and-stick" postage.

USPS offered collectors the option of purchasing the Madison stamp in uncut press sheets of six panes, or 120 stamps, at face value of $40.80.

James Madison was born March 16, 1751, in Port Conway, Virginia, the eldest of 12 children of James Madison Sr. and Eleanor Rose (Nellie) Conway Madison. He graduated in two years from the College of New Jersey, now known as Princeton University, in 1771, and turned his attention to public affairs. He was elected to the Virginia Convention in 1776 and to the Continental Congress in 1779.

Madison was instrumental in organizing the convention that wrote the U.S. Constitution in 1787, and his extensive study of ancient republics underlay some of his many contributions to that document. According to the Montpelier Foundation, "While the Constitution flowed from the political ideals of the American Revolution, the genius of one individual — James Madison — was the driving force behind its final shape."

During the convention, Madison took detailed notes that provide a unique glimpse of those historic deliberations. The notes, filling more than 1,000 pages, are held at the Library of Congress. Afterward, with Alexander Hamilton and John Jay, he authored the series of 85 essays now known as the Federalist Papers that were published in New York newspapers to explain the new Constitution to New Yorkers and help persuade them to ratify it.

Later, as a member of the first U.S. House of Representatives, Madison played a key role in the creation and passage of the 10 constitutional amendments defining Americans' basic rights, including freedom of speech, press, assembly and religion. The amendments were proposed in

1789 and adopted in 1791.

After serving as President Thomas Jefferson's secretary of state for eight years, Madison was elected president in 1808. In June 1812, near the end of his first term, he called on Congress to declare war on Great Britain, which had been attacking American shipping and seizing American sailors. That fall, he won re-election. In 1814, he and his wife Dolley had to flee the White House, which was burned by British troops who had captured Washington, D.C. Nevertheless, when the treaty of Ghent that ended the war was signed in 1814, Americans felt they had won, and Madison's popularity was high.

Upon leaving office in 1817, Madison retired to Montpelier, his Virginia estate. His last political activity was as a member of the Virginia Constitutional Convention of 1829. He died at Montpelier June 28, 1836, at the age of 85.

Madison has appeared on several U.S. postage stamps, beginning with $2 definitives in 1894, 1895, 1902 and 1917. He was depicted on the 4¢ value of the Presidential series of 1938-39, and on a 22¢ stamp of the Ameripex 86 miniature sheets of 1986 that depicted all the deceased presidents. In 1994, USPS commemorated the 100th anniversary of stamp production by the Bureau of Engraving and Printing by issuing a souvenir sheet of four $2 Madison stamps using the original die BEP had prepared for the Madison stamp of 1894.

His wife, Dolley, was depicted on an experimental 15¢ miniature commemorative stamp in 1980 that is considered the prototype for the Great Americans definitive series of 1980-99. A 15¢ postal card marking the 200th anniversary of the Federalist Papers and bearing the names of Madison, Hamilton and Jay was issued in 1988.

The Design

After CSAC approved Philip Meggs' proposal for a James Madison 250th anniversary stamp, Carl Herrman, who had been art director for the James Polk commemorative, took from his files the preliminary sketches John Thompson had made in 1998 for a Madison stamp in the Polk style and asked Thompson to prepare a finished design.

Thompson is a staff artist for the Hillman Group, a design firm and advertising agency of Waterloo, Iowa. In addition to the Polk stamp, he created the triangular designs for the 32¢ Pacific 97 commemoratives of 1997. At one time he made extensive use of the scratchboard technique, and still employs it for stamps, but he now does most of his commercial work on a computer.

Scratchboard is unlike traditional drawing and painting in that it consists of subtraction, not addition. Thompson coats a plaster-coated posterboard with black ink, then scratches away portions of it with an Exacto knife, leaving the remaining lines and shapes to form the picture.

"I think I'm more proficient with scratchboard than with traditional pen and ink," he said. "I like the control I have over the linework with scratch-

This is John Thompson's completed scratchboard drawing of a Madison stamp, done in October 2000. The portrait, lettering and ornamentation all were done by hand; the background cross-hatching and horizontal rules were created on a computer. The frame is similar to that of the 6¢ Washington Bicentennial commemorative of 1932.

board. I can get extremely fine lines, and also coarse, grainy ones. For me, there's a lot more versatility than with pen and ink. I don't have to rely on stippling or crosshatching to get my effects.

"It's kind of a strange process, but interesting. I work with my face about an inch away from the board when I'm doing the scratching, and as I scratch I'm continually making a little pile of dust in front of the blade as I push it over the board, so I'm constantly giving puffs of air to blow the dust away so I can see what I'm working on.

"Back when I was doing scratchboard all day, every day, it was giving me some carpal tunnel [trouble] because of the grip I had to have on the knife and the constant similar movements. So it was painful at times. But now I do so little of it that it's a lot of fun again."

For the Polk stamp, Thompson had drawn an ornate frame inspired by the ½¢ stamp of the Washington Bicentennial commemorative set of 1932. For Madison, he adapted another frame from that series, that of the 6¢ value, which included an arch and a ribbon bearing the subject's name and the years of his birth and death.

"The committee loved it," McCaffrey recalled. "But because it looked so similar to the Polk stamp, we knew people would say, 'Aha, you ARE doing a series, but you forgot Millard Fillmore.' We needed a different kind of design. So Carl [Herrman] had to go back and start over."

Herrman's solution was to create a new design, in commemorative size and arranged horizontally, using Thompson's already-completed portrait of Madison, and add a background scene based on period images of Montpelier, the Madison estate in Virginia. Thompson made a scratchboard drawing of the estate, eliminating some of the details, such as outbuildings, for the sake of simplicity.

"I wasn't exactly sure where Madison was going to fall [in the stamp design]," Thompson said. "I made the ground and trees and sky continue all the way across the piece, so no matter where the portrait was placed there would be a full background behind him."

Because he had drawn Madison to fit inside a narrow frame on a definitive-size stamp, Thompson said, he had to "add some ink down on the shoulder and chest area and to continue the linework down so that it would work in the new format."

In depicting his subject, Thompson relied on a painting by Gilbert Stu-

Carl Herrman experimented with this alternative design layout for the Madison stamp as a semi-jumbo size.

This is the Gilbert Stuart painting of Madison on which John Thompson based his scratchboard portrait for the stamp. The painting was made in 1805-07, when Madison was secretary of state in President Thomas Jefferson's cabinet.

art, done in the period 1805-07, when Madison was secretary of state in President Thomas Jefferson's Cabinet, and on an engraving made from that portrait by the Bureau of Engraving and Printing. The painting, now in the collection of the Bowdoin College Museum of Art, was commissioned by Major General Henry Dearborn, secretary of war, on behalf of James Bowdoin III, the U.S. minister to Spain and a friend and admirer of Madison. Most of the previous U.S. stamps that had pictured the fourth president were based on the same painting. (Stuart also painted the portrait of Dolley Madison on which the design of her 1980 commemorative stamp was based.)

Thompson's two separate drawings — portrait and background — then were joined, and the combined image was photoengraved by BCA. Philip Meggs, whose advocacy led to the issuance of the Madison stamp, pointed out that photoengraving is well suited for scratchboard art because the artist's lines, dots and shapes are faithfully reproduced on the intaglio die without being "translated" by a human engraver.

Herrman originally had wanted the Montpelier background to be offset-printed in a soft color, for a stronger contrast with the engraved portrait. However, BCA officials protested that to juxtapose intaglio and offset lines so closely would create an extremely difficult registration problem. In the end, USPS officials agreed to an all-intaglio image, but with the background portion lightened in the photoengraving process.

This is the scratchboard drawing of Montpelier that John Thompson created to be combined with the Madison portrait he had drawn earlier.

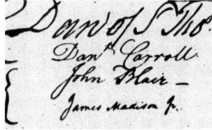

Madison signed his name "James Madison Jr." on the U.S. Constitution. In his autograph shown on the stamp, the "Jr." is omitted.

"I think it's spectacular," Herrman admitted. "It wasn't what I intended, but it worked perfectly."

The inscriptions below the vignette — the "2001" year date on the left and "JAMES MADISON 1751-1836" on the right — are intaglio, as well. All the engraved portions of the design are printed in a dark green, which Herrman chose because it imparts the dignified look of currency.

Madison's name appears a second time, more prominently and in autograph form, printed in black offset just below the mansion. In his youth, Madison signed his name "James Madison Jr.", and that is how his signature appears on the U.S. Constitution, but he also omitted the "Jr." on occasion, and Herrman chose to show it that way for optimum legibility.

"USA 34," in Goudy Old Style type, is printed in black offset, on the white cloud at the upper right.

First-day Facts

Vinnie Malloy, New York District postmaster, dedicated the stamp at the opening of the fall Postage Stamp Mega-Event show at Jacob K. Javits Convention Center in New York City. Speakers were Lloyd DeVries, secretary of the American Philatelic Society, which with the American Stamp Dealers Association (ASDA) sponsored the show; John Thompson, the stamp's illustrator; Mike Quinn, president of the Montpelier Foundation; and Joseph Cinadr, president, National League of Postmasters. Jackson Taylor, ASDA president, gave the welcome, and an actor, John Douglas Hall, playing James Madison, put in an appearance.

NONDENOMINATED (34¢) LOVE LETTERS
CONVERTIBLE BOOKLET OF 20

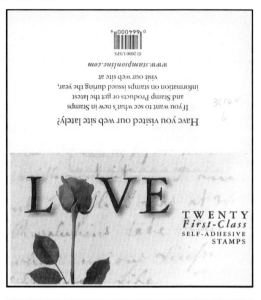

Date of Issue: January 19, 2001

Catalog Numbers: Scott 3496, single stamp; 3496a, pane of 20

Colors: black, cyan, magenta, yellow

First-Day Cancel: Tucson, Arizona

First-Day Cancellations: 30,214

Format: Convertible booklet pane of 20, vertical, 5 across, 4 down, with horizontal peel-off strip between horizontal rows 2 and 3. Offset printing plates of 400 subjects (25 across, 16 around).

Gum Type: self-adhesive

Overall Stamp Size: 0.91 by 1.19 inches; 23.11 by 30.23mm

Pane Size: 4.55 by 5.00 inches; 115.57 by 127.00mm

Perforations: 11¼ (die-cut simulated perforations) (rotary die cutter). Rouletting under peel-off strip.

Selvage Markings: plate numbers and " • Peel here to fold • Self-adhesive stamps • DO NOT WET • © 2000 USPS" on peel-off strip

Back Markings: "LOVE/TWENTY/First-Class/SELF-ADHESIVE/STAMPS." Promotion for www.stampsonline.com web site. "© 2000 USPS." Universal Product Code (UPC) "0 664000 4."

Photographer: Renee Comet of Washington, D.C.

Designer and Typographer: Lisa Catalone of Bethesda, Maryland

Art Director: Ethel Kessler of Bethesda, Maryland

Stamp Manufacturing: Stamps printed by Banknote Corporation of America, Browns Summit, North Carolina, on Goebel 670 offset press. Stamps finished by BCA.

Quantity Ordered: 500,000,000 stamps

Plate Number Detail: 1 set of 4 plate numbers preceded by the letter B on peel-off strip.

Plate Number Combinations Reported: B1111, B2222

Paper Supplier: Paper Corporation of the United States/Spinnaker Coatings

Tagging: phosphored paper

34¢ LOVE LETTERS
CONVERTIBLE BOOKLET OF 20

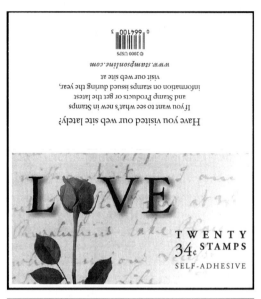

Date of Issue: February 14, 2001

Catalog Numbers: Scott 3497, single stamp; 3497a, pane of 20

Colors: black, cyan, magenta, yellow

First-Day Cancel: Lovejoy, Georgia

First-Day Cancellations: 181,746 (includes 34¢ Love Letters vending booklet, 55¢ Love Letters stamp and 34¢ Lovebirds envelope)

Format: Convertible booklet pane of 20, vertical, 5 across, 4 down, with horizontal peel-off strip between horizontal rows 2 and 3. Offset printing plates of 400 subjects (25 across, 16 around).

Gum Type: self-adhesive

Overall Stamp Size: 0.91 by 1.19 inches; 23.11 by 30.23mm

Pane Size: 4.55 by 5.00 inches; 115.57 by 127.00mm

Perforations: 11¼ (die-cut simulated perforations) (rotary die cutter). Rouletting under peel-off strip.

Selvage Markings: plate numbers and " • Peel here to fold • Self-adhesive stamps • DO NOT WET • © 2000 USPS" on peel-off strip

Back Markings: "LOVE/TWENTY/34¢ STAMPS/SELF-ADHESIVE." Promotion for www.stampsonline.com web site. "© 2000 USPS." Universal Product Code (UPC).

Photographer: Renee Comet of Washington, D.C.

Designer and Typographer: Lisa Catalone of Bethesda, Maryland

Art Director: Ethel Kessler of Bethesda, Maryland

Stamp Manufacturing: Stamps printed by Banknote Corporation of America, Browns Summit, North Carolina, on Goebel 670 offset press. Stamps finished by BCA.

Quantity Ordered: 1,500,000,000 stamps

Plate Number Detail: 1 set of 4 plate numbers preceded by the letter B on peel-off strip.

Plate Number Combinations Reported: B1111, B2222, B3333, B4444, B5555

Paper Supplier: Paper Corporation of the United States/Spinnaker Coatings

Tagging: phosphored paper

34¢ LOVE LETTERS
VENDING BOOKLET OF 20

Date of Issue: February 14, 2001

Catalog Numbers: Scott 3498, single stamp; 3498a, booklet pane of 4; 3498b, booklet pane of 6

Colors: black, cyan, magenta, yellow

First-Day Cancel: Lovejoy, Georgia

First-Day Cancellations: 181,746 (includes 34¢ Love Letters convertible booklet, 55¢ Love Letters stamp and 34¢ Lovebirds envelope)

Format: Vending booklet of 20, vertical, 2 across, 10 down, with stamps arranged in blocks of 4, 6, 6 and 4, with horizontal peel-off strips between horizontal rows 2 and 3, 5 and 6, and 8 and 9. Offset printing plates of 400 subjects (20 across, 20 around).

Gum Type: self-adhesive

Overall Stamp Size: 0.87 by 0.98 inches; 22.10 by 24.89mm

Pane Size: 1.74 by 10.98 inches; 44.20 by 278.89mm

Perforations: 11½ by 10¾ die-cut simulated perforations) (rotary die cutter).

Selvage Markings: "Peel here to fold • Self-adhesive stamps • DO NOT WET" on first and third peel-off strips. "© 2000 USPS • Peel here to fold • Self-adhesive stamps • DO NOT WET" on second peel-off strip.

Back Markings: "TWENTY 34¢/SELF-ADHESIVE/STAMPS/$6.80." USPS logo. Promotion for www.stampsonline.com web site. "© 2000 USPS." Universal Product Code (UPC) "0 666100 7."

Photographer: Renee Comet of Washington, D.C.

Designer and Typographer: Lisa Catalone of Bethesda, Maryland

Art Director: Ethel Kessler of Bethesda, Maryland

Stamp Manufacturing: Stamps printed by Banknote Corporation of America, Browns Summit, North Carolina, on Goebel 670 offset press. Stamps finished by BCA.

Quantity Ordered: 80,000,000 stamps

Plate Number Detail: 1 set of 4 plate numbers preceded by the letter B on bottom left stamp of pane

Plate Number Combination Reported: B1111

Paper Supplier: Paper Corporation of the United States/Spinnaker Coatings

Tagging: phosphored paper

55¢ LOVE LETTERS
PANE OF 20

Date of Issue: February 14, 2001

Catalog Number: Scott 3499

Colors: black, cyan, magenta, yellow

First-Day Cancel: Lovejoy, Georgia

First-Day Cancellations: 181,746 (includes 34¢ Love stamp in 2 formats and 34¢ Lovebirds envelope)

Format: Pane of 20, horizontal, 4 across, 5 down. Offset printing plates printing 240 stamps per revolution.

Gum Type: self-adhesive

Overall Stamp Size: 1.19 by 0.91 inches; 30.23 by 23.11mm

Pane Size: 5.95 by 5.46 inches; 151.13 by 138.68mm

Perforations: 11¼ (die-cut simulated perforations) (rotary die cutter)

Selvage Markings: "©/2000/USPS." ".55/x20/$11.00." "PLATE/POSITION" and diagram. Universal Product Code (UPC) "561200" in 2 positions.

Photographer: Renee Comet of Washington, D.C.

Designer and Typographer: Lisa Catalone of Bethesda, Maryland

Art Director: Ethel Kessler of Bethesda, Maryland

Stamp Manufacturing: Stamps printed by Banknote Corporation of America, Browns Summit, North Carolina, on Goebel 670 offset press. Stamps finished by BCA.

Quantity Ordered: 180,000,000 stamps

Plate Number Detail: 1 set of 4 plate numbers preceded by the letter B in selvage above or below each corner stamp

Plate Number Combination Reported: B1111

Paper Supplier: Paper Corporation of the United States/Spinnaker Coatings

Tagging: phosphored paper

57¢ LOVE LETTERS
PANE OF 20

Date of Issue: November 19, 2001

Catalog Number: Scott 3551

Colors: gray (PMS 441), black, cyan, magenta, yellow

First-Day Cancel: Lovejoy, Georgia

First-Day Cancellations: 15,259

Format: Pane of 20, horizontal, 4 across, 5 down. Offset printing plates of 320 subjects (16 across, 20 around)

Gum Type: self-adhesive

Overall Stamp Size: 1.19 by 0.91 inches; 30.23 by 23.11mm

Pane Size: 5.95 by 5.46 inches; 151.13 by 138.68mm

Perforations: 11¼ (die-cut simulated perforations) (Heidelberg rotary die cutter)

Selvage Markings: "©/2000/USPS." ".57/x20/$11.40." "PLATE/POSITION" and diagram. Universal Product Code (UPC) "565700" in 2 positions.

Photographer: Renee Comet of Washington, D.C.

Designer and Typographer: Lisa Catalone of Bethesda, Maryland

Art Director: Ethel Kessler of Bethesda, Maryland

Stamp Manufacturing: Stamps printed by Banknote Corporation of America, Browns Summit, North Carolina, on MAN Roland 300 offset press. Stamps finished by BCA.

Quantity Ordered: 100,000,000 stamps

Plate Number Detail: 1 set of 5 plate numbers preceded by the letter B in selvage above or below each corner stamp

Plate Number Combination Reported: B11111

Paper Supplier: Paper Corporation of the United States/Spinnaker Coatings

Tagging: phosphored paper

The Stamps

In 2001 the Postal Service issued five varieties of Love stamp in two different designs. Their common theme celebrated what USPS called "the cherished tradition of love letters."

The designs, one vertical, one horizontal, display the word "LOVE," with the blossom of a rose forming the "O." In each case, the word is superimposed on a portion of a letter from the voluminous 18th-century correspondence of John Adams and his future wife, Abigail Smith.

The first stamp was issued January 19 at the Aripex 2001 stamp show in Tucson, Arizona. It was nondenominated and sold for 34¢ to cover the first-class rate that had taken effect 12 days earlier. A self-adhesive, it is of the special-stamp size, vertically arranged, and was produced in a convertible booklet of 20.

The varieties that came later, also self-adhesives, were:

• 34¢, same design and size as the nondenominated stamp, convertible booklet of 20, issued February 14, Valentine's Day, in Lovejoy, Georgia.

• 34¢, same design, vending booklet of 20, same date and place. The stamp is somewhat smaller than the stamp in the convertible booklet and its die-cut simulated perforations are of a different gauge.

• 55¢, horizontally arranged, special-stamp size, pane of 20, same date and place. The denomination covered the two-ounce first-class rate, which customarily is needed for wedding invitations that include RSVP cards and envelopes.

• 57¢, same design and size as the 55¢, issued November 19 in Washington, D.C. The denomination covered the higher two-ounce first-class rate that took effect July 1, 2001.

All five varieties were printed by the offset process by Banknote Corporation of America.

The total of five Love stamps in one year was topped only in 1995, a

year that saw six Love stamps, including two that were nondenominated, all depicting one or both the child angels from Raphael's painting *Sistine Madonna*.

The *Postal Bulletin* for December 14, 2000, had reported that the forthcoming nondenominated Love stamp would be issued January 10 in Lovejoy. However, the issue date was postponed nine days and the site changed to Tucson. USPS said the postponement was due to concerns about production schedules and stamp availability.

Plans to issue the 57¢ variety were

announced July 10, after the second-ounce postage rate had risen from 21¢ to 23¢, making the 55¢ stamp obsolete as a stand-alone. At that time, USPS said the denomination of the new stamp would be printed in green, to differentiate it from the 55¢ value. However, on the issued stamp, the denomination is in black, the same as on the 55¢ stamp. There is a color difference between the two stamps: On the 55¢, the background color is a light tan and the rose is pink, while on the 57¢ the background color is gray

and the rose is red, similar to the color of the rose on the 34¢ stamp.

The Designs

The designs for the 2001 Love stamps emerged from a lengthy process involving Ethel Kessler of Bethesda, Maryland, one of the Postal Service's part-time art directors, and a former associate, Lisa Catalone, who now operates her own firm, Catalone Design Co., also in Bethesda.

Catalone is a stamp collector, and thus Kessler felt it would be particularly appropriate to call on her for help to fill an ongoing Postal Service need: a need for designs for holiday stamps and Love stamps.

"The Love stamp is a perfect place where people can play with ideas a little bit and feel free in terms of what techniques they use," Kessler said. "I knew Lisa had an appreciation for stamps and for the scale of them, and she's a terrific designer.

"So I gave her the challenge of working on a Love stamp."

Among the approaches tried by Catalone was a montage in which objects associated with love and romance — hearts, wedding rings, seals, ribbons — were incorporated in the word "LOVE" as replacements for the "O" or the "V," all photographed against a background of calligraphy.

"When I presented that direction to the [Citizens' Stamp Advisory] Committee, they were interested, but they wanted the writing to be more legible," Kessler recalled. "Well, the copy Lisa used wasn't meant to be readable; it was meant to be background texture. But one of the members said something about how frustrating it was not to be able to read it, and it was suggested that Lisa get something that one could read, something handwritten.

"And then, all of a sudden, it made all the sense in the world. It was one of those group light bulbs going off. Love letters!"

This is one of Catalone's early essays incorporating a montage as a Love stamp design.

Before she decided to use a long-stemmed rose for the "O" in "LOVE," Lisa Catalone experimented with other objects to replace the "O" or "V," including a felt heart, twin wedding rings, a rose blossom and ribbons with sealing wax, and different script backgrounds, including one of fabric.

Among those who suggested using the Adams-Smith letters were Virginia Noelke, chair of CSAC, and Louis Plummer, a co-owner of PhotoAssist, the Postal Service's research firm. Ethel Kessler believes that the idea was validated in her own mind because she had met author David McCullough at the first-day ceremony for the Library of Congress stamp in April 2000 and learned that he was completing a biography of John Adams that would be published in 2001. "Definitely, there was a cosmic coincidence there someplace," she laughed.

John Adams, who served as the second president of the United States (1797-1801), and Abigail were married October 25, 1764, and their union lasted more than 50 years. Both before their marriage and afterward, when John's political duties required him to be away from home for long periods, letters served as their link and kept their love and affection for one another strong. At times intimate and frank, their correspondence provides a window for viewing the lives of two strong and fascinating individuals. Both have been pictured on U.S. stamps: John, on the 2¢ Presidential stamp of 1938 (Scott 806) and a 22¢ Ameripex 86 miniature-sheet commemorative (Scott 2216b); Abigail, on a 22¢ commemorative in 1985 (Scott 2146).

In choosing letters for the project, Kessler said, "We were more interested in texture for the background than in content. The researchers got copies of several letters and that's what we worked with. So it wasn't so much that we were going for 'What does the sentence say?' Rather, it was 'Get us authentic letters from John to Abigail and Abigail to John.'

"It's not as if one letter answers a question from the other letter. That would be way too much to ask for. Also, some of the letters had folds in them and ink blots and there was a question as to what we were going to be able to use at stamp size."

PhotoAssist asked the Massachusetts Historical Society, which has custody of the Adams papers, to photograph the first pages of five different letters from the couple's courtship, and Catalone then selected the two she thought worked best. The letter that is excerpted on the nondenominated and 34¢ stamps was written by John April 20, 1763, from his home in Braintree, Massachusetts, to Abigail in Weymouth, Massachusetts. It includes this passage:

"I am at Braintree but I wish I was at Weymouth! What strange Revolutions take Place in our Breasts, and what curious Vicissitudes in every Part of human Life. This summer I shall like Weymouth better than Braintree but something prompts me to believe I shall like Braintree next Winter better than Weymouth. Writers who procure Reputation by flattering human Nature, tell us that Mankind grows wiser and wiser: whether they lie, or speak the Truth, I know I like it, better and better. — I would feign make an original, an Exemplar, of this Letter but fear I have not an original Genius."

The letter used for the two-ounce rate stamps was written by Abigail August 11, 1763, from Weymouth and contains these paragraphs:

"My Friend

"If I was sure your absence to day was occasioned, by what it generally is, either to wait upon Company, or promote some good work, I freely confess my Mind would be much more at ease than at present it is — yet this uneasiness does not arise from any apprehension of Slight or neglect, but a fear lest you are indisposed — for that you said should be your only hindrance.

"Humanity obliges us to be affected with the distresses and miserys of our fellow creatures. Friendship is a band yet stronger, which causes us to [fee]l with greater tenderness the afflictions of our Friends."

Once it was determined that the visual elements of each design would be the letter, the word "LOVE" minus the "O" and a long-stemmed rose,

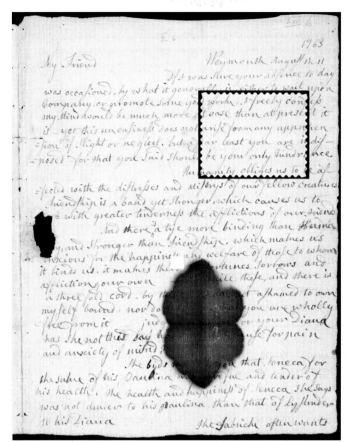

This is a photographic copy of the original letter, stained and torn, written by Abigail Smith to John Adams August 11, 1763. The portion that appears on the 55¢ and 57¢ Love stamps is shown in outline.

Shown here are the component parts of the photographic montage that Renee Comet assembled to create the design for the nondenominated and 34¢ Love stamps. The rose was photographed against a photocopy of the portion of the John Adams letter that was to appear on the stamp; note

the masking tape holding the paper to the mounting board and the shadows cast by the flower. Then an acetate overlay with a reproduction of the hand-lettered word "LOVE," minus the "O," was photographed and combined with the first composite photograph so that the letters also cast shadows. The result is a three-dimensional effect.

the design team set about assembling them.

From the transparencies of the letters furnished by the Massachusetts Historical Society, PhotoAssist had large prints made on heavy cotton rag paper to create a look as close to the originals as possible. An artist was hired to create the typography by hand, giving it an old-fashioned, serifed look. Renee Comet, a Washington, D.C., photographer who specializes in still life and whose photos have been used on several U.S. stamps in recent years, was brought into the project to film the elements, to be combined on film or electronically in a way that would show them all at the same scale.

The result, in both the vertical and horizontal designs, is a three-dimensional effect in which the typography and the rose cast shadows on the paper of the letters behind them.

"It was a far more complicated little project than it might seem," Kessler said.

Catalone noted with regret that after all the effort that was made to obtain appropriate letters for the designs, the stamps bore no indication of their source. "It's too bad that people don't know that they're historic letters," she said.

The nondenominated stamp bears the inscription "USA First-Class" in black italics in the lower-right corner of the design. This type, unlike the "LOVE," is conventionally set. The denominated stamps display hand-drawn value figures and "USA" in two lines in the lower-right corner.

Because all the Love stamps were printed by offset, a method USPS considers less secure than intaglio or gravure, the microprinted letters "USPS" can be found in the design of each one.

On the nondenominated (34¢) stamp and both formats (pane of 20 and vending booklet of 20) of the 34¢ stamp, the microprinting is found along the stem of the leaf closest to the bottom frameline. On the 55¢ stamp, it is outside the bottom serif of the letter "E" in "LOVE," and on the 57¢, it is outside the main stem of the rose just below the blossom.

Varieties

A miscut convertible booklet of the nondenominated (34¢) stamp was found with five vertical pairs missing their horizontal die cuts. The error pairs comprise the stamps in the second and third rows of the pane. Scott assigned the catalog number 3496a to the error pair.

First-Day Facts

The nondenominated Love stamp was issued January 19 on the first day of the Aripex 2001 show at the Tucson Convention Center.

Alvaro A. Alvarez, Tucson's postmaster, dedicated the stamps. The speaker was Gordon C. Morison, a former assistant postmaster general who headed the stamp program during his final years at USPS. Morison took part in the program as president of Nordia 2001, which sponsored a Nordic stamp exhibition at Aripex. Betsy Towle, executive director of the

On the nondenominated (34¢) stamp, shown here, and on both formats (pane of 20 and vending booklet of 20) of the 34¢ stamp, the microprinted letters "USPS" are found along the stem of the leaf closest to the bottom frameline.

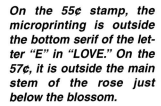

On the 55¢ stamp, the microprinting is outside the bottom serif of the letter "E" in "LOVE." On the 57¢, it is outside the main stem of the rose just below the blossom.

This miscut convertible booklet of nondenominated Love stamps contains five die-cut-missing vertical pairs, comprising the stamps in the second and third rows that show complete stamp designs. Note that the peel-off selvage strip is near the top of this pane. A normal pane has the strip in the middle, with two rows of five stamps each at the top and two rows of five stamps each at the bottom. Bernard Lenz of Georgia brought this item to the attention of Linn's Stamp News.

Postal History Foundation, gave the welcome, and Gregory Lehner, manager of customer service operations for USPS, was master of ceremonies.

The 34¢ and 55¢ Love stamps and the 34¢ Lovebirds stamped envelope were dedicated February 14 in a ceremony at the Lovejoy High School in Lovejoy, Georgia, by William J. Brown, USPS vice president for Southeast Area operations. He was introduced by Anderson Hodges Jr., Atlanta District manager for USPS.

Candle Bray, chairman of the Clayton County Board of Commissioners, was the speaker. Evelyn Florin, principal of Lovejoy High School, gave the welcome, and members of the Lovejoy High Drama Club in period costumes read portions of letters exchanged by John Adams and Abigail Smith. Lisa Catalone, the stamp's designer, was an honored guest.

No first-day ceremony was held November 19 for the 57¢ Love stamp.

The earliest-known prerelease use of a 34¢ Love stamp from a pane of 20 was on covers with machine cancellations from Las Vegas, Nevada, dated February 7, seven days before the official first day of issue.

The earliest-known prerelease use of a 34¢ Love stamp from a vending booklet was on a blue utility payment envelope with a machine cancellation from the Suburban Maryland Processing and Distribution Center dated February 12, two days before the official sale date.

The earliest-known prerelease use of a 55¢ Love stamp was on a rigid document mailer bearing a double-outline circular hand cancellation from Smith, Nevada, dated February 12, two days before the official first day of issue.

34¢ EID
HOLIDAY CELEBRATIONS SERIES

Date of Issue: September 1, 2001

Catalog Number: Scott 3532

Colors: gray (PMS 300), blue (PMS 424), gold (PMS 871)

First-Day Cancel: Des Plaines, Illinois

First-Day Cancellations: 107,142

Format: Panes of 20, vertical, 5 across, 4 down. Gravure printing cylinders printing 240 stamps per revolution, 2 panes across, 6 panes around, manufactured by Armotek Industries.

Gum Type: self-adhesive

Overall Stamp Size: 0.91 by 1.19 inches; 23.114 by 30.226mm

Pane Size: 5.375 by 5.875 inches; 136.53 by 149.23mm

Perforations: 11¼ (die-cut simulated perforations) (Comco Commander rotary die cutter). Die cuts in backing paper.

Selvage Markings: "© 2000/USPS." ".34/x 20/$6.80." "PLATE/POSITION" and diagram. Universal Product Code (UPC) "562100."

Designer, Calligrapher and Typographer: Mohamed Zakariya of Arlington, Virginia

Art Director: Phil Jordan of Falls Church, Virginia

Stamp Manufacturing: Stamps printed by Avery Dennison Security Printing Division, Clinton, South Carolina, on 8-color Dia Nippon Kiko webfed gravure press. Stamps processed by Avery Dennison.

Quantity Ordered: 75,000,000

Plate Number Detail: 1 set of 3 plate numbers preceded by the letter V in selvage next to each corner stamp

Plate Number Combination Reported: V111

Paper Supplier: Fasson Division of Avery Dennison

Tagging: block tagging over stamps

The Stamp

In recent years, the Citizens' Stamp Advisory Committee, with the encouragement of Postal Service management, has placed increasing emphasis on reflecting the diversity of the American people in the U.S. stamp program. Thus, in 1996 USPS launched a new series it called "Holiday Celebration" (it has since made the noun a plural) to honor religious and cultural holidays other than Christmas, which had inspired an annual stamp or stamps since 1962.

The first stamp in the series featured Hanukkah, the Jewish Festival of Lights. This was followed with stamps for the nonreligious African-American holiday Kwanzaa (1997) and the Mexican and Mexican-American holiday Cinco de Mayo (1998). All three later were reissued with higher denominations to reflect increases in the first-class rate (see separate chapters on the 34¢ Hanukkah and Kwanzaa stamps).

The Citizens' Stamp Advisory Committee soon began receiving requests from the American Muslim community, which numbers an estimated 6 million to 7 million, for a stamp honoring an Islamic holiday. Among those weighing in early was a 10-year-old stamp collector in Sparks, Nevada, named Muhib Beekun.

According to an article in *Saudi Aramco World*, a bimonthly magazine published and distributed by the Saudi Aramco oil company, young Muhib decided in 1996 that there should be a stamp for an Islamic holiday like those for Christmas and Hanukkah. With the help of a family friend, Aminah Assilmi, director of the International Union of Muslim Women, he launched what the magazine described as "a letter, e-mail, phone, petition and postcard campaign [that] gradually gained the enthusiastic support of thousands of Muslim children across the nation."

Terrence McCaffrey, manager of stamp development for USPS, confirmed that "thousands of letters" were received. "Phil Meggs, who is chair of the CSAC subcommittee for holiday stamps, looked into it, along with PhotoAssist [the Postal Service's research firm], and determined that the demographics were there to do an Islamic holiday stamp. The requests certainly were there," McCaffrey said.

Meggs recommended that a stamp for the Muslim holy month of Ramadan be approved, and the committee agreed. Phil Jordan, one of the Postal Service's part-time art directors, was assigned to oversee the design process.

Because of strict Islamic prohibitions on the use of images, the question of what to depict on the stamp was a tricky one. "I had a couple of books on the tradition of Islamic calligraphy," Jordan said, "and from the very start I thought, this is the only way out of the dilemma. We'll do a calligraphic design."

PhotoAssist put Jordan in touch with Mohamed Zakariya, an internationally known Islamic calligrapher who lives in Arlington, Virginia, a short distance from Jordan's home in Falls Church. Zakariya accepted the assignment, and in October 1999 he produced a design based on the mes-

171

sage "Ramadan Greetings" in Arabic calligraphy, with the same words in English.

At this point, a USPS official who is a Muslim learned of the project and insisted that the subject of the stamp be changed. He told members of CSAC and the USPS staff that a Ramadan stamp would be inappropriate and widely regarded as offensive. Ramadan is a month of fasting — analogous, as he saw it, to the Christian Lenten season — and the official felt they should be no more willing to approve a stamp for the one observance than for the other.

As an alternative, he proposed that the stamp celebrate the two most important festivals, or "eids" (rhymes with "beads"), in the Islamic calendar. These, like Ramadan itself, occur at 354-day rather than 365-day intervals because of Islam's use of a lunar calendar.

The Eid al-Fitr, the first day of the Muslim lunar month of Shawwal, signifies "the feast of breaking the fast" and marks the end of Ramadan at sundown of the preceding day. Eid al-Adha, "the feast of the sacrifice," which occurs approximately two months and 10 days after Eid al-Fitr, comes at the end of the hajj — the annual period of pilgrimage to the holy city of Mecca — and commemorates Ibrahim's willingness to sacrifice his son Ismail. The latter is the Muslim account of the Judeo-Christian story of Abraham and Isaac.

CSAC and the USPS staff accepted the suggestion, and Jordan and Zakariya created a design similar to the one they had prepared for Ramadan, with a different calligraphic message in Arabic and the words "Eid" and "Greetings" in English.

Avery Dennison's Security Printing Division printed 75 million self-

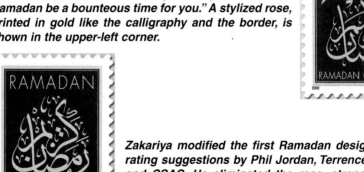

The Eid stamp originally was intended to celebrate Ramadan, the Islamic month of fasting. This is Mohamed Zakariya's first version of a calligraphic design conveying the message "Ramadan Karim" in Arabic, which translates literally to "May the month of Ramadan be a bounteous time for you." A stylized rose, printed in gold like the calligraphy and the border, is shown in the upper-left corner.

Zakariya modified the first Ramadan design, incorporating suggestions by Phil Jordan, Terrence McCaffrey and CSAC. He eliminated the rose, strengthened the principal calligraphic lines and rearranged the non-Arabic type. Later, the subject of the stamp was changed from Ramadan to the two eids, or Islamic festivals.

172

adhesive Eid stamps by the gravure process for sale in panes of 20. The design was unveiled in November 2000, and the stamps were issued nationwide September 1, 2001, with the first-day ceremony held at the annual convention of the Islamic Society of North America in Des Plaines, Illinois. The first Eid al-Fitr thereafter was celebrated on December 16, 2001, and the first ensuing Eid-al-Adha was February 23, 2002.

Ten days after the first day of issue, Muslim terrorists attacked the World Trade Center and the Pentagon, killing thousands of Americans and fueling anti-Muslim sentiment that targeted, among other things, the Eid stamp.

Mekeel's and *Stamps* magazine published editorials urging Muslims and others not to use the Eid stamp but instead to use the United We Stand definitive depicting the U.S. flag that was issued in the aftermath of the attacks (see separate chapter). And in November, the Free Congress Foundation, a conservative policy group, asked Republican congressional leaders to repudiate the Eid stamp.

"I am writing to suggest that the current stamps be withdrawn, to be overprinted with the image of the Twin Towers and then reissued," Paul M. Weyrich, president of the foundation, wrote in letters to House Speaker J. Dennis Hastert, Majority Leader Richard K. Armey and Majority Whip Tom DeLay. "I have no doubt a majority of Americans would find the altered stamps a more appropriate commemoration of Islam than the current celebratory version."

In response, Aly R. Abuzaakouk, executive director of the American Muslim Council, told *The Washington Post* that anyone who looked at the Arabic script in the Eid design and equated it with terrorism was "really playing into the hands of the terrorists."

"Who dares to associate negativity with something that celebrates a religious festival?" he said. "The Eid has nothing to do with the terrorists, and we thank God that all of those ... suspected to have done this have nothing to do with our community."

Abuzaakouk's organization and other Islamic groups told *The Post* they had received reports from members that some post offices weren't selling the Eid stamp. They urged people to forward such complaints to the Postal Service and to order the stamp online or through the USPS toll-free number.

Postal officials told *The Post* there was no attempt to cut back on the stamp's distribution. "As far as we're concerned, it's going to stay on sale and should be in stock at post offices around the country," said David Failor, USPS manager of community relations.

Shortly afterward, Muslim leaders voiced another grievance to the Postal Service. USPS printed for distribution to its 38,000 post offices a poster promoting the use of holiday stamps and depicting Christmas, Kwanzaa and Hanukkah stamps — but omitting the Eid stamp. On November 13, the American Muslim Council called for a national protest over the omission, and hundreds of e-mails reportedly were sent to Postmaster General John E. Potter in response.

The next day, Azeezaly S. Jaffer announced that the Eid stamp had been left off the posters "due to an oversight," one that the Postal Service "deeply regrets." He said the posters would be reprinted with Eid included, and this was done, although *Linn's Stamp News* was unable to report any sightings of revised posters until mid-January 2002.

The American Muslim Council commended USPS officials "for their immediate response to what was an oversight and in the caring way that they communicated the error and the correction." The council urged Muslims to ask for and use the stamps, saying that "U.S. stamps are a time-honored symbol of American life."

A footnote to the story was the results of the *Linn's* U.S. Stamp Popularity Poll for 2001. *Linn's* writer Charles Snee provided it in a sidebar to his article about the poll results published April 15, 2002.

"A determined group of voters went to extraordinary lengths to ensure that the 34¢ Eid stamp came out on top in online balloting for the favorite 2001 United States stamp," Snee wrote. "... [T]he Eid stamp garnered nearly 14,000 online votes as the favorite U.S. stamp of 2001. The four 34¢ Carnivorous Plants stamps came in a very distant second, with 241 votes.

"The impressive tally for the Eid stamp represents the enthusiastic voting of many individuals who identify in some fashion with the Muslim community in the United States, as some of the voters told *Linn's*.

"About one week before the March 4 deadline for casting ballots (both mail-in and online) in the 2001 poll, *Linn's* began receiving a steady stream of e-mail messages from readers who pointed out that online voting appeared to be favoring the Eid stamp to an unusual degree. A number of these messages also included the transcript of a message purportedly from the American Muslim Council. 'Vote in favor of the Eid stamp by March 4,' the message directed.

"*Linn's* attempted several times to contact the AMC to verify the authenticity of the message. No reply was received.

"The message instructed the reader how to move through the four online voting screens (one screen each for commemoratives, definitive and special stamps, postal stationery and favorite stamp). ... 'The fourth screen is extremely important. This is where you will vote for "my favorite 2001 stamp." Please vote ... for the Eid stamp,' the message stated.

"Regardless of the source of the message, numerous voters evidently received it and took its directions to heart. The voters' eagerness can't be faulted, but none of the online votes are counted in the final tallies recorded [by *Linn's*]. Similar dedicated but weaker voting in other categories also skewed the figures."

The 2001 online votes were counted separately from the mail-in ballots, as happened in 1999, when votes for the Tropical Flowers stamps skewed the results, Snee wrote.

In the mail-in portion of the poll for Overall Favorite U.S. Stamp of

174

2001, Eid placed 12th with 67 votes; the American Illustrators pane won with 368. The mail-in competition among U.S. definitive and special stamps produced wildly diverse results. Here, Eid placed third out of 24 in the "Most Important" category, first in the "Least Necessary" category, 10th in "Best Design" and second in "Worst Design."

The Design

Mohamed Zakariya was born in California in 1942, raised as what he calls "a sometime Christian," toured Morocco as a teenager and converted to Islam shortly thereafter. He learned calligraphy from masters in Tangier, London and Istanbul and has refined his art through extensive study abroad and at home. His work has been displayed in such venues as the Smithsonian Institution and the Metropolitan Museum of Art, and he has lectured and written extensively. Skilled as a woodworker and machinist as well as an artist, Zakariya also custom-makes working examples of antique-style timepieces and scientific instruments, such as astrolobes, quadrants and sundials.

The Ramadan and Eid designs produced by Zakariya, in consultation with Phil Jordan, were for a stamp of the special size the Postal Service uses for most of its Christmas, Holiday Celebrations and Love stamps, vertically arranged. Zakariya's artwork was in black and white, with the color added by computer. The calligraphy and a single-line border are printed in metallic gold on a background of deep blue, which Jordan describes as a "lapis lazuli" shade. The English words and "USA 34" are in gray.

In a letter to PhotoAssist dated October 29, 1999, Zakariya discussed the art of calligraphy and his original design for a Ramadan stamp.

"In classical terms, Islamic calligraphy is the primary visual art of the Muslim peoples, because it is considered to partake of some of the sanctity that clothes the source scripture, the Quran," he wrote. "It is an art that

has evolved over 14 centuries, from its primitive origins in the Arabian peninsula to the highly developed and subtle forms and methods of 19th- and 20th-century Ottoman Turkey.

"Since the 1930s, calligraphy has declined somewhat in most Islamic regions, although it has remained a prestigious art. During the last 15 years or so — thanks in large part to the

Calligrapher Mohamed Zakariya at work. Zakariya uses traditional methods and instruments, including hand-cut bamboo and reed pens, homemade black ink and specially prepared paper.

175

efforts of the Research Centre for Islamic History, Art and Culture in Istanbul — there has been a revival of the art worldwide. Consequently, the Turkish style is no longer a regional approach but has become what one could call the universal style.

"I am a specialist in this style of calligraphy, having been awarded two icazets (diplomas) by masters in Turkey. Most of my work is in the Turkish style.

"For the Ramadan stamp, I selected the *celi sulus* [in Turkish; in Arabic, *thuluth*] script for the inscription, using the clearest, most classical, yet fully legible form for the composition. This script is, traditionally, the most appropriate for such an inscription. The primary difficulty was composing the inscription in such a way that it remained completely distinct in the micro-reduction required for the stamp.

"As for the salutation itself, I think it is appropriate that we chose the simplest and most direct greeting, 'Ramadan Karim.' This is the phrase that Muslims commonly use to greet one another during the month of fasting. Even though it is in Arabic, which is the *lingua franca* of Islam, this phrase is used widely in Muslim societies both here and abroad. The literal translation is, 'May the month of Ramadan be a bounteous time for you,' but I chose to render it more simply as 'Ramadan Greetings,' which should have an appeal to Muslims and non-Muslims alike.

"Through consultation with Phil Jordan, I decided that it would be most effective to keep the entire design spare and clean, rather than distracting the eye with stereotypical Islamic decoration. I chose a slim sans-serif typeface [Futura] for the English salutation to complement the curvilinear Arabic and a simple color scheme that echoes the tonalities in many compositions from the classical period.

"In all stages of developing this composition, I used traditional methods and instruments, including hand-cut bamboo and reed pens and homemade black ink. The semi-finals and the final artwork were done on my own specially prepared ahar paper; that is, paper that has been sized with starch, coated with a mixture of egg whites and alum, burnished with an agate burnisher, and aged for at least one year."

After the subject of the stamp was changed to Eid, and Zakariya created a new design, the artist provided additional information to PhotoAssist in a letter dated December 15, 1999.

"The phrase [featured in the calligraphy] transliterates as 'Eid mubarak,' which translates literally as 'blessed or fortunate festival,' " he wrote. "It could be paraphrased as 'May your religious festival be blessed,' but because that is cumbersome, I suggest that the stamp say 'Eid Greetings.' One nice feature about this phrase is that it is not restricted to Eid al-Fitr, the festival that ends Ramadan. It is also used at Eid al-Adha ... Moreover, even Arabic-speaking Jews and Christians may use the phrase for their own religious holidays.

"Phil Jordan and I have concluded that a blue background is best for the job. In the classical art of Islamic calligraphy, most of the great works were done in gold over a colored background — often blue — which gives beauty and elegance to the composition and enhances its legibility."

Additional information on Zakariya and Islamic calligraphy can be found on his Web site at www.zakariya.net.

First-day Facts

Azeezaly S. Jaffer, USPS vice president for public affairs and communications, dedicated the Eid stamp in a ceremony at the Donald E. Stephens Convention Center in Des Plaines, site of the Islamic Society of North America's convention.

The speakers were the American Muslim Council's Aly R. Abuzaakouk; Imam W. Deen Mohammed, a spokesman for the Muslim American Society; and stamp designer Mohamed Zakariya. Sayyid Muhammad Syeed, secretary general of the Islamic Society of North America, gave the welcome, and Muzammil H. Siddiqi, the society's president, offered a prayer. The master of ceremonies was Danny Jackson, USPS vice president for the Great Lakes Area.

The earliest-known prerelease use of an Eid stamp was on a cover machine-canceled in Portland, Oregon, August 31, one day prior to the official first day of issue.

34¢ HOLIDAY SANTAS (4 DESIGNS) PANE OF 20

Date of Issue: October 10, 2001

Catalog Numbers: Scott 3537-3540, single stamps; 3540b, block of 4

Colors: magenta, black, cyan, yellow

First-Day Cancel: Santa Claus, Indiana

First-Day Cancellations: 376,615 (includes all versions of Holiday Santas stamps)

Format: Pane of 20, vertical, 5 across by 4 down. Gravure printing cylinders printing 320 stamps per revolution manufactured by Armotek Industries.

Gum Type: self-adhesive

Overall Stamp Size: 0.91 by 1.19 inches; 23.11 by 30.22mm

Pane Size: 5.4600 by 5.8125 inches; 138.68 by 147.63mm

Perforations: 10¾ by 11 (die-cut simulated perforations) (Comco custom rotary die cutter)

Selvage Markings: ".34/x20/$6.80" "©1999/USPS." "PLATE/POSITION" and diagram. Universal Product Code (UPC) 551500 in 2 positions.

Designer, Art Director and Typographer: Richard Sheaff of Scottsdale, Arizona

Modeler: Donald Woo of Sennett Security Products of Chantilly, Virginia

Stamp Manufacturing: Stamps printed for Sennett Security Products by American Packaging Corp. of Columbus, Wisconsin, on Rotomec 3000 gravure press. Stamps finished by Unique Binders of Fredericksburg, Virginia.

178

Quantity Ordered: 125,000,000 stamps

Cylinder Number Detail: 1 set of 4 cylinder numbers preceded by the letter S in selvage above or below each corner stamp

Cylinder Number Combination Reported: S1111

Paper Supplier: Maclac

Tagging: phosphored paper

34¢ HOLIDAY SANTAS (4 DESIGNS) CONVERTIBLE BOOKLET OF 20

Date of Issue: October 10, 2001

Catalog Numbers: Scott 3537a-3540a, single stamps; 3540c, block of 4; 3540d, pane of 20; 3537b-3539b, 3540e, single stamps with large "2001" yeardate; 3540f, block of 4; 3540g, pane of 20

Colors: magenta, black, cyan, yellow

First-Day Cancel: Santa Claus, Indiana

First-Day Cancellations: 376,615 (includes all versions of Holiday Santas stamps)

Format: Convertible booklet pane of 20, vertical. Stamps on both sides, 8 (2 across by 4 down) plus nonstamp label (booklet cover) on one side, 12 (2 across by 6 down) on other side, with 2 horizontal peel-off strips on each side. Gravure printing cylinders printing 21 booklets in a press sheet.

Gum Type: self-adhesive

Overall Stamp Size: 0.91 by 1.19 inches; 23.11 by 30.22mm

Pane Size: 1.82 by 7.45 inches; 46.22 by 189.23mm

Perforations: 10¾ by 11 (die-cut simulated perforations) (Comco custom rotary die cutter). Backing paper scored under peel-off strips.

Selvage Markings: "© 1999 USPS • Peel here to fold • Self-adhesive stamps • DO NOT WET" on first peel-off strip on all-stamp side; cylinder numbers and • Peel here to fold • Self-adhesive stamps • © 1999 USPS" on second peel-off strip on all-stamp side.

Back Markings: "Holiday Greetings/Twenty 34¢/Self-adhesive stamps/Four different designs/$6.80" plus Universal Product Code (UPC) "0 665100 0" on booklet cover.

Designer, Art Director and Typographer: Richard Sheaff of Scottsdale, Arizona

Modeler: Donald Woo of Sennett Security Products of Chantilly, Virginia

Stamp Manufacturing: Stamps printed for Sennett Security Products by American Packaging Corp. of Columbus, Wisconsin, on Rotomec 3000 gravure press. Stamps finished by Unique Binders of Fredericksburg, Virginia.

Quantity Ordered: 1,500,000,000 stamps

Cylinder Number Detail: 1 set of 4 cylinder numbers preceded by the letter S on 1 peel-off strip.

Cylinder Number Combinations Reported: S1111, S3333, S4444

Paper Supplier: Kanzaki/Nichemen

Tagging: phosphored paper. Phosphate blocker applied to the cover portion of the pane.

34¢ HOLIDAY SANTA (4 DESIGNS) VENDING BOOKLET OF 20

Date of Issue: October 10, 2001

Catalog Numbers: Scott 3541-3544, single stamps; 3544a, block of 4; 3544b, booklet pane of 4; 3544c, booklet segment of 6, 3543, 3544, 2 each 3541-3542; 3544d, booklet segment of 6, 3541, 3542, 2 each 3543-3544; BK266, vending booklet containing 3544c, 3544d, 2 3544b

Colors: magenta, cyan, black, yellow

First-Day Cancel: Santa Claus, Indiana

First-Day Cancellations: 376,615 (includes all versions of Holiday Santas stamps)

Format: Vending booklet of 20, vertical, 2 across by 10 down, in 4 segments: 4 (2 by 2), 6 (2 by 3), 6 (2 by 3) and 4 (2 by 2). Gravure printing cylinders of 300 (5 panes across, 3 panes around) printing 15 panes, manufactured by Armotek Industries.

Gum Type: self-adhesive

Overall Stamp Size: 0.870 by 0.982 inches; 22.098 by 24.943mm

Pane Size: 1.740 by 10.375 inches; 44.196 by 263.530mm

Perforations: 11 (die-cut simulated perforations) (Comco Commander rotary die cutter). Backing paper rouletted between booklet segments.

Selvage Markings: none

Back Markings: "Holiday/Greetings/$6.80/Four/different/designs/Twenty 34¢ self-adhesive stamps" on front cover. Promotion for www.stampson-line.com web site, "©2000 USPS," USPS logo, cylinder numbers and Universal Product Code (UPC) "0 665000 1" on back cover.

Designer, Art Director and Typographer: Richard Sheaff of Scottsdale, Arizona

Stamp Manufacturing: Stamps printed by Avery Dennison Security Printing Division, Clinton, South Carolina, on Dia Nippon Kiko gravure press. Stamps finished by Avery Dennison.

Quantity Ordered: 201,000,000 stamps

Cylinder Number Detail: 1 set of 4 cylinder numbers preceded by the letter V on back of backing paper, behind top 4-stamp segment

Cylinder Number Combination Reported: V1111

Paper Supplier: Fasson Division of Avery Dennison

Tagging: phosphored paper

The Stamps

Richard Sheaff, one of the Postal Service's part-time art directors, is a collector of ephemera — antique printed paper products — and has designed numerous holiday and Love stamps for USPS reproducing pictures from such sources. One of the advantages postal officials find in using images from ephemera is that most copyrights, if any, have long since expired.

On October 10, USPS issued a block of four holiday stamps depicting the character now known as Santa Claus. The images, from 80 to 110 years old, came from chromolithographs in Sheaff's collection. Chromolithography is a color printing process that was developed in the early 19th century and became more efficient and very popular as the century progressed.

Holiday stamps have been issued for many years as companions to the annual Madonna and Child stamps. Originally, they were called "contemporary" Christmas stamps, meaning they

have a nonreligious design theme. The four Santa Claus stamps were unveiled in 1999 for release in 2000. But in April 2000 the Postal Service announced that the set would be postponed for a year to allow existing stocks of the 1999 Deer stamps to be used up, with supplementary printings of those designs if necessary. As a result, 2000 was the first year since 1961 — the year before the first U.S. Christmas stamp was issued — with no new stamp in that category.

Each of the four Santas depicted in 2001 has a characteristic flowing white beard and carries a small Christmas tree or holly bush and an assortment of toys. In the block of four designs, the Santas on the stamps in the upper left (gold cap and holly bush) and lower right (gold costume) probably date from the 1880s, according to USPS. They may have been designed in England and printed in Germany. People may have purchased these images and placed them in keepsake scrapbooks. The Santas in the upper right (blue costume) and lower left (black trim on cap) were printed in Germany and probably date between 1915 and 1920. Santas such as these may have been used to decorate "lebkuchen," a traditional German cookie.

The stamps are self-adhesive, printed by the gravure process by two different contractors and issued in three formats, an arrangement that produced 16 collectible varieties. The designs, vertically arranged, are the same for all formats. They are:

• Pane of 20 (Scott 3537-40), printed by Sennett Security Products. The stamps are arranged on the pane in four rows of five stamps each and have die-cut simulated perforations on all four sides. The "34" denomination and "USA" are in black. USPS ordered 125,000,000 stamps in this format.

• Double-sided pane (convertible booklet) of 20 (Scott 3537a-40a, and 3537b-39b, 3540e). One side bears two vertical rows of four stamps each and a large label, while the other side has two vertical rows of six stamps each. Horizontal strips can be peeled off to facilitate folding, after which the label serves as a booklet cover. This product also was printed by Sennett. The Scott catalog says the designs are slightly taller than those on the

184

Here are three 34¢ Santas stamps from three different formats: pane of 20, double-sided pane of 20 and vending booklet of 20. The text explains how to easily tell them apart.

pane of 20, hence the separate listing. Because of the stamps' arrangement on the pane, each has a straight edge on one or two sides. The denomination and "USA" are in black. The print order was 1,500,000,000 stamps.

Two sizes of the "2001" year date have been identified on stamps from this format: a smaller size, printed from cylinder-number combination (plate number) S1111, and a larger size, from plate number S3333.

• Vending booklet of 20 (Scott 3541-44), printed by Avery Dennison Security Products. The booklet comes prefolded. Individual stamps are readily distinguishable from their Sennett counterparts by their much smaller size and by the fact that the "34" is printed in green and the "USA" in red. Each stamp has a straight edge on one or two sides. The four gravure cylinder numbers preceded by the letter V appear on the printed side of the liner paper. Avery Dennison supplied 201,000,000 booklet stamps.

The Santas designs also appear on a set of four 21¢ picture postal cards that were sold in packages of 20 cards each (see separate chapter).

Collectors reported a problem with the Sennett double-sided pane that occurs from time to time with modern U.S. self-adhesive stamps: difficulty in soaking used specimens from envelope paper. (The problem was especially acute with two stamps issued in 2000, the 33¢ Coral Pink Rose definitive from a double-sided pane and the 33¢ Adoption Awareness commemorative.)

Linn's Stamp News writer Charles Snee and *Stamp Collector* writer Fred Baumann responded to readers' complaints by conducting experiments of their own. Both reported that Santa stamps from the other formats came off their corners easily after a brief soak, but those from the double-sided pane were virtually impossible to remove. Rather than separate from their envelope paper after a period in the water, the stamps tended to delaminate, or shear in two along the plane of the paper, Baumann wrote. (One *Stamp Collector* reader, however, did report success when he soaked the stamps in lighter fluid.)

In a follow-up article in *Linn's* several months later, Snee announced

Shown here are greatly magnified images of the "2001" year dates on Santas stamps from the double-sided pane of 20 printed by Sennett Security Products. The smaller year date on the left is from panes printed by gravure cylinder number combination S1111. Used stamps from these panes are notoriously difficult to soak from their envelope paper. The larger year date on the right is from panes printed by combination S3333. Stamps from these panes are easy to remove from their envelope corners after a short time in the water.

that the soaking problem associated with the double-sided pane was limited to stamps bearing the smaller "2001" year date. "Stamps bearing a noticeably larger '2001' year date are excellent for soaking," Snee wrote.

Linn's asked USPS spokesman Don Smeraldi for an explanation of the difficulty soaking the small-date Santas and received this reply:

"The reason for the soaking differences is that the Santas stamps were produced using two batches of paper. Both batches were from International Paper, but the first batch dates back to summer 2000. It was originally intended for double-sided panes of the 33¢ Coral Pink Rose stamp.

"But with the January 7, 2001, rate increase looming at that time, the Postal Service canceled the projected print quantities for the Coral Pink Rose and instructed printer Sennett Security Products to use this first batch of paper on a future issue, which turned out to be the Santas stamps.

"This first batch of paper later was found to have problems meeting water removability requirements, and that is why collectors experienced problems soaking Santas stamps from double-sided panes bearing plate number S1111.

"The second batch of paper, which was delivered to Sennett for the remainder of the Santas print order, was processed by International Paper with revised formulations that met water removability requirements. Double-sided Santas panes printed using this batch of paper bear plate number S3333."

The Designs

For this set, Richard Sheaff made stamp mockups of several Santa images from his ephemera collection, including Santas with sleighs and Santas with children, and added to the mix a handful of Christmas angels.

The Citizens' Stamp Advisory Committee "felt that while the Santas with the kids were interesting, they were very busy," said Terrence McCaffrey, manager of stamp development. CSAC decided that the designs showing Santa Claus alone would work better. Sheaff had developed some of these as commemorative-size designs, but USPS is committed to the

Shown here are several other vintage Santa Claus images that Sheaff mocked up in commemorative size.

CSAC found these Santa stamp designs interesting, but pronounced them too "busy," especially at the special size in which Sheaff laid them out.

Sheaff showed CSAC designs incorporating images of Christmas angels from his ephemera collection, but the committee preferred Santa Claus.

Happy Holiday Season!

Close to the ultimate in "busyness" is this image of Santa Claus dressed in furs and floating a balloon labeled "God bless the children" over the heads of a sleeping brother and sister.

Richard Sheaff developed these two Santa images in the commemorative size. Later, he cropped them to fit the smaller special size, and they became the designs of two of the four issued stamps.

smaller and more economical "special" size for its holiday and Love stamps. "The committee asked Dick to recrop them or find similar images that would work well in the special size," McCaffrey said.

First-day Facts

Wayne Gardner, marketing manager for the USPS Great Lakes Area, dedicated the stamps in a ceremony at the theater in Holiday World, an amusement park in Santa Claus, Indiana.

The principal speaker was Patricia Koch of Santa's Elves Inc. Will Koch, president and general manager of Holiday World and Splashin' Safari, gave the welcome. Dawna Fornter, manager of post office operations for the USPS Great Lakes Area, was master of ceremonies.

Previous Christmas stamps that had their first-day sale in Santa Claus were the 1963 issue, which pictured the National Christmas Tree and the White House, and the 1983 Christmas contemporary stamp, bearing Santa's portrait.

34¢ CHRISTMAS MADONNA AND CHILD
CONVERTIBLE BOOKLET OF 20

Seasons Greetings

Twenty **34** cent
First-Class
Self-adhesive
Stamps

$**6**.80

B1 11 • Peel here to fold • Self-adhesive stamps • DO NOT WET • © 2000 USPS

Date of Issue: October 10, 2001

Catalog Number: Scott 3536, single stamp; 3536a, pane of 20

Colors: black, yellow, cyan, magenta

First-Day Cancel: Philadelphia, Pennsylvania

First-Day Cancellations: 106,169

Format: Convertible booklet of 20, vertical, 5 across, 4 down, with horizontal peel-off strip between horizontal rows 2 and 3. Gravure printing cylinders manufactured by Acitronics printing 500 stamps per revolution.

Gum Type: self-adhesive

Overall Stamp Size: 0.91 by 1.19 inches; 23.11 by 30.23mm

Pane Size: 4.55 by 5.00 inches; 115.57 by 127.00mm

Perforations: 11½ (die-cut simulated perforations)

Selvage Markings: Cylinder numbers and "• Peel here to fold • Self-adhesive stamps • DO NOT WET • © 2000 USPS."

Back Markings: "Seasons Greetings/Twenty 34 cent/First-Class/Self-adhesive/stamps/$6.80." Promotion for The Postal Store web site. "© USPS 2000." Universal Product Code (UPC) "0 665200 9."

Designer, Typographer and Art Director: Richard Sheaff of Scottsdale, Arizona

Stamp Manufacturing: Stamps printed for Banknote Corporation of America, Browns Summit, North Carolina, by Guilford Gravure, Guilford, Connecticut, on Cerutti R118 gravure press. Stamps finished by BCA.

Quantity Ordered: 800,000,000

Cylinder Number Detail: 1 set of 4 cylinder numbers preceded by the letter B on peel-off strip

Cylinder Number Combination Reported: B1111

Tagging: phosphored paper

The Stamp

On October 10, 2001, the Postal Service issued a 34¢ "traditional" Christmas stamp featuring a detail from Lorenzo Costa's painting *Virgin and Child* that hangs in the Philadelphia Museum of Art. Its issuance was the result of two changes in plans by USPS.

Two years earlier, officials had unveiled the design of a traditional Christmas stamp to be issued in 2000 featuring a Madonna and Child painting by Netherlandish artist Jan Gossaert

This was the preliminary design for a Madonna and Child stamp featuring a painting by Jan Gossaert that was unveiled in 1999 for a 2000 issue. The Gossaert design then was postponed to 2001 and later replaced for that year's Christmas stamp by a design reproducing art by Lorenzo Costa. The Gossaert design was rescheduled for 2002.

that is part of the collection of the Art Institute of Chicago. But on April 4, 2000, USPS announced that there would be no new traditional or contemporary Christmas stamp that year. Instead, the 1999 stamps would be offered again for the 2000 holiday season "in a move to continue prudently managing inventories." The designs that had been announced for 2000 would be used later, USPS said.

When the designs for the 2001 stamp program were disclosed on November 13, 2000, however, the traditional Christmas stamp that was included didn't depict the Gossaert Madonna painting, but instead showed a painting of the same subject by Italian Renaissance artist Lorenzo Costa.

"The Philadelphia Museum of Art had petitioned the Citizens' Stamp Advisory Committee for a stamp honoring its 125th anniversary," said Terrence McCaffrey, manager of stamp development for USPS. "It was turned down, based on our criterion of only marking anniversaries in 50-year increments." (Another CSAC criterion bars stamps to honor "primary or secondary schools, hospitals, libraries or similar institutions.")

The museum "had proposed using one of Vincent Van Gogh's flower paintings as the basis for the art," McCaffrey continued. "But we had recently issued the Four Centuries of American Art Classic Collection, and didn't wish to do a separate stamp featuring a foreign artist.

"Someone made the suggestion that we check with the museum to see if they had any Madonna and Child paintings that could work as a Christmas stamp. Upon exploration, we discovered the Lorenzo Costa painting. When Dick Sheaff [USPS art director Richard Sheaff] received a copy of it and worked upon it, we found we had a very acceptable design. It was shared with the committee and approved.

"Because the committee had seen and approved numerous Madonna and Child paintings for future issuance, it revisited the group of approved designs and slotted the Costa for 2001 to accommodate the museum's anniversary. That is why the Gossaert Madonna, which would have been issued in 2001, was moved to 2002."

The Costa stamp, a self-adhesive, was printed by the gravure process by Guilford Gravure of Guilford, Connecticut, for Banknote Corporation of America. It was the first Madonna and Child Christmas stamp to be gravure-printed since 1987; in the interim, all the Madonnas were produced by offset or an offset-intaglio combination. BCA issued the stamp in a pane of 20 that USPS calls a convertible booklet, meaning that buyers could remove the pane's single peel-off strip and fold it along a rouletted line into a more convenient size.

The stamp features a detail of Costa's *Virgin and Child*, circa 1490, that is part of the collection of 1,200 items of art that prominent Philadelphia lawyer John G. Johnson willed to the Philadelphia museum in 1917. Few Costa works are owned by American museums, although the artist is well represented in major European galleries. In this oil-on-panel depiction, the Madonna is seated behind a waist-high, pearl gray parapet upon which she holds her standing child. She wears a dark blue mantle over a white kerchief and red dress.

Lorenzo Costa (1460-1535) was born in the northern Italian town of Ferrara. In the 1480s he moved to Bologna, where he received the patronage of the ruling Bentivoglio family. Costa's work included altarpieces, frescoes, portraits and allegories, and his major commissions for Bolognese churches are considered among his best. In 1506, Costa succeeded Andrea Mantegna as the court painter to the ruling Gonzaga family in Mantua, where he remained until his death in 1535.

Officials of the Philadephia Museum of Art pointed out that the Costa painting was not the first work from the museum's collection to be depicted on a stamp. In 1998, Marcel Duchamp's 1912 masterpiece, *Nude Descending a Staircase, No. 2*, was illustrated on a stamp in the Celebrate the Century pane for the 1910s that commemorated the 1913 Armory Show in New York, where the painting was exhibited.

The Design

Richard Sheaff's design follows a now-standard formula for traditional Christmas stamps. The detail from the painting, in a vertical rectangle, occupies most of the design area. Across the top, in black Garamond type on a white strip, is the word "CHRISTMAS." In a corresponding strip across the bottom, in smaller Garamond letters, are the words "L. Costa Philadelphia Museum of Art." Just below the artist's name is the tiny year date, "2001." The "34 USA" is in the upper-right corner of the picture area, in two lines dropped out of the black background.

Sheaff cropped the image just below Mary's hands holding the Christ child, omitting the lower part of the child's legs and the parapet on which he is standing.

The booklet cover reproduces the stamp design in color. Like the cover of the 1999 Madonna and Child booklet, it bears the inscription "Seasons Greetings," omitting the apostrophe.

First-day Facts

S. David Fineman, vice chairman of the USPS Board of Governors, dedicated the stamp in a ceremony at the Philadelphia Museum of Art.

Carl Strehlke, adjunct curator of the museum's John G. Johnson Collection, was the principal speaker. Alexander Lazaroff, USPS Philadelphia District manager, was master of ceremonies, and Gail Harrity, the museum's chief operating officer, gave the welcome. Honored guests included two other museum officials: Joseph J. Rishel, senior curator of European painting before 1900, and Teresa Lignelli, associate conservator of paintings.

34¢ WE GIVE THANKS
HOLIDAY CELEBRATIONS SERIES

Date of Issue: October 19, 2001

Catalog Number: Scott 3546

Colors: black, cyan, magenta, yellow; tan (PMS 453), selvage only

First-Day Cancel: Dallas, Texas

First-Day Cancellations: 114,931

Format: Panes of 20, horizontal, 4 across, 5 down. Offset printing plates of 180 subjects, 15 across, 12 around.

Gum Type: self-adhesive

Overall Stamp Size: 1.19 by 0.91 inches; 30.226 by 23.114mm

Pane Size: 5.95 by 5.46 inches; 151.130 by 138.684mm

Perforations: 11¼ (die-cut simulated perforations) (Arpeco die cutter)

Selvage Markings: "©/USPS/1999." ".34/x 20/$6.80." "PLATE/POSITION" and diagram. Universal Product Code (UPC) "551000" in 2 locations.

Illustrator and Typographer: Margaret Cusack of Brooklyn, New York

Designer and Typographer: Richard Sheaff of Scottsdale, Arizona

Modeler: Joseph Sheeran of Ashton-Potter (USA) Ltd., Williamsville, New York

Stamp Manufacturing: Stamps printed by Ashton-Potter on offset portion of Stevens Variable Size Security Documents webfed 6-color offset, 3-color intaglio press. Stamps finished by Ashton-Potter.

Quantity Ordered: 69,000,000

Plate Number Detail: 1 set of 4 plate numbers preceded by the letter P in selvage opposite each corner stamp

Plate Number Combinations Reported: P1111, P2222

Paper Supplier: Flexcon/Tullis Russell

Tagging: block tagging over stamps

The Stamp

On October 19, the Postal Service issued a stamp in the Holiday Celebrations series recognizing the American holiday of Thanksgiving, which originated in a three-day harvest feast shared by colonists and native Americans at Plymouth, Massachusetts, 380 years earlier.

The stamp's design — a wicker basket shaped like a cornucopia, or horn of plenty, overflowing with fruits and vegetables, under the words "We Give Thanks" — was created in machine-appliqued needlework. A full pane of 20, four across by five down, with selvage gives the visual effect of a quilt.

USPS said the design, which was the fifth in the Holiday Celebrations series, would be the last new one in the series, although some of the designs would continue to be recycled with new denominations to correspond to increases in the first-class rate.

The We Give Thanks design, with a 33¢ denomination, actually was unveiled in October 1999 with the announcement that the stamp would be issued the following year to coincide with the United Nations proclamation of 2000 as the International Year of Thanksgiving. But in September 2000, USPS postponed the issuance. A 1¢ rate hike was expected in early 2001, and officials didn't want to be left holding additional millions of

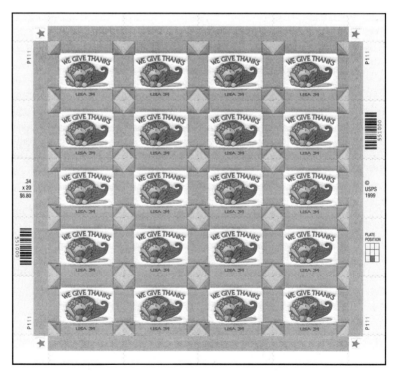

A full pane of the We Give Thanks stamps, with a border pattern in the selvage and a star in each corner, gives the visual impression of an old-fashioned quilt.

holiday stamps that no longer fulfilled an exact rate and eventually would have to be destroyed.

The Pilgrims' first Thanksgiving in Plymouth Colony in 1621 celebrated a dramatic change for the better in the fortunes of the colonists.

Following a 66-day crossing of the Atlantic in the *Mayflower*, 104 Pilgrims set foot in Massachusetts December 21, 1620. The first winter was one of hardship, as disease reduced the population by more than half. William Bradford, the colony's governor, wrote in March: "This month thirteen of our number die ... scarce fifty remain, the living scarce able to bury the dead."

However, the crops flourished in 1621. Members of the Wampanoag tribe, led by their chief, Massasoit, provided seeds for corn and taught the Pilgrims how to fertilize the land. Barley also was available.

"Our harvest being gotten in," colonist Edward Winslow wrote to a friend in England, "our governor sent four men on fowling, that so we might after a special manner rejoice together after we had gathered the fruit of our labors." The men brought back enough waterfowl and wild turkeys to last a week. Fishermen pulled in cod and bass. Indian hunters contributed five deer. Ninety Indians, with Massasoit, feasted with the colonists for three days.

The date of that first feast isn't known, but it occurred before December 11, the date of Winslow's letter. The complete menu was a full one: venison, roast duck, roast goose, clams and other shellfish, eels, corn bread, leeks and watercress, plums and dried berries, and wine fermented from wild grapes from the forest.

"Although it be not always so plentiful as it was at this time with us," Winslow concluded, "yet by the goodness of God, we are so far from want that we often wish you partakers of our plenty."

There is no record that the feast was called a "thanksgiving." Appointing special days for giving special thanks was a custom of the Puritans, but the first record of such a day was two years later, in 1623. Then the Pilgrims "set apart a day of thanksgiving" for rain that ended a severe drought.

In the third year of the Civil War, President Abraham Lincoln, believing that the Union had been saved, proclaimed a national Thanksgiving to be celebrated on Thursday, November 26, 1863. He also named the last Thursday in November as a day to be observed every year. Since 1941, Thanksgiving has been observed on the fourth Thursday of November, which isn't always the last.

The Design

At the outset, art director Richard Sheaff developed several conventional designs for the We Give Thanks stamp for consideration by the Citizens' Stamp Advisory Committee. These included material from his own ephemera collection, in vintage seed catalogs and other sources, as well as an abstract turkey that he sketched on his computer and a stylized sheaf of

Before the decision was made to use a fabric design for the We Give Thanks stamp, art director Richard Sheaff developed these more conventional designs for CSAC's consideration. The images include material from vintage seed catalogs and other sources, an abstract turkey that Sheaff sketched on his computer, and a stylized sheaf of grain similar to the logo Sheaff uses for his own design firm in Scottsdale, Arizona.

grain similar to the logo he uses for his own design firm.

But Sheaff had been looking for an opportunity to use the work of Margaret Cusack of Brooklyn, New York, who creates stitched illustrations with needle and thread. Cusack's art has appeared, among other places, in ads, children's books, greeting cards, a 1997 *Time* magazine cover, the 1986 Avon calendar and the poster for the Broadway musical *Shenandoah*. When Sheaff telephoned her to ask if she would like to try her hand at a postage stamp, she welcomed the challenge.

During the design process, Cusack hand-embroidered a sampler that was bordered by x-stitches and dominated by the words "We Give Thanks" above a small house and stylized trees. CSAC preferred a cornu-

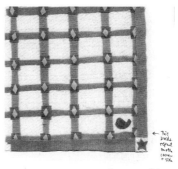

Rough fabric paste-up of quilt block of stamps

Margaret Cusak submitted for CSAC's consideration this hand-embroidered sampler bordered by x-stitches and dominated by the words "We Give Thanks" above a small house and stylized trees.

During the design process, Margaret Cusack made this rough fabric paste-up to show how a pane of stitched stamps laid out as a quilt might look.

copia theme with somewhat smaller wording, however, and Cusack's final product conformed to these specifications.

She made an 8-inch by 10-inch miniature quilt, using old and new fabrics, on her Bernina sewing machine. The horn of plenty is quilted, and the words "We Give Thanks" and "USA 34" are stitched above and below it, respectively. (She had to resew the denomination when it was changed from 33¢ to 34¢.)

Using a color transparency of Cusack's original and his computer, Sheaff translated the stitchery into a finished stamp design. The stamp is in the special size used for Christmas stamps and the Holiday Celebrations series. The "2001" year date is visible in the triangular corner of the fabric in the lower-left part of the design. Because Ashton-Potter (USA) Ltd. produced the stamp by the offset process, it includes microprinting, consisting of the letters "USPS" on the round orange vegetable in the center of the cornucopia.

To convey the impression of the larger quilt, Sheaff incorporated into the selvage of the pane a border with a star in each of the four corners, also sewn by Cusack. Ashton-Potter used the standard four process colors to

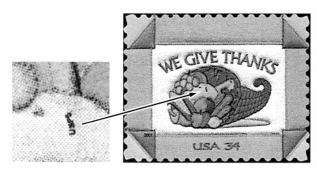

The microprinted letters "USPS" can be found on the round orange vegetable in the center of the cornucopia.

print the stamp, plus a fifth color, tan (PMS 453), for the selvage area. Because a tan plate number on a tan background would not have been visible, the four-digit plate number represents the process colors only

First-day Facts

Einar V. Dyhrkopp, a member of the USPS Board of Governors, dedicated the stamp in a ceremony at the Center for World Thanksgiving at Thanks-Giving Square in Dallas, Texas. The Center, according to USPS, "is an international resource devoted to gathering and sharing the thanksgivings of the United States and the world," while the Square, formally established in 1981, "serves as the sponsor or site for a variety of ongoing activities dedicated to revitalizing the spirit of thanksgiving."

The principal speaker was Carl T. January Jr., USPS Dallas District manager. David Martin, Dallas postmaster, opened the program, and Mary Poss, mayor pro tem, Dallas City Council, was master of ceremonies. Charles J. Wyly Jr., honorary chairman of Thanks-Giving Square, gave the welcome. Stamp illustrator Margaret Cusack was present and, while in Dallas, gave a slide lecture on her work, "Illustrating the Fabric of Life." She also attended a second-day ceremony at Borough Hall in Brooklyn the following day.

34¢ HANUKKAH
HOLIDAY CELEBRATIONS SERIES

Date of Issue: October 21, 2001

Catalog Number: Scott 3547

Colors: yellow, magenta, cyan, black, red

First-Day Cancel: New York, New York

First-Day Cancellations: 29,754 (includes 34¢ Kwanzaa)

Format: Panes of 20, horizontal, 4 across, 5 down. Gravure printing cylinders of 200 subjects (2 panes across, 5 around) manufactured by Southern Graphic systems.

Gum Type: self-adhesive

Overall Stamp Size: 1.56 by 0.99 inches; 39.624 by 25.146mm

Pane Size: 6.500 by 5.875 inches; 165.100 by 149.225mm

Perforations: 11 (die-cut simulated perforations) (Comco Commander rotary die cutter)

Selvage Markings: "© 1995 USPS." "$0.34 x 20 = $6.80." "PLATE/POSITION" and diagram. Universal Product Code (UPC) "561900" in 2 locations.

Illustrator and Typographer: Hannah Smotrich of Washington, D.C.

Art Director: Derry Noyes of Washington, D.C.

Stamp Manufacturing: Stamps printed by Avery Dennison Security Printing Division, Clinton, South Carolina, on an 8-color Dia Nippon Kiko webfed gravure press. Stamps processed by Avery Dennison.

Quantity Ordered: 40,000,000

Cylinder Number Detail: 1 set of 5 cylinder numbers preceded by the letter V in selvage above or below each corner stamp

Cylinder Number Combination Reported: V11111

Paper Supplier: Fasson Division of Avery Dennison

Tagging: phosphored paper

The Stamp

In 1996, the Postal Service launched what it now calls its Holiday Celebrations series with a 32¢ self-adhesive stamp, part of a joint issue with Israel, honoring Hanukkah, the Jewish Festival of Lights. Three years later, after the first-class rate rose to 33¢, USPS reissued the stamp with the higher value. And on October 21, 2001, following another rate increase, the stamp was reissued again, at 34¢.

The three stamps are identical in appearance except for two sets of numbers: the denomination and the tiny year date. All three were printed by the gravure process by Avery Dennison Security Printing Division and issued in panes of 20. Only 40 million were ordered in the initial printing, however, compared to 65 million for the 33¢ version and 103.52 million for the 32¢ original.

On the same day, USPS issued a 34¢ Kwanzaa stamp, another Holiday Celebrations stamp that had previously appeared in 32¢ and 33¢ versions (see separate chapter).

Catherine Caggiano, USPS director of stamp services, announced plans for the two stamps during a January 20, 2001, meeting in Tucson, Arizona, involving philatelic journalists and Postal Service officials. She acknowledged that public pressure to continue making the holiday stamps available influenced the decision to reissue them, and praised the familiar designs of the two issues.

Hanukkah's origins can be traced back some 2,165 years to 164 B.C., when Judah the Maccabee and his followers liberated Jerusalem from the Syrian Greeks and set about to purify and rededicate the city's ancient temple.

However, when the time came to light the menorah, only one jar of pure olive oil could be found, enough to burn for a single day. Miraculously, the light burned for eight days and nights, long enough to prepare a supply of fresh consecrated oil.

Today Hanukkah is celebrated for eight days, beginning at sundown on the 25th of the Hebrew month Kislev, which in 2001 was December 9. Each night the family gathers around the menorah, exchanges gifts, chants blessings and lights candles — one the first night, two the second night, and so on, until eight candles are lit the final night. The ninth candle in the menorah is called the Shamash, meaning "helper," and is used to light the other candles.

The Design

Hannah Smotrich, 35, a Washington, D.C., graphic designer, created the 1996 Hanukkah stamp design that was reycled for the 1999 and 2001 versions. She cut colored paper to create the nine candles of a stylized menorah, each of a different color and with a flickering flame at the top, on a horizontal gold bar against a plain white background. The slate-green Shamash candle in the center, taller than the rest, stands in a small red candleholder. Across the top of the stamp are the word "HANUKKAH," in red Lithos type, and "USA 34" in black.

First-day Facts

The 34¢ Hanukkah stamp had its first-day sale Sunday, October 21, at the 2001 Postage Stamp Mega-Event show in New York City. There was no official first-day ceremony.

The release originally was scheduled for Friday, October 19, the first day of the show. Don Smeraldi, a USPS spokesman, told *Linn's Stamp News* that the change was made because officials felt sales at the show would be better on a Sunday than a Friday. Issuing the stamps on Saturday, October 20, would have conflicted with the Jewish Sabbath, Smeraldi said.

34¢ KWANZAA
HOLIDAY CELEBRATIONS SERIES

Date of Issue: October 21, 2001

Catalog Number: Scott 3548

Colors: yellow, magenta, cyan, black

First-Day Cancel: New York, New York

First-Day Cancellations: 29,754 (includes 34¢ Hanukkah)

Format: Panes of 20, horizontal, 4 across, 5 down. Gravure printing cylinders of 240 subjects (2 panes across, 6 panes around) manufactured by Southern Graphic Systems.

Gum Type: self-adhesive

Overall Stamp Size: 1.19 by 0.91 inches; 30.230 by 23.114mm

Pane Size: 5.35 by 5.75 inches; 135.89 by 146.05mm

Perforations: 11 (die-cut simulated perforations) (Comco Commander rotary die cutter)

Selvage Markings: "© 1996 USPS." "$0.34 x 20 = $6.80." "PLATE/POSITION" and diagram. Universal Product Code (UPC) "561800" in 2 locations.

Illustrator: Synthia Saint James of Los Angeles, California

Typographer and Art Director: Derry Noyes of Washington, D.C.

Stamp Manufacturing: Stamps printed by Avery Dennison Security Printing Division, Clinton, South Carolina, on an 8-color Dia Nippon Kiko webfed gravure press. Stamps processed by Avery Dennison.

Quantity Ordered: 40,000,000

Cylinder Number Detail: 1 set of 4 cylinder numbers preceded by the letter V in selvage above or below each corner stamp

Cylinder Number Combination Reported: V1111

Paper Supplier: Fasson Division of Avery Dennison

Tagging: phosphored paper

The Stamp

On October 21, the Postal Service issued a 34¢ self-adhesive stamp in its Holiday Celebrations series to honor the African-American festival of Kwanzaa.

The stamp incorporated the design of two earlier Kwanzaa stamps: the original, which USPS issued in 1997 with a 32¢ denomination, and a 33¢ version that appeared in 1999. The 1999 and 2001 versions were issued to reflect increases in the first-class postage rate.

All three Kwanzaa stamps were printed by the gravure process by Avery Dennison Security Printing Division. The new stamp, like the 33¢ version, was issued in panes of 20. The original 32¢ Kwanzaa stamp had been distributed in panes of 50 and, unlike its two successors, had been made available to collectors in uncut press sheets.

USPS ordered 40 million 34¢ Kwanzaa stamps, reflecting a continuing decrease in anticipated demand. It had printed 133 million 32¢ Kwanzaa stamps in 1997 and 95 million 33¢ stamps in 1999.

The new stamp had its first-day sale at the 2001 Postage Stamp Mega-Event in New York City. On the same day and at the same place, USPS issued a 34¢ Hanukkah stamp, another Holiday Celebrations stamp that previously had appeared in 32¢ and 33¢ versions (see separate chapter).

Kwanzaa is an "invented" holiday. Created in 1996 by Maulana Karenga, chairman of the Department of Black Studies at California State University-Long Beach, it is a seven-day cultural celebration that takes its name from the Swahili phrase meaning "first fruits" and honors the African tradition of celebrating the harvest.

According to USPS, the festival, which begins December 26 and ends January 1, celebrates and reinforces family, community and culture through practices and affirmations related to the Nguzo Saba, or seven principles. These principles, observed during Kwanzaa, are Umoja (unity), Kujichagulia (self-determination), Ujima (collective work and responsibility), Ujamaa (cooperative economics), Nia (purpose), Kuumba (creativity) and Imani (faith).

Kwanzaa has seven basic symbols that represent its spirit and focus: the Mkeka, the straw mat on which all other objects are placed; the Mazao, which symbolize the harvest origins of the holiday; the Kinara, a candleholder that holds seven candles and represents the ancestral stalk from which African-American people come; Mishumaa, the candles (three green, three red and one black) that represent the Nguzo Saba; Muhindi, ears of corn representing the children in the house and community; Kikombe Cha Umoja, the Unity Cup that is used to pour libation and passed to each member of the family to sip from in a gesture of unity and commitment to Kwanzaa; and Zawidi, culturally based gifts for children, which must include a book and heritage symbol. A Karamu, an African feast, is held on December 31. The final day of Kwanzaa is a day of meditation (Taamuli) dedicated to sustained reflection on human life and purpose and the central values of African culture.

The Design

The designs of the 34¢, 33¢ and 32¢ Kwanzaa stamps are identical except for the denominations and the year dates in the lower-left corner, which are "2001," "1999" and "1997," respectively. All three utilize artist Synthia Saint James' simple, posterlike illustration showing a man, woman and three children in profile, clad in African costume. Also shown are the Kwanzaa symbols: the straw mat; the candleholder with seven candles; a bowl of fruit and ears of corn; the unity cup; wrapped gifts; and a flag with three horizontal stripes, black, red and green. The typeface is called Lithos.

First-day Facts

No official first-day ceremony was held at the Postage Stamp Mega-Event.

34¢ STATUE OF LIBERTY COIL (SELF-ADHESIVE) ROUNDED CORNERS ROLLS OF 3,000 AND 10,000

Date of Issue: January 7, 2001

Catalog Number: Scott 3466

Colors: yellow, magenta, cyan, black

First-Day Cancel: Washington, D.C.

First-Day Cancellations: 35,301 (includes Federal Eagle envelope)

Format: Coils of 3,000 and 10,000, vertical format.

Gum Type: self-adhesive

Overall Stamp Size: 0.87 by 0.96 inches; 22.1 by 24.4mm

Perforations: 9¾ (die-cut simulated perforations)

Photographer: Paul Hardy of New York, New York

Designer, Art Director and Typographer: Derry Noyes of Washington, D.C.

Stamp Manufacturing: Stamps printed by Bureau of Engraving and Printing on 7-color Andreotti gravure press (601)

Quantity Ordered: 120,000,000 (in rolls of 3,000) and 300,000,000 (in rolls of 10,000)

Cylinder Number Detail: 1 set of 4 numbers on every 21st stamp

Cylinder Number Combinations Reported: 1111, 2222

Counting Number Detail: 1 4-digit counting number on back of every 20th stamp

Tagging: phosphored paper

34¢ STATUE OF LIBERTY COIL (WATER-ACTIVATED GUM) ROLLS OF 100, 3,000 AND 10,000

Date of Issue: February 7, 2001

Catalog Number: Scott 3476, phosphored coated paper (grainy solid tagging); 3476a, phosphored coated paper (solid tagging)

Colors: yellow, magenta, cyan, black

First-Day Cancel: New York, New York

First-Day Cancellations: 178,635 (includes all varieties of nondenominated Statue of Liberty, Flowers and Flag Over Farm stamps)

Format: Coils of 100, 3,000 and 10,000, vertical format. Gravure cylinders printing 432 stamps per revolution (24 by 18)

Gum Type: water-activated

Overall Stamp Size: 0.87 by 0.96 inches; 22.1 by 24.4mm

Perforations: 9¾

Photographer: Paul Hardy of New York, New York

Designer, Art Director and Typographer: Derry Noyes of Washington, D.C.

Stamp Manufacturing: Stamps printed by Bureau of Engraving and Printing on 7-color Andreotti gravure press (601)

Quantity Ordered: 400,000,000 in rolls of 3,000; 100,000,000 in rolls of 10,000

Cylinder Number Detail: 1 set of 4 numbers on every 24th stamp

Cylinder Number Combinations Reported: 1111

Counting Number Detail: 1 4-digit counting number on back of every 20th stamp

Paper Suppliers: Spinnaker Coatings (grainy solid tagging); Tullis Russell Coaters (solid tagging)

Tagging: phosphored paper

34¢ STATUE OF LIBERTY COIL (SELF-ADHESIVE) SQUARE CORNERS ROLL OF 100

Date of Issue: February 7, 2001

Catalog Number: Scott 3477

Colors: yellow, magenta, cyan, black

First-Day Cancel: New York, New York

First-Day Cancellations: 178,635 (includes all varieties of nondenominated Statue of Liberty, Flowers and Flag Over Farm stamps)

Format: Coil of 100, vertical. Gravure cylinders printing 480 stamps per revolution (24 by 20).

Gum Type: self-adhesive

Overall Stamp Size: 0.87 by 0.96 inches; 22.1 by 24.4mm

Perforations: 9¾ (die-cut simulated perforations)

Photographer: Paul Hardy of New York, New York

Designer, Art Director and Typographer: Derry Noyes of Washington, D.C.

Stamp Manufacturing: Stamps printed by Bureau of Engraving and Printing on 7-color Andreotti gravure press (601)

Quantity Ordered: 8,865,000,000

Cylinder Number Detail: 1 set of 4 numbers on every 24th stamp

Cylinder Number Combinations Reported: 1111, 2222, 3333, 4444, 5555, 6666, 7777

Tagging: phosphored paper

34¢ STATUE OF LIBERTY
CONVERTIBLE BOOKLET OF 10

Date of Issue: February 7, 2001

Catalog Number: Scott 3485, single stamp; 3485a, pane of 10

Colors: yellow, magenta, cyan, black

First-Day Cancel: New York, New York

First-Day Cancellations: 141,634 (includes other varieties of Statue of Liberty, plus Flag Over Farm and Four Flowers stamps)

Format: Convertible booklet pane of 10, horizontal, 5 across, 2 down, with vertical peel-off strip between second and third vertical rows. Gravure printing cylinders printing 44 panes per revolution (2 across, 22 around) manufactured by Southern Graphics Systems.

Gum Type: self-adhesive

Overall Stamp Size: 0.982 by 0.870 inches; 24.948 by 22.098mm

Pane Size: 6.50 by 1.74 inches; 165.1 by 44.2mm

Perforations: 11 (die-cut simulated perforations) (Comco Commander rotary die cutter). Bull's-eye die cuts on top selvage. Cover scored for folding.

Selvage Markings: "Peel this strip and fold here" on peel-off strip. USPS logo, "© 2000 USPS" and cylinder numbers on top selvage.

Back Markings: "The Statue/of Liberty/Twenty 34 cent/Self-adhesive/ Stamps/$3.40" on front of cover. Promotion for www.usps.com web site and Universal Product Code (UPC) "0 669500 4" on back of cover.

Photographer: Paul Hardy of New York, New York

Designer, Art Director and Typographer: Derry Noyes of Washington, D.C.

Stamp Manufacturing: Stamps printed by Avery Dennison Security Division, Clinton, South Carolina, on an 8-color Dia Nippon Kiko webfed gravure press. Stamps processed by Avery Dennison.

Quantity Ordered: 400,000,000 stamps

Cylinder Number Detail: 1 set of 4 cylinder numbers preceded by the letter V on top selvage.

Cylinder Number Combinations Reported: V1111, V1221

Paper Supplier: Fasson Division of Avery Dennison

Tagging: phosphored paper

34¢ STATUE OF LIBERTY
CONVERTIBLE BOOKLET OF 20

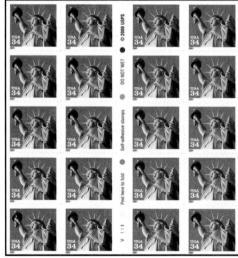

Date of Issue: February 7, 2001

Catalog Number: Scott 3485, single stamp; 3485b, pane of 20

Colors: yellow, magenta, cyan, black

First-Day Cancel: New York, New York

First-Day Cancellations: 141,634 (includes other varieties of Statue of Liberty, plus Flag Over Farm and Four Flowers stamps)

Format: Convertible booklet pane of 20, horizontal, 4 across, 5 down, with vertical peel-off strip between second and third vertical rows. Gravure printing cylinders printing 24 panes per revolution (3 across, 8 around) manufactured by Southern Graphics Systems.

Gum Type: self-adhesive

Overall Stamp Size: 0.982 by 0.870 inches; 24.948 by 22.098mm

Pane Size: 4.125 by 4.350 inches; 104.78 by 110.49mm

Perforations: 11 (die-cut simulated perforations) (Comco Commander rotary die cutter). Cover scored for folding.

Selvage Markings: "Peel here to fold • Self-adhesive stamps • DO NOT WET" • © 2000 USPS" plus cylinder numbers on peel-off strip

Back Markings: "The Statue/of Liberty/Twenty 34 cent/Self-adhesive/ Stamps/$6.80" on front of cover. Promotion for www.usps.com web site and Universal Product Code (UPC) "0 669800 1" on back of cover.

Photographer: Paul Hardy of New York, New York

Designer, Art Director and Typographer: Derry Noyes of Washington, D.C.

Stamp Manufacturing: Stamps printed by Avery Dennison Security Division, Clinton, South Carolina, on an 8-color Dia Nippon Kiko webfed gravure press. Stamps processed by Avery Dennison.

Quantity Ordered: 2,700,000,000 stamps

Cylinder Number Detail: 1 set of 4 cylinder numbers preceded by the letter V on peel-off strip.

Cylinder Number Combinations Reported: V1111, V1211, V1221, V2111, V2112, V2121, V2122, V2212, V2222

Paper Supplier: Fasson Division of Avery Dennison

Tagging: phosphored paper

34¢ STATUE OF LIBERTY VENDING BOOKLET OF 20

Date of Issue: February 7, 2001

Catalog Number: Scott 3485, single stamp; 3485c, booklet pane of 4; 3485d, booklet pane of 6; BK283, 2 each 3485c, 3485d

Colors: yellow, magenta, cyan, black

First-Day Cancel: New York, New York

First-Day Cancellations: 141,634 (includes other varieties of Statue of Liberty, plus Flag Over Farm and Four Flowers stamps)

Format: Vending booklet of 20, horizontal, in 4 segments: 6 (3 by 2), 4 (2 by 2), 4 (2 by 2) and 6 (3 by 2). Gravure printing cylinders of 300 (5 panes across, 3 panes around), manufactured by Southern Graphics Systems.

Gum Type: self-adhesive

Overall Stamp Size: 0.982 by 0.870 inches; 24.948 by 22.098mm

Booklet Size: 10.40 by 1.74 inches (unfolded)

Perforations: 11 (die-cut simulated perforations) (Comco Commander rotary die cutter). Cover scored for folding.

Selvage Markings: none

Back Markings: "The Statue/of Liberty/Twenty 34 cent/Self-adhesive/ Stamps/$6.80" on front cover. Promotion for www.usps.com web site, "© 2000 USPS" and Universal Product Code (UPC) "0 669000 9" on back cover. USPS logo on back of second 4-stamp segment.

Photographer: Paul Hardy of New York, New York

Designer, Art Director and Typographer: Derry Noyes of Washington, D.C.

Stamp Manufacturing: Stamps printed by Avery Dennison Security Division, Clinton, South Carolina, on an 8-color Dia Nippon Kiko webfed gravure press. Stamps processed by Avery Dennison.

Quantity Ordered: 800,000,000 stamps

Cylinder Number Detail: 1 set of 4 cylinder numbers preceded by the letter V on bottom-right stamp on first 4-stamp segment

Cylinder Number Combinations Reported: V1111, V2212, V2222

Paper Supplier: Fasson Division of Avery Dennison

Tagging: phosphored paper

The Stamps

Six different formats of the denominated version of the 34¢ Statue of Liberty stamp were issued by USPS in early 2001. The stamps' designs were taken from a waist-up photograph of the American icon taken by Paul Hardy of New York.

The same design was used for the nondenominated Statue of Liberty stamps placed on sale by the Postal Service December 15, 2000. The non-denominated stamps were intended as a stopgap for use immediately after the increase in the first-class letter rate January 7, 2001.

Two printers produced the denominated Statue of Liberty stamps in six different formats. All formats were printed by the gravure process.

On January 7, a single self-adhesive coil stamp (Scott 3466) was issued in rolls of 3,000 and 10,000. The vertically arranged stamps were printed by the Bureau of Engraving and Printing. The stamps are separated from each other on their backing paper and have rounded corners. A four-digit cylinder number appears on every 21st stamp, and an aqua four-digit counting number is on the back of every 20th stamp.

On February 7, USPS issued additional formats of the 34¢ Statue of Liberty stamp. These formats were:

• Rolls of 100, 3,000 and 10,000 vertically arranged coil stamps, with water-activated gum and conventional perforations (Scott 3476). A four-digit cylinder number appears on every 24th stamp and an aqua four-digit counting number is on the back of every 20th stamp. The BEP printed the stamps.

• Roll of 100 vertically arranged self-adhesive coil stamps (Scott 3477). The stamps abut each other on the coil, with no backing paper visible between, above or below them, and have square corners. A four-digit cylinder number is found on every 24th stamp. There are no counting numbers on the back. Again, BEP printed the stamp.

• Pane (convertible booklet) of 20 horizontally arranged self-adhesive stamps, four across by five down, with a vertical peel-off strip and scoring to allow the pane to be folded. The stamp (Scott 3485) was printed by Avery Dennison Security Printing Division. The four-digit cylinder number combination is printed on the peel-off strip.

• The same stamp as above in a pane (convertible booklet) of 10 horizontally arranged self-adhesive stamps, two across by five down, with a vertical peel-off strip and scoring to allow the pane to be folded. The four-digit cylinder number combination is printed on the peel-off strip.

• The same stamp as above in a vending-machine booklet of 20 self-adhesive stamps. The booklet pane, 10 across by two down, is divided into segments of four, six, six and four stamps. It is folded in the middle, between two six-stamp segments, and the four-stamp segments on each end are folded inside, making a flat palm-sized packet. The cylinder-number combination is printed on the bottom-right corner stamp, below the frameline on the right side, opposite the "2001" year date.

The Statue of Liberty coil varieties were the only postage stamps issued in 2001 to be printed by the Bureau of Engraving and Printing. BEP, once the exclusive manufacturer of U.S. postage stamps, could be out of the stamp printing business after 2005, a source close to the Bureau told *Linn's Stamp News* in early June 2001. BEP is located a few blocks from USPS headquarters in Southeast Washington, D.C.

Today, the task of printing U.S. postage stamps has been taken over by private-sector companies.

Like their nondenominated counterparts, individual Statue of Liberty stamps from the three varieties of booklets are indistinguishable from each other except in two instances. A stamp with die-cut simulated perforations on all four sides can come only from the interior of the convertible booklet of 20, and a stamp with cylinder numbers at the bottom can come only from the vending-machine booklet.

Unlike their nondenominated counterparts, however, no differences were found in the "2001" year date. Two different types of the "2000" year date were found on the nondenominated Statue of Liberty self-adhesive coil stamps.

The denominated Statue of Liberty stamp in vending-booklet format is the fifth U.S. booklet stamp that can be found with plate numbers printed on the stamp itself. The first four were the Yellow Rose of 1996 (Scott 3049), printed by Stamp Venturers, and the Statue of Liberty stamp of 1997 (3122), the Flag Over City stamp of 1999 (Scott 3278) and the non-denominated Statue of Liberty stamp of 2000 (Scott 3451), all printed by Avery Dennison.

The Design

The design for the denominated versions of the 34¢ Statue of Liberty stamp is from the same waist-up photograph used for the nondenominated versions issued in 2000. Art director Derry Noyes chose a photograph supplied by The Stock Market. The photographer, Paul Hardy, made his shot in 1996 from near the statue's feet on Liberty Island, looking up at the head, crown and uplifted torch.

Noyes adapted the photo for use as a definitive-size stamp in horizontal format, cropping it at the waist so that the picture included not only the head, crown, right arm and torch, but also the tablet of law that Liberty grips in her left hand.

Noyes inserted the inscription "USA/34" in dropout white Clarendon type in the lower-left corner of the design.

214

Her horizontal layout was used for the stamps in the booklet formats. For coil use, a vertical layout was required. The photo was reduced in size and recropped for that purpose. The vertical version shows slightly more of the waist area of the statue.

Varieties

A dramatic freak of the 34¢ Statue of Liberty coil stamp appeared on a cover. A misregistration between the die-cutting mat and the printed paper web (continuous roll) caused portions of two stamp images to appear on a single stamp. Gregg Ford of Florida sent the cover to *Linn's*, along with a plate-number strip of four similarly misregistered stamps. Ford stated that the bizarre strip (and the stamp on the cover) came from a complete roll of 100 that he purchased at a local post office. The plate number of the roll is 4444.

Stamp dealer and columnist Robert Rabinowitz, writing in the June 24, 2002, *Linn's Stamp News*, reported that two distinct tagging types exist for the water-activated 34¢ Statue of Liberty coil stamp (Scott 3476). Rabinowitz referred to an article by Richard Nazar in the May issue of *Coil Line*, the monthly publication of the Plate Number Coil Collectors Club. In the article, Nazar reported that during the summer of 2001, a third production run of the 34¢ coil in lick-and-stick rolls of 100, 300 and 10,000 was completed.

According to Nazar, BEP used paper from two sources approved by USPS: Spinnaker Coatings of Troy, Ohio, and Tullis Russell Coaters Limited of the United Kingdom.

The use of two different paper types resulted in two different tagging types. According to Rabinowitz, "Collectors likely will find the two different paper types easier to distinguish by observing the tagging under shortwave ultraviolet light."

Tagging is a chemical compound applied to stamp paper (either before or after stamps are printed, or both) that activates automated sorting and canceling equipment.

Rabinowitz explained that when most modern U.S. stamps are viewed under shortwave ultraviolet light, the tagging appears as a yellow-green glow. The Liberty stamps printed on Spinnaker paper exhibit a distinct mottled appearance. The stamps printed on Tullis Russell paper show solid tagging.

Rabinowitz noted that other recent U.S. coil stamps, such as the 23¢ Lunch Wagon (Scott 2464) and the 29¢ Mount Rushmore (2523), are known both with mottled and solid tagging.

"When comparing stamps," Nazar wrote, "the printed image on the Spinnaker Coating paper appears purplish-blue and the image printed on the Tullis Russell Coaters paper appears bright blue." Nazar also noted that the color of the Spinnaker paper is "somehat browner (less white) on the front and the back" than the color of the Tullis Russell paper.

Rabinowitz cautioned that collectors should not rely on the color vari-

These two strips of five 34¢ Statue of Liberty coil stamps, shown under short-wave ultraviolet light, exhibit two discernable tagging types: mottled, top, and solid, bottom.

ations as an absolute distinction between stamps printed on the two papers. "Minor color variations during a given print run are the norm for many U.S. stamps issued in recent years," he said.

Nazar wrote that the Spinnaker paper is responsive to longwave UV (glows white), while the Tullis Russell paper "is almost nonreactive (or 'dead')."

First-day Facts

No first-day ceremonies were held for the denominated rate-change stamps issued January 7 in Washington, D.C. and February 7 in New York, New York. The stamps were placed on sale nationwide.

34¢ FLAG OVER FARM

Date of Issue: February 7, 2001

Catalog Number: Scott 3469

Colors: black, cyan, magenta, yellow

First-Day Cancel: New York, New York

First-Day Cancellations: 141,634 (includes all varieties of 34¢ Statue of Liberty and Flowers stamps issued February 7)

Format: Pane of 100 stamps, vertical, 10 across, 10 down. Offset printing plates printing 200 subjects per revolution.

Gum Type: water-activated

Overall Stamp Size: 0.84 by 0.99 inches; 21.336 by 25.146mm

Pane Size: 9.06 by 10.25 inches; 229.92 by 260.12mm

Perforations: 11¼ (Wista stroke perforator)

Selvage Markings: "© 2000 USPS." ".34x100=$34.00" "PLATE/POSITION" and diagram. Universal Product Code (UPC) "100940" in 2 positions.

Illustrator: Hiro Kimura of Brooklyn, New York

Designer, Art Director and Typographer: Richard Sheaff of Scottsdale, Arizona

Modeler: Joseph Sheeran of Ashton-Potter (USA) Ltd., Williamsville, New York

Stamp Manufacturing: Stamps printed by Ashton-Potter on offset portion of Stevens Variable Size Security Documents webfed 6-color offset, 3-color intaglio press. Stamps processed by Ashton-Potter.

Quantity Ordered: 25,000,000

Plate Number Detail: 1 set of 4 plate numbers preceded by the letter P in selvage next to 1 corner stamp

Plate Number Combinations Reported: P1111, P2222

Paper Supplier: Tullis Russell

Tagging: overall tagging

34¢ FLAG OVER FARM
PANE OF 20, SELF-ADHESIVE

Date of Issue: March 6, 2001

Catalog Number: Scott 3470

Colors: black, cyan, magenta, yellow

First-Day Cancel: Lincoln, Nebraska

First-Day Cancellations: 72,407 (includes Nine Mile Prairie and Apple and Orange convertible booklet stamps)

Format: Pane of 20 stamps, vertical, 5 across, 4 down. Offset printing plates printing 240 subjects per impression (15 across, 16 around).

Gum Type: self-adhesive

Overall Stamp Size: 0.84 by 0.99 inches; 21.336 by 25.146mm

Pane Size: 5.04 by 4.95 inches; 128.016 by 125.730mm

Perforations: 11¼ (die-cut simulated perforations) (Arpeco die cutter)

Selvage Markings: "©2000/USPS." ".34/x20/=$6.80." "PLATE/POSITION" and diagram. Universal Product Code (UPC) "561000" in 2 positions.

Illustrator: Hiro Kimura of Brooklyn, New York

Designer, Art Director and Typographer: Richard Sheaff of Scottsdale, Arizona

Modeler: Joseph Sheeran of Ashton-Potter (USA) Ltd., Williamsville, New York

Stamp Manufacturing: Stamps printed by Ashton-Potter on offset portion of Stevens Variable Size Security Documents webfed 6-color offset, 3-color intaglio press. Stamps processed by Ashton-Potter.

Quantity Ordered: 200,000,000

Plate Number Detail: 1 set of 4 plate numbers preceded by the letter P in selvage above or below each corner stamp

Plate Number Combinations Reported: P1111, P2222, P3333, P4444, P5555

Paper Supplier: Glatfelter/Fasson

Tagging: phosphored paper

34¢ FLAG OVER FARM
PANE OF 18, ATM-VENDED

Date of Issue: December 17, 2001

Catalog Number: Scott 3495, single stamp; 3495a, pane of 18

Colors: yellow, magenta, cyan, black

First-Day Cancel: Washington, D.C.

First-Day Cancellations: 12,101

Format: Pane of 18, vertical, arranged vertically 3 across by 6 down, with horizontal peel-off strip between horizontal rows 3 and 4. Gravure printing cylinders printing 30 panes per revolution (5 across, 6 around) manufactured by Southern Graphics Systems.

Gum Type: self-adhesive

Overall Stamp Size: 0.870 by 0.982 inches; 20.098 by 24.942mm

Pane Size: 2.610 by 6.125 inches; 66.294 by 155.100mm

Perforations: 8 (die-cut simulated perforations) (Comco Commander rotary die cutter)

Front Markings: on peel-off strip: "Peel here to fold • Self-adhesive stamps • DO NOT WET," color registration dots and cylinder numbers

Back Markings: "Farm Flag/Eighteen Self-Adhesive Stamps/$6.12." "©USPS 2000." USPS logo. Universal Product Code (UPC) "0 560900 8." Promotion for www.stampsonline.com web site. Disclaimer of any amount charged over stamps' face value.

Illustrator: Hiro Kimura of Brooklyn, New York

Designer, Art Director and Typographer: Richard Sheaff of Scottsdale, Arizona

Stamp Manufacturing: Stamps printed by Avery Dennison Security Printing Division, Clinton, South Carolina, on a Dia Nippon Kiko 8-station gravure press. Stamps lacquer coated, front and back, die cut, processed and shipped by Avery Dennison.

Quantity Ordered: 300,024,000

Cylinder Number Detail: 1 group of 4 gravure cylinder numbers preceded by the letter V on peel-off strip

Cylinder Number Combination Reported: V1111

Paper Supplier: Avery Dennison Fasson Division

Tagging: phosphor added to lacquer coating applied to front of pane

The Stamp

In 2001 the Postal Service issued its second set of denominated rate-change definitives featuring a design that had been used previously for nondenominated stamps issued in late 2000.

On February 7, a single 34¢ Flag Over Farm definitive in a pane of 100 was released. The stamp has water-activated gum and conventional perforations. The design shows a U.S. flag in full color waving over stylized rows of green crops. Farm buildings are tucked into the background at upper right, beneath a turquoise-blue sky and puffy clouds.

The pane-of-100 format previously was used for the water-activated 33¢ Flag Over City stamp of 1999.

USPS placed an initial order of only 25 million water-activated Flag Over Farm stamps with printer Ashton-Potter (USA) Ltd. of Williamsville, New York. Historically, this is a low number for a modern U.S. definitive, but USPS anticipated that the public would continue to prefer self-adhesives over the once-traditional lick-and-stick stamps. The stamp (Scott 3469) was printed using offset lithography.

The Flag Over Farm design continued the Postal Service's policy of always having available a first-class-rate definitive that shows the U.S. flag in full color waving over a national landmark or against a generic backdrop, in this case a farm scene.

The design was an appropriate successor to the Flag Over City image that was featured on various 33¢ sheet, coil and booklet stamps in 1999, and was the work of the same artist, Hiro Kimura, and art director, Richard Sheaff.

On March 6, USPS repeated the design on a pane of 20 34¢ Flag Over Farm self-adhesive stamps (Scott 3470), with die-cut simulated perforations. Ashton-Potter printed the stamps by offset lithography.

The designs of the water-activated and self-adhesive stamps are identical, as are the selvage markings, with the exception of the Universal Product Code, which has different bar arrangements and UPC numbers on the two panes. The water-activated stamp is overall tagged; the self-adhesive is printed on phosphored paper.

Late in 2001, on December 17, USPS issued a third denominated pane, a self-adhesive pane of 18 (Scott 3495) with die-cut simulated perforations. This pane was made for sale through automated teller machines (ATMs). The stamp in this format was printed by the gravure process by Avery Dennison Security Printing Division in Clinton, South Carolina. Like all panes made for ATMs, it has the dimensions and thickness of U.S. currency and is printed on nonphosphored paper. To prevent curling, a lacquer coating was applied to the pane after printing. This coating, on the front, contained the tagging material.

The Design

Designer Hiro Kimura of Brooklyn, New York, began his professional career designing video game packaging and has become a successful creator of book covers, magazines and advertising material. He characterizes his work as "graphic stylized," and for years his preferred medium was acrylic paint, although he since has turned to computers to create his "painting look."

In 1995, working with art director Richard Sheaff, Kimura sketched numerous American flag designs for use on definitive stamps as needed. Out of them came three finished pieces of art. One became the design for the 33¢ Flag Over City stamps, issued in sheet, booklet and coil formats in 1999. The second, showing a flag in a schoolroom (Flag Over Chalkboard), was used on a 33¢ ATM-vended stamp, also in 1999. The third was the Flag Over Farm image. Kimura created these in the traditional way: paint on canvasboard.

A rippling American flag occupies the lower half of Kimura's Flag Over Farm illustration, with a narrow portion of the flag's blue field curving around to the upper-left corner. Behind it is a farm scene, with neat rows of green crops stretching away to the horizon. Rural buildings, including a silo and red barn, are in the distance at the upper right, and at the top is a blue sky with puffy white clouds. "FIRST-CLASS" and "USA," in a typeface called Gill Sands, is dropped out of this blue background.

Single stamps of the three varieties of Flag Over Farm stamps can be easily distinguished from one another. A stamp from the pane of 100 with

On both the self-adhesive and conventionally gummed versions of the Flag Over Farm 34¢ stamp printed by Ashton-Potter, the microprinted letters "USPS" can be found on the white wall of the low farm building, between the two doors.

water-activated gum has conventional perforation teeth on all four sides. A stamp from the self-adhesive pane of 20 has die-cut simulated perforations on all four sides. These have a relatively fine gauge, defined in the Scott catalogs as 11¼. A stamp from the self-adhesive pane of 18 also has die-cut simulated perforations, but of a coarser gauge, listed as 8 by Scott. Furthermore, 14 of the 18 stamps on the pane have a straight edge on either one or two sides.

The stamps from Ashton-Potter's 20-stamp and 100-stamp panes, which were printed by offset with a 300-line screen, have a somewhat sharper and more distinct look than Avery Dennison's gravure-printed ATM stamp. The "2001" year date beneath the design is small and clear on the offset-printed stamps, larger and heavier on the gravure product.

Because USPS considers offset a somewhat less secure printing method than gravure, it requires stamp printers using offset to incorporate microprinting in the designs as a safeguard against counterfeiting. On Ashton-Potter's two 34¢ Flag Over Farm stamps, the letters "USPS," in microtype, can be found on the white wall of the low building, between the two doors. There is no microprinting on the Avery Dennison ATM stamp.

First-day Facts

No first-day ceremony was held for the denominated rate-change stamps, which were placed on sale nationwide. First-day covers for the pane of 100 were postmarked New York, New York. FDCs for the Ashton-Potter pane of 20 were postmarked Lincoln, Nebraska. FDCs for stamps from the Avery Dennison pane of 18 were postmarked Washington, D.C.

$3.50 CAPITOL DOME

Date of Issue: January 29, 2001

Catalog Number: Scott 3472

Colors: black, cyan, magenta, yellow

First-Day Cancel: Washington, D.C.

First-Day Cancellations: 22,803 (includes $12.25 Washington Monument stamp)

Format: Pane of 20, vertical, 5 across, 4 down. Offset printing plates printing 120 stamps per revolution (10 across, 12 around).

Gum Type: self-adhesive

Scrambled Indicia: PRIORITY MAIL

Overall Stamp Size: 1.23 by 1.56 inches; 31.24 by 39.62mm

Pane Size: 7.13 by 7.26 inches; 181.1 by 184.4mm

Perforations: 11¼ by 11½ (die-cut simulated perforations) (rotary die cutter)

Selvage Markings: "©/2000/USPS." "3.50/x20/$70.00." "PLATE/POSITION" and diagram. Universal Product Code (UPC) "111900" in 2 locations.

Photographer: Robert Llewellyn of Earlysville, Virginia

Designer, Art Director and Typographer: Derry Noyes of Washington, D.C.

Stamp Manufacturing: Stamps printed by Banknote Corporation of America, Browns Summit, North Carolina, on Goebel 670 offset press. Stamps processed by BCA.

Quantity Ordered: 125,000,000

Plate Number Detail: 1 set of 4 plate numbers preceded by the letter B in selvage above or below each corner stamp

Plate Number Combinations Reported: B1111, B2222

Paper Supplier: Paper Corporation of the United States/Spinnaker Coatings

Tagging: phosphored paper

The Stamp

USPS marked the departure from Space Shuttle designs January 29 when it issued stamps for Priority Mail and Express Mail rates depicting historic landmarks in Washington, D.C. From 1995-98, space shuttles graced the stamps used for these special classes of mail.

"When the Citizens' Stamp Advisory Committee asked the design group to begin development of future designs for Priority Mail and Express Mail stamps, they asked us to recommend different thematic subjects for these rates, because the space shuttle designs had been exhausted as far as new ways to depict the theme was concerned," said Terrence McCaffrey, manager of stamp development.

Derry Noyes, one of the Postal Service's art directors, returned with a National Monument theme and showed the committee designs featuring the U.S. Capitol Dome and Washington Monument as examples. "The committee was very favorable to this theme and these designs," McCaffrey said. "It approved both designs and asked that we develop future Priority Mail and Express Mail designs with this theme."

The new stamps featured two of the most prominent and easily recognizable structures in Washington. The $3.50 Priority Mail stamp, satisfying the new one-pound Priority Mail rate implemented January 7, features the Capitol dome. The $12.25 Express Mail stamp, good for the eight-ounce Express Mail rate that went into effect the same day, shows the Washington Monument (see related chapter).

Both stamps were sold in panes of 20, the same format that was used for the $3.20 Space Shuttle Landing stamp of 1998 (Scott 3261). They were printed by offset lithography by Banknote Corporation of America, Browns Summit, North Carolina. Both are self-adhesive with die-cut perforations.

The vertically oriented $3.50 Capital Dome stamp pictures the central dome of the legislative building that is home to the House of Representatives and the Senate. The nighttime view of the illuminated dome fills most of the stamp.

An example of 19th-century neoclassical architecture, the building covers about four acres of ground in the Capitol Complex. The original building was designed by Scottish physician William Thorton. Thorton's plan called for a building made up of three sections. The central section, topped by a low dome, was to be flanked by two rectangular wings (one for the Senate and one for the House of Representatives) on the north and south.

In 1793 George Washington laid the cornerstone of the Capitol, located in the building's southeast corner.

Architect Benjamin Henry Latrobe modified Thorton's design and directed the construction of the Capitol. Latrobe was the first fully trained professional architect to work in America and was one of the founders of professional architects in the country. Construction of the Capitol proceeded for the better part of 20 years.

During the War of 1812, British troops set fire to the building, causing significant damage. A sudden rainstorm is credited with preventing complete destruction. Latrobe was called upon to lead the restoration. He resigned his position in 1817 after he came under fire for delays and increasing costs of the project, much of which was beyond his control. Charles Bulfinch, a prominent Boston architect, succeeded Latrobe as lead architect of the restoration.

Bulfinch completed construction of the Capitol in 1826. His position as Capitol architect was terminated in 1829.

The Capitol was placed under the care of the commissioner of public buildings. The building continued to be expanded to meet the needs of the increasing numbers of senators and representatives from states newly admitted to the Union.

Bulfinch replaced the original dome with a larger, copper-covered wooden dome. In 1855 a new, fireproof cast-iron dome, designed by Thomas Ustick Walter, replaced the Bulfinch wooden dome. This massive dome, weighing nearly nine million pounds, was hoisted atop the Capitol using steam-powered derricks.

In 1863 the Statue of Freedom, designed by Thomas Crawford and cast in bronze by Clark Mills, was lifted into place atop the dome. The statue weighs in at nearly 15,000 pounds and is 19½ feet tall.

In 1983, the west front of the Capitol underwent renovation to restore and preserve the structure.

On May 9, 1993, the bronze Statue of Freedom, the crowing glory of the Capitol, was removed from its pedestal by helicopter for restoration. The statue was showing extensive pitting and corrosion on the surface of the bronze and the cast-iron pedestal had begun to crack and rust. The United States Capitol Preservation Commission provided $780,000 in privately raised funds, which covered the restoration.

The statue was returned to its place atop the dome less than six months later, on October 23, 1993, during the celebration of the bicentennial of the Capitol.

The U.S. Capitol has appeared on more than 20 previously issued U.S. stamps. The first was the 4¢ Electric Automobile stamp from the 1901 Pan-American issue (Scott 296). A portion of the building is visible behind the auto in the vignette (central image) of the stamp.

The most recent issue to show the Capitol is the 29¢ District of Columbia Bicentennial stamp of 1991 (Scott 2561). The stamp shows a stylized view of Pennsylvania Avenue in the early 20th century and includes the image of the Capitol dome in the background.

Other stamps showing the Capitol include the $2 United States Capitol stamp of 1923 (Scott 572); 1928 2¢ and 5¢ Aeronautics Conference (649-50); 1950 3¢ Statue of Freedom (989), 3¢ National Capital Sesquicentennial (992); 1952 3¢ Service Women (1013); 1962 4¢ Sam Rayburn (1202); 1969 6¢ Beautification of America (1365); 9¢ Capitol Dome stamps released from 1975-77 (Scott 1590, 1590A, 1591, 1591a, 1616); 1980 15¢ National Letter Writing Week (1809); three varieties of Flag Over Capitol stamps issued in 1985 (Scott 2114-16); 1991 50¢ Switzerland (2532); and two 1962 8¢ Jet Airliner Over Capitol airmail stamps (C64-65).

The Design

The idea for a National Monument stamp theme grew out of the commemorative stamp Derry Noyes had designed for the 200th anniversary of the White House in 2000, featuring a winter photograph of the executive mansion at twilight.

"When I designed it, I came upon photographs of other buildings in Washington that I thought were particularly beautiful," she said.

The White House stamp was issued in the special size used for USPS holiday and Love stamps, and Noyes mocked up stamp designs incorporating other Washington photographs in that size as well. She did so regretfully, she said, "because the photographs were so beautiful and, as was the case with the White House stamp, the small size didn't do them justice." She included in the designs inscriptions identifying the landmarks in the same uppercase and lowercase Garamond type she had used to inscribe "The White House" on the earlier stamp.

To her satisfaction, however, CSAC asked her to redesign them in the semijumbo size that has become standard for Priority Mail and Express Mail postage. She also was asked to simplify the designs by eliminating the identifying type, which the committee members felt was unnecessary for such familiar buildings.

"PhotoAssist [the Postal Service's research firm] found hundreds of photographs for me from stock companies," Noyes said. "I was looking for pictures that would hold up at stamp size, that weren't too complicated, that had backgrounds that weren't too busy, and that were somewhat unusual — like a photograph of the White House at dusk with a blanket of snow on the ground.

"These particular photos just caught my eye."

Her design for the $3.50 Priority Mail stamp shows the dome of the U.S. Capitol against a dark blue night sky. Only the dome is shown, and it fills much of the design. The dome is illuminated by external lights, and interior light shows through its windows.

The photograph, made in April 1981, is unusual in that it shows the dome at eye level. To obtain it, photographer Robert Llewellyn took his Nikon camera and telephoto lens to the roof of the Library of Congress, which is a short walk from the Capitol's East Front. The photo was one of a series Llewellyn was shooting for a book titled *Washington, The Capitol*, but had never been published until it appeared on the stamp.

The "USA" and denomination are in dropout white in a typeface called Serifa Bold. Noyes included a horizontal dash of a lighter blue over the denomination to "get a little emphasis," she said.

The Capitol Dome stamp and its companion, the $12.25 Washington Monument stamp, incorporate what USPS calls "scrambled indicia" in their designs. Scrambled indicia, which can be read only by using a spe-

Designer Derry Noyes originally incorporated Robert Llewellyn's Capitol Dome photograph in a special-size stamp layout with an identifying inscription.

The scrambled-indicia message on the $3.50 Capitol Dome stamp, as viewed through a USPS acrylic decoder, is PRIORITY MAIL.

cial acrylic decoder lens sold by Stamp Fulfillment Services, are placed on certain stamps both as a security device and to attract collector interest. The last stamps to feature scrambled indicia were the four Xtreme Sports commemoratives that were issued June 25, 1999. On the Capitol Dome stamp, the hidden image consists of the words "PRIORITY MAIL" in a single line near the top of the design.

First-day Facts

No official first-day ceremony was held for the Capitol Dome and Washington Monument stamps. The Capitol Dome stamp originally was scheduled to be issued January 19 at the Aripex 2001 stamp show in Tucson, Arizona.

The earliest-known prerelease use of a Capitol Dome stamp was on a cover bearing a double-outline circular datestamp from the Salem, Ohio, post office. The cover was mailed January 12, 17 days before the official first day of issue.

$12.25 WASHINGTON MONUMENT

Date of Issue: January 29, 2001

Catalog Number: Scott 3473

Colors: black, cyan, magenta, yellow

First-Day Cancel: Washington, D.C.

First-Day Cancellations: 22,803 (includes $3.50 U.S. Capitol stamp)

Format: Pane of 20, vertical, 5 across, 4 down. Offset printing plates printing 120 stamps per revolution (10 across, 12 around).

Gum Type: self-adhesive

Scrambled Indicia: EXPRESS MAIL

Overall Stamp Size: 1.23 by 1.56 inches; 31.24 by 39.62mm

Pane Size: 7.13 by 7.26 inches; 181.1 by 184.4mm

Perforations: 11¼ by 11½ (die-cut simulated perforations) (rotary die cutter)

Selvage Markings: "©/2000/USPS." "12.25/x20/$245.00." "PLATE/POSITION" and diagram. Universal Product Code (UPC) "112000" in 2 locations.

Photographer: Patricia Fisher of Washington, D.C.

Designer, Art Director and Typographer: Derry Noyes of Washington, D.C.

Stamp Manufacturing: Stamps printed by Banknote Corporation of America, Browns Summit, North Carolina, on Goebel 670 offset press. Stamps processed by BCA.

Quantity Ordered: 35,000,000

Plate Number Detail: 1 set of 4 plate numbers preceded by the letter B in selvage above or below each corner stamp

Plate Number Combination Reported: B1111

Paper Supplier: Paper Corporation of the United States/Spinnaker Coatings

Tagging: phosphored paper

The Stamp

A 50¢ jump in the basic (8-ounce) domestic Express Mail rate January 7, 2001, prompted the Postal Service to release a $12.25 Express Mail stamp January 29 depicting the Washington Monument. The stamp was issued together with a $3.50 Priority Mail stamp showing the Capitol dome. (See related chapter.) The new stamps feature two of the most prominent and easily recognizable structures in Washington, D.C.

Both the Washington Monument and Capitol Dome stamps were sold in panes of 20. They were printed by offset lithography by Banknote Corporation of America, Browns Summit, North Carolina. Both are self-adhesive with die-cut perforations.

The Washington Monument stamp's vertical design is similar to the Capitol Dome stamp, with the "USA" and denomination located in approximately the same positions on the stamps. The Washington Monument stamp shows an eastward view of a silhouetted monument at sunrise, with the Capitol silhouetted in the background, just to the left of the base of the monument.

Various hues of orange and yellow dominate the sky behind the monument. They reflect off the water of the Reflecting Pool in the foreground.

Nearly 50 years after his death in 1799, construction began on the 555-foot obelisk that pays tribute to George Washington, the first president of the United States. The monument, one of the nation's most recognizable, was first considered by the Continental Congress in 1783. However, Congress neglected to take action on the project.

In 1832, the 100th anniversary of George Washington's birth, the Washington National Monument Society was organized by a group of concerned citizens with the express purpose of raising funds for the building of a monument to pay tribute to Washington. By 1847 the society had raised $87,000.

Architect Robert Mills designed the structure, an obelisk nearly 600 feet high. Mills envisioned the monument as an American pantheon with a colonnade that would house statues of presidents and national heroes. The top of the colonnade would feature Washington standing in a chariot.

The cornerstone of the monument was laid July 4, 1848, but the monument was to take on a form much different than what Mills had envisioned. The idea of a colonnade was abandoned.

The great obelisk is classical in style, rivaling any of those in Egypt. The inside of the monument is hollow. The inner walls are set with 193 carved memorial stones, donated by individuals, states, cities and other countries.

The most controversial stone was that given by Pope Pius IX. The memorial stone halted the construction of the monument in March 1854. At the time, the monument was only 152 feet high. A group believed to be Know-Nothings, an anti-immigrant and anti-Catholic American party, stole the stone and supposedly threw it in the Potomac River.

Contributions stopped, and Congress rescinded its contribution of

$200,000. Work did not resume until 1879.

Evidence of the 25-year construction gap can be seen on the monument. Marble used to finish the structure came from the same Maryland quarry, but it came from a different stratum, which resulted in a slightly different color and consequently a noticeable ring on the monument.

The 3,300-pound capstone was set in place on December 6, 1884. The capstone was capped with a 9-inch tall aluminum pyramid, marking the completion of the work. The monument was dedicated on February 21, 1885, and opened to the public on October 9, 1888.

Today, the top of the monument may be reached by elevator or by an iron stairway. The monument has more than 800,000 visitors a year.

The Washington Monument is an imposing structure that stands near the Potomac River, about halfway between the U.S. Capitol and the Lincoln Memorial. The 50 U.S. flags that encircle the base of the Monument represent the 50 states.

George Washington has appeared on numerous U.S. stamps, but the Washington Monument is depicted on just a handful. The $12.25 Express Mail stamp is the first to show the structure as the central focus of the design.

The first stamps to picture the monument were the 2¢ and 5¢ Aeronautics Conference stamps of 1928 (Scott 649-50). The Aeronautics stamps also show the Capitol.

The Capitol and Washington Monument are featured in the background on separate stamps in the 1969 Beautification of America set (1365-68). The 6¢ Plant For More Beautiful Cities stamp (1365) shows the Capitol. The Washington Monument can be seen on the 6¢ Plant For More Beautiful Parks stamp (1366).

Other stamps showing the monument include the 1960 4¢ United States-Japan Treaty (1158); five 6¢ Flag Over White House stamps issued from 1968-71 (1338, 1338A, 1338D, 1338F, 1338G); 1985 22¢ Flag Over Capitol (2116); and 1985 18¢ George Washington stamps (2149 and 2149a).

The Design

The striking photograph chosen by Derry Noyes to illustrate the stamp captures images of the National Mall silhouetted against the sky at dawn. The obelisk of the Washington Monument dominates the picture. Trees are seen on either side, and in the distance are the Capitol dome, which marks the east axis of the Mall; the dome of the Library of Congress, which stands beyond the Capitol; and the tower of the Smithsonian Institution "castle," which is on the south side of the Mall. The sun, halfway over the horizon, is seen just to the right of the Smithsonian tower. The scene is partly reflected in the Reflecting Pool in the foreground, most prominently in the dark shaft of the Washington Monument and the glowing smudge of the rising sun.

The photograph was made by Patricia Fisher, a Washington, D.C., pho-

230

tographer whose photo of the White House on a winter evening formed the design of the White House Bicentennial commemorative stamp of 2000. Because of the sun's position, Fisher knows it was taken around March 21, the vernal equinox, or around September 21, the autumnal equinox, but she doesn't remember which.

"Normally, I go down there at the time of the equinoxes, when the sun is rising most directly to the east of the Monument," she said. "The vantage point for this picture is a little up, so I'm probably on the steps of the Lincoln Memorial, shooting with my Canon 35mm camera with a long lens. At that time of day, the scrubbers and cleaners probably would be there with their mops and brooms — that's when they traditionally clean the statue, when there aren't many people around — and I'd be dodging hoses and things.

"For this picture, I'm standing actually to the left of the Reflecting Pool, which means I'm on the north side of the steps. If it's the fall, it's after September 21, because the sun has already moved south of the Capitol. If it's the spring, it's before March 21, because the sun is still moving north, toward the Capitol.

"We photographers who shoot a lot of stock photography of Washington are always looking for opportunities to get good views, and there are certain times of year when the sun is in a position that we like, and certain vantage points within and outside of the city that give us good shots at dawn.

"Once I went to the other famous vantage point, which is the grounds of the Iwo Jima Memorial in Arlington, Virginia, overlooking the city. There was a group of us there — I think it was September equinox time — and we were all waiting for the dawn. The mist came up off the Potomac River and obscured everything for about 15 minutes and we missed the sunrise! So everybody agreed we'd be back the next morning, and someone would bring doughnuts and someone else would bring coffee.

"A good stock photo brings all the elements together, and you can pick the spot, but you have to wait for something wonderful to happen at that spot."

The golden glow that suffuses the picture is in the photo negative and wasn't electronically enhanced for the stamp image. "The light is normally that color at dawn or sunset," Fisher said. "It has something to do with the way the light refracts and shines off the dust in the atmosphere."

She pointed out that the scene captured in the photograph can never be duplicated. The Reflecting Pool in the foreground is being altered by work now in progress on the nation's World War II Memorial that will occupy space on the Mall between the Washington Monument and Lincoln Memorial.

Fisher said she was happy to have two of her photographs chosen for postage stamps within a few months of each other, but wished the stamps could have had a longer useful life. The White House stamp's 33¢ denom-

As she did with the Capitol Dome photograph used on the $3.50 stamp, designer Derry Noyes originally incorporated Patricia Fisher's Washington Monument photograph in a special-size stamp layout with an identifying inscription.

The scrambled-indicia message on the $12.25 Washington Monument stamp, as viewed through a USPS acrylic decoder, is EXPRESS MAIL.

ination was made obsolete by the increase in the first-class rate to 34¢ less than three months after its October 18, 2000, issue date, and the $12.25 basic Express Mail rate covered by the Washington Monument stamp was increased to $12.45 July 1, 2001, slightly more than five months after the stamp's debut.

The "USA" and denomination are in dropout white in a typeface called Serifa Bold. Noyes included in the design a horizontal line in a darker orange against the sky over the denomination to add graphic interest.

The scrambled indicia on the Washington Monument stamp, visible only through a special acrylic decoder lens sold by Stamp Fulfillment Services, consists of the words "EXPRESS MAIL" in a single line near the top of the design.

First-day Facts

No official first-day ceremony was held for the Washington Monument and Capitol Dome stamps.

34¢ FLOWERS (4 DESIGNS)
CONVERTIBLE BOOKLET OF 20

Date of Issue: February 7, 2001

Catalog Numbers: Scott 3487-3490, single stamps; 3490a, same stamps, block of 4; 3490e, double-sided pane of 20 consisting of 5 3490a; BC161, convertible booklet cover containing 5 3490a

Colors: magenta, black, cyan, yellow

First-Day Cancel: New York, New York

First-Day Cancellations: 141,634 (includes all varieties of 34¢ Flowers, Statue of Liberty and Flag Over Farm stamps)

Format: Convertible booklet pane of 20, vertical. Stamps on both sides, 8 (2 across by 4 down) plus label (booklet cover) on one side, 12 (2 across by 6 down) on other side, with 2 horizontal peel-off strips between blocks of 4 on each side. Gravure printing cylinders of 192 (16 across, 12 around), cover side; 288 (16 across, 18 around), all-stamp side.

Gum Type: self-adhesive

Overall Stamp Size: 0.870 by 0.982 inches; 22.09 by 24.94mm

Pane Size: 1.7400 by 6.2083 inches; 44.19 by 157.69mm

Perforations: 10¼ by 10¾ (die-cut simulated perforations) (Comco custom rotary die-cutter)

Selvage Markings: "© 2000 USPS • Peel here to fold • Self-adhesive stamps • DO NOT WET" on first peel-off strip on all-stamp side; "• Peel here to fold • Self-adhesive stamps • © 2000 USPS" plus cylinder numbers on second peel-off strip on all-stamp side.

Back Markings: "4 Flowers/Twenty 34 cent/Self-adhesive Stamps/© 2000 USPS" and Universal Product Code (UPC) "0 669200 7" on label (booklet cover).

Photographer: Robert Peak of Winter Park, Florida

Designer, Art Director and Typographer: Derry Noyes of Washington, D.C.

Modeler: Donald Woo of Sennett Security Products of Chantilly, Virginia

Stamp Manufacturing: Stamps printed for Sennett Security Products by American Packaging Corp. of Columbus, Wisconsin, on Rotomec 3000 gravure press. Stamps finished by Unique Binders of Fredericksburg, Virginia.

Quantity Ordered: 1,150,000,000 stamps

Cylinder Number Detail: 1 set of 4 cylinder numbers preceded by the letter S on 1 peel-off strip.

Cylinder Number Combinations Reported: S1111, S2222

Paper Supplier: Paper Corporation of the United States/Spinnaker Coatings

Tagging: phosphored paper with phosphate blocker applied to the label (booklet cover) portion of the pane

34¢ FLOWERS (4 DESIGNS)
VENDING BOOKLET OF 20

Date of Issue: February 7, 2001

Catalog Numbers: Scott 3487-3490, single stamps; 3490b, booklet pane of 4; 3490c, booklet pane of 6, 3489, 3490, 2 each 3487-3488; 3490d, booklet pane of 6, 3487, 3488, 2 each 3489-3490; BK284, vending booklet containing 2 3490b, 3490c, 3490d

Colors: magenta, black, cyan, yellow

First-Day Cancel: New York, New York

First-Day Cancellations: 141,634 (includes all varieties of 34¢ Flowers, Statue of Liberty and Flag Over Farm stamps)

Format: Vending booklet of 20, vertical, 2 across, in 4 segments: 6 (2 by 3), 6 (2 by 3), and 2 4-stamp segments (2 by 2) attached back to back. 1 4-stamp segment is on its own backing paper, separate from backing paper of main booklet. Gravure printing cylinders of 480 subjects (24 across, 20 around) printing 24 panes.

Gum Type: self-adhesive

Overall Stamp Size: 0.870 by 0.982 inches; 22.09 by 24.94mm

Pane Size: 1.739 by 10.375 inches; 44.17 by 263.52mm

Perforations: 10¼ by 10¾ (die-cut simulated perforations) (Comco custom rotary die-cutter)

Selvage Markings: none

Back Markings: "4 Flowers/Twenty 34 cent/Self-adhesive/Stamps" on front cover. "© 2000 USPS," USPS logo, Universal Product Code (UPC) "0 669400 5" and promotion for www.usps.com web site on back cover.

Photographer: Robert Peak of Winter Park, Florida

Designer, Art Director and Typographer: Derry Noyes of Washington, D.C.

Modeler: Donald Woo of Sennett Security Products of Chantilly, Virginia

Stamp Manufacturing: Stamps printed for Sennett Security Products by American Packaging Corp. of Columbus, Wisconsin, on Rotomec 3000 gravure press. Stamps finished by Unique Binders of Fredericksburg, Virginia.

Quantity Ordered: 200,000,000 stamps

Cylinder Number Detail: 1 set of 4 cylinder numbers preceded by the letter S on back of main booklet backing paper, behind 4-stamp segment

Cylinder Number Combination Reported: S1111

Paper Supplier: Paper Corporation of the United States/Spinnaker Coatings

Tagging: phosphored paper

34¢ FLOWERS (4 DESIGNS), COIL

Date of Issue: February 7, 2001

Catalog Numbers: Scott 3478-3481, single stamps; 3481a, strip of 4

Colors: black, cyan, magenta, yellow

First-Day Cancel: New York, New York

First-Day Cancellations: 141,634 (includes all varieties of 34¢ Flowers, Statue of Liberty and Flag Over Farm stamps)

Format: Coil of 100, vertical. Gravure cylinders printing 384 subjects per revolution (16 across, 24 around) manufactured by Acitronics.

Gum Type: self-adhesive

Overall Stamp Size: 0.870 by 0.965 inches; 22.10 by 24.51mm

Perforations: 8½ (die-cut simulated perforations) (George Schmitt & Co. rotary die cutter)

Photographer: Robert Peak of Winter Park, Florida

Designer, Art Director and Typographer: Derry Noyes of Washington, D.C.

Stamp Manufacturing: Stamps printed by Guilford Gravure, Guilford, Connecticut, for Banknote Corporation of America, Browns Summit, North Carolina, on Cerrutti R118 gravure press. Stamps finished by Guilford Gravure.

Quantity Ordered: 1,500,000,000

Cylinder Number Detail: 1 set of 4 cylinder numbers preceded by the letter B on every 12th stamp (numbers appear only on Scott 3480)

Cylinder Number Combinations Reported: B1111, B2111, B2122, B2211, B2222

Paper Supplier: Paper Corporation of the United States/Spinnaker Coatings

Tagging: phosphored paper

The Stamp

On February 7, USPS released the third set of denominated stamps featuring the same designs as previous nondenominated rate-change stamps issued in late 2000. The stamps carried a denomination of 34¢ to meet the new first-class rate. They incorporated four different flower designs arranged se-tenant in three formats, similar to their nondenominated counterparts.

The designs used photographs rather than illustrations of flowers. The four pastel-colored flowers — not identified on the stamps themselves — are the freesia, Asian hybrid lily, cymbidium orchid and longiflorum lily.

The stamps are self-adhesives, with die-cut simulated perforations, and were printed by the gravure process on phosphored paper. The formats, the same as for the nondenominated stamps, are:

• Two-sided pane (convertible booklet) of 20, 12 stamps on one side, eight on the other, printed by American Packaging Corporation for Sennett Security Products. On one side of the pane are three blocks of four, separated by horizontal peel-off strips, one of which has the cylinder-number combination, preceded by the letter S. On the other side are two blocks of four plus the booklet cover, which actually is a large peelable label. The top two stamps of the blocks of four are longiflorum lily (Scott 3487) at left and cymbidium orchid (3488) at right; the pair beneath are the freesia (3489) at left and Asian hybrid lily (3490) at right. A phosphor blocker was applied to the cover to prevent its use as a postage stamp. All the stamps have either one or two straight edges.

• Vending-machine booklet of 20, also printed by American Packaging Corporation for Sennett Security Products. The booklet pane is two stamps across by 10 stamps down. Each stamp has either one or two straight edges. The top pair of stamps is longiflorum lily and cymbidium orchid, the pair beneath it is freesia and Asian hybrid, and these pairings alternate to the bottom of the pane, which is divided into segments of four, six, six and four stamps. The pane is folded in the middle, between the two six-stamp segments, and the four-stamp segments on each end are folded inside, making a flat palm-sized packet.

The gauge of the die-cut simulated perfs, by *Linn's Stamp News'* measure, is 10¼ by 10¾. The four cylinder numbers, preceded by the letter S for Sennett, are not on the stamps or interior selvage, but are printed across the top of the reverse of the booklet.

• Coil of 100, printed by Guilford Gravure for Banknote Corporation of America and finished by BCA. The order of the stamps on the coil is: freesia (3478), Asian hybrid lily (3479), cymbidium orchid (3480) and longiflorum lily (3481). The stamps abut each other on the backing paper with no spaces between, above or below them. The four-digit cylinder number combination, preceded by the letter B for BCA, appears on every 12th stamp, which is always a cymbidium orchid. As with the nondenominated coil stamps, many collectors of plate number coils, or PNCs, opted to collect these coil stamps in symmetrical strips of nine, with the plate-number stamp in the center and a non-numbered cymbidium orchid stamp on either end.

The Design

The designs for the four 34¢ Flowers stamps are the same as those used for the nondenominated Flowers stamps issued in 2000, except that the year date in the lower-left corner is 2001 and the inscription "USA/34" appears in the lower right-hand corner in place of the words "first class usa." The type is in dropout white Garamond italic letters.

The designs are based on photographs taken by Robert Peak of Winter Park, Florida. Prior to the release of the nondenominated Flowers definitives, USPS had never used flower photos on stamps before, according to art director Derry Noyes.

Each of the four stamps has a distinctive background color. For the freesia it is green; Asian hybrid lily, red; cymbidium orchid, tan; and longiflorum lily, purple.

A comparison of the booklet and coil stamps shows that the printing on the coil version is somewhat crisper and clearer than on the booklets. The year date "2001" is slightly wider on the booklet stamps and has rounder zeroes than on the coils. This was also true of the nondenominated stamps.

First-day Facts

No first-day ceremony was held for the denominated Four Flowers stamps.

The earliest-known prerelease use of a Four Flowers coil stamp (Scott 3478-81) was a plate number single of the cymbidium orchid stamp on a cover mailed to *Linn's Stamp News* with an Austin, Texas, machine cancellation dated February 6, one day before the official first day of issue. The cancellation tied to the same cover a 34¢ Statue of Liberty coil stamp (Scott 3476), also a plate number single and also an earliest-known prerelease use.

76¢ HATTIE W. CARAWAY
DISTINGUISHED AMERICANS SERIES

Date of Issue: February 21, 2001

Catalog Number: Scott 3431, die-cut gauge 11; 3432, die-cut gauge 11 by 11.5

Colors: black, red (PMS 1797) (offset); black (intaglio)

First-Day Cancel: Little Rock, Arkansas

First-Day Cancellations: 18,626

Format: Pane of 20, vertical, 5 across, 4 down. Offset and intaglio printing plates of 240 subjects, 15 across, 16 around.

Gum: self-adhesive

Overall Stamp Size: 0.84 by 0.99 inches; 21.34 by 25.15mm

Pane Size: 5.04 by 4.95 inches; 128.02 by 125.73mm

Perforations: 11 (die-cut simulated perforations) (rotary die cutter)

Selvage Markings: "©USPS/2000." ".76/x20/$15.20." "Plate/Position" and diagram. Universal Product Code (UPC) "101400" in 2 locations.

Illustrator: Mark Summers of Waterdown, Ontario, Canada

Designer, Art Director and Typographer: Richard Sheaff of Scottsdale, Arizona

Engraver: Chemically engraved by Banknote Corporation of America, Browns Summit, North Carolina

Stamp Manufacturing: Stamps printed by BCA on Goebel 670 offset press and Epikos 5009 intaglio press. Stamps processed by BCA.

Quantity Ordered and Distributed: 100,000,000

Plate Number Detail: 2 offset plate numbers preceded by the letter B and 1 intaglio plate number in selvage above or below each corner stamp

Plate Number Combination Reported: B11-1

Paper Supplier: Paper Corporation of the United States/Spinnaker Coatings

Tagging: phosphored paper

The Stamp

On February 21, the Postal Service issued a 76¢ definitive stamp depicting Hattie W. Caraway of Arkansas, the first woman elected to the U.S. Senate.

The stamp was the third in the Distinguished Americans series, following stamps in 2000 honoring General Joseph W. Stilwell (10¢) and U.S. Senator Claude Pepper (33¢). The first two had water-activated gum and were conventionally perforated; this one was a self-adhesive with die-cut simulated perfs.

The Caraway stamp's 76¢ denomination covered the three-ounce rate for first-class mail that had taken effect the preceding month. Its effectiveness for that purpose lasted only a little more than four months, however. On July 1, USPS increased the rate for each ounce of first-class mail after the first ounce from 21¢ to 23¢, a step that raised the three-ounce rate to 80¢.

Hattie Caraway's chief advocate on the Citizens' Stamp Advisory Committee had been Ronald Robinson, a fellow Arkansan and former advertising executive from Little Rock. "The committee asked, 'Who was Hattie Caraway?' " recalled Terrence McCaffrey, manager of stamp development for USPS. "Ron was quick to tell us."

CSAC approved her inclusion in the then-current Great Americans series of definitive stamps in 1997, and illustrator Keith Birdsong made a pencil sketch of the senator, to be developed into a design in the Great Americans style. The committee approved several other subjects at the same time, to be used as needed for future rate changes. But USPS terminated the Great Americans and launched the Distinguished Americans before Caraway's stamp could be issued. Art director Richard Sheaff then asked Mark Summers to make a new portrait that could be adapted to the design style of the new series, which he did.

The Distinguished Americans are bicolors, black and red, rather than monochromatic, as the Great Americans were. The portraits are produced by the scratchboard technique, in which the artist begins with a completely black surface and scratches away the unwanted color with a pointed tool, leaving the remaining lines and shapes to form the picture. Like the

In 1997 CSAC approved Hattie Caraway as a Great Americans series subject, and this design was prepared, using a pencil sketch of the senator by Keith Birdsong of Muskogee, Oklahoma. The Great Americans series was terminated before the Caraway stamp could be issued. Caraway was shifted to the new Distinguished Americans series, with a new portrait done in scratchboard by Mark Summers.

241

first two stamps in the series, the Hattie Caraway was printed by Banknote Corporation of America by a combination of intaglio and offset and distributed in panes of 20.

Hattie Ophelia Wyatt was born February 1, 1878, near Bakerville, Tennessee. She grew up there and in nearby Hustburg, Tennessee. In 1896 she graduated from Dickson Normal School in Dickson, Tennessee, and taught school for a brief time thereafter.

In 1902 she married Thaddeus Caraway, and devoted her time to their children and the farm while her husband practiced law. Thaddeus Caraway later became a Democratic congressman and a U.S. senator from Arkansas.

He died in 1931 and a few days later, November 13, 1931, Hattie Caraway was appointed by Arkansas governor Harvey Parnell to fill his empty seat. The appointment made her the second woman — after Rebecca Latimer Felton in 1922 — to be seated in the U.S. Senate, although Felton's was a courtesy appointment and lasted just one day.

On January 12, 1932, Caraway won a special election to serve the remaining months of her husband's term, and subsequently she was elected to two six-year terms. She was a strong backer of the New Deal and other legislative initiatives of President Franklin D. Roosevelt's administration. She supported veterans and organized labor and opposed isolationism.

In 1933 Caraway became the first woman to chair a Senate committee. On October 19, 1943, in the absence of Vice President Henry A. Wallace and Senator Carter Glass of Virginia, the Senate's president pro tempore, she was appointed acting president pro tempore, the first woman to preside formally over the Senate.

Her attempt to win a third term failed when she finished fourth in the 1944 Arkansas Democratic Senate primary, which was won by Representative J. William Fulbright. On December 19, 1944, her last day at work in the Senate chamber, she received a standing ovation from her colleagues. After her service officially ended in January 1945, President Roosevelt appointed her to the Federal Employees' Compensation Commission.

A stroke ended Hattie Caraway's public career in January 1950, and she died December 21, 1950, in Falls Church, Virginia.

The Design

Mark Summers of Waterdown, Ontario, created the head-and-shoulders portrait for the Hattie Caraway stamp, as he had done for the Stilwell and Pepper stamps that inaugurated the series. Summers is well known for the scratchboard portraits of literary personalities — some verging on caricature — he has created for the chain bookseller, Barnes & Noble. His art, characterized by a dense network of horizontal lines, also has appeared in *The New York Times Book Review* and elsewhere.

Summers and Keith Birdsong, who had made the pencil sketch for the unused earlier Caraway stamp design, both based their portraits on a

242

Mark Summers based his scratchboard portrait of Hattie W. Caraway on this photograph, made October 21, 1943, of Senator Caraway in her role as acting president pro tempore of the U.S. Senate.

UPI/Corbis-Bettman photograph made October 21, 1943, in Washington, of Caraway as the Senate's acting president pro tempore. She wears a dark suit with a string of pearls and is holding aloft a presiding officer's gavel.

The stamp shows its subject against a white background. The portrait is engraved, as is the "USA" and "76" in black Minion regular type. All other design elements are printed by offset: the hairline partial frame in black, the name "Hattie W. Caraway," in red Minion bold italic that runs up the left side outside the frameline, and the word "Senator" in black Minion display italic running down the right side.

Varieties

A horizontal die-cut variety of the Caraway stamp was discovered in Alabama in March 2002 by collector Kathleen Campbell, who notified *Linn's Stamp News* of the variety. The die cuts on "normal" specimens measure gauge 11, while the variety gauges 11.5 horizontally by 11 vertically. Scott assigned it a catalog listing of 3432.

According to *Linn's*, the key to identifying the variety is the bottom-right corner of the stamp. This corner on the 11.5 specimen is much broader than the same corner on the 11 (see illustration).

USPS spokesman Don Smeraldi told Fred Baumann of *Stamp Collector* that the variety didn't come from a second printing, but "was more of a die cut registration variance."

"BCA used separate horizontal and vertical die cutting plates rather than a combined plate [to make the cuts]," Smeraldi said. "During the printing process, they sometimes have to replace a horizontal plate and/or a vertical plate but not necessarily both at the same time. These changes can create a range of variation within a certain tolerance, which can lead to relatively small differences between the serpentine cuts on stamps printed during the same run."

As with other inadvertent die-cut varieties produced by USPS contract printers, the Caraway variety wasn't placed on sale by Stamp Fulfillment Services as a separate item. "SFS doesn't have the staffing to dedicate people to manually measuring perforations before shipping out items," Smeraldi said. "And ... they won't list an additional Caraway because there wasn't a second printing, and we don't consider it a variety."

The used Hattie Caraway stamp at left, discovered by collector Kathleen Camp-bell, has horizontal die cuts that gauge 11.5, whereas the Caraway stamp at right has horizontal die cuts that gauge 11. The bottom-right corner of the 11.5 stamp is much broader than the same corner on the 11.

First-Day Facts

Deborah Willhite, USPS senior vice president for government relations, dedicated the stamp in the rotunda of the Arkansas state capitol in Little Rock. The speakers were Arkansas' two U.S. senators, Democrat Blanche L. Lincoln and Republican Tim Hutchinson, and U.S. Representative Vic Snyder. Arkansas Lieutenant Governor Winthrop Rockefeller gave the welcome, and Jeff Taylor, Little Rock's postmaster, presided.

A second-day ceremony was held the next day in Jonesboro, Arkansas, where Caraway lived and is buried.

20¢ GEORGE WASHINGTON
CONVERTIBLE BOOKLET OF 10

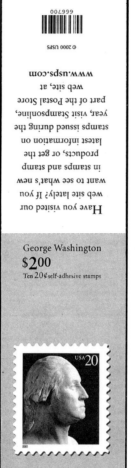

Date of Issue: February 22, 2001

Catalog Numbers: Scott 3482, single stamp, die cut perf 11¼; 3483, single stamp, die cut perf 10½ by 11¼; 3482a, booklet pane of 10 3482; 3482b, booklet pane of 4 3482; 3482c, booklet pane of 6 3482; 3483a, booklet pane of 4, 2 3482 at left, 2 3483 at right; 3483b, booklet pane of 6, 3 3482 at left, 3 3483 at right; 3483c, booklet pane of 10, 5 3482 at left, 5 3483 at right; 3483d, booklet pane of 4, 2 3483 at left, 2 3482 at right; 3483e, booklet pane of 6, 3 3483 at left, 3 3482 at right; 3483f, booklet pane of 10, 5 3483 at left, 5 3482 at right; 3483g, pair, 3482 at left, 3483 at right; 3483h, pair, 3483 at left, 3482 at right

Color: red (PMS 202), stamp; black, blue (PMS 540), red (PMS 202), cover

First-Day Cancel: Wall, South Dakota

First-Day Cancellations: 90,746 (includes all varieties of 20¢ George Washington and 21¢ Bison, 55¢ Art Deco Eagle and 70¢ Badlands postal card)

Format: Convertible booklet pane of 10, vertical, 2 across, 10 down, with horizontal peel-off strip covering roulettes between second and third horizontal row. Offset printing plates of 330 subjects, 15 across, 22 around.

Gum Type: self-adhesive

Overall Stamp Size: 0.875 by 0.990 inches; 22.225 by 25.146mm

Pane Size: 1.75 by 6.50 inches; 44.45 by 165.10mm

Perforations: 10½ by 11¼ or 11¼ (die-cut simulated perforations) (Arpeco custom stroke die-cutter). Two bull's-eye die-cuts in top selvage.

Selvage Markings: USPS logo, "© 2000 USPS" and plate number in top selvage. "Peel this strip and fold here" on horizontal peel-off strip.

Back Markings: "George Washington/$2.00/Ten 20¢ self-adhesive stamps" on front cover. Promotion for Stampsonline web site, "© 2000 USPS" and Universal Product Code (UPC) "666700" on back cover.

Photo Source: Mount Vernon Ladies Association

Designer, Art Director and Typographer: Richard Sheaff of Scottsdale, Arizona

Modeler: Joseph Sheeran of Ashton-Potter (USA) Ltd., Williamsville, New York

Stamp Manufacturing: Stamps printed by Ashton-Potter on offset portion of Stevens Variable Size Security Documents webfed 6-color offset, 3-color intaglio press. Stamps finished by Ashton-Potter.

Quantity Ordered: 500,000,000 stamps

Plate Number Detail: 1 plate number preceded by the letter P on top selvage

Plate Number Combinations Reported: P1, P2, P3

Paper Supplier: Fasson/Glatfelter

Tagging: phosphored paper

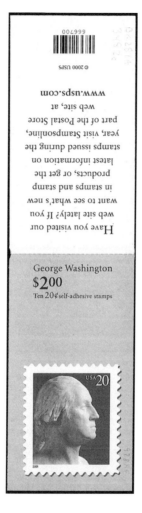

Date of Issue: February 22, 2001

Catalog Numbers: Scott 3482, single stamp, die cut perf 11¼; 3483, single stamp, die cut perf 10½ by 11¼; 3482a, booklet pane of 10 3482; 3482b, booklet pane of 4 3482; 3482c, booklet pane of 6 3482; 3483a, booklet pane of 4, 2 3482 at left, 2 3483 at right; 3483b, booklet pane of 6, 3 3482 at left, 3 3483 at right; 3483c, booklet pane of 10, 5 3482 at left, 5 3483 at right; 3483d, booklet pane of 4, 2 3483 at left, 2 3482 at right; 3483e, booklet pane of 6, 3 3483 at left, 3 3482 at right; 3483f, booklet pane of 10, 5 3483 at left, 5 3482 at right; 3483g, pair, 3482 at left, 3483 at right; 3483h, pair, 3483 at left, 3482 at right

Color: red (PMS 202), stamp; black, blue (PMS 540), red (PMS 202), cover

First-Day Cancel: Wall, South Dakota

First-Day Cancellations: 90,746 (includes all varieties of 20¢ George Washington and 21¢ Bison, 55¢ Art Deco Eagle and 70¢ Badlands postal card)

Format: Vending booklet of 10, vertical, 2 across, 10 down, with rouletted space between second and third horizontal row. Offset printing plates of 330 subjects, 15 across, 22 around.

Gum Type: self-adhesive

Overall Stamp Size: 0.875 by 0.990 inches; 22.225 by 25.146mm

Pane Size: 1.75 by 6.50 inches; 44.45 by 165.10mm

Perforations: 10½ by 11¼ or 11¼ (die-cut simulated perforations) (Arpeco custom stroke die-cutter). Two bull's-eye die-cuts in top selvage.

Selvage Markings: USPS logo, "© 2000 USPS" and plate number in top selvage.

Back Markings: "George Washington/$2.00/Ten 20¢ self-adhesive stamps" on front cover. Promotion for Stampsonline web site, "© 2000 USPS" and Universal Product Code (UPC) "666700" on back cover.

Photo Source: Mount Vernon Ladies Association

Designer, Art Director and Typographer: Richard Sheaff of Scottsdale, Arizona

Modeler: Joseph Sheeran of Ashton-Potter (USA) Ltd., Williamsville, New York

Stamp Manufacturing: Stamps printed by Ashton-Potter on offset portion of Stevens Variable Size Security Documents webfed 6-color offset, 3-color intaglio press. Stamps finished by Ashton-Potter.

Quantity Ordered: 60,000,000 stamps

Plate Number Detail: 1 plate number preceded by the letter P on top selvage

Plate Number Combinations Reported: P1, P2, P3

Paper Supplier: Fasson/Glatfelter

Tagging: phosphored paper

The Stamps

For 142 years, George Washington's face was never absent from a current U.S. stamp. Between 1908 and 1921, in fact, all U.S. definitive stamps carried the profile of either Washington or his fellow Founding Father, Benjamin Franklin. Washington's run began in 1842, when he looked out from the first stamp ever issued in America, New York's City Despatch Post local (Scott 40L1), and ended May 31, 1984, when the Postal Service withdrew the 5¢ Prominent Americans coil (Scott 1304C) bearing his picture.

The disappearance of the Father Of His Country from the postal portrait gallery shocked collectors and patriotic groups and was the subject of disapproving editorials in the philatelic press. Washington made a brief return to definitive postage in 1985, when USPS put his face on an 18¢ coil stamp (Scott 2149) covering the basic presort rate for first-class mail. But this stamp was meant for use primarily by bulk mailers, not the general public, and had only a three-year life before the presort rate went up and it was replaced by a 21¢ stamp in the Transportation coil series. In 1994, Washington was allowed to share a still-current but little-seen $5 diamond-shaped definitive with one of his presidential successors, Andrew Jackson (Scott 2592).

Finally, in 2001, George Washington returned to active service in U.S. postage. A 20¢ self-adhesive Washington stamp was issued February 22, his birthday. It came in two formats, vending booklet of 10 and flat pane (convertible booklet) of 10 (which the Postal Service was aware of and announced in advance) and two varieties of die-cut simulated perforations (which it wasn't and didn't).

The stamp's 20¢ denomination met the postcard rate. However, its usefulness for that purpose lasted only a little more than four months. On July 1, 2001, the rate was increased to 21¢, and demand for booklets of 20¢ stamps disappeared.

The Washington design grew out of a June 1999 meeting among the Postal Service art directors and the Citizens' Stamp Advisory Committee's design subcommittee at Newport Beach, California. Such meetings, according to Terrence McCaffrey, manager of stamp development, are retreats at which "we sit down and think about where to take the stamp program next, and discuss issues we don't normally have time to talk about" at regular CSAC sessions.

On this occasion, it was decided to develop a U.S. counterpart of Great Britain's "Machin heads," a long-running series much admired by the Postal Service group. The Machins, which first appeared in 1967, are single-color stamps with a simple design, a plaster profile bust of Queen Elizabeth II created by artist Arnold Machin.

"We don't have a queen, but we had, in effect, a king — George Washington," McCaffrey said. Washington was quickly chosen as the design subject, he said, after which the question arose: "Why not do Franklin, too? So we developed two designs, Washington and Franklin. We didn't have an immediate need for Franklin, so we put that design in the 'bank.' "

In his design for the Washington stamp, art director Richard Sheaff placed a photograph of a bust of the first president by Jean-Antoine Houdon against a solid background. To achieve the classic look the design group wanted, the members proposed that it be printed in single-color intaglio, using the services of the famous Czeslaw Slania, court engraver of Sweden, to produce the die. In March 2000, McCaffrey showed the design to Slania himself during a trip to Stockholm to plan the joint U.S.-Swedish commemorative issue marking the centennial of the Nobel Prizes (see separate chapter).

However, a combination of lack of time and Slania's own reservations about the wisdom of engraving the design led to the decision to print the stamp by offset lithography instead — much to Sheaff's and McCaffrey's disappointment.

"Slania pointed out that we couldn't get the solid background color of the design by engraving," McCaffrey said. "He would have to use cross-hatching, and that would give us only about 70 percent of the color. When I told the committee this, they said, 'No, what's great about this design is the rich strong background color. If we're going to lose that, let's just photograph it.' "

The printing assignment went to Ashton-Potter (USA) Ltd., which produced the two kinds of booklet required by USPS: the convertible booklet, a flat pane of 10 with a peel-off strip that allowed the pane to be folded, and a prefolded booklet of 10 for vending-machine distribution. Because the stamps are arranged two across by five down on the panes, all specimens have a straight edge on either the right or left side.

After the stamp was placed on sale, collectors discovered what the Postal Service hadn't known, let alone announced: that it came in two different gauges of die-cut simulated perforation, with the two varieties coexisting in some cases in the same booklet. The variation was in the horizontal "perfs," with some measuring 11¼, the same gauge as the vertical "perfs," and others measuring 10½.

James E. Kloetzel, Scott catalog editor, wrote in the 2002 Scott *Specialized Catalogue of U.S. Stamps & Covers*:

"Fortuitously, the problem ... was discovered right here in the Scott offices when Charles Snee, an associate editor of *Linn's Stamp News,* dropped by to question our proposed die cut measurements of the 20¢ Washington convertible booklet. As it turns out, Scott had received from [Stamp Fulfillment Services at] Kansas City booklets of the variety that eventually would be listed as No. 3483f, containing five stamps die cut 10½ by 11¼ at the left and five stamps die cut 11¼ at the right. Our new-issues editor, Marty Frankevicz, had measured the upper-left stamp from the pane for listing purposes.

"Meanwhile, Snee had measured stamps from a 'normal' die cut 11¼ pane, and when the panes were compared side by side, the die-cutting variations were noted. Later, the other variety showing the die cut 11¼ stamps at the left and the die cut 10½ by 11¼ stamps at the right was discovered. Still later, when the Washington vending booklets hit post offices, it was discovered that all three varieties also existed in these booklets. ...

"The Postal Service had no idea that the stamps they were accepting from their contractors had these die-cutting variations, and they did not (and still do not) offer these as separate items. Collectors were left to their

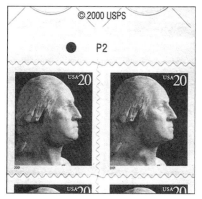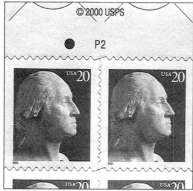

Close-up images of the top row of two stamps from the Washington vending booklet, left, and the Washington convertible booklet, right. There are noticeable differences in the die-cut corners of stamps from each format, making it possible for collectors to look at a single stamp and know from which format it came.

own devices to try to find the combination varieties, which have turned out to be much scarcer than the normal varieties. Many collectors are upset that they cannot go into a post office and buy the varieties, or that they cannot order them from Kansas City."

Snee, in *Linn's,* explained the problem that this created for collectors "who strive for completeness."

"For example," he wrote, "if you collect intact Washington panes and vending booklets and want to be complete for the die-cut arrangements, you need to acquire six items ($12 worth of stamps, at $2 per pane or booklet of 10): one 11¼L/11¼R pane, one 10½L/11¼R pane, one 11¼L/10½R pane, one 11¼L/11¼R vending booklet, one 10½L/11¼R vending booklet and one 11¼L/10½R vending booklet. If you decide to collect both [existing] plate numbers and the die cuts, you must acquire six panes and six vending booklets, for a total of $24.

"Most collectors probably won't find all versions at post offices. Some will have to enlist the services of a new-issue dealer if they want to fill the spaces in their albums. And they will pay a premium above face value for the dealer's services."

In another article, Snee informed collectors how to determine whether a single specimen of the 20¢ Washington stamp came from a convertible booklet or vending booklet. The difference is illustrated in the images, shown here, of the first row of Washington stamps from the vending booklet (left) and the convertible booklet (right).

The top-right corner of the left stamp from a vending booklet slopes down to the right and the top-left corner of the right stamp slopes up to the left. The situation is reversed for Washington stamps from a convertible booklet: The top-right corner of the left stamp slopes up to the right, and the top-left corner of the right stamp slopes down to the left.

The Design

The 20¢ Washington stamp is brick-red in color. Its design is the essence of simplicity, like that of the British Machins that inspired it. The Houdon bust of Washington is seen in profile, facing right. The only typography, in the upper-right corner, is "USA 20," in a font called Minion, dropped out of the solid background.

Houdon busts of Washington are familiar to stamp collectors, having been depicted on many U.S. definitives since 1851 and on the 1¢ Washington Bicentennial commemorative of 1932. This particular bust, in terra cotta and undraped, is at Mount Vernon, where Washington lived, died and is buried. Signed and dated "HOUDON F. 1785," it is one of several made by the sculptor in different materials, including plaster, marble and bronze. Washington sat for the famous French sculptor at Mount Vernon in October 1785.

The photograph used on the stamp was furnished by the Mount Vernon Ladies Association, which has owned and operated Mount Vernon since 1858. Richard Sheaff also worked up alternative designs, using photographs of the bust from different angles. In some of these designs he included the name "George Washington," but in the end it was decided that identification was unnecessary. "We wanted to make the design as simple and clean as we could," Sheaff said.

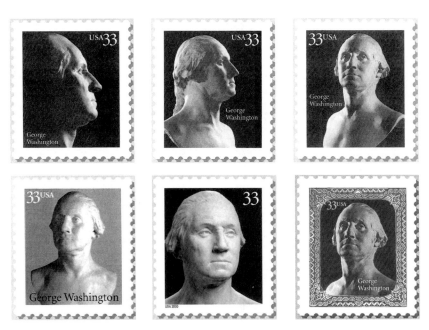

Richard Sheaff used a variety of photographs of the Houdon bust of Washington for alternative stamp designs, some of which included the first president's name. One of these unused designs incorporated an ornate frame, in contrast to the classic simplicity of the design that ultimately was approved.

252

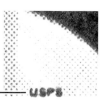

The microprinted letters "USPS" can be found on Washington's left shoulder, along the bottom edge of the stamp design.

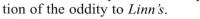

Because the stamp was a single-design, offset-printed issue, the Postal Service required microprinting as a design element. The letters "USPS" can be found on Washington's left shoulder, along the bottom edge of the stamp design.

Varieties

The discovery of an interesting freak vending booklet of the 20¢ Washington stamp by the friend of a *Linn's* reader was reported in the April 15, 2002, issue of the publication. Opened out, the booklet reveals a "stowaway" — a miscut pair of stamps affixed atop the bottom pair of stamps in the booklet (see illustration).

The pair has no vertical die cutting between the stamps, and is shifted noticeably to the right in relation to the other stamps in the booklet, revealing a portion of the underlying stamp on the left side. The horizontal die cuts of the overlying stamps nearly match the horizontal die cuts of the two stamps beneath them; those two underlying stamps have normal die cuts, as do the other eight stamps in the booklet.

Ashton-Potter (USA), through the Postal Service, provided an explanation of the oddity to *Linn's*.

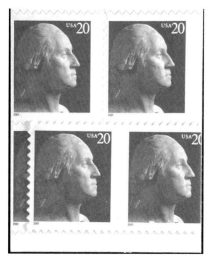

"The two extra stamps were most likely applied during the folding, gluing and slitting operation, when mount units of five booklets are processed," the printer said. "Occasionally the

This is a close-up view of the bottom of a freak George Washington booklet. The errant pair affixed to the bottom two stamps of the booklet pane has no vertical die-cut simulated perforations. Ashton-Potter, the printer, provided an explanation for the production mishap that produced the oddity.

mount unit will come down the feeder table at an awkward angle, causing it to hit the folding plate and buckle the mount unit.

"This buckle sometimes causes the die-cut stamps to peel away from the liner paper. These stamps will float and, at times, adhere to either a roller, folding plate, conveyor or, as in the case of this booklet, the mount unit.

"This is the reason there is no [serpentine] die cutting between the two [extra] stamps; they come from another position on the mount unit where it was to be slit [into two booklets]. This means that two booklets from this mount unit are both missing one stamp.

"The mount unit was then folded, glued shut and slit into individual booklets, all in one pass.

"This does occasionally happen, but most of the time [an errant] stamp ends up on the roller or folding plate, making it visible to the operators, who would then remove the damaged mount unit.

"The fact that the horizontal die cuts of the overlying stamps appear close to lining up with the horizontal die cuts of the underlying stamps is a simple coincidence."

First-day Facts

The Washington stamp in both formats, the 21¢ Bison stamp in both formats, the 55¢ Art Deco Eagle stamp and the 70¢ Badlands postal card were issued February 22 in Wall, South Dakota, and were placed on sale nationally the next day. For details on the event, see the chapter on the Bison stamp varieties.

21¢ BISON
PANE OF 20

Date of Issue: February 22, 2001

Catalog Number: Scott 3468

Colors: yellow, magenta, cyan, purple

First-Day Cancel: Wall, South Dakota

First-Day Cancellations: 90,746 (includes all varieties of 21¢ Bison and 23¢ George Washington, 55¢ Art Deco Eagle and 70¢ Badlands postal card)

Format: Pane of 20 stamps, vertical, 4 across, 5 down. Gravure printing cylinders printing 200 subjects per press sheet (2 panes by 5 panes)

Gum Type: self-adhesive

Overall Stamp Size: 0.870 by 0.982 inches (22.098 by 24.943mm)

Pane Size: 4.350 by 5.875 inches (110.490 by 149.225mm)

Perforations: 11 (die-cut simulated perforations) (Comco Commander rotary die cutter)

Selvage Markings: "©2000/USPS." ".21 x 20/= $4.20." "PLATE/POSITION" and diagram. Universal Product Code (UPC) "101100" in 2 locations.

Illustrator: Tom Nikosey of Bell Canyon, California

Designer, Art Director and Typographer: Carl Herrman of Carlsbad, California

Stamp Manufacturing: Stamps printed by Avery Dennison Security Printing Division, Clinton, South Carolina, on Dia Nippon Kiko gravure press. Stamps finished by Avery Dennison.

Quantity Ordered: 200,000,000

Cylinder Number Detail: 1 set of 4 cylinder numbers preceded by the letter V in selvage next to each corner stamp

Cylinder Number Combinations Reported: V1111, V1112, V2222

Paper Supplier: Fasson Division of Avery Dennison

Tagging: phosphored paper

21¢ BISON
COIL OF 100

Date of Issue: February 22, 2001

Catalog Number: Scott 3475

Colors: yellow, magenta, cyan, purple

First-Day Cancel: Wall, South Dakota

First-Day Cancellations: 90,746 (includes all varieties of 21¢ Bison and 23¢ George Washington, 55¢ Art Deco Eagle and 70¢ Badlands postal card)

Format: Coil of 100 stamps, vertical. Gravure printing cylinders printing 385 subjects per revolution (11 across, 35 around).

Gum Type: self-adhesive

Overall Stamp Size: 0.870 by 0.982 inches (22.098 by 24.943mm)

Perforations: 8½ (die-cut simulated perforations) (Comco Commander rotary die cutter)

Illustrator: Tom Nikosey of Bell Canyon, California

Designer, Art Director and Typographer: Carl Herrman of Carlsbad, California

Stamp Manufacturing: Stamps printed by Avery Dennison Security Printing Division, Clinton, South Carolina, on Dia Nippon Kiko gravure press. Stamps finished by Avery Dennison.

Quantity Ordered: 600,000,000

Cylinder Number Detail: 1 set of 4 cylinder numbers preceded by the letter V on every 5th stamp

Cylinder Number Combinations Reported: V1111, V2222

Paper Supplier: Fasson Division of Avery Dennison

Tagging: phosphored paper

21¢ BISON
PANE OF 100

Date of Issue: September 20, 2001

Catalog Number: Scott 3467

Colors: black, cyan, magenta, yellow, orange (PMS 152), purple (PMS 269)

First-Day Cancel: Washington, D.C.

First-Day Cancellations: 82,371 (includes all varieties of 21¢ Bison, 23¢ George Washington and 21¢ White Barn postal card, and 57¢ Art Deco Eagle)

Format: Pane of 100 stamps, vertical, 10 across, 10 down. Offset printing plates printing 400 subjects per revolution (20 across, 20 around).

Gum Type: water-activated

Overall Stamp Size: 0.84 by 0.99 inches (21.336 by 25.146mm)

Pane Size: 9.00 by 10.18 inches (228.6 by 258.57mm)

Perforations: 11¼ (Wista stroke perforator)

Selvage Markings: "©2000 USPS." ".21 x 100 = $21.00." "PLATE/POSITION" and diagram. Universal Product Code (UPC) "102100."

Illustrator: Tom Nikosey of Bell Canyon, California

Designer, Art Director and Typographer: Carl Herrman of Carlsbad, California

Modeler: Joseph Sheeran of Ashton-Potter (USA) Ltd., Williamsville, New York

Stamp Manufacturing: Stamps printed for Ashton-Potter by Sterling Sommer, Tonawanda, New York, on Heidelberg 840 offset press. Stamps finished by Ashton-Potter.

Quantity Ordered: 25,000,000

Plate Number Detail: 1 set of 6 plate numbers preceded by the letter P in selvage next to 1 corner stamp

Plate Number Combination Reported: P111111

Paper Supplier: Tullis Russell

Tagging: phosphored paper

21¢ BISON
CONVERTIBLE BOOKLET OF 10

 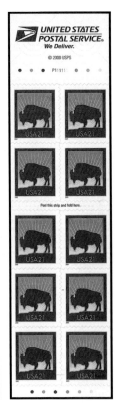

Date of Issue: September 20, 2001

Catalog Numbers: Scott 3484, single stamp, die cut perf 11¼; 3484A, single stamp, die cut perf 10½ by 11¼; 3484b, booklet pane of 4 3484; 3484c, booklet pane of 6 3484; 3484d, booklet pane of 10 3484; 3484Ae, booklet pane of 4, 2 3484 at left, 2 3484A at right; 3484Af, booklet pane of 6, 3 3484 at left, 3 3484A at right; 3484Ag, booklet pane of 10, 5 3484 at left, 5 3484A at right; 3484Ah, booklet pane of 4, 2 3484A at left, 2 3484 at right; 3484Ai, booklet pane of 6, 3 3484A at left, 3 3484 at right; 3484Aj, booklet pane of 10, 5 3484A at left, 5 3484 at right; 3484Ak, pair, 3484 at left, 3484A at right; 3484Al, pair, 3484A at left, 3484 at right.

Colors: black, orange (PMS 152), purple (PMS 369), cyan, magenta, yellow. Same colors for outside cover.

First-Day Cancel: Washington, D.C.

First-Day Cancellations: 82,371 (includes all varieties of 21¢ Bison, 23¢ George Washington and 21¢ White Barn postal card, and 57¢ Art Deco Eagle)

Format: Convertible booklet pane of 10, vertical, 2 across, 10 down, with horizontal peel-off strip covering roulettes between second and third horizontal row. Offset printing plates of 360 subjects, 15 across, 24 around.

Gum Type: self-adhesive

Overall Stamp Size: 0.875 by 0.982 inches; 22.225 by 24.942mm

Pane Size: 1.75 by 6.50 inches; 44.45 by 165.10mm

Perforations: 10½ by 11¼ or 11¼ (die-cut simulated perforations) (Arpeco custom stroke die-cutter). Two bull's-eye die cuts in top selvage.

Selvage Markings: USPS logo, "© 2000 USPS" and plate number in top selvage. "Peel this strip and fold here" on horizontal peel-off strip.

Back Markings: "BISON/Ten 21 cent/Self-adhesive/Stamps/$2.10" on front cover. Promotion for Postal Service web site, "© 2000 USPS" and Universal Product Code (UPC) "0 662800 2" on back cover.

Illustrator: Tom Nikosey of Bell Canyon, California

Designer, Art Director and Typographer: Carl Herrman of Carlsbad, California

Modeler: Joseph Sheeran of Ashton-Potter (USA) Ltd., Williamsville, New York

Stamp Manufacturing: Stamps printed by Ashton-Potter on offset portion of Stevens Variable Size Security Documents webfed 6-color offset, 3-color intaglio press. Stamps finished by Ashton-Potter.

Quantity Ordered: 300,000,000 stamps

Plate Number Detail: 1 set of 6 plate numbers preceded by the letter P on top selvage

Plate Number Combinations Reported: P111111, P222222, P333333

Paper Supplier: Fasson/Glatfelter

Tagging: phosphored paper

21¢ BISON
VENDING BOOKLET OF 10

 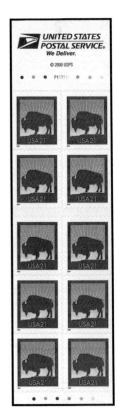

Date of Issue: September 20, 2001

Catalog Numbers: Scott 3484, single stamp, die-cut perf 11¼; 3484A, single stamp, die-cut perf 10½ by 11¼; 3484b, booklet pane of 4 3484; 3484c, booklet pane of 6 3484; 3484d, booklet pane of 10 3484; 3484Ae, booklet pane of 4, 2 3484 at left, 2 3484A at right; 3484Af, booklet pane of 6, 3 3484 at left, 3 3484A at right; 3484Ag, booklet pane of 10, 5 3484 at left, 5 3484A at right; 3484Ah, booklet pane of 4, 2 3484A at left, 2 3484 at right; 3484Ai, booklet pane of 6, 3 3484A at left, 3 3484 at right; 3484Aj, booklet pane of 10, 5 3484A at left, 5 3484 at right; 3484Ak, pair, 3484 at left, 3484A at right; 3484Al, pair, 3484A at left, 3484 at right.

Colors: black, orange (PMS 152), purple (PMS 369), cyan, magenta, yellow. Same colors for outside cover.

First-Day Cancel: Washington, D.C.

First-Day Cancellations: 82,371 (includes all varieties of 21¢ Bison, 23¢ George Washington and 21¢ White Barn postal card, and 57¢ Art Deco Eagle)

Format: Vending booklet pane of 10, vertical, 2 across, 10 down, with space and roulettes between second and third horizontal row where booklet is folded. Offset printing plates of 360 subjects, 15 across, 24 around.

Gum Type: self-adhesive

Overall Stamp Size: 0.875 by 0.982 inches; 22.225 by 24.942mm

Pane Size: 1.75 by 6.50 inches; 44.45 by 165.10mm

Perforations: 10½ by 11¼ or 11¼ (die-cut simulated perforations) (Arpeco custom stroke die cutter). Two bull's-eye die cuts in top selvage.

Selvage Markings: USPS logo, "© 2000 USPS" and plate number in top selvage.

Back Markings: "BISON/Ten 21 cent/Self-adhesive/Stamps/$2.10" on front cover. Promotion for Postal Service web site, "© 2000 USPS" and Universal Product Code (UPC) "0 662900 1" on back cover.

Illustrator: Tom Nikosey of Bell Canyon, California

Designer, Art Director and Typographer: Carl Herrman of Carlsbad, California

Modeler: Joseph Sheeran of Ashton-Potter (USA) Ltd., Williamsville, New York

Stamp Manufacturing: Stamps printed by Ashton-Potter on offset portion of Stevens Variable Size Security Documents webfed 6-color offset, 3-color intaglio press. Stamps finished by Ashton-Potter.

Quantity Ordered: 80,500,000 stamps

Plate Number Detail: 1 set of 6 plate numbers preceded by the letter P on top selvage

Plate Number Combinations Reported: P111111, P222222, P333333

Paper Supplier: Fasson/Glatfelter

Tagging: phosphored paper

The Stamp

On February 22, the Postal Service issued a 21¢ definitive stamp depicting a bison in silhouette. The stamp came in two formats, a pane of 20 and a coil of 100, both self-adhesive.

Its denomination covered the rate that had gone into effect the preceding January 7 for each additional ounce of first-class mail after the first ounce. No stocks of 21¢ stamps existed at the time; the most recent stamp of that denomination had been the Chester Carlson Great Americans definitive of 1988.

A little more than four months later, on July 1, USPS increased the additional-ounce rate to 23¢, making the Bison stamp obsolete for that purpose. However, on the same day, it raised the postcard rate from 20¢ to 21¢, thus giving the stamp a new reason for being.

On September 20, the Bison was issued in three additional formats: pane of 100 and two booklets of 10, convertible and machine-vended.

Details on the stamp's five formats follow:

• Pane of 20, self-adhesive (Scott 3468). It was printed by gravure by Avery Dennison Security Printing Division in four colors, yellow, magenta, cyan and purple, and has die-cut simulated perforations with a gauge of 11.

• Coil of 100, self-adhesive (Scott 3475). Like the first one, it was gravure-printed by Avery Dennison in yellow, magenta, cyan and purple, and has gauge 8½ die-cut simulated perfs. It is the first small-roll, self-adhesive coil stamp to be produced by Avery Dennison. Stamps abut each other on the roll, and no backing paper shows from the front. Cylinder numbers are found on every fifth stamp, resulting in an unusually large number of PNCs (plate number coil stamps). According to dealer-specialist Stephen G. Esrati, Avery Dennison explained that five was the only interval it could devise for the rows of 35 stamps around the printing cylinders.

Soon after the coil stamp was issued, collectors discovered that some rolls displayed a large nine-digit number printed at 35-stamp intervals on the backing paper of two or three adjacent stamps. The number is printed by black dot matrix, usually has one or more leading zeros and is always inverted in relation to the stamp face. Its value increases by one with each appearance and, because of the 35-stamp spacing, it can be found no more than three times in a roll of 100.

"This number serves as an internal accounting device," Alan Thomson wrote in the *United States Specialist* (June 2001). "It is not just a record of cylinder impressions per se. Avery is using it as a waste control and to track the quantity of stamps processed and shipped.

"The number is applied only to the bottom [11th] row in the web and starts at zero when the first run of the design is printed. The value of the number at the beginning of subsequent runs picks up where the last run stopped. Lower numbers come from earlier runs ...

"Plate number strips with this back number carry a premium in the current market."

• Pane of 100, water-activated gum (Scott 3467). This stamp was printed for Ashton-Potter (USA) Ltd. by Sterling Summer on a Heidelberg 840 offset press, using the four standard process colors, black, cyan, magenta and yellow, plus orange (PMS 152) and purple (PMS 269). Because USPS considers offset printing less secure than gravure, the design includes the microprinted letters "USPS" in black on the orange outline of the bison's rear hoof.

A new type of control number appears on the back of the liner paper at 35-stamp intervals on every 11th roll of Bison coil stamps.

• Convertible booklet of 10, self-adhesive. This time, Ashton-Potter itself was the printer, also using the offset method (but with a Stevens Varisize Security Press) and the same colors that are on the pane of 100. The microprinting is in the same location, as well. Each stamp has a straight edge on either the left or right side. The pane is sold flat, with a horizontal strip between the second and third horizontal pairs of stamps that can be peeled off to allow it to be folded into booklet form.

• Vending booklet of 10, self-adhesive. The printer, the printing method, the colors and the microprinting are the same as those of the convertible booklet, and the two kinds of booklet are identical in appearance except that the vending booklet has no horizontal peel-off strip and comes already folded.

Like the 20¢ George Washington stamp issued on the same day, also in two 10-stamp booklet formats that were produced by Ashton-Potter, the stamps from the two Bison booklets come in two different gauges of die-cut simulated perforations (which USPS hadn't announced and in fact hadn't known about.)

Some specimens were found with horizontal "perfs" measuring 11¼, the same gauge as the vertical perfs, while others have horizontal perfs measuring 10½. In some cases, these two varieties coexist in the same booklet, while other booklets contain only the all-perf 11¼ variety. Scott assigned the number 3484 to the all-perf 11¼ stamp and 3484A to the 11¼ by 10½.

In the case of the 20¢ George Washington, a mint or used single stamp from a convertible booklet can be distinguished from a single stamp from a vending booklet because the horizontal die-cutting between two adjacent stamps on a pane has a transition, or separator, that slopes in different directions on the two types of booklet (see chapter on the George Washington stamps). However, no such transition difference exists in the Bison booklets, meaning that stamps from the two formats are indistinguishable once they have been removed from the backing paper.

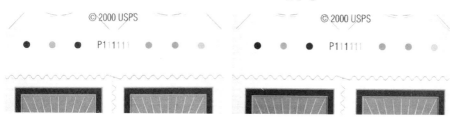

Close-up images of the top row of two stamps from a Bison convertible booklet, left, and vending booklet, right. Each booklet displays both of the two die-cut gauge varieties of the Bison stamp. The convertible booklet has an 11¼-gauge stamp on the left and a 10½-gauge stamp on the right; on the vending booklet, the two varieties are reversed. Note that the transition in the horizontal die-cutting between the paired stamps in each format slopes down from left to right, making it impossible to tell which format a single stamp came from after it has been separated from its backing paper.

The Design

A continuing assignment for the Postal Service's art directors is to come up with "American" subjects and themes that haven't been overused and turn them into designs for definitive and bulk-rate stamps. One such subject was the bison, or American buffalo, and illustrator Tom Nikosey developed the Bison stamp design under the art direction of Carl Herrman.

Nikosey's graphic design credits include the logos for several Super Bowls, the Grammy Awards and Tony Awards, the San Diego Padres baseball team and several musical groups. For USPS, he illustrated and designed the four Holiday Deer stamps of 1999 that reappeared as picture postal cards in 2000.

"I chose Tom because he does these bold logolike creations that hold up nicely at stamp size," Herrman said.

Nikosey's inspiration for the Bison illustration was the herd of buffaloes on Catalina Island, some 26 miles off the coast of Southern California. "They brought bisons to Catalina to film a movie back in the 1920s and left them there," Herrman said. "The herd survived, because two-thirds of the island is an ecological preserve. For some reason, Tom was thinking of the Catalina buffaloes when he came up with this design."

Nikosey, who uses a computer to create his artwork, drew a "three-legged bison" (one of its forelegs is concealed behind the other one), facing left, in a stance similar to that of the animal on the old buffalo nickel. The bison is completely dark except for the horn facing the viewer, which is white, and stands on an irregular hilltop.

In one of his early treatments, Nikosey showed the animal against a solid dark blue sky with a crescent moon in the upper-right corner. In his final version, the background is a rising or setting sun with yellow rays radiating to the edges of the design. The bison, hilltop and a wide frameline are purple, outlined in orange. "USA 21," in light blue Futura medium type, is at the bottom.

"It was a very simple, clean design, but everybody loved it," Herrman said. "It had an easy ride through the [Citizens' Stamp Advisory] Committee. And it reproduced magnificently."

First-Day Facts

The first two formats of the 21¢ Bison stamp, along with the 20¢ George Washington varieties, the 55¢ Art Deco Eagle stamp and the 70¢ Badlands postal card, had their first-day sale in Wall, South Dakota February 22. They were placed on nationwide sale the next day.

No official USPS dedication ceremony was held, but local and district postal officials organized an event. Pete Dunker, Wall's postmaster, was master of ceremonies and oversaw the first-day cancellation operation. Other participants included Dave Hahn, mayor of Wall; William P. Supernaugh Jr., superintendent of Badlands National Park; and schoolchildren from Wounded Knee High School in Kyle, South Dakota.

This early version shows the bison against a dark blue sky with a crescent moon. The inscription indicates that the design was under consideration for a nondenominated bulk-rate stamp.

At one point, the bison design was considered for use as a nondenominated first-class rate stamp during a future rate-change transition. The typeface is Franklin condensed.

The microprinted letters "USPS" can be found in the same location on stamps from the pane of 100 and the convertible and vending booklets of 10: in the orange outline of the bison's rear hoof.

The stamps and card originally were scheduled for release February 21 in Interior, a tiny town of fewer than 70 residents near the national park headquarters. But the date and location were changed because of staffing considerations, USPS said. "The Interior post office is basically a one-person operation," explained Postal Service spokesman Don Smeraldi.

When the ceremony was moved to Wall, a somewhat larger community some 30 miles away on the north side of the national park, the place chosen was the dining room of the Wall Drug Store, a well-known stopping place for tourists since 1931. But that plan, too, was changed because of space considerations, and the event was moved across the street to the Wall Community Center. "We were a bit uncertain as to how many people might attend the ceremony," Postmaster Dunker told *Linn's Stamp News*, "so we wanted to be sure we would have enough room."

When the three additional formats of the 21¢ Bison stamp were placed on sale September 20, no first-day ceremony was held. The official first-day cancellation was Washington, D.C.

55¢ ART DECO EAGLE

Date of Issue: February 22, 2001

Catalog Number: Scott 3471

Colors: magenta, yellow, cyan, process black, black

First-Day Cancel: Wall, South Dakota

First-Day Cancellations: 90,746 (includes all varieties of 20¢ George Washington and 21¢ Bison, and 70¢ Badlands postal card)

Format: Pane of 20, vertical, 5 across by 4 down. Gravure printing cylinders printing 120 stamps per revolution manufactured by Southern Graphic Systems.

Gum Type: self-adhesive

Overall Stamp Size: 0.84 by 0.99 inches; 21.33 by 25.14mm

Pane Size: 4.96 by 5.04 inches; 125.98 by 128.01mm

Perforations: 10¾ (die-cut simulated perforations) (Comco custom rotary die cutter)

Selvage Markings: "©2000/USPS." ".55/x20/$11.00." "PLATE/POSITION" and diagram. Universal Product Code (UPC) "101200" in 2 locations.

Illustrator: Nancy Stahl of New York, New York

Designer, Art Director and Typographer: Carl Herrman of Carlsbad, California

Modeler: Donald Woo of Sennett Security Products of Chantilly, Virginia

Stamp Manufacturing: Stamps printed for Sennett Security Products by American Packaging Corp. of Columbus, Wisconsin, on Rotomec 3000 gravure press. Stamps finished by Unique Binders of Fredericksburg, Virginia.

Quantity Ordered: 100,000,000 stamps

Cylinder Number Detail: 1 set of 5 cylinder numbers preceded by the letter S in selvage above or below each corner stamp

Cylinder Number Combination Reported: S11111

Paper Supplier: Paper Corporation of the United States/Spinnaker Coating

Tagging: phosphored paper

57¢ ART DECO EAGLE

Date of Issue: September 20, 2001

Catalog Number: Scott 3472

Colors: magenta, yellow, cyan, process black, black

First-Day Cancel: Washington, D.C.

First-Day Cancellations: 82,371 (includes all varieties of 21¢ Bison, 23¢ George Washington and 21¢ White Barn postal card)

Format: Pane of 20, vertical, 5 across by 4 down. Gravure printing cylinders printing 320 stamps per revolution (20 across, 16 around) manufactured by Southern Graphic Systems.

Gum Type: self-adhesive

Overall Stamp Size: 0.84 by 0.99 inches; 21.33 by 25.14mm

Pane Size: 4.96 by 5.04 inches; 125.98 by 128.01mm

Perforations: 10¾ (die-cut simulated perforations) (Comco custom rotary die cutter)

Selvage Markings: "©2001/USPS." ".57/x20/$11.40." "PLATE/POSITION" and diagram. Universal Product Code (UPC) "105800" in 2 locations.

Illustrator: Nancy Stahl of New York, New York

Designer, Art Director and Typographer: Carl Herrman of Carlsbad, California

Modeler: Donald Woo of Sennett Security Products of Chantilly, Virginia

Stamp Manufacturing: Stamps printed for Sennett Security Products by American Packaging Corp. of Columbus, Wisconsin, on Rotomec 3000 gravure press. Stamps finished by Unique Binders of Fredericksburg, Virginia.

Quantity Ordered: 100,000,000 stamps

Cylinder Number Detail: 1 set of 5 cylinder numbers preceded by the letter S in selvage above or below each corner stamp

Cylinder Number Combination Reported: S11111

Paper Supplier: Paper Corporation of the United States/Spinnaker Coating

Tagging: phosphored paper

The Stamps

On February 22, the Postal Service issued a 55¢ self-adhesive stamp to cover the rate for a first-class letter weighing between one and two ounces. The stamp depicted a sculpted eagle in the Art Deco style.

Although USPS billed the stamp as a rate-change item, the two ounce letter rate hadn't changed. In fact, it had remained at 55¢ through two increases in the basic first-class rate. The reason was that when the basic rate went up by a penny, on January 10, 1999, and did so again (to 34¢) on January 7, 2001, the rate for an additional ounce was reduced each time by the same amount.

However, in a little more than four months after the Art Deco Eagle stamp was issued, the two-ounce letter rate did change. On July 1, USPS increased the rate for each additional ounce after the first ounce from 21¢ to 23¢. This resulted in an increase to 57¢ of the cost of mailing a letter weighing between one and two ounces.

On July 10, USPS announced that it would meet the need for a new two-ounce rate stamp by issuing a 57¢ definitive with the same Art Deco Eagle design that had been on the 55¢, but in a different color. The stamp was issued September 20.

Both stamps were printed by the gravure process by American Packaging Corporation for Sennett Security Products and distributed in panes of 20.

The Design

Terrence McCaffrey, manager of stamp development for USPS, had asked his art directors to develop designs for definitive stamps with patriotic themes. In response, illustrator Nancy Stahl of New York City prepared the Art Deco eagle design under the supervision of art director Carl Herrman. Herrman adapted the design for various postal uses before it was decided to give it a first-class mail denomination.

The 55¢ stamp, printed in warm oranges and yellows suggestive of gold, shows a highly stylized, angular eagle, its wings spread, head turned to the left and claws gripping a perch of horizontal parallel lines, with a triangular shield over its breast.

Stahl previously had illustrated the nondenominated coil stamp of 2000 that depicts one of the two stone lions outside the New York Public Library. She found her inspiration for her new assignment in another piece of New York City sculpture. Her computer-created artwork was based on a photograph she took of an eagle on a mailbox in the lobby of the Chanin Building on East 42nd Street near Grand Central Terminal.

The Chanin Building, at 56 stories and 649 feet in height, was the third

This is the full illustration that Nancy Stahl based on sculptor Rene Chambellan's art deco eagle decoration for a mailbox in the lobby of New York City's Chanin Building. It includes details that art director Carl Herrman wanted to show in the stamp design, including a sealed envelope beneath the eagle's perch. However, Herrman had to crop the image tightly around the eagle to make the image effective at the small size of a definitive stamp.

Herrman included a large part of Stahl's full illustration in this layout for a nondenominated first-class presort stamp, but it was felt that the treatment didn't do justice to the center figure, the eagle.

Presorted First-Class

tallest building in the world when it was completed in 1930. Designed by Sloan and Robertson, it was built by Irwin S. Chanin, a major New York developer in the 1920s. The lobby, a showplace of the art deco style, was designed by set designer Jacques Delamarre, while sculptor Rene Chambellan created the floor and screens of gilded bronze, the elevator doors and mailboxes, including the one that commanded Nancy Stahl's attention. Its eagle is surrounded by dramatic three-dimensional shapes, including triangles, circles and lightning bolts, and the function of the mailbox is evoked by a sealed envelope beneath the bird's talons.

"The envelope formed beautiful diagonal lines," Herrman said. "I really wanted to get it into the design because it had such a nice connection to being on a stamp. But we found that we had to crop the image so that it would hold up when reduced to stamp size, and so, unfortunately, we had to give up the envelope. We were left with a panel just above it, and I put the USA and denomination there.

"The complete image had so many good things in it! If the stamp had been a commemorative, and we could have designed it as a semijumbo, it would have been magnificent. But it was a definitive, so we had to keep cropping tighter and tighter. We did keep the essence of it, which was a really neat eagle."

For the USA and denomination, Herrman chose an unusual typeface called Gabriel that was compatible with the design's art deco theme.

When officials decided to repeat the design on a 57¢ stamp, the predominant color chosen for the new version was a bluish-green. Unlike the gold tones of the original, the green had no logical connection to the stamp's subject matter.

First-Day Facts

For information on the first-day sale of the 55¢ Art Deco stamp at Wall, South Dakota, February 22, see the chapter on the 21¢ Bison stamps.

No first-day ceremony was held September 20 for the 57¢ Art Deco Eagle stamp. The first-day postmark was Washington, D.C.

34¢ OFFICIAL MAIL COIL STAMP

Date of Issue: February 27, 2001

Catalog Number: Scott O158

Colors: red, blue, black

First-Day Cancel: Washington, D.C.

First-Day Cancellations: 26,675 (includes Official Mail stamped envelope)

Format: Coils of 100, vertical. Offset printing plates of 432 subjects (18 across, 24 around).

Gum Type: water-activated

Overall Stamp Size: 0.99 by 0.84 inches; 25.14 by 21.33mm

Perforations: 9¾ (stroke perforator)

Designer and Typographer: Bradbury Thompson

Art Director: Joe Brockert, USPS

Modeler: John Murray of the Bureau of Engraving and Printing

Stamp Manufacturing: Stamps printed by BEP, Washington, D.C., on Optiforma offset press. Stamps processed by BEP.

Quantity Ordered and Distributed: 5,000,000

Plate Number Detail: no plate number

Tagging: phosphored paper

The Stamp

On February 27, USPS issued a 34¢ Official Mail coil stamp for use by authorized federal agencies to carry government correspondence. The stamp, offset printed by the Bureau of Engraving and Printing and produced in rolls of 100, has water-activated gum and conventional perforations.

272

Official Mail stamps and envelopes have been used since 1983 as a means of holding federal agencies accountable for their exact postage use. The new stamp and a 34¢ Official Mail stamped envelope released the same day (see separate chapter) were issued despite reports in 1997 and 1999 that the Official Mail program in the United States was about to be replaced by a new system that would eliminate Official Mail stamps and postal stationery.

The Federal Postal Payment Card was being developed for use by federal agencies to obtain regular postage stamps at local post offices in lieu of Official Mail stamps.

Problems with the FPPC program delayed a planned implementation in January 1999 and additional snags continued to keep the program on hold.

In the February 26, 2001, issue of *Linn's Stamp News*, writer Michael Baadke reported that Tom Dale, manager of the USPS Official Mail program, told *Linn's* that the FPPC is still being tested but that full development has been pushed back indefinitely.

"This delay has caused us to continue the existing penalty mail stamp program until either the card is adopted or an alternative process is put into place," Dale told *Linn's*.

Like all Official Mail stamps since 1985, this stamp has no plate numbers. When the no-number practice was instituted, W.L. (Pete) Davidson, director of stamps and philatelic marketing for USPS, explained the reason:

"Because Official stamps cannot be used by regular mailers and collectors, the Postal Service waived the minimum purchase requirements that usually apply. When collectors purchased plate blocks or plate-number coils, a large amount of broken panes and coil strips resulted. Elimination of plate numbers ... represents an effort to reduce the waste and destruction caused by this situation."

The Design

The stamp's design is basically the one developed by Bradbury Thompson, the late longtime design coordinator and typographer for USPS. It was first used on Official Mail stamps in 1983. The design features a modified Great Seal of the United States in drop-out white against a blue rectangular background. The words "Official Mail USA" and "Penalty for Private Use $300" appear in red across the top and bottom of the stamp, respectively. The denomination, "34," is printed in black and centered beneath the vignette. The tiny year date "2001" also is in black and is located in the lower-left corner.

Like other recent offset-printed U.S. Official Mail stamps, this one incorporates in its design a line of microprinted blue type directly below the Great Seal vignette. The line consists of the inscription "USA2001" repeated 10 times.

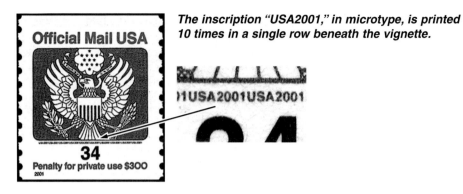

The inscription "USA2001," in microtype, is printed 10 times in a single row beneath the vignette.

First-day Facts

No first-day ceremony was held for the Official Mail stamp or stamped envelope. First-day covers of the stamp bear a Washington, D.C., postmark. For a limited time, Stamp Fulfillment Services offered uncacheted first-day covers for sale at 52¢ each.

34¢ APPLE AND ORANGE (2 DESIGNS)
CONVERTIBLE BOOKLET OF 20

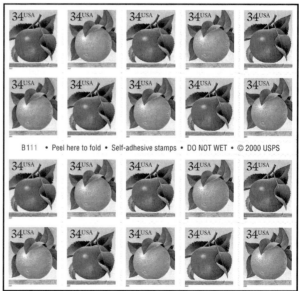

Date of Issue: March 6, 2001

Catalog Numbers: Scott 3491-3492, single stamps; 3492a, pair; 3492b, pane of 20

Colors: black, cyan, magenta, yellow

First-Day Cancel: Lincoln, Nebraska

First-Day Cancellations: 72,407 (includes 70¢ Nine Mile Prairie and 34¢ Flag Over Farm pane of 20)

Format: Convertible booklet pane of 20, vertical, 5 across, 4 down, with horizontal peel-off strip between horizontal rows 2 and 3. Offset printing plates of 500 subjects (25 across, 20 around).

Gum Type: self-adhesive

Overall Stamp Size: 0.72 by 0.83 inches; 18.29 by 21.08mm

Pane Size: 4.35 by 4.13 inches; 110.49 by 104.90mm

Perforations: 11¼ (die-cut simulated perforations) (rotary die-cutter). Rouletting under peel-off strip.

Selvage Markings: plate numbers and " • Peel here to fold • Self-adhesive stamps • DO NOT WET • © 2000 USPS" on peel-off strip

Back Markings: "Apple & Orange/Twenty 34-cent First-Class/Self-adhesive/ Stamps/2/different/stamp designs/$6.80." Promotion for www.stamps-online.com web site. "© 2000 USPS." Universal Product Code (UPC) "0 669600 3."

Illustrator and Designer: Ned Seidler of Hampton Bays, New York

Art Director and Typographer: Howard Paine of Delaplane, Virginia

Stamp Manufacturing: Stamps printed by Banknote Corporation of America, Browns Summit, North Carolina, on Goebel 670 offset press. Stamps finished by BCA.

Quantity Ordered: 3,000,000,000 stamps

Plate Number Detail: 1 set of 4 plate numbers preceded by the letter B on peel-off strip.

Plate Number Combinations Reported: B1111, B2222, B3333, B4444, B5555, B6666, B7777

Paper Supplier: Paper Corporation of the United States/Spinnaker Coatings

Tagging: phosphored paper

34¢ APPLE AND ORANGE (2 DESIGNS)
VENDING BOOKLET OF 20

Date of Issue: late April 2001

Catalog Numbers: Scott 3493-3494, single stamps; 3494a, pair; 3494b, booklet pane of 4, with or without plate number single; 3494c, booklet pane of 6, 3493 at upper left; 3494d, booklet pane of 6, 3494 at upper left

Colors: black, cyan, magenta, yellow

First-Day Cancel: none

First-Day Cancellations: none

Format: vending booklet of 20, vertical, 2 across, 10 down, with stamps arranged in blocks of 4, 6, 6 and 4, with horizontal peel-off strips between horizontal rows 2 and 3, 5 and 6, and 8 and 9. Offset printing plates of 480 subjects (24 across, 20 around).

Gum Type: self-adhesive

Overall Stamp Size: 0.87 by 0.98 inches; 22.10 by 24.89mm

Pane Size: 1.74 by 10.98 inches; 44.20 by 278.89mm

Perforations: 11½ by 10¾ (die-cut simulated perforations)

Selvage Markings: On first and third peel-off strips: "Peel here to fold • Self-adhesive stamps • DO NOT WET." On second peel-off strip: "© 2000 USPS • Peel here to fold • Self-adhesive stamps • DO NOT WET."

Back Markings: "Apple & Orange/Twenty 34 cent/Self-adhesive/Stamps/ $6.80/2/different/stamp designs." USPS logo. Promotion for www.stamps-online.com web site. "© 2000 USPS." Universal Product Code (UPC) "0 669700 3."

Illustrator and Designer: Ned Seidler of Hampton Bay, New York

Art Director and Typographer: Howard Paine of Delaplane, Virginia

Stamp Manufacturing: Stamps printed by Banknote Corporation of America, Browns Summit, North Carolina, on Goebel 670 offset press. Stamps finished by BCA.

Quantity Ordered: 201,000,000 stamps

Plate Number Detail: 1 set of 4 plate numbers preceded by the letter B on bottom-left stamp of pane

Plate Number Combination Reported: B1111

Paper Supplier: Paper Corporation of the United States/International Paper (face paper)/Glatfelter (liner)/Spinnaker Coatings (converting)

Tagging: phosphored paper

The Stamp

USPS issued a se-tenant pair of 34¢ definitive stamps March 6, one depicting a bright red apple, the other a ripe orange.

The stamps were issued in a pane (convertible booklet) of 20 stamps (Scott 3491-92). The vertical stamps are arranged horizontally four down by five across, separated by a horizontal peel-off strip between the second and third rows. When the peel-off strip is removed, the pane can be folded into a compact booklet, with the imprinted liner paper serving as the cover. To facilitate folding, the backing paper is scored with dashlike cuts that penetrate the peel-off strip. Most collectors keep these panes intact and store them flat.

The Postal Service's initial order called for 3 billion Apple and Orange stamps. The self-adhesive stamps were printed by offset lithography by Banknote Corporation of America, Browns Summit, North Carolina.

In late April, without any announcement, the Postal Service issued a vending booklet of 20 of the Apple and Orange stamps. Again, the stamps

carried a denomination of 34¢.

The new format went virtually unnoticed by collectors until a collector notified *Linn's Stamp News* that he had purchased a vending booklet (Scott 3493-94) in late May at a post office in Virginia.

Associate editor Charles Snee reported the discovery in the June 11, 2001, issue of *Linn's*. According to Snee, the booklet was purchased by Bob Derkits, a *Linn's* reader.

Derkits sent computer images of the booklet to *Linn's*. Snee reported that *Linn's* contacted the Postal Service about the heretofore unknown new format for these stamps, "only to learn that the Postal Service itself initially was unaware that the booklet had reached at least one collector's hands."

USPS spokesman Don Smeraldi told *Linn's* at the time, "The technical specifications we have say that the Apple and Orange stamps were issued March 6 in one format — a convertible booklet [flat] pane of 20."

Linn's also spoke with BCA, which confirmed that the printer had produced the Apple and Orange vending booklet at the request of USPS. A BCA spokesman told *Linn's*, "We've been shipping Apple and Orange vending booklets for about a month now."

According to Snee, Smeraldi later told *Linn's* that USPS had ordered 201 million stamps (10.05 million vending booklets) from BCA.

"The vending booklets were shipped from BCA to our stamp distribution offices, beginning April 23. Sales at some post offices started some time after that," Smeraldi said. He added, "Shipments are almost 50 percent complete and more will go out to the SDOs on July 30."

When the vending booklet is opened, it reveals a pane of 20, two across by 10 down, with the stamps separated into groups of four by three peel-off selvage strips. From top to bottom, the groups consist of four stamps, six stamps, six stamps and four stamps.

The format is similar to the vending booklet of 20 of the 34¢ Rose and Love Letter stamp issued February 14 and also printed by BCA.

The bottom-left stamp (an Orange stamp) bears plate number B1111 in the bottom-right corner. The "B" prefix denotes BCA as the printer.

In the July 23, 2001, issue of *Linn's*, Snee explained how to distinguish a single stamp from the convertible booklet from a single stamp from the vending booklet. Six of the 20 stamps from a flat pane have die-cut simulated perforations all around. The other 14 stamps have die cuts on two sides or three sides, depending on their positions in the pane.

Stamps from the vending booklet have a single straightedge at left or right, except for the bottom two stamps, which have two straightedges.

Snee noted that a plate number is printed in the bottom-right corner of the bottom-left stamp only from the vending booklet. The plate number on the convertible booklet pane of 20 is found only on the selvage strip. "Thus, if you find an Orange stamp without a plate number that has straightedges at left and bottom, it came from a pane of 20," Snee said.

The die-cut gauge of stamps from the pane of 20 measures 11¼; the vending booklet, 11½ by 10¾.

Snee also pointed out that a quick visual check will aid in identification. On stamps from the convertible booklet pane, the top-left side ends with a peak, whereas on the vending booklet stamp, the top-left side ends with a valley.

The die-cut corners of a stamp from the convertible booklet appear more spadelike than those from the vending booklet. The straightedges appear smoother on the convertible booklet stamps.

Because USPS considers offset a less-secure printing, the stamps each contain a line of microprinting reading "USPS." The microprinting on both formats of the 34¢ Apple and 34¢ Orange stamps is relatively easy to spot. "USPS" appears just to the right and near the bottom of the large, upturned leaf on the Orange stamp, and right above and slightly to the right of the top of the fruit on the Apple stamp.

Apple and Orange stamps from a pane of 20 differ in the gauge of their die-cut perforations from stamps from a vending booklet of 20, but the differences also can be distinguished visually. The 34¢ Apple stamp shown on the left is from a pane, while the one on the right is from a vending booklet. Both have straightedges along the right side, but the shapes of the die-cut corners of the two stamps are distinctly different. The corners of a stamp from a pane appear more spadelike than the corners of a stamp from a vending booklet.

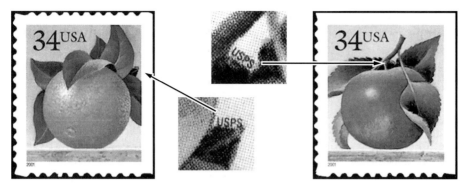

The microprinting on the Apple and Orange stamps consist of the letters "USPS" along the edges of leaves. The microprinting is on the right side on the Orange stamp and in the center between two stems on the Apple stamp.

The Design

The first stamp illustration created by Ned Seidler of Hampton Bays, New York, for USPS was of a person: Francis of Assisi, whose 20¢ commemorative was issued in 1982. Since then, however, Seidler has specialized in postal botany.

His gouache and watercolor paintings of garden flowers of the four seasons were reproduced on four five-stamp se-tenant booklet panes between 1993 and 1996. Definitives and special stamps displaying his art include the 29¢ African Violet (1993), the 32¢ American Holly (1997), the 33¢ Coral Pink Rose (1999) and the four 33¢ Fruit Berries (1999).

Seidler also created illustrations for two se-tenant 32¢ stamps showing a peach and a pear that were issued in 1995 in the form of a self-adhesive convertible booklet of 20, a self-adhesive coil of 5,000 and a conventional booklet of 20 with water-activated gum. These stamps were "colorful, neutral and message-free," as the art director, Howard Paine, put it, and Seidler was asked to provide two more paintings of the same type for future stamp use. These paintings became the Apple and Orange stamps.

Like the peach and pear stamps, the apple and orange are seen at eye level against a light blue background, sitting on a ledge in which the wood grain is slightly visible. The edge of the ledge is bluish green on the 1995 set, brown on this one. The apple is red with a tinge of green in the lower-left corner; the orange is of the navel variety. Green leaves garnish each fruit. Of the earlier pair, the peach and pear, Howard Paine said, "I love the way the leaves have a surreal look to them. They just wrap around the fruit like a cloak or a cape."

The inscription "34 USA" is in black Galliard type in the upper-left corner of each stamp.

Varieties

Specimens of the convertible booklet stamps were found with the black ink omitted, creating designs without the "34 USA" inscription.

A progressive block of 10 of the error (Scott 3492c) was offered in the September 5, 2002, mail sale of Nutmeg Mail Auctions.

A die-cut-missing error of the 34¢ Apple and 34¢ Orange stamps of 2001 was discovered in Washington state in spring 2002, *Linn's* learned in summer. Collector Bob Lodge told *Linn's* that he purchased four self-adhesive panes of 20 from the Wenatchee, Washington, post office that bear no die cuts between any of the stamps.

Linn's closely examined the pane under 30X magnification and detected no trace of die cutting anywhere on the front of the pane, according to associate editor Snee.

The printing on the back of the liner-release paper (side away from the stamps) appears normal, said Snee. The backing paper also bears traces of the normal scoring that makes a self-stick convertible pane of stamps easier to fold once the peel-off selvage strip is removed from the front of the pane.

On normal Apple and Orange panes of 20, the selvage strip runs horizontally through the middle of the pane.

Snee said, "The scoring on Lodge's pane strongly suggests that the roll of stamp paper, called a web, from which the pane originated went through normal printing and finishing processes at the printer. In other words, Lodge's pane most likely is not an example of printer's waste that somehow left the printer by other-than-normal means.

"The pane also is free of wrinkles, creases, stains or other marks (such as fingerprints), all of which are telltale signs of printer's waste."

Scott catalog editor James Kloetzel also scrutinized Lodge's pane and agreed that it is a legitimate major error.

The Apple and Orange die-cut-missing error pane is listed as 3492d in the 2003 Scott *Specialized Catalogue of United States Stamps and Covers*.

Lodge told *Linn's* that other die-cut-missing Apple and Orange panes were discovered at the Wenatchee post office about a year before he made his own find.

"The first error panes were found in March 2001," Lodge stated. "A friend of mine has a pane from that first find. I found out too late to acquire one. A few more panes showed up a little more than a year later. I didn't note the date, but it was sometime in spring 2002.

"I purchased four die-cut-missing panes, one of which had been folded by a postal patron who had brought the pane back to the post office because he could not peel the stamps from the pane."

Lodge decided to cut singles, pairs and strips of three from the folded pane. He then offered a pair of stamps from this pane on the Internet auction house eBay. The pair sold July 10 for $107.50. Seven different bidders placed a total of 12 bids.

Lodge also used on covers nine singles and one pair from the folded pane.

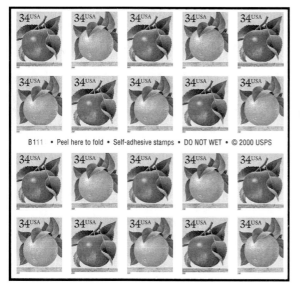

This pane of 20 34¢ Apple and 34¢ Orange stamps shows no evidence of die cutting. The new error is listed as 3492d in the 2003 Scott Specialized Catalogue of United States Stamps & Covers.

"I cut through the horizontal selvage between the second row and third row of stamps, yielding 10 stamps with selvage lettering in either the top margin or bottom margin," Lodge said. "All of the covers were made by gluing the stamps to their envelopes using an archival glue stick." Lodge said he did this because he was unable to separate the die-cut-missing stamps from their backing paper.

The stamp corner of one of Lodge's covers is shown nearby. Note the uneven margins around the Apple stamp and the partial lettering in the bottom margin. The lettering establishes that the stamp on this cover is the second stamp from the second row of stamps in the pane.

Lodge stated that he was aware of only a small number of die-cut-missing panes, in addition to the four in his possession.

"Based on my conversations with other local collectors," said Lodge, "my best estimate is that somewhere between 12 panes and 20 panes were sold, probably much closer to 12. This total includes the panes discovered in 2001 and in 2002, about a year apart."

An unusual inking freak was found on a convertible booklet pane of 20. On the freak pane, nearly all the magenta ink is missing from many of the stamps in the first four vertical rows. Some freak stamps seem to picture

Stamp corner of cover bearing a 34¢ Apple stamp that was cut from a die-cut-missing pane of 20 Apple and Orange stamps that was found in Washington state in spring 2002.

round lemons rather than oranges; others seem to picture Granny Smith apples rather than Red Delicious.

The pane was illustrated in the January 21, 2002, issue of *Linn's Stamp News* after being brought to the attention of the editors by stamp dealer and auctioneer Jacques C. Schiff. According to *Linn's*, the striking appearance of the offset-printed Apple and Orange stamps likely resulted because the metal plate that applied the magenta ink wore out. Another explanation could be a problem with the blanket cylinder or with the plate-making processes.

The article in *Linn's* explained, "Offset lithography, based on the principle that ink and water do not mix, uses one flexible metal plate for each ink. The inks are offset to secondary cylinders (blankets) that apply the inks to the paper."

First-day Facts

No official first-day ceremony was held for the Apple and Orange convertible booklet, which went on sale in Lincoln, Nebraska, March 6, or for the unannounced vending-booklet version, which made its appearance in late April.

70¢ NINE-MILE PRAIRIE
SCENIC AMERICAN LANDMARKS SERIES

Date of Issue: March 6, 2001

Catalog Number: Scott C136

Colors: black, cyan, magenta, yellow, metallic silver

First-Day Cancel: Lincoln, Nebraska

First-Day Cancellations: 72,407 (includes 34¢ Apple and Orange convertible booklet and 34¢ Flag Over Farm pane of 20)

Format: Panes of 20, horizontal, 4 across, 5 down. Offset printing plates of 180 subjects.

Gum Type: self-adhesive

Overall Stamp Size: 1.56 by 0.99 inches; 39.624 by 25.146mm

Pane Size: 7.135 by 5.900 inches; 181.229 by 149.860mm

Perforations: 11¼ by 11½ (die-cut simulated perforations) (Arpeco die cutter)

Selvage Markings: "© 2000/USPS." ".70/x20/$14.00." "PLATE/POSITION" and diagram. Universal Product Code (UPC) "561400" in 2 positions.

Photographer: Michael Forsberg of Lincoln, Nebraska

Designer, Art Director and Typographer: Ethel Kessler of Bethesda, Maryland

Modeler: Joseph Sheeran of Ashton-Potter (USA) Ltd., Williamsville, New York

Stamp Manufacturing: Stamps printed by Ashton-Potter on offset portion of Stevens Variable Size Security Documents webfed 6-color offset, 3-color intaglio press. Stamps finished by Ashton-Potter.

Quantity Ordered: 85,000,000

Plate Number Detail: 1 set of 5 plate numbers preceded by the letter P in selvage above or below each corner stamp

Plate Number Combinations Reported: P11111, P22222

Tagging: block tagging

The Stamp

On March 6, the Postal Service issued a 70¢ self-adhesive stamp featuring a photo of Nebraska's Nine-Mile Prairie, a surviving example of the tallgrass prairie that once covered the landscape from Ohio to eastern Nebraska.

The stamp was part of the Scenic American Landmarks series of international-rate stamps and postal stationery that are intended to photographically showcase America's beauty for overseas recipients of mail. The 70¢ denomination covered the rate for postcards addressed to countries other than Canada and Mexico and for aerograms to all countries under a revised schedule of international postage rates that took effect January 7, 2001.

The stamp had its first-day sale in Lincoln, Nebraska, home of the University of Nebraska Foundation, which owns the 228 acres that compose Nine-Mile Prairie — 210 of which have never been plowed — and preserves it for teaching, research and nature study.

Nine-Mile Prairie, northwest of Lincoln, was so named in the 1930s because it is exactly nine miles from the Lincoln City Square. It was a principal site for pioneering studies of plant ecology by Dr. John E. Weaver of the University of Nebraska, and has been the property of the foundation since the 1980s. The preserve is managed by a committee of university officials and community representatives.

The stamp was printed by Ashton-Potter (USA) Ltd. by the offset method and distributed in panes of 20.

The Scenic American Landmarks series was launched in 1999 with stamps for Niagara Falls and the Rio Grande and a postal card showing Mount Rainier. It was continued with a Grand Canyon stamp in 2000 and a 70¢ Badlands postal card issued March 6, 2001 (see separate chapter). A 1999 aerogram depicting scenes from Voyageurs National Park is listed by USPS as part of the series, although the design of its imprinted stamp is different in style from the designs of the stamps and postal cards.

The Postal Service intends to continue the series, according to Terrence McCaffrey, manager of stamp development. Ethel Kessler, art director for the series, and Louis Plummer, co-owner of PhotoAssist, the Postal Service's research firm, have compiled a list of potential places to show on future stamps and reviewed the color photography available on each one.

"They just had to be places — given that this was a series of international rate stamps — to which people would go naturally, and then, in addition, places that they would visit if they knew how gorgeous they were," Kessler explained. "Color was important, because I think one of the things that worked was that Niagara Falls was this really dreamy sort of blue color, and the Grand Canyon stamp was purples and violets and yellows and oranges. We wanted to avoid having mountains all be snow-capped — and that's hard.

"The challenge we took on was how visually diverse could we get and, whether these were all known places or not, how could we have people from other countries understand the beauty that was here?"

To ensure that all areas of the United States would be represented in the series, Kessler and Plummer marked a map with the locations of the landmarks that have been depicted to date and then added the locations of another dozen or more places for which they had found colorful and dramatic photo images that could be used on future stamps and postal cards. The latter group includes scenes in Alaska, Arizona, California, Georgia, New York, North Carolina, Tennessee, Utah, Virginia, Wyoming and offshore territories.

The Design

The stamp's design conforms to a style established by Ethel Kessler in 1999 with the first stamp in the Scenic American Landmarks series. It is horizontally arranged, with the entire design area occupied by the photograph of the scenic subject. "USA" (vertical) and the denomination (horizontal), in thin sans-serif type, are dropped out of opposite corners — in this case, the lower left and upper right. The scene is identified in very small black type in the bottom-right margin ("Nine-Mile Prairie, Nebraska"). Kessler said her intention was to get the typography "out of the way of the image and let the image have as much space on that stamp as possible." The design includes a tiny jet-plane silhouette printed in silver next to the denomination, indicating that the stamp is meant for mail sent abroad by air.

For her central subject, Kessler chose a photo by Michael Forsberg of Lincoln, Nebraska, a specialist in photographing the wildlife and landscapes of the Great Plains. In the photo, which Forsberg titled *October in the Tallgrass*, a sea of high, amber-colored grass stretches from immediately in front of the viewer to the distant horizon, broken by a row of trees that crosses the image in the middle distance. According to USPS, Forsberg described the grass as "six-foot-high big bluestem." Overhead is a blue sky streaked with cirrus clouds.

"It is so painterly, and so beautiful, that at first look we couldn't tell if it was a painting or a photograph," Kessler said.

An article on Forsberg's web site, which includes excerpts from an interview in *The Omaha World Herald* by Julie Anderson, quotes the photographer as saying he took the picture in the fall of 1994 from a stepladder on which he stood to give the camera some elevation.

"What I wanted to do was give people a sense of the tallgrass prairie, particularly what it would have been like for a person on horseback or in a covered wagon 150 years ago as they were rolling across Nebraska," Forsberg said. Few such views can be found anymore without telephone poles or buildings, he said, adding, "It's almost like we're chasing ghosts out here on the landscape."

On the stamp, the microprinted letters "USPS" are at the top of the line of trees on the left side of the design. Microprinting is a security device used on single-design stamps that are produced by offset.

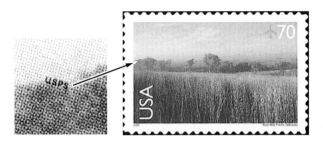

The microprinted letters "USPS" can be found at the top of the line of trees on the left side of the design.

First-Day Facts

No official dedication ceremony was held for the Nine-Mile Prairie stamp, the 34¢ Apple and Orange convertible booklet or the 34¢ Flag Over Farm pane of 20, all of which had their first-day sale in Lincoln March 6. Michael Forsberg autographed pictures and Nine-Mile Prairie stamps March 8 at the Great Plains Art Collection in Lincoln's Hewit Place Gallery.

80¢ MOUNT McKINLEY
SCENIC AMERICAN LANDMARKS SERIES

Date of Issue: April 17, 2001

Catalog Number: Scott C137

Colors: yellow, magenta, cyan, black, metallic silver

First-Day Cancel: Fairbanks, Alaska

First-Day Cancellations: 20,660

Format: Panes of 20, horizontal, 4 across, 5 down. Gravure printing cylinders of 200 subjects, 2 panes across, 5 panes around.

Gum Type: self-adhesive

Overall Stamp Size: 1.560 by 0.990 inches; 39.624 by 25.146mm

Pane Size: 6.500 by 5.875 inches; 165.100 by 149.225mm

Perforations: 11 (die-cut simulated perforations) (Comco Commander rotary die cutter)

Selvage Markings: "© 2000 USPS." "$0.80 x 20 = $16.00." "PLATE/POSI-TION" and diagram. Universal Product Code (UPC) "561500" in 2 locations.

Photographer: John Eastcott and Yva Momatiuk of Hurley, New York

Designer, Art Director and Typographer: Ethel Kessler of Bethesda, Maryland

Stamp Manufacturing: Stamps printed by Avery Dennison Security Printing Division, Clinton, South Carolina, on 8-color Dia Nippon Kiko webfed gravure press. Stamps processed by Avery Dennison.

Quantity Ordered: 85,000,000

Plate Number Detail: 1 set of 5 plate numbers preceded by the letter V in selvage next to each corner stamp

Plate Number Combination Reported: V11111

Paper Supplier: Fasson Division of Avery Dennison

Tagging: phosphored paper

The Stamp

On April 17, the Postal Service issued an 80¢ self-adhesive stamp depicting Alaska's Mount McKinley, the highest mountain in North America. It was the fifth in the Scenic American Landmarks series of stamps issued to cover international mail rates.

When the stamp was placed on sale, its 80¢ denomination covered the rate, effective January 7, 2001, for letters of one ounce or less addressed to all countries except Canada and Mexico. However, it acquired an added reason for being on July 1, when the rate for first-class domestic mail weighing between two and three ounces rose from 76¢ to 80¢. Because no new 80¢ definitive was issued, the Mount McKinley became the stamp of choice for that purpose.

Avery Dennison Security Printing Division printed the stamp by the gravure process and distributed it in panes of 20.

Terrence McCaffrey, manager of stamp development for USPS, explained how Mount McKinley came to be included in the group of subjects being developed for the Scenic American Landmarks series.

"We had received word that Postmaster General [William] Henderson had spoken with Senator Ted Stevens of Alaska, who had requested a stamp honoring Mount McKinley," McCaffrey said. Senator Stevens, a key legislator in postal matters and a stamp collector, has had a longstanding interest in the U.S. stamp program, particularly in stamps related to his home state.

"We informed the postmaster general that we had already issued two stamps featuring that peak, but he said that he had already promised the senator that it would happen," McCaffrey continued. "We also pointed out that in the upcoming Greetings From America series to be issued in 2002, the Greetings from Alaska stamp would feature Mount McKinley.

"This information was shared with the senator, who thought it was wonderful. But he still wanted an individual stamp honoring Mount McKinley."

The two previous Mount McKinley stamps to which McCaffrey referred were a 3¢ commemorative in the Territorial series of 1937 (Scott 800) and a 15¢ stamp in the National Parks Centennial issue of 1972 (Scott 1454).

Mount McKinley, named for the 25th president of the United States, William McKinley, is known to the Athabaskan people as Denali, or "High One." It rises 20,320 feet above sea level in Denali National Park and Preserve and is part of the 600-mile Alaska Range.

Because the countryside to Mount McKinley's north and west is rolling plateau, from that vantage point one can look up at 17,000 or more feet of mountain. Its spectacular beauty masks weather conditions that can be extreme. Winter lows can fall to minus 95 degrees Fahrenheit, and storm winds can gust to more than 150 mph.

In some places, ice hundreds of feet thick enrobes the mountain's granite and slate core. Numerous glaciers that ring Mount McKinley's base are

Mount McKinley's massive bulk previously was shown on a 3¢ stamp of 1937 in the Territorial series (Scott 800) and a 15¢ stamp in the National Parks Centennial issue of 1972 (Scott 1454).

supplied from the permanent snowfields that cover more than 50 percent of the mountain.

Initially established February 16, 1917, Mount McKinley National Park was designated a wilderness area and incorporated into Denali National Park and Preserve in 1980. The Denali park's more than 6 million acres encompass a complete sub-arctic ecosystem with large mammals such as bears, wolves, Dali sheep, caribou and moose.

The stamp, like all stamps in the Scenic American Landmarks series, carries a line of very small type below the bottom frameline of the design identifying the landmark — in this case, "Mount McKinley, Alaska."

"When the first-day event took place, we found out that we had not pleased everyone," Terrence McCaffrey said, in that some of Alaska's Native Americans were "very upset" that the name "Denali" didn't appear on the stamp. "A protest was mounted and a group of individuals boycotted the stamp ceremony," McCaffrey said.

The Design

Ethel Kessler's stamp design presents a photograph of Mount McKinley on a clear day, with sunlight shining on its snowy slopes. Shades of blue, ranging from dark to pale, dominate the stamp. The silhouette of a stylized jet airplane that is part of every Scenic American Landmarks design is printed in silver next to the "80" denomination.

Kessler selected the photo from a variety of stock images obtained by PhotoAssist, the Postal Service's research firm. This one came from the National Geographic Image Collection and was taken on a summer morning in 1997 or 1998 by John Eastcott and Yva Momatiuk of Hurley, New York, a husband-and-wife nature-photography team for the National Geographic Society.

"We go to Denali park a lot," Momatiuk said. "Like almost everybody else, we just watch for a glimpse of the big one. We have to wait for the clouds to lift because it is so tall that many kinds of clouds just naturally cover it. It's always a wonderful thing when the mountain shows up.

"This picture was taken from a place called Stony Pass, which is one of the prime viewing points. The park is the size of Massachusetts, and only one road, much of it gravel, leads into it. The closest you can get to the mountain is perhaps 20 or 25 miles. You're never really near it, but it is so enormous it appears to be right there. We used a Canon camera on a tripod with one of the long telephoto lenses to make this picture.

"It's a wonderful mountain, and it changes all day long. If the clouds aren't upon it, you can observe it all day long from actually two sides, the side you are looking at [on the stamp], which is basically the eastern face, and the north face, which is also visible from the road. You can drive around and look at the light changing on it. In the evening you have to go to another face, because this face will be in shadow.

"If you have a full moon floating over Denali, then you are really in hog heaven!"

Momatiuk and Eastcott didn't learn that their photograph had been selected for the stamp, she said, "until one day I got a telephone call from the Anchorage post office saying that they were preparing this little exhibit for the stamp's unveiling."

First-Day Facts

Postmaster-General William J. Henderson dedicated the Mount McKinley stamp in a ceremony at the International Arctic Research Center of the University of Alaska in Fairbanks. The speakers were U.S. Senator Ted Stevens, whose request to Henderson led to the issuance of the stamp, and Kathy Blair Wilson, deputy director of the Fairbanks Native Association. Syun-Ichi Akasofu, director of the research center, gave the welcome, and Fairbanks Postmaster Raymond E. Clark presided.

The earliest-known use of a Mount McKinley stamp was on a cover machine-canceled in Columbus, Ohio, March 19, nearly a month before the April 17 official first day of issue.

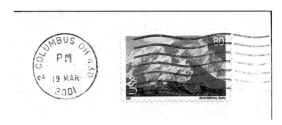

The earliest-known use of a Mount McKinley stamp was on a cover machine-canceled in Columbus, Ohio, March 19, nearly a month before the April 17 official first day of issue.

60¢ ACADIA NATIONAL PARK
SCENIC AMERICAN LANDSCAPES SERIES

Date of Issue: May 30, 2001

Catalog Number: Scott C138

Colors: black, cyan, magenta, yellow

First-Day Cancel: Bar Harbor, Maine

First-Day Cancellations: 22,933

Format: Pane of 20, horizontal, 4 across, 5 down. Offset printing plates of 180 subjects, 15 across, 12 around.

Gum Type: Self-adhesive

Overall Stamp Size: 1.56 by 0.99 inches; 39.62 by 25.15mm

Pane Size: 7.25 by 6.00 inches; 184.15 by 152.40mm

Perforations: 11¼ by 11½ (die-cut simulated perforations) (rotary die cutter)

Selvage Markings: "©/USPS/200." ".60/x20/$12.00." "PANE POSITION" and diagram. Universal Product Code (UPC) "561300" in 2 locations.

Photographer: Carr Clifton of Taylorsville, California

Designer, Typographer and Art Director: Ethel Kessler of Bethesda, Maryland

Stamp Manufacturing: Stamps printed by Banknote Corporation of America (BCA), Browns Summit, North Carolina, on a Goebel 670 offset press. Stamps processed by BCA.

Quantity Ordered: 100,000,000

Cylinder Number Detail: 1 set of 4 cylinder numbers preceded by the letter B in selvage above or below each corner stamp

Cylinder Number Combination Reported: B1111

Paper Supplier: Paper Corporation of the United States/P.H. Glatfelter/Consolidated Papers/Spinnaker Coatings

Tagging: phosphored paper

The Stamp

On May 30, in Bar Harbor, Maine, the Postal Service issued a 60¢ definitive stamp reproducing a photograph of a scene in nearby Acadia National Park. Its 60¢ denomination covered the rate for a letter weighing one ounce or less addressed to Canada or Mexico.

The stamp was part of a series of stamps and postal stationery that USPS previously had called "Scenic American Landmarks." However, on May 1, the name of the series was changed to "Scenic American Landscapes." According to *Stamp Collector*, the Postal Service said the new name "better reflects existing and upcoming images." Two other stamps in the series, the 70¢ Nine-Mile Prairie and 80¢ Mount McKinley, had been issued earlier in 2001 under the original series designation.

The Acadia stamp, a self-adhesive, was printed by the offset process by Banknote Corporation of America and distributed in panes of 20. The first in the series to replace an existing stamp of the same denomination, it took the place of the 60¢ Grand Canyon stamp of 2000, which had been issued to cover the rate then in effect for a half-ounce letter to any country other than Canada or Mexico.

The Grand Canyon stamp had been a jinxed issue. Its first printing bore the wrong inscription — "Grand Canyon, Colorado," instead of "Grand Canyon, Arizona" — and had to be destroyed. After the stamp was printed with the correct inscription and placed on sale, it was discovered that the photographic transparency used to create its design had been inadvertently flopped, or reversed, when the printing plates were made.

Acadia National Park encompasses 47,633 acres of granite-domed mountains, woodlands, lakes, ponds and ocean shoreline on Maine's Mount Desert Island and several smaller islands. It includes Cadillac Mountain, at 1,532 feet the highest point along the Atlantic coast of North America.

The park owes its creation to the efforts of George B. Dorr, an affluent conservationist who spent 43 years working to preserve the Acadian landscape. In 1901, concerned over the growing development of the Bar Harbor area and the dangers he foresaw in the newly invented gasoline-powered portable sawmill, Dorr and others established the Hancock County Trustees of Public Reservations with the sole purpose of preserving land for the perpetual use of the public.

By 1913 the trustees had acquired 6,000 acres, which Dorr offered to the federal government. In 1916 President Woodrow Wilson announced the creation of the Sieur de Monts National Monument. Dorr continued to obtain property and work to obtain full national park status for his preserve. In 1919 President Wilson signed the act establishing Lafayette National Park, the first national park east of the Mississippi River, and Dorr became the first park superintendent.

In 1929 the park's name was changed to Acadia. This is the English equivalent of Acadie, which the French had called the large region south of the Gulf of St. Lawrence that includes what is now the Canadian

This 1934 National Parks series stamp (Scott 746) depicts a rocky promontory in Acadia National Park called the Great Head.

provinces of Nova Scotia and New Brunswick.

Besides Dorr, other major benefactors of the park were Charles W. Eliot, a former president of Harvard University, and John D. Rockefeller, who gave more than 11,000 acres of land and directed and financed the construction of a network of more than 45 miles of rustic carriage roads. The roads still are closed to automobile traffic and are used by hikers, runners, horseback riders and bicyclists.

Acadia National Park had previously been featured on the 7¢ black stamp of the 1934 National Parks issue (Scott 746). That stamp depicted an engraving of a rocky promontory called the Great Head at Bar Harbor, based on a National Park Service photograph. A ship offshore was added by the engraver, reportedly at the suggestion of President Franklin D. Roosevelt as a way to balance the design. Like the 2001 Acadia stamp, its 1934 predecessor had its first-day sale in Bar Harbor.

The Design

The photograph chosen by art director Ethel Kessler for the stamp shows a misty autumn landscape in Acadia park. A lichen-covered granite hilltop is in the foreground, with brown grass growing from its crevices, behind which are bright red huckleberry bushes and fog-shrouded spruce trees.

PhotoAssist, the Postal Service's research firm, obtained the photo from Minden Pictures, a stock supplier in Aptos, California. The picture was made by Carr Clifton of Taylorsville, California, a large-format landscape photographer whose work has been widely published in books, magazines, posters and calendars.

A spokeswoman for Clifton said the photographer took the photo in the fall of 1992 "somewhere in the higher regions of the park," but was unable to recall the specific location. Clifton "frequently goes back East," she said. "He loves the East Coast, and especially Maine. He goes to New England — Maine, New Hampshire — because of the fall colors."

She said the photo probably was made with a four-by-five Toyo 45AR camera equipped with a 90-millimeter Schneider lens.

Kessler placed the vertical "USA" in the stamp's upper-left corner and the denomination and jet-plane silhouette in the lower-right corner. On the first five stamps in the series, those graphic elements were shown at the lower left and upper right, respectively.

The microprinted letters"USPS" can be found on the stone outcropping to the left of the stamp's center.

When the series was launched in 1999, the stated intention of Stamp Services officials was to include the silhouette of a stylized jet plane on each stamp to indicate that its principal use was for international mail, and to print the jet in metallic silver. So far, that has been done with four of the stamps: the 40¢ Rio Grande and 48¢ Niagara Falls of 1999 and the 70¢ Great Plains Prairie and 80¢ Mount McKinley of 2001. However, on the two 60¢ stamps, the Grand Canyon and now the Acadia, no silver was used and the jet was printed in gray (actually, a screened black).

Because the Acadia stamp was offset-printed, its design includes microprinting as a security device. The letters "USPS" can be found on the granite surface to the left of the center of the stamp.

First-Day Facts

No official first-day ceremony was held by USPS headquarters. However, the Maine District of the Postal Service, along with the Friends of Acadia, collaborated on a ceremony at the Jordan Pond House in the park and produced a ceremony program. Participants included U.S. Senator Olympia J. Snowe, Republican of Maine, and Joan Benoit Samuelson, Olympic marathon gold medalist. First-day cancellations were available at the event and at the post office in Bar Harbor.

NONDENOMINATED (10¢) ATLAS STATUE STANDARD MAIL PRESORT RATE COIL AMERICAN CULTURE SERIES

Date of Issue: June 29, 2001

Catalog Number: Scott 3520

Colors: black, cyan, magenta, yellow

First-Day Cancel: New York, New York

First-Day Cancellations: 17,714

Format: Coils of 10,000, vertical. Gravure printing cylinders of 400 subjects (20 across, 20 around) made by Acitronics.

Gum Type: self-adhesive

Overall Stamp Size: 0.870 by 0.982 inches; 22.10 by 24.94mm

Perforations: 8½ (die-cut simulated perforations) (George Schmitt & Co. rotary die cutter)

Designer: Kevin Newman of Santa Monica, California

Art Director and Typographer: Carl Herrman of Carlsbad, California

Stamp Manufacturing: Stamps printed for Banknote Corporation of America, Browns Summit, North Carolina, by Guilford Gravure, Guilford, Connecticut, on Cerrutti R118 gravure press. Stamps processed by Guilford Gravure.

Quantity Ordered and Distributed: 800,000,000

Cylinder Number Detail: 1 group of 4 cylinder numbers preceded by the letter B on every 20th stamp

Cylinder Number Combination Reported: B1111

Counting Number Detail: 1 5-digit counting number in black on back of liner paper behind every 10th stamp.

Paper Supplier: Paper Corporation of the United States/Spinnaker Coatings

Tagging: untagged

The Stamp

On June 29, the Postal Service issued a nondenominated self-adhesive coil stamp depicting the well-known statue in New York City's Rockefeller Center of Atlas bearing the weight of the heavens on his shoulders.

The stamp sold for 10¢ and bears the service inscription "PRESORT-ED STD," indicating that it was created for a class of quantity mail called "standard" that formerly was known as third-class bulk mail. Many direct-mail advertisers prefer stamps to printed indicia because of evidence that stamps increase the rate of favorable responses.

Stamps such as this one bear inscriptions describing the mail classification for which they are intended, but have no denominations. They are used under an arrangement collectors call false franking. The user, at the time of mailing, pays the difference between the cost of the stamp and the actual postage charged for the item to which it is affixed, a charge that varies depending on the degree to which the mail is presorted and other factors.

The Postal Service considers service inscriptions such as the wording on the Atlas stamp to be precancels. These stamps are untagged, and mail bearing them bypasses the post office canceling machines.

Guilford Gravure Inc. of Guilford, Connecticut, printed the Atlas stamp for Banknote Corporation of America by the gravure process in rolls of 10,000. The individual stamps are attached to their backing paper with spaces above, between and below them. Cylinder numbers appear on the stamps at intervals of 20, and 5-digit counting numbers in black are printed on the backing paper at 10-stamp intervals.

In addition to full rolls at $1,000 per roll, Stamp Fulfillment Services offered plate-number strips of 25 stamps to collectors at $2.50 per strip.

The Atlas stamp was the second nondenominated coil stamp in less than a year to be issued for use on standard mail and sell for 10¢. The first, also a self-adhesive, made its debut November 9, 2000, and depicted one of the two stone lions that guard the entrance to the New York Public Library in New York City.

According to the Postal Service, the Atlas stamp would replace the nondenominated (10¢) Green Bicycle coil stamp that was issued in 1998 with two types of gum, self-adhesive and water-activated. The Lion coil was meant to replace the various nondenominated Eagle and Shield coil stamps issued in the 1990s.

"It is intended that two nondenominated coils with the same face value but different designs be in circulation at the same time," Don Smeraldi, a Postal Service spokesman, told *Linn's Stamp News*.

USPS had stated in June 2000 that a version of the Lion coil with water-activated gum would be released later, perhaps in 2001. A year later, Smeraldi told *Linn's* that "a nondenominated (10¢) coil with water-activated gum, probably in rolls of 3,000, is tentatively scheduled for release this year [2001]." The Postal Service's plans changed, however, and no water-activated version of either the Lion or Atlas had appeared as of late

Shown here is a photograph of Lee Lawrie's Atlas statue and the armillary sphere created by Kenneth Lynch.

in 2002.

The Atlas design was the fifth in the American Culture series of non-denominated bulk-rate coil stamps, some of which were issued both as conventionally gummed stamps and self-adhesives. The series began in 1995 with the (15¢) Auto Tail Fin and continued with the (25¢) Juke Box, the (25¢) Diner and the (10¢) New York Public Library Lion. The Postal Service included the last-mentioned stamp in the series retroactively.

The bronze Atlas statue was created by sculptor Lee Lawrie in 1937 and stands in front of the International Building at Fifth Avenue and 50th Street in Manhattan, across from St. Patrick's Cathedral. The complex armillary sphere that sits atop Atlas' shoulders was made by Kenneth Lynch.

An armillary sphere, or spherical astrolabe, was used to teach the concepts of astronomy. It consists of a number of interlocking, graduated rings representing the fundamental circles of the heavens. The armillary sphere held by Lawrie's Atlas contains the 12 signs of the zodiac.

In Greek mythology, Atlas was a member of the Titans, a group of immense gods who warred with Zeus. As punishment, Zeus condemned him to uphold the heavens on his shoulders. A book of maps is called an atlas because the figure of Atlas with the universe on his back was put on the title page by Rumold Mercator when he published his father's maps in 1595.

The Design

The Postal Service's part-time art directors have a continuing assignment: to work with illustrators to develop designs for definitive and special stamps and postal stationery that can be used as needed. As part of this process, artist Kevin Newman of Santa Monica, California, produced a number of design concepts under the supervision of art director Carl Herrman. One of these became the nondenominated Diner coil stamp for presorted first-class mail that was issued in 1998. Another provided the basis for the Atlas Statue stamp.

Herrman had asked Newman to pursue the theme "American icons," and one of the sketches produced by the artist depicted a ground view of a towering Atlas and armillary sphere, rendered as masses and lines of green, black and white highlights. Instead of a literal background, Newman painted a flat orange backdrop surrounding a red pentagon that merely suggests the cityscape. The finished art was done in acrylic.

Newman based his illustration on a photo by Horst Hamann, a German photographer who is known for his wide-angle photos of city skylines and well-known urban buildings and other landmarks. Hamann used a panoramic camera tilted 90 degrees to capture some unusual images of New York City, many of them contained in his 1998 book *New York Vertical*.

"The [Citizens' Stamp Advisory] Committee instantly liked Kevin's picture for its simplicity and unique angle," said Terrence McCaffrey, manager of stamp development.

Herrman placed the "PRESORTED STD" inscription at the bottom of the stamp in dropout white Fritz Quadrata type. "I was lucky," Herrman said. "All the little counters [enclosed spaces of letters] happened to land on dark areas where they would stand out." "USA" is in black in the upper-right corner.

However, the stamp as issued included a design element that hadn't been part of the illustration released in advance: a line of black type on a white panel across the top that read "Atlas, Rockefeller Center, New York City."

"After the design was approved and completed, the final negotiations were handled by our office to obtain the rights," said McCaffrey. "The rights holders asked that we identify the subject matter and especially the location. We agreed that the average customer may not be familiar with this particular statue, so we added a line of type at the top identifying the statue and its location."

Carl Herrman was enthusiastic about the finished product, even with the added typography. "Of all the small bulk-rate stamps I've ever done, this one probably worked out the best, because of the strong colorful background and the dark foreground silhouette image that is so graphic," he said. "In a way, it's pretty just as a piece of abstract art, and it reproduced fantastically well.

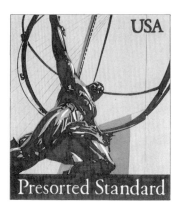

Kevin Newman's original color sketch of the Atlas statue, except for the hand-lettered inscriptions, is very close in appearance to the finished stamp.

300

This picture of the Atlas Statue stamp, released by the Postal Service in advance, didn't include the line of descriptive type that appeared at the top of the issued stamp. To make room for it, the illustration was cropped slightly at the bottom.

"I would think it would be popular with mailers. It would be especially good for investment companies and companies of that kind. It's like the Library Lion stamp; it suggests loyalty and trust and strength and all those good characteristics."

First-Day Facts

The stamp had its first-day sale in New York City with no ceremony. Collectors preparing their own covers for first-day cancellation had to make certain the total face value of the stamps on the envelopes equaled the 34¢ first-class rate or more. Stamp Fulfillment Services sold uncacheted first-day covers bearing a single Atlas coil stamp and a single non-denominated (25¢) Diner coil stamp for 56¢.

NONDENOMINATED (15¢) WOODY WAGON POSTCARD PRESORT RATE COIL AMERICAN CULTURE SERIES

Date of Issue: August 3, 2001

Catalog Number: Scott 3522

Colors: green (PMS 561), magenta, black, cyan, yellow

First-Day Cancel: Denver, Colorado

First-Day Cancellations: 21,160

Format: Coils of 10,000, vertical. Gravure printing cylinders of 420 subjects (21 across, 20 around) manufactured by Armotek Industries.

Gum Type: self-adhesive

Overall Stamp Size: 0.870 by 0.982 inches; 22.09 by 24.94mm

Perforations: 11½ (die-cut simulated perforations) (Comco rotary die cutter)

Designer: Kevin Newman of Santa Monica, California

Art Director and Typographer: Carl Herrman of Carlsbad, California

Modeler: Donald H. Woo of Sennett Security Products, Chantilly, Virginia

Stamp Manufacturing: Stamps printed for Sennett Security Products by American Packinging Corporation, Columbus, Wisconsin, on Rotomec 3000 gravure press. Stamps processed by Unique Binders, Fredericksburg, Virginia.

Quantity Ordered and Distributed: 310,000,000

Cylinder Number Detail: 1 group of 5 cylinder numbers preceded by the letter S on every 21st stamp

Cylinder Number Combination Reported: S11111

Counting Number Detail: 1 5-digit counting number in magenta on back of liner paper behind every 10th stamp.

Paper Supplier: Paper Corporation of the United States/Spinnaker Coating

Tagging: untagged

The Stamp

On August 3, the Postal Service issued a nondenominated self-adhesive coil stamp depicting a wood-paneled station wagon known to car collectors as a "woody" (alternatively spelled "woodie"). The stamp sold for 15¢ and was intended for use on presorted first-class postcards.

The Woody Wagon design was the sixth in the American Culture series and the second to be issued in 2001. Its immediate predecessor in the series was the Atlas Statue stamp for standard mail, issued June 29, 2001.

USPS offers various bulk-mail discounts from the basic 23¢ postcard rate, depending on the degree of presorting. The Woody Wagon stamp was meant for use in any of these discounted categories. The mailer affixes the stamps to his postcards and pays the post office the difference between the cost of the stamps and the total cost of the mailing.

Previous coil stamps issued for use on quantity-mailed postcards include the 13¢ Patrol Wagon stamp of 1988, in the Transportation series, and the nondenominated (15¢) Automobile Tail Fin stamp of 1995, in the American Culture series.

The Woody Wagon stamp was printed by the gravure process by American Packaging Corporation for Sennett Security Products and distributed in rolls of 10,000. Stamp Fulfillment Services sold the stamp to collectors in strips of 25, which included one stamp with a plate number.

For several years, the Citizens' Stamp Advisory Committee had received requests for a woody wagon stamp or stamps from members of the National Woodie Club, Inc. The club is an association of owners, restorers and admirers of the wood-bodied vehicles that had their heyday in the 1930s and 1940s. The April 1995 issue of *Woodie Times*, the club's official publication, reproduced on its cover a proposed 25¢ commemorative stamp depicting a 1939 Ford woody painted by artist and club member John Hutchinson of Salem, Massachusetts.

The stamp, when finally issued, was a product of the Postal Service's policy of changing the designs of its bulk-mail stamps periodically and the continuing effort of its art directors to come up with colorful new ones. The developer of this design was Carl Herrman, who is an expert on southern California "beach culture" and its artifacts, including surfboards and the woodies often used to transport them.

Herrman started surfing nearly 50 years ago, contributed articles to surfing magazines, and still frequents the beaches near his hometown of Carlsbad, California. "Back in the late '50s all the surfers had woodies," he said. "They were the cheapest car you could find, because the wood was hard to maintain, and on many of them it had rotted out and the cars were crummy looking. Today, people restore them and maintain them, and they sell for as much as $60,000."

The Beach Boys celebrated the woody wagon in their 1962 song *Surfin' Safari*: "Early in the morning we'll be startin' out/Some honeys will be coming along/We're loading up our Woody/With our boards inside/And headin' out singing our song."

The Design

To illustrate the Woody Wagon stamp, Herrman commissioned Kevin Newman, who had created the painting for the Atlas Statue coil stamp that was issued earlier in the year. Newman made several color sketches, but didn't hit on a satisfactory image until Herrman spotted an "absolutely perfect woody" in a marina parking lot at Dana Point, California, took a photo of it and sent it to the artist. The car was a 1941 Ford with red fenders, red spare-tire cover and white sidewall tires, and Herrman's photo showed it from behind and to the right.

Newman made an acrylic painting based on the photograph and added a white surfboard protruding through the car's right rear window and a subtle background of palm trees and sky. "He kept all the tones simple so it would reproduce nicely at stamp size," Herrman said. "There wasn't a lot of discussion about getting this through the [Citizens' Stamp Advisory Committee] because it sold itself."

There was one problem, however: Newman's painting showed the surfboard thrusting through the car's closed two-panel rear window in a way that challenged physics. After the anomaly was pointed out to Herrman by Louis Plummer, the co-owner of PhotoAssist, the Postal Service's research firm, Herrman corrected the image electronically, using Photoshop software. "I lifted the window up a notch," he said, "and then redrew the surfboard underneath the window, in the space between the top and bottom panels, so the surfboard went into the rear of the car the way it should."

The letters "USA" are dropped out of the design at the upper right, and "PRESORTED FIRST-CLASS CARD" is in two lines at the bottom. The typeface is called Trajon. American Packaging Corporation used five inks to print the stamp: the four standard process colors, plus green (PMS 561) for the service inscription.

The "2001" year date appears halfway up the left side of the design, underneath the block of colors constituting the scene's background. Normally the year date is located beneath the design on the left, but Herrman moved it to a different spot to leave the bottom of the stamp uncluttered.

The October 2001 issue of *Woodie Times* depicted the stamp on its cover, while an article inside told the story of the photograph Herrman had taken at Dana Point. "Herrman didn't get the name of the woody's owner, but the personal tag read

Carl Herrman mocked up this design, using one of Kevin Newman's early sketches with no foliage in the background and a "Presorted First-Class" inscription.

41 SURFR," the article said. "We imagine about a hundred of you will claim it's yours!"

A hundred didn't come forward, but the car's real owner did. David Brobeck of Dana Point sent a follow-up article to *Woodie Times*, which published it in the March 2002 issue.

"Just before my wife, Gaye, and I left for a vacation overseas, I received the October issue of *Woodie Times* with the cover picture of the new U.S. stamp," Brobeck wrote. "Gaye and I thought the graphics on the stamp were terrific, particularly since we own a red Ford woodie. However, it was not until returning ... that I read your article ... entitled 'A Woodie Stamp Is Born.' "

Brobeck "just about fell over," he continued, when he read about the "41 SURFR" tag. "That is when I grabbed my wife and said 'It is ours!' " he wrote.

"Anyway, we were excited about this development, and a friend of ours even created a large poster of the stamp taken off the cover of *Woodie Times*. We would appreciate your passing along a message to Mr. Herrman, thanking him for the honor of having our car on a U.S. stamp. (We promise we won't ask for any royalties!) ...

"Gaye and I both grew up surfing in Southern California, and her brother, Greg MacGillivray, is well-known to our club members who are old surfers. Greg and his partner, Jim Freeman, created some of the best-known classic surfing movies of all time, including *Five Summer Stories*

Shown here are photos of the 1941 Ford woody wagon illustrated on the stamp, including the photo taken by Carl Herrman on which Kevin Newman based his painting. The other one shows David and Gaye Brobeck posing beside the vehicle outside their Dana Point, California, home. In that picture, a white surfboard similar to the one shown in the stamp design protrudes from the rear window, and David holds one of the "41 SURFR" vanity license plates that confirmed that the car Herrman photographed was his. Woodie Times published the photo of the Brobecks and their woody on the back cover of the March 2002 issue.

The first version of Kevin Newman's finished painting, shown here mocked up as a sheet stamp for presorted first-class mail, depicted a physical impossibility: the surfboard passing through the closed rear window of the woody wagon. Carl Herrman altered the image on his computer to raise the window slightly and put the surfboard through the resulting open space.

and *Free and Easy*. (Greg has since become the foremost IMAX filmmaker in the world, receiving Academy Award nominations for *Everest* and *The Living Sea*.)

"We have enjoyed our '41 Ford woodie for almost 10 years, drive it most weekends, and still think that it looks best with a longboard on top or sticking out the rear window!"

Brobeck sent *Woodie Times* a photograph of himself and Gaye posing beside their car, with "the same surfboard protruding from the rear window" and the poster depicting the stamp prominently displayed. The magazine published it on the back cover of the issue in which Brobeck's article appeared.

Carl Herrman said his only regret was that because the Woody Wagon stamp is in a special category that requires a precancel permit to use, lovers of woodies in southern California and the rest of the nation were unable to use it on their personal mail.

First-Day Facts

George A. Boettger, Colorado-Wyoming District manager for USPS, dedicated the stamp in a ceremony at the Denver Marriott Tech Center Hotel in Denver, Colorado, site of the Americover 2001 stamp show. Two vintage woodies were on display on the exhibition floor during the show and 11 others were shown in the hotel parking lot.

John Blachowski, president of the Hi-Country Chapter of the National Woodie Club in Aurora, Colorado, was the principal speaker. Michael Litvak of the American First Day Cover Society, sponsor of Americover, gave the welcome, and Denver Postmaster Lloyd Wilkinson was master of ceremonies.

Collectors preparing their own covers for first-day cancellations were required to use three Woody Wagon stamps or one Woody Wagon and other postage totaling 19¢ in order to cover the 34¢ first-class rate. Stamp Fulfillment Services sold uncacheted first-day covers bearing one Woody Wagon and one 20¢ Ring-Necked Pheasant coil stamp for 56¢.

23¢ GEORGE WASHINGTON
PANE OF 20

Date of Issue: September 20, 2001

Catalog Number: Scott 3468A

Colors: green (modified PMS 561), gray (modified PMS 430), black

First-Day Cancel: Washington, D.C.

First-Day Cancellations: 82,371 (includes 21¢ Bison and 57¢ Art Deco Eagle stamps and 21¢ White Barn postal card)

Format: Pane of 20, vertical, 5 across, 4 down. Offset printing plates of 240 subjects, 12 across, 20 around.

Gum Type: self-adhesive

Overall Stamp Size: 0.84 by 0.99 inches; 21.34 by 25.15mm

Pane Size: 5.04 by 4.83 inches; 128.02 by 122.68mm

Perforations: 11¼ by 11¾ (die-cut simulated perforations) (rotary die cutter).

Selvage Markings: "© 2000 USPS." ".23/x20/$4.60." "Plate/Position" and diagram. Universal Product Code (UPC) "102300" in 2 positions.

Photo Source: Mount Vernon Ladies Association

Designer, Art Director and Typographer: Richard Sheaff of Scottsdale, Arizona

Stamp Manufacturing: Stamps printed by Banknote Corporation of America, Browns Summit, North Carolina, on Goebel 670 offset press. Stamps finished by BCA.

Quantity Ordered: 200,000,000 stamps

Plate Number Detail: 1 set of 3 plate numbers preceded by the letter B above or below each corner stamp

Plate Number Combination Reported: B111

Paper Supplier: Paper Corporation of the United States/Spinnaker Coatings

Tagging: phosphored paper

23¢ GEORGE WASHINGTON COIL OF 100

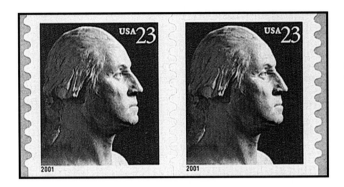

Date of Issue: September 20, 2001

Catalog Number: Scott 3475A

Colors: green (PMS 561), gray (PMS 5665)

First-Day Cancel: Washington, D.C.

First-Day Cancellations: 82,371 (includes 21¢ Bison and 57¢ Art Deco Eagle stamps and 21¢ White Barn postal card)

Format: Coil of 100, vertical. Gravure printing cylinders printing 384 stamps per revolution.

Gum Type: self-adhesive

Overall Stamp Size: 0.870 by 0.965 inches; 22.10 by 24.51mm

Perforations: 9¾ (die-cut simulated perforations)

Photo Source: Mount Vernon Ladies Association

Designer, Art Director and Typographer: Richard Sheaff of Scottsdale, Arizona

Stamp Manufacturing: Stamps printed by Guilford Gravure, Guilford, Connecticut, for Banknote Corporation of America, Browns Summit, North Carolina, on Cerrutti R118 gravure press. Stamps finished by Guilford Gravure.

Quantity Ordered: 300,000,000 stamps

Plate Number Detail: 2 plate numbers preceded by the letter B on every 24th stamp

Plate Number Combination Reported: B11

Tagging: phosphored paper

The Stamp

A new George Washington stamp was released September 20, this time green in color with a denomination of 23¢. The stamp again featured the bust by sculptor Jean-Antoine Houdon. The bust is in right profile, the same orientation used for the convertible booklet and vending booklet stamps released earlier in the year (see separate chapter).

The 23¢ self-adhesive stamp satisfied the additional-ounce rate for a first-class domestic letter that went from 21¢ to 23¢, effective July 1. USPS released two formats of the stamp — a pane of 20 (Scott 3468A) and a coil of 100 (3475A). The pane of 20 with die-cut simulated perforations was offset-printed by Banknote Corporation of America, based in Browns Summit, North Carolina. The pane had an initial printing of 200 million stamps.

BCA subcontracted the printing of the Washington coil of 100 to Guilford Gravure of Guilford, Connecticut. The stamp was printed by gravure. The initial printing for the coil stamps was 300 milllion.

The Washington, Art Deco Eagle and Bison stamps released September 20 all used designs that had appeared on stamps that were issued earlier in the year. There are precedents for using the same design on different U.S. stamps. The best-known example is the lengthy and perplexing Washington-Franklin-head series of definitives, the series of look-alike stamps that was issued from 1908 to 1922.

In 1981 USPS issued the James Hoban stamp in denominations of 18¢ and 20¢. Three versions of the 29¢ Eagle and Shield stamp were issued in 1994, each with the "USA 29" inscription printed in a different color — red, green or brown.

The design of the 29¢ Statue of Liberty stamp of 1994 was used again on two similar 32¢ stamps issued in 1997.

The Design

In addition to the modified Pantone Matching System 561 green, the technical details released by USPS stated that two distinct shades of gray were used to print the Washington stamps released September 20: PMS 5665 gray for the coil stamps and modified PMS 430 gray for stamps from the pane of 20.

In an article in the September 17, 2001, issue of *Linn's Stamp News*, associate editor Charles Snee quoted USPS spokeman Don Smeraldi, who explained, "There are differences in the PMS gray colors for the Washington pane and coil stamps because they were printed on two different presses."

Smeraldi also told Snee that the PMS colors for the Washington stamps from panes of 20 were intentionally modified. "This simply means that the colors were adjusted very slightly to better match the colors of the artwork," Smeraldi stated.

Black ink was used to print the panes of 20 but not the coil stamps. The black appears as a microprinted "USPS" on stamps from a pane of 20. The

The microprinted letters "USPS" can be found directly above the "2" of the "2001" year date in the bottom-left corner, just below the design.

microprinting appears directly above the "2" of the "2001" year date in the bottom-left corner, just below the design.

Because the coil stamp was printed by the gravure process, which USPS believes is a more secure printing process than offset, no microprinting is included in the design of the coil stamp.

First-day Facts

The 23¢ Washington stamp in both formats, the 21¢ Bison stamp in three formats, the 57¢ Art Deco Eagle stamp and 21¢ White Barn postal card were issued September 20, 2001, in Washington, D.C., and were placed on sale nationally the next day. There was no official ceremony.

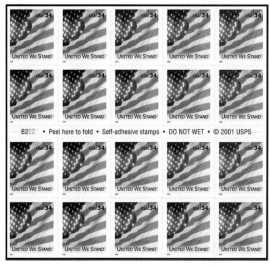

Date of Issue: October 24, 2001

Catalog Number: Scott 3549, single stamp; 3549a, pane of 20

Colors: black, cyan, magenta, yellow

First-Day Cancel: Stamps placed on sale at post offices in Washington, D.C., New York, New Jersey, Pennsylvania, Connecticut and Washington metropolitan area ZIP codes beginning with 200-212, 214-230, 232-239 and 244. Stamps sold nationwide beginning November 5.

First-Day Cancellations: 451,053 (includes coil versions)

Format: Convertible booklet pane of 20, vertical, 5 across, 4 down, with horizontal peel-off strip between second and third horizontal rows. Offset printing plates printing 500 subjects per revolution.

Gum Type: self-adhesive

Overall Stamp Size: 0.87 by 0.98 inches; 22.10 by 24.89mm

Pane Size: 4.35 by 4.13 inches; 110.49 by 104.90mm

Perforations: 11¼ (die-cut simulated perforations). Cover scored for folding.

Selvage Markings: "Peel here to fold • Self-adhesive stamps • DO NOT WET • © 2001 USPS" plus plate numbers on peel-off strip

Back Markings: "UNITED WE STAND/Twenty 34 cent first-class stamps/Self-adhesive Stamps/$6.80" on front of cover. USPS logo, "© 2001 USPS" and Universal Product Code (UPC) "0 661200 1" on back of cover.

Photographer: Lawrence Manning of Hermosa Beach, California

Designer, Art Director and Typographer: Terrence McCaffrey, USPS

Stamp Manufacturing: Stamps printed by Banknote Corporation of America, Browns Summit, North Carolina, on Goebel webfed 670 offset press.

Quantity Ordered: 2,250,000,000

Plate Number Detail: 1 set of 4 plate numbers preceded by the letter B on peel-off strip.

Plate Number Combinations Reported: B1111, B2222, B3333, B4444

Tagging: phosphored paper

34¢ UNITED WE STAND
COIL OF 100

Date of Issue: October 24, 2001

Catalog Number: Scott 3550

Colors: yellow, magenta, cyan, black

First-Day Cancel: Stamps placed on sale at post offices in Washington, D.C., New York, New Jersey, Pennsylvania, Connecticut and Washington metropolitan area ZIP codes beginning with 200-212, 214-230, 232-239 and 244. Stamps sold nationwide beginning November 5.

First-Day Cancellations: 451,053 (includes 10,000-stamp coil version and convertible booklet version)

Format: Coil of 100, vertical. Gravure cylinders printing 480 stamps per revolution. Stamps abut each other on coil and have right-angle corners.

Gum Type: self-adhesive

Overall Stamp Size: 0.84 by 0.99 inches; 21.33 by 25.10mm

Perforations: 9¾ (die-cut simulated perforations)

Photographer: Lawrence Manning of Hermosa Beach, California

Designer, Art Director and Typographer: Terrence McCaffrey, USPS

Stamp Manufacturing: Stamps printed by Bureau of Engraving and Printing on 7-color Andreotti gravure press (601)

Quantity Ordered: 4,700,000,000

Cylinder Number Detail: 1 set of 4 numbers on every 24th stamp

Cylinder Number Combinations Reported: 1111, 2222, 3333

Tagging: phosphored paper

34¢ UNITED WE STAND
COIL OF 10,000

Date of Issue: October 24, 2001

Catalog Number: Scott 3550A

Colors: yellow, magenta, cyan, black

First-Day Cancel: Stamps placed on sale at post offices in Washington, D.C., New York, New Jersey, Pennsylvania, Connecticut, and Washington metropolitan area ZIP codes beginning with 200-212, 214-230, 232-239 and 244. Stamps sold nationwide beginning November 5.

First-Day Cancellations: 451,053 (includes 100-stamp coil version and convertible booklet version)

Format: Coil of 10,000, vertical. Gravure cylinders printing 432 stamps per revolution. Stamps are spaced approximately 2mm apart on backing paper and have rounded corners.

Gum Type: self-adhesive

Overall Stamp Size: 0.87 by 0.96 inches; 22.1 by 24.4mm

Perforations: 9¾ (die-cut simulated perforations)

Photographer: Lawrence Manning of Hermosa Beach, California

Designer, Art Director and Typographer: Terrence McCaffrey, USPS

Stamp Manufacturing: Stamps printed by Bureau of Engraving and Printing on 7-color Andreotti gravure press (601)

Quantity Ordered: 75,000,000

Cylinder Number Detail: 1 set of 4 numbers on every 21st stamp

Cylinder Number Combination Reported: 1111

Counting Number Detail: 1 5-digit counting number on back of every 20th stamp

Tagging: phosphored paper

The Stamp

On September 12, with smoke from the terrorist-damaged Pentagon still visible from Postal Service headquarters in Washington, D.C., Terrence McCaffrey, manager of stamp development for USPS, heard from some of the members of the Citizens' Stamp Advisory Committee.

"They said, 'We need to do a stamp for this,' " McCaffrey recalled, meaning the September 11 terrorist attacks on the Pentagon, New York's World Trade Center and the jetliner that crashed in Pennsylvania. "I said, 'Stop and think, people. Breathe deeply. I know this has been a bad thing, but we don't do stamps for disasters. Let's get a focus here.' There were a few choice words said back and forth, but in the end everybody seemed to calm down a little bit.

"But then, a couple of days later, it started up again. We were getting a lot of e-mail messages, letters and phone calls saying we had to do something in response to the tragedy. I had a conversation with Virginia Noelke [chair of CSAC] and she said, 'I think we need to do a stamp, but it has to be on a positive note. What can we do?'

"I said, 'I'm seeing American flags on the overpasses on the way to work. What if we do a flag stamp?' She said, 'What would we call it?' She added, 'I've heard this phrase, United We Stand, all of a sudden, everywhere.' I said, 'That's fine with me. Let's make that a working concept.' "

Thus was born the United We Stand stamp, swiftly prepared and printed by USPS as a contribution to national unity in the wake of the September 11 tragedies, and issued in the billions.

Its design was approved by CSAC by e-mail Wednesday, September 19, and immediately approved by Postmaster General John E. Potter. "By Friday morning [September 21] we had a high-resolution electronic file in hand and turned it over to the two printers we had selected," McCaffrey said. "So, in a week and a half we had the stamp designed and it was at the printers'. They worked over the weekend, and by Tuesday [September 25], two weeks after the attack, one of them had it on the presses."

The stamp, a 34¢ definitive, was announced and unveiled October 2 in a ceremony outside USPS headquarters in Washington, D.C., with Postmaster General Potter and the USPS Board of Governors participating. The unveiling was done by Patricia Jenkins and Linda Washington, two

Postmaster General John Potter applauds as Linda Washington, near right, and Patricia Jenkins, postal workers from the Pentagon post office, unveil the design of the United We Stand stamp during a ceremony October 2, 2001.

315

employees at the Pentagon post office who survived the attack on the building, and Potter was presented with the flag that flew over the Church Street Station in New York, the post office closest to the World Trade Center. It still bore the dust generated by the collapse of the Twin Towers.

"They may be small, but they're powerful," Potter said of postage stamps. He called the new stamp "a ballot for freedom" and appealed for its use by the public "to spread our national message of unity and resolve with every letter we send."

"It is fitting that the U.S. Postal Service — which has served the people of this nation since the dawn of our republic — is planning to issue the United We Stand stamp," added Robert F. Rider, chairman of the Board of Governors. "For our primary job has always been to bind the nation together. Today, more than ever, the people of America are united in their purpose, their pride and their determination. This postage stamp is graphic representation of that unity."

The official issue date was October 24, 43 days after the terrorist attacks. The stamp was first placed on sale in the areas most directly affected by the terrorism: Washington, D.C., specified ZIP codes in the Washington metropolitan area, and the states of New York, Pennsylvania, New Jersey and Connecticut. New Jersey was added in a USPS press release October 17, while Connecticut was added at literally the last minute, in a press release that actually was dated October 25. On November 5, the stamp went on sale nationwide.

Three varieties were produced by two printers.

• Banknote Corporation of America printed a convertible booklet of 20 on its offset press. BCA was the first to get its stamp on press, on September 25, and its stamp was the only variety available October 24. Stamps from the convertible booklet have simulated perforations on all four sides or straight edges on one side or two adjacent sides.

• The Bureau of Engraving and Printing used the gravure process to make self-adhesive coil rolls of 100 and 10,000. Coil stamps, of course, have straight edges at the top and bottom. The stamps on the smaller rolls abut each other, with no backing paper visible from the front; those on the larger rolls are spaced about 2 millimeters apart and have backing paper showing above and below each stamp, a configuration that allows them to be used in automated equipment that removes individual stamps from a roll and affixes them to envelopes for bulk mailings. Although the gauge of their die-cut simulated perfs is the same, the stamps have differently shaped corners — square on the small rolls, rounded on the large rolls — and because of that difference Scott Publishing Company assigned them separate major catalog numbers.

The Postal Service's plan to produce coils of 10,000 wasn't announced until October 31, and neither type of coil was available until several days after the official first day of issue. The 100-stamp rolls were distributed to authorized first-day sites October 29, and the 10,000-stamp rolls were placed on sale at Stamp Fulfillment Services in Kansas City, Missouri,

November 5.

Issuance of the United We Stand stamp wiped out plans to order additional printings of the 34¢ Apples and Oranges booklet stamps and 34¢ Four Flowers booklets and coils, the Postal Service said. The United We Stand stamp became the only American flag stamp at the current first-class rate of 34¢ to be produced in coil format. The Flag Over Farm stamp issued earlier in 2001 was made only in panes and convertible booklets.

The phrase on the stamp, "United We Stand," is part of a motto and leaves the other half, "Divided We Fall," unspoken. The motto, which predates the United States, is attributed, in a less euphonious version, to *The Liberty Song* of 1768 by statesman and journalist John Dickinson in Pennsylvania. Ironically, in 1776 Dickinson led the debate against the Declaration of Independence in the Continental Congress.

The present form of the motto was popularized before the Civil War by the poet, songwriter and journalist George Pope Morris in his poem *The Flag of Our Union.*

McCaffrey was quoted in *The New York Times Magazine* of October 21 as saying that the elapsed time of less than two months from concept to first day of sale for the United We Stand stamp was "a record" in terms of speed. It may have been a modern record, but a handful of earlier U.S. stamps had been produced more rapidly, as philatelic writer Kathleen Wunderly and others pointed out to *Linn's Stamp News.*

The nation's first airmail stamp, the 24¢ carmine-rose and blue Curtiss Jenny (Scott C3), was issued May 13, 1918, only seven days after Congress set the airmail rate of 24¢ per ounce on May 6. Other stamps that beat the United We Stand record were the 2¢ Lincoln Birth Centenary commemorative (Scott 367), authorized by a joint resolution of Congress January 22, 1909, and issued February 12, just 21 days later, and the 2¢ black Harding Memorial stamp (Scott 610), issued September 1, 1923, just 30 days after President Warren G. Harding's sudden death August 2 in California.

Also, the 5¢ United Nations Conference stamp (Scott 928), issued April 25, 1945, was modified to carry the name of President Franklin D. Roosevelt, who had died April 12, 13 days earlier. The revised model and die proof were approved by Postmaster General Frank C. Walker April 16, nine days before the first-day sale.

The Design

On Friday, September 14, McCaffrey telephoned PhotoAssist, the Postal Service's research firm, and asked for a selection of flag images from stock companies to be e-mailed to him the following Monday. Eight flag photographs awaited him when he arrived at work that day.

He discarded some of them early on because they were "standard flag-waving-in-the-breeze images," he said, or couldn't be cropped suitably to the size and shape of a definitive stamp. "I wanted something that had life to it, that had excitement," McCaffrey said. Ultimately, he narrowed the

McCaffrey tried this photograph of a folded flag in stamp format but wasn't satisfied with the result.

McCaffrey laid out this flag photograph as a horizontal definitive-sized stamp, then decided it would work better by rotating the image 90 degrees and making it a vertical. With the addition of the type and with the bottom portion of the design lightened to provide greater contrast to the words "UNITED WE STAND," it became one of the two finalists sent to CSAC for a decision.

field to three, then to two. He rotated one of the two finalists 90 degrees so the blue field of stars was at the top.

McCaffrey stripped in the words "UNITED WE STAND" in black capitals across the bottom of each design, trying both bold and regular type. Because both flag photos had a shadow in the lower part of the cropped area, the wording was difficult to read. McCaffrey asked Dodge Color, the Bethseda, Maryland, firm that does the Postal Service's prepress work, to "screen back" that portion of the designs to provide more contrast.

"I liked the light version of the letters better," McCaffrey said. "The bold type was just too heavy. I had Dodge put together the two light-letter versions in final form and electronically send them to me.

"I attached them to a message that I sent to all the members of CSAC on Tuesday [September 18], saying, 'Here are two versions. I've discussed this with Virginia Noelke. This is what we want to say; we want a positive upbeat thing. I need your concurrence. Please choose one of these designs within 24 hours.'

"Everyone picked the same image. The final design was rushed to the postmaster general, who approved it instantly."

During the same period, McCaffrey's art directors were telephoning with offers of help. One of them, Richard Sheaff, mocked up a photograph of a fireman with the word "America," and also adapted one of his Stars and Stripes Classic Collection designs of 2000 by adding the words "United We Stand" to a flat illustration of the American flag. But the decision was made to stay with a flag photograph.

The chosen photo appealed to McCaffrey, he said, because of its "soft focus and ripple effect." "It's not the standard roll," he told one interviewer. "It looked like it was being whipped around in a strong wind ... an

318

Art director Richard Sheaff volunteered these two design concepts: a mood photograph of a firefighter with the word "AMERICA," and an adaptation of his design for the Stars & Stripes Classic Collection stamps of 2000 with the words "United We Stand."

effect that is powerful and dramatic."

The picture was made by Lawrence Manning, a 56-year-old commercial photographer from Hermosa Beach, California, who learned photography while a Peace Corps volunteer in Africa in the 1970s. Manning didn't know that his four-year-old picture had been used on the most significant postage stamp of the year until October 30, four days after its issue date, when a representative of the stock company, Corbis Corporation, telephoned him to ask his permission to release his name to the public. The Postal Service, through PhotoAssist, had tried vainly to learn the photographer's identity, but it took the persistence of a reporter from *Photo District News* — a publication described by Manning as "the Bible of professional photographers" — who wanted to write the story of the person behind the image to persuade Corbis that it should cooperate.

"When they called me to ask if it would be OK to give out my name, I felt like saying, 'Why haven't you already done this?' " Manning laughed.

In 1997, Manning, then living in Redondo Beach, California, had been making pictures of the flags of some 15 major nations for stock purposes. Assisted by his daughter Sara, then 14, he tried shooting the flags on poles outdoors in the sunlight, but wasn't getting the effect he wanted.

Inside his garage studio, he suspended a U.S. flag, approximately 3½ feet by 5 feet, with clamps and bungee cords attached to poles "to create the ripple effect." Then, using a heavy 4 by 5 Sinar view camera on a tripod, with a macrolens, he took three exposures that blended together on the film to create the finished photograph.

One exposure was taken with backlighting through a sheet of milky plexiglass to provide a "nice glow." Another was a slow exposure made with a diffusion filter and lit by several tungsten lights, while Sara gently tugged at the flag to "create the soft blur effect where it looks as if it's waving." The third exposure lit up the stars from above.

"The American flag was perfect for that technique," Manning said.

Shown here is the photograph of the American flag taken by Lawrence Manning and provided to CSAC by Corbis Corporation, a stock photo house, that Terrence McCaffrey adapted for what ultimately became the United We Stand stamp design.

"When I shot something like the French flag or the Belgian flag, with just three linear colors, it was much harder to make a graphic statement. The American flag with the stars and stripes gave me a lot to work with. It became really obvious that this was the best image I made, and it was because of how intriguing our flag is."

Manning and his girlfriend, graphic designer-illustrator Betty Malorca, quickly educated themselves about first-day covers and other details of stamp collecting and decided to create some customized covers to give to family members, friends and associates. They designed a 5-inch by 7-inch card depicting the full photograph, outlining the portion cropped for the stamp image. They ordered 2,000 from a printer and obtained an equal number of United We Stand stamps from the post office.

The Postal Service had allowed collectors 60 days, rather than the usual 30, to send stamped covers to the postmaster in Washington, D.C., for the first-day cancellation. Even so, the December 23 postmark deadline was closing in when Manning and Malorca took their supplies to their local tavern and enlisted the patrons to address cards and apply stamps. "We set up an assembly line to get this project out the door," Manning laughed. "Some of the people got to address their own cards. By noon the next day, we had just made the deadline, and we were exhausted!"

One of the people to whom Manning gave a card was his letter carrier. "He was practically in tears," the photographer recalled. "For so many of the people who work for the Postal Service, this stamp meant so much."

Manning remains astonished and humbled, he said, at the way his photo became the

Lawrence Manning displays one of the postcards he created for first-day covers of the United We Stand stamp, showing on the picture side the stamp design superimposed over his larger, uncropped flag photograph. Behind him hangs the flag that is shown on the photo.

320

The microprinting on the BCA convertible booklet version of the United We Stand stamp consists of the letters "USPS," in black, reading up the left side of the design, just below the second star from the top.

graphic center of a stamp of such importance. "I just made an image and put the image out there, and something great happened to it," he said. "I've been saying, it was a great picture, but they made it incredible by the way it was used. It's such a positive thing to be part of.

"As a creator, would I have ever in the wildest part of my imagination submitted a piece of artwork to the Postal Service thinking a stamp would be made? The answer is probably 'No.' You never think of such things."

Manning still has the flag that he photographed, but he has promised to give it to his son Jake, 25, who when younger had often assisted him with his photo projects.

McCaffrey, like Manning, felt a sense of connection with something extremely important. "I've worked for the post office for 31 years and have personally designed 14 stamps," he told *The New York Times Magazine*, "but I'm most proud of this one."

In his design, McCaffrey included a black vertical line between the "USA" and "34" in the upper-right corner. "I had it in as a horizontal line underneath and I didn't like it, so I just divided the two elements," he said. "I upset so many people with that little thing; one guy actually thought it was there to symbolize one of the Twin Towers! I said, no, it's a simple design device, and I won't do it again."

BCA's convertible-booklet version of the stamp, printed by offset, has a somewhat crisper image than that of the Bureau's coil version, which was produced on the BEP's old Andreotti gravure press. Because the Postal Service considers offset a less secure form of printing than gravure, it requires that single-design stamps produced by that process include microprinting in the design. The BCA stamp contains the letters "USPS" in black type reading up the left side, just below the second star from the top.

First-day Facts

Deputy Postmaster General John Nolan dedicated the United We Stand stamp October 24 in a ceremony in the Mike Mansfield room on the Senate side of the Capitol.

"We hope the stamp's simple yet powerful message helps bring our country closer together in this time of crisis," Nolan said.

Some 100 persons attended, mostly members of Congress and their aides, postal officials and media representatives. The Capitol had been closed to the public because of the anthrax-by-mail threat, and attendance was by invitation only. The only member of the stamp-collecting community present was Thomas Beschorner, editor of the *Ceremonial*, the publication of the American Ceremony Program Society.

Speakers were Senators Daniel Akaka, D-Hawaii; Max Cleland, D-Georgia; George Allen, R-Virginia; Ted Stevens, R-Alaska; and Joseph Lieberman, D-Connecticut. They addressed the events of the past two months, the symbolism of the flag and the true meaning of patriotism.

The speakers mentioned by name Joseph Curseen Jr. and Thomas Morris, the two postal workers at Washington's main post office, the Brentwood facility, who had been killed by the anthrax attack. "They and the nearly 800,000 men and women of the Postal Service have suddenly found themselves on the front lines," Lieberman said. Rank-and-file postal workers from Brentwood and Alexandria, Arlington and Falls Church, Virginia, stood in a line behind the rostrum.

Richard J. Strasser, USPS executive vice president and chief financial officer, was master of ceremonies, substituting for Deborah K. Willhite, USPS senior vice president for government relations and public policy. Senate chaplain Lloyd Ogilvie delivered the invocation.

Only the printed insert of the ceremony program with the stamp and cancel added was distributed at the event. The normal generic first-day-ceremony folder for the insert wasn't used.

First-day cancellations were available to the general public under the supervision of the Washington special cancellation unit headed by Lee Carmichael. With Washington's main post office, the Brentwood facility, closed by anthrax contamination, the North Capitol Station was chosen for the public first-day site. Late on the preceding day, however, it was decided to close North Capitol for anthrax tests, and the first-day site was changed to the Ben Franklin Station at 12th and Pennsylvania Avenues.

In addition to the normal large, straight-line first-day-of-issue cancel and the small circular datestamp cancel, the Pentagon and State Department double-ring plug cancels also were available for those who wished to service their covers with an appropriate unofficial first-day marking. The White House Visitor's Center, just up Pennsylvania Avenue, provided the National Park Service datestamp.

$15 MIGRATORY BIRD HUNTING (DUCK) STAMP 2001-2002

Date of Issue: June 29, 2001

Catalog Number: Scott RW68

Colors: Face: magenta, yellow, cyan, black (offset), black (intaglio). Back: black (offset).

First-Day Cancel: June 29, 2001, Washington, D.C.; artist's hometown event, September 8, 2001, New London, Minnesota

Format: Panes of 20, horizontal, 5 across, 4 down. Offset printing plates of 80 subjects (8 across, 10 around); intaglio printing sleeves of 160 subjects (8 across, 20 around); flexographic back plate of 80 subjects (8 across, 10 around).

Gum Type: water-activated

Overall Stamp Size: 1.96 by 1.41 inches

Pane Size: 10.220 inches by 7.045 inches

Perforations: 11¼ (Eureka stroke perforator)

Selvage Markings: "ARTIST/ROBERT HAUTMAN" in 4 locations. "DEPARTMENT OF THE INTERIOR/20 x $15.00" in 4 locations. "PLATE/POSITION" and diagram.

Back Inscription (printed on top of gum): "INVEST IN AMERICA'S FUTURE/BUY DUCK STAMPS AND/SAVE WETLANDS/SEND IN OR REPORT ALL/BIRD BANDS TO/1-800-327-BAND/IT IS UNLAWFUL TO HUNT WATERFOWL OR USE THIS STAMP/AS A PASS TO A NATIONAL WILDLIFE REFUGE UNLESS/YOU SIGN YOUR NAME IN INK ON THE FACE OF THIS STAMP."

Stamp Artist: Robert Hautman of Delano, Minnesota

Stamp Design, Typography and Modeling: Brian Thompson, Bureau of Engraving and Printing

Engravers: Thomas Hipschen, BEP, picture; Dixie O. March, BEP, lettering

Stamp Manufacturing: Stamps printed by BEP on the 4-color offset, 3-color intaglio webfed F press (801)

Quantity Ordered: 1,194,000

Sleeve Number: 1 6-digit intaglio sleeve number printed in selvage above or below each corner stamp

Sleeve Number Reported: 199613

Paper Supplier: Glatfelter/Spinnaker Coating

Tagging: untagged

$15 MIGRATORY BIRD HUNTING (DUCK) STAMP 2001-2002 (SELF-ADHESIVE)

Date of Issue: June 29, 2001

Catalog Number: Scott RW68A

Colors: Front: magenta, yellow, cyan, black (offset), black (intaglio). Back: black (offset).

First-Day Cancel: June 29, 2001, Washington, D.C.; artist's hometown event, September 8, 2001, New London, Minnesota

Format: Sold in single-stamp panes. Offset printing plates of 24 subjects (3 across, 8 around) and intaglio printing sleeves of 48 subjects (3 across, 16 around).

Gum Type: self-adhesive

Overall Stamp Size: 1.96 by 1.41 inches

Pane Size: 6.14 by 2.60 inches

Perforations: 10 (die-cut simulated perforations) (Goebel stroke die cutter)

Selvage and Back Markings: see illustrations above

Stamp Artist: Robert Hautman of Delano, Minnesota

Stamp Design, Typography and Modeling: Brian Thompson, Bureau of Engraving and Printing

Engravers: Thomas Hipschen, BEP, picture; Dixie O. March, BEP, lettering

Stamp Manufacturing: Stamps printed by BEP on the 4-color offset, 3-color intaglio webfed F press (801)

Quantity Ordered: 2,806,000

Sleeve Number: none

Paper Supplier: Glatfelter/Spinnaker Coating

Tagging: untagged

The Stamps

The remarkable domination of the annual federal duck stamp competition by the three Hautman brothers of Minnesota was extended on November 8, 2000, when Robert Hautman's acrylic painting of a swimming northern pintail took first place out of 316 entries in that year's contest. As a result, the painting was reproduced on the $15 stamp that was issued June 29, 2001, for use on hunters' licenses during the following year.

Robert Hautman had won in 1996 and was back in the contest in his first year of re-eligibility under a rule that excludes winners for three years after their victory. His younger brother Jim won the 1989 competition at age 21 and went on to win the 1994 and 1998 contests as well, and the oldest brother, Joe, won in 1991.

The 2001 stamp was issued in two formats, conventionally gummed and self-adhesive, for the fourth consecutive year. It was printed by a combination of intaglio and offset by the Bureau of Engraving and Printing, the producer of all the duck stamps since the first one in 1934.

That 68-year streak would end with the 2001 stamp, however. In the fall of 2001, Banknote Corporation of America outbid BEP for the contract to print the 2002-2003 duck stamps.

The competition to design the 2001 stamp was held over a three-day period at the Department of the Interior auditorium in Washington, D.C. Contestants were instructed to paint one of five species of waterfowl: northern pintail, American green-winged teal, black duck, ruddy duck and American wigeon.

Pintails (121) were the most frequently chosen subject. Like Robert Hautman's winning entry, the second-place and third-place paintings also

This is Robert Hautman's contest-winning acrylic painting of a northern pintail on the surface of a pond.

Acrylic paintings of pintails by Gerald Mobley (left) and Joe Hautman (right) placed second and third, respectively, in the competition to create the artwork for the 2001 federal duck stamp.

depicted swimming pintails. They were by Gerald Mobley of Oklahoma, the 1984 contest winner, and Joe Hautman, respectively.

The contest judges were Carol Baker-Jones, vice president of the board of directors of the Easton, Maryland, Waterfowl Festival; Ed Bierly, a wildlife artist and three-time winner of the federal duck stamp contest; Charles Ekstrom, a stamp collector, exhibitor and waterfowler; Charles Sauer, past executive director of the Wisconsin Waterfowl Association; and Jimmie Vizier, a prominent decoy carver.

Out of a possible 25 points in the final round of judging, Robert Hautman's entry scored 24, beating Mobley's painting by a single point. The scores awarded by judge Bierly — 5 to Hautman, 4 to Mobley — made the difference.

Besides the two Hautmans and Mobley, nine other previous federal contest winners participated in the 2000 contest: Arthur Anderson, Neal Anderson, Al Gilbert, Wilhelm Goebel, Ron Jenkins, Bruce Miller, Martin Murk, Richard Plasschaert and Dan Smith. Jim Hautman was sitting out his three-year period of winner's ineligibility.

The duck stamp, officially known as the Migratory Bird Hunting and Conservation stamp, is issued by the Fish and Wildlife Service, a branch of the Interior Department, to raise money to buy waterfowl habitat. The cost of the first one was $1, and has been increased periodically since. It has been $15 since 1991.

Each year a current stamp must be purchased by waterfowl hunters over 16 years of age. Duck stamps also are popular with stamp collectors, wildlife artists and conservationists. The stamps are sold at post offices, national wildlife refuges and some national retail chain stores and sporting-goods stores.

Ninety-eight cents of each duck stamp dollar goes to buy wetlands habitat for the National Wildlife Refuge System, which includes 514 national wildlife refuges and 37 wetlands management districts. To date, more than $500,000,000 raised from duck stamp sales has been used to acquire some 5,000,000 acres for the system.

The duck stamp contest, with an entry fee of $100, is the only federally sponsored art competition. Winning artists receive no prize money, but the professional recognition is extremely valuable, and they also stand to earn hundreds of thousands of dollars from the sale of limited-edition prints of their artwork to collectors and licensed products bearing the image of their stamp designs.

The conventionally gummed and perforated version of the 2001 stamp was distributed in panes of 20 with four sets of plate numbers. The self-adhesive, with die-cut simulated perfs, was printed on a piece of dollar-sized backing paper from which the buyer could peel it and affix it to his or her hunting license.

The selvage of the conventionally gummed stamp, for the second consecutive year, contains the name of the artist, which is contained in the tab next to each set of plate numbers. Before 2000, no duck stamp's pane had displayed such information. Also in the selvage are a plate-position diagram, "Department of the Interior," "20 x $15.00," and two sets of five duck silhouettes printed in the stamp's four offset process colors and one intaglio color. The selvage is the traditional white; the preceding year's issue had been strongly criticized for its purple selvage and purple border around each stamp.

For the first time in 15 years, the federal duck stamp office did not sell a souvenir card reproducing the stamp image. "The numbered, mint and canceled cards are not a profitable product for us to carry and sell," explained Robert C. Lesino, chief of the office, before he left that post in September 2001. "They are being discontinued in their entirety."

However, the office did sell a so-called artist's commemorative card to which was affixed the 2001 $15 Northern Pintail stamp and a 1998-99 $15 Barrow's Goldeneye stamp (Scott RW65). Both stamps bear a June 29, 2001 cancellation, the first day of sale for the 2001 stamp and the last day of sale for the 1998-99 stamp. The card sold for $50 and only 500 were issued.

The only version of the stamp sold by the duck stamp office was the self-adhesive. A $2 fee was added for artist-signed specimens, which went to the migratory bird fund. Collectors wanting to buy the conventionally gummed stamp had to obtain them from Stamp Fulfillment Services of the Postal Service, from philatelic windows at selected post offices or from Amplex, which runs the duck stamp consignment program.

The northern pintail (Anas acuta) is a popular game bird because of its tasty flesh and fast flight, and as a result is one of the wariest ducks. It is widely distributed, breeding from Alaska east to Labrador and south to California, Nebraska and Maine and wintering south to Central America and the West Indies.

The pintail is slim and graceful, with a slender neck. The male has a brown head and white neck with a white line extending onto the side of the head; the central tail feathers are long, black and pointed, hence the bird's name. The female is mottled brown, with a brown speculum bordered with white at the rear edge.

Its habitat is marshes, prairie ponds and tundra, and sometimes salt marshes in winter. A dabbler, the pintail dines primarily on seeds of aquatic plants, but in winter it also eats small aquatic animals. When freshwater habitats freeze over, it turns to tidal flats, where it feeds on snails and small crabs.

A pair of pintails was shown on the fifth federal duck stamp, in 1938, and the species also appeared on duck stamps in 1962 and 1983.

The Design

Robert Hautman's painting depicts a male pintail gliding across a pond, its reflection wavering in the greenish water below. A few reeds are visible at the right, and the duck's head is set off by a greenish, misty background.

In translating the painting to a stamp image, Thomas Hipschen, BEP's top engraver, engraved extensive areas of the bird's body and neck, head, beak and tail, as well as its reflection in the water. The intaglio portion also includes the stamp's lettering. Bob Dumaine, duck stamp author and dealer who pays close attention to the finished product each year, pronounced the stamp "very well engraved."

The BEP framed the vignette in black and displayed the words "U.S. DEPARTMENT OF THE INTERIOR" and "MIGRATORY BIRD HUNTING AND CONSERVATION STAMP" on orange bands on the right side of the stamp and across the bottom. "Northern Pintail" in italics and "$15," both in a lighter orange, are dropped out of the image at the bottom, and "Void after June 30, 2002" is in black italics at the top.

Hautman told *The Yearbook* the pintail is one of his favorite ducks and he considers it quite beautiful. For reference, he said, he used a mounted pintail that his brother Jim had borrowed from a friend, "and I had a wing I got somewhere along the line, and photos, which I've been taking and collecting my whole life — kind of a mixture of everything."

He decided to place the bird on the water after making sketches of flying pintails. "Pintails are pretty tough to do flying," he explained. "They've just got such a different look, and none of them worked out the way I wanted, so I just went with a sitting bird."

He chose a greenish background after examining photographs of pintails on a neighboring pond where the surrounding trees impart a green tone to the water. "The photos are so striking — the orange of the pintail's head really contrasts with the green," he said.

Asked about the bird's reflection, Hautman said: "When you have a bird on the water, one of the things that really gives it life is the reflection. I spent a lot of time on it, and I'm glad I did, because after the contest several judges told me that they really liked the reflection.

"They can be so different. One time a reflection can be fuzzy, where

you're kind of seeing through it, and another time it will be an exact reproduction of the bird on a perfectly calm day.

"It's worth the time you take. If it's just not right, it looks bad. It's just
a matter of trial and error. I don't know that there's a trick to it; just keep
working on it until it looks good is my theory."

Hautman said the painting took two to three months to complete, and
he concentrated on the details until every feather was perfect and the color
exact.

Bob Dumaine identified some minor color variations in both the conventionally gummed and self-adhesive versions of the stamp. In both
instances, the green color in the offset-printed areas is more pronounced
than in the normal varieties.

First-day Facts

The Federal Duck Stamp Office held the first-day-of-sale and signing
ceremony for the 2001 stamps on June 29 at the National Postal Museum
in Washington, D.C. Only the self-adhesive version was available for sale
after the ceremony. Robert Hautman was on hand to sign stamps and covers.

The traditional second, "artist's hometown" ceremony was held September 8 in New London, Minnesota, some 60 miles west of Hautman's
own hometown of Delano, at a Minnesota Waterfowl Association celebration called "Prairie Pothole Days."

34¢ FEDERAL EAGLE ENVELOPE

Date of Issue: January 7, 2001

Catalog Number: Scott U646

Colors: "postal blue" (PMS 549) and "postal gray" (PMS 5645)

First-Day Cancel: Washington, D.C.

First-Day Cancellations: 35,301 (includes 34¢ Statue of Liberty coil, rounded corners)

Sizes: numbers 6¾, 9 (security) and 10, each with or without windows

Watermark: none

Markings: "© USPS 2000" under flap. "THIS ENVELOPE IS RECYCLABLE AND MADE WITH 100%/RECYCLED PAPER, 30% POST-CONSUMER CONTENT" and recycling symbol. Security envelopes have patterned interior.

Designer and Typographer: Michael Doret of Hollywood, California

Art Director: Richard Sheaff of Scottsdale, Arizona

Envelope Manufacturing: envelopes printed by Westvaco of Williamsburg, Pennsylvania, by flexography on a VH-1 machine

Quantity Ordered: 20,000,000 number 6¾; 20,000,000 number 6¾ with window; 2,500,000 number 9; 1,800,000 number 9 with window; 75,000,000 number 10; 29,000,000 number 10 with window.

Tagging: vertical bar to right of stamp

The Envelope

On January 7, the day the first-class postage rate was increased from 33¢ to 34¢, the Postal Service issued a 34¢ envelope with an imprinted stamp depicting a stylized bald eagle described as a "federal eagle."

The Federal Eagle envelope replaced the 33¢ Flag envelope of 1999 as

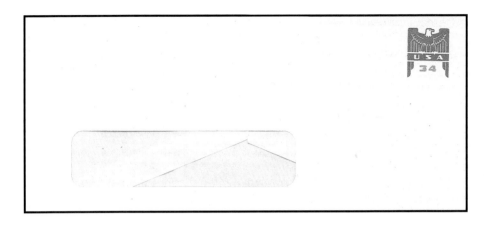

the definitive stamped envelope for the first-class rate. It was manufactured in three sizes, 6¾, 9 and 10, with each being available with and without a window. The number 9 sizes are security envelopes with patterned liners to prevent anyone from holding them to the light and discerning their contents.

Like other recent U.S. stamped envelopes, this one was produced by the flexography process by Westvaco at its Williamsburg, Pennsylvania, plant. There is no embossing.

Single envelopes sold for 42¢. USPS also sold boxes of 500 for $182 (number 6¾) and $184 (other sizes).

Several months after its issuance, the Federal Eagle envelope was burdened with an unwelcome distinction. It became known as the "anthrax envelope" because it was used by the unknown person or persons who sent letters with anthrax spores to U.S. Senate Majority Leader Tom Daschle, NBC newsman Tom Brokaw and *The New York Post* in the fall of 2001. The mail-processing centers in Washington, D.C., and Hamilton Township, New Jersey, through which the number 6¾ envelopes passed became massively contaminated with the spores, several postal workers contracted the disease and two died. It was speculated that the spores had escaped into the processing areas through microscopic openings in the envelope paper.

On October 31, USPS abruptly withdrew all stamped envelopes from sale at post offices nationwide. In response to questions, the Postal Service issued this statement:

"Many customers and employees have expressed concern about our temporary suspension of the sale of prestamped envelopes. Some have heard rumors that they were suspended because of possible contamination. There is absolutely no truth to any of those rumors.

"We are studying the design and construction

of the envelopes."

Nine days later, the envelopes were put back on sale. In its announcement, USPS said:

"The Postal Service has completed its review of the design and composition of its stamped envelopes. The results indicate that they are consistent with industry standards and are completely safe. The temporary suspension of stamped envelopes for sale at post offices and other postal retail locations was lifted effective November 9. However, the suspension of stamped envelope sales at vending machines will continue until further notice.

"Customers who have purchased personalized stamped envelopes or nonpersonalized stamped envelopes are reminded that they are perfectly safe. The Postal Service apologizes for any inconvenience this might have caused."

The Design

The eagle in the envelope's imprinted stamp perches on a panel on which "USA" is lettered in dropout white. It looks to the right, its wings are spread, its shoulders are elevated and its pinions form patterns of parallel vertical bars. Its color is a light blue, described by USPS as "postal blue." The denomination, "34," in "postal gray," floats in the open space below the eagle and between the tips of its long outer wing feathers.

Credit for the artwork went to Michael Doret of Hollywood, California, a graphic designer, logo maker and specialist in modern typography. For the Postal Service, Doret previously had provided the lettering that accompanied illustrations by his wife, Laura Smith, for the Florida and Texas statehood commemorative stamps of 1995.

Doret actually had created the Federal Eagle design several years earlier under the supervision of art director Richard Sheaff for a variable-rate coil stamp. Variable-rate coils were used in an experimental program launched by USPS in 1992 in which custom-built machines vended stamps in denominations that were punched in by the customer and imprinted by the machine. After the program was abandoned, the Federal Eagle and another Doret design went into the USPS "bank" for possible future use in some other form.

Terrence McCaffrey, manager of stamp development, found the Federal Eagle and asked Sheaff to revise it to meet a forthcoming need for a definitive stamped envelope. Sheaff removed the pattern of zigzag security lines that Doret had included as a backdrop for the imprinted variable-rate denomination and inserted in its place a "34" provided by the artist. He also chose a combination of colors that was more subtle than the red and blue of Doret's original stamp design, which McCaffrey rejected as "a little too jarring" for envelope use.

"Little did we know that the envelope was going to be all over the news," McCaffrey said. Given the exposure it had received, he said, "I wish we had had something more attractive out there. I thought the enve-

Several years earlier, Michael Doret had created these red, white and blue designs for a variable-rate coil stamp that never was issued. When a design was needed for a 34¢ definitive stamped envelope, art director Richard Sheaff adapted the Federal Eagle stamp art, eliminating the security pattern of zigzag lines, inserting a "34" denomination in its place and changing the colors to a more subtle blue and gray.

lope was a good one at the time, but every time I see it now I think how bureaucratic it looks, how federal."

Numerous color variations of the imprinted stamp on the envelope have been found by collectors, including eagles in various degrees of gray.

First-Day Facts

No first-day ceremony was held for the Federal Eagle envelope. For a limited time, Stamp Fulfillment Services sold uncacheted first-day covers of all six formats of the envelope for 52¢ each.

34¢ LOVE ENVELOPE

Date of Issue: February 14, 2001

Catalog Number: Scott U647

Colors: pink (PMS 205 uncoated) and violet (PMS 526 uncoated)

First-Day Cancel: Lovejoy, Georgia

First-Day Cancellations: 181,746 (includes 34¢ Love Letters stamps)

Sizes: numbers 6¾ and 10

Watermark: none

Markings: "THIS ENVELOPE IS RECYCLABLE AND MADE WITH 100%/RECYCLED PAPER, 30% POST-CONSUMER CONTENT" and recycling symbol on back of envelope. "© USPS 2000" under flap.

Designer: Robert Brangwynne of Boston, Massachusetts

Art Director and Typographer: Richard Sheaff of Scottsdale, Arizona

Envelope Manufacturing: Envelopes printed by Westvaco of Williamsburg, Pennsylvania, by offset

Quantity Ordered: 30,000,000 (15,000,000 of each size)

Tagging: vertical bar to right of stamp

The Envelope

On February 14, the Postal Service issued a 34¢ Love stamped envelope at Lovejoy, Georgia. Also issued at Lovejoy that day were two Love stamps, in 34¢ and 55¢ denominations (see separate chapter).

Four previous Love envelopes had been issued, for the 25¢ first-class rate (1989), the 29¢ rate (1991), the 32¢ rate (1995) and the 33¢ rate (1999).

The new envelope was offset-printed by Westvaco on 100 percent recycled paper and was available in the number 6¾ and number 10 sizes, with no window. USPS ordered 15 million of each size. Individual envelopes cost 42¢ each; the 8¢ premium charged for envelope production was a penny more than the 7¢ surcharge that had been imposed on the 33¢ Love envelopes. USPS also offered 500 Love envelopes for $182 (number 6¾) or $184 (number 10).

The Design

The stamped design portion of the envelope features a line drawing of mirror images of two birds, head to head, that also form the outline of a heart. Although the USPS news release describes the birds as "lovebirds," they appear more to resemble doves. The release said the design "embodies the intimacy of true love."

The idea behind the illustration is somewhat similar to that of Marvin Mattelson's 1997 Love stamps, on which the arched necks of two swans form the shape of a heart.

It was the work of the late Robert Brangwynne of Boston, Massachusetts, and was one of several design concepts for definitive and special stamps and stationery prepared under the direction of Richard Sheaff, one of the Postal Service's part-time art directors, that USPS kept in reserve for use as needed. This one was developed around 1994. Brangwynne's stamp design credits included the 25¢ Rhode Island Statehood Bicentennial stamp of 1990.

In developing the Brangwynne drawing as a stamped envelope, Sheaff experimented with adding the word "Love" in italics and calligraphy. "The [Citizens' Stamp Advisory] Committee said the calligraphy was overkill, it was a little too schmaltzy," said Terrence McCaffrey, manager of stamp development for USPS. Eventually the word was dropped altogether. "Everybody felt that with the heart and doves, it said 'Love' enough," McCaffrey said. "We didn't need to repeat it."

The heart-birds image is printed in violet and the "34 USA," in two lines on the left side, is pink.

Art director Richard Sheaff incorporated the word "Love" into early design variations, but it was decided that the word wasn't needed.

336

First-day Facts

For information on the first-day ceremony, see the chapter on the 34¢ Love Letters stamps. Stamp Fulfillment Services offered uncacheted first-day covers of the Love envelope for 52¢.

34¢ COMMUNITY COLLEGES ENVELOPE

Date of Issue: February 20, 2001

Catalog Number: Scott U648

Colors: blue (PMS 2955), orange (PMS 159)

First-Day Cancel: Joliet, Illinois

First-Day Cancellations: 15,076

Sizes: numbers 6¾ and 10, each with or without windows

Watermark: none

Markings: "© USPS 2000" under flap. "THIS ENVELOPE IS RECYCLABLE AND MADE WITH 100%/RECYCLED PAPER, 30% POST-CONSUMER CONTENT" and recycling symbol.

Illustrator and Typographer: Steve McCracken of Washington, D.C.

Art Director and Designer: Howard Paine of Delaplane, Virginia

Envelope Manufacturing: envelopes printed by Westvaco of Williamsburg, Pennsylvania, by flexography on a VH-1 machine

Quantity Ordered: 6,000,000 number 6¾; 4,000,000 number 6¾ with window; 12,000,000 number 10; 6,000,000 number 10 with window.

Tagging: vertical bar to right of stamp

The Envelope

On February 20, the Postal Service issued a 34¢ stamped envelope to honor the nation's community colleges on the 100th anniversary of the oldest one, Joliet Junior College in Joliet, Illinois. The envelope had its first-day sale at Joliet.

A community college, as defined by the American Association of Community Colleges, is a publicly supported, regionally accredited institution of higher education that offers the associate's degree as its highest degree

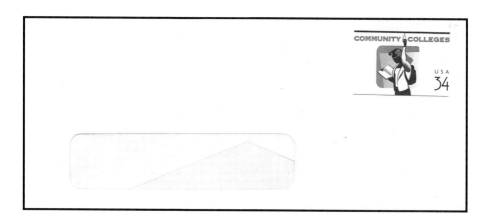

and primarily serves commuter students.

The envelope was manufactured in two sizes, 6¾ and 10, each available with or without a window. Like other recent U.S. stamped envelopes, it was produced by the flexography process by Westvaco at its Williamsburg, Pennsylvania, plant. It has no embossing.

Single envelopes sold for 42¢. USPS also sold boxes of 500 for $182 (number 6¾) and $184 (other sizes).

Joliet Junior College began in 1901 as an experimental postgraduate high school program conceived by J. Stanley Brown, superintendent of Joliet Township High School, and William Rainey Harper, president of the University of Chicago. Private two-year colleges existed before 1901, but a publicly funded program such as Joliet's was an innovation. The initial enrollment was six. Today JJC serves more than 10,000 students in credit classes and another 21,000 taking noncredit courses.

Norma Kent, director of communications for the American Association of Community Colleges, asked that USPS not "single out Joliet" in the envelope's design, but rather "celebrate America's community colleges in general in 2001, the centennial of Joliet's founding." "Diversity, civic responsibility and affordable, quality education are three of the prominent features that make community colleges distinctive and noteworthy American institutions," she said.

Approximately 1,000 public community colleges exist today with a combined enrollment of some 5 million, which represents nearly half the country's total college population. An additional 5 million Americans take non-credit courses at community colleges. The institutions serve 46 percent of all African-American college students, 55 percent of all Hispanic students, 55 percent of all Native American students and 46 percent of Asian/Pacific Islander students.

The Design

Steve McCracken, whom art director Howard Paine selected to illustrate the envelope, is a Washington, D.C. artist whose previous assignment for USPS was to create the airbrush paintings for the block of four 29¢ Circus commemoratives of 1993. He now works almost exclusively on a Macintosh computer, using programs such as Adobe Photoshop, Adobe Illustrator and Adobe Painter.

"I realized early on that we didn't want a building, because every community college across the country is of a different design," Paine said. "Mostly, the buildings are low, flat, modern — nondescript, if you will — with no historic tower or architectural purity. And even if there were, what's at one school isn't like what's at another.

"My thought was that 'community college' means an urban situation where students live at home and go to school on the bus. Very early on, I said, this has got to show a straphanger. We don't want a kid sitting at the foot of a tree on a lovely, idyllic campus reading a book or whatever; we want to show somebody in an urban setting going between point A and point B."

To "make this image as universal as we could," in Paine's words, McCracken depicted a woman of indeterminate ethnicity, her face in shadow. "We put a backpack on her, and had her hanging on the strap of a bus or trolley," Paine continued. "In one version, Steve had four straps hanging down, but I told him we really only needed one. We had her reading a book, as though preparing for class. Steve put a rectangle behind her, with rounded corners, that suggests a bus window. I think it works very nicely."

This is one of several rough pencil sketches sent by Howard Paine to Steve McCracken in June 1999 to start the design process for the Community Colleges envelope.

Shown here are two earlier versions of Steve McCracken's strap-hanging student. In one, she is holding the book away from her body; in the revised art, she holds it in a more natural position along her forearm. The four straps in the other version were reduced in number to the one to which the student clings.

340

The student and "USA 34" are printed in dark blue; the rectangle and the words "COMMUNITY COLLEGES," in a brownish orange. Until the very end of the design process, McCracken had included the inscription "Serving America 100 Years." Then the Citizens' Stamp Advisory Committee decreed that the line be dropped, a decision that simplified the design but left the user of the envelope with no information as to why it had been issued.

First-Day Facts

The envelope was dedicated by James M. Holmes, lead executive and district manager of the Central Illinois Performance Cluster, in a ceremony on the bridge at Joliet Junior College.

The speakers were J.D. Ross, president of the college; Norma Kent, director of communications for the American Association of Community Colleges; and U.S. Representative Jerry Weller, Republican of Illinois.

Lisa Hellman, Joliet Junior College's centennial celebration event specialist, gave the welcome and introduced the guests. Lolita Rice, Joliet postmaster, presided.

34¢ OFFICIAL MAIL ENVELOPE

Official Mail

USA
34

OFFICIAL BUSINESS
PENALTY FOR PRIVATE USE $300

Date of Issue: February 27, 2001

Catalog Number: Scott UO90

Colors: blue, red

First-Day Cancel: Washington, D.C.

First-Day Cancellations: 26,675 (includes Official Mail stamp)

Size: number 10, without window

Watermark: none

Markings: "© USPS 1988" under flap. "OFFICIAL BUSINESS/PENALTY FOR PRIVATE USE $300." Recycled logo and "THIS ENVELOPE IS RECYCLABLE AND MADE WITH 100% RECYCLED PAPER, 30% POST-CONSUMER CONTENT."

Designer and Typographer: Bradbury Thompson

Art Director: Joe Brockert, USPS

Envelope Manufacturing: Envelopes printed by Westvaco of Williamsburg, Pennsylvania, by flexography and embossing on a VH-1 machine.

Quantity Ordered: 2,000,000

Tagging: vertical bar to left of stamp

The Stamp

In response to the January 7 increase in the domestic postal rate to 34¢, the Postal Service issued a 34¢ Official Mail stamped envelope to cover the new rate. The envelope was placed on sale February 27 in Washington, D.C., without a first-day ceremony. The envelope, along with a 34¢ Official Mail coil stamp issued the same day (see related chapter), was available nationwide the following day.

Official Mail

USA
34

The designs of both the envelope and stamp show the eagle and shield of the Great Seal of the United States. The same basic design has appeared with some modifications on most modern U.S. Official Mail postal items since 1983.

The envelope was issued in the number 10 size only, without a window. It was printed by Westvaco on 100 percent recycled paper by two-color flexography with embossing. Individual envelopes sold for 42¢.

The envelope was a surprise addition to the 2001 U.S. stamp program. Although a list of upcoming stamps released in early January 2001 by USPS included a February 27 listing for "34¢ Official Mail," there was no indication that both a stamp and a stamped envelope would be released.

It wasn't until February 6 that a Postal Service announcement specifically noted that an Official Mail stamped envelope was to be issued.

The Design

Since 1983, the year the current series of Official Mail stamps, envelopes and postal cards began, all Official Mail items, with two exceptions, have carried designs by the late Bradbury Thompson featuring the Great Seal of the United States. The exceptions, 52¢ and 75¢ stamped envelopes issued in 1992 for passports, had designs commemorating the 200th anniversary of the U.S. Consular Service.

The Great Seal on the 34¢ Official Mail envelope is shown in dropout white. All other elements are printed in blue, with the exception of the 34¢ denomination, which appears in red.

In addition, details of the Great Seal design are embossed, including the eagle's features, the stripes of the shield and the stars above the eagle's head.

Embossing is a type of security feature used on U.S. stamped paper. Once a customary element of U.S. stamped envelopes, it is now used only occasionally.

First-day Facts

No first-day ceremony was held for the 2001 Official Mail envelope. For a limited time, Stamp Fulfillment Services offered uncacheted envelopes with first-day cancellations for 52¢ each.

70¢ BADLANDS NATIONAL PARK POSTAL CARD
SCENIC AMERICAN LANDMARKS SERIES

Date of Issue: February 22, 2001

Catalog Number: Scott UXC28

Colors: magenta, yellow, cyan, black

First-Day Cancel: Wall, South Dakota

First-Day Cancellations: 90,746 (includes 55¢ Art Deco Eagle, 20¢ George Washington and 21¢ Bison stamps)

Format: Cards printed in 80-subject sheet but available only as single-cut cards. Offset printing plates of 80 subjects (8 across, 10 down).

Size: 5.5 by 3.5 inches

Marking: "©2000 USPS." Recycled logo followed by "recycled."

Photographer: David Muench of Santa Barbara, California

Designer, Art Director and Typographer: Ethel Kessler of Bethesda, Maryland

Card Manufacturing: Cards printed by the Government Printing Office in Washington, D.C., on a 5-color MAN Roland sheetfed offset press. Cards processed and shipped by GPO.

Quantity Ordered: 6,000,000

Paper Type: 22-pound bright white

Tagging: vertical bar to right of stamp

The Card

On February 22, the Postal Service issued a 70¢ postal card with an imprinted stamp depicting a scene from the Badlands in South Dakota.

The card was part of a series of international-rate stamps and postal stationery called Scenic American Landmarks.

The 70¢ denomination covered the rate that took effect the preceding January 7 for postcards to countries other than Canada and Mexico. The one previous postal card in the series, a 55¢ card depicting Mount Rainier that was issued in 1999, had met the old international postcard rate.

The card was the first of four items in the Scenic American Landmark series to be issued in 2001. The others, all stamps, depicted scenes from Nine-Mile Prairie, Nebraska; Mount McKinley, Alaska; and Acadia National Park, Maine (see separate chapters).

The Badlands, in southwest South Dakota, derives its name from the English equivalent of both the old Lakota Sioux name for the region, "mako sica," and the early French trappers' description, "les mauvaises terres a traverser," or "the bad terrain to travel through." Badlands National Park consists of nearly 244,000 acres of sharply eroded buttes, pinnacles and spires blended with the largest protected mixed-grass prairie in the United States.

Water runoff erodes large amounts of sediment, creating remarkable natural sculptures. The soft rocks are composed of mixtures of sand, silt, clay and volcanic ash and erode so quickly that one thunderstorm can virtually change the landscape overnight. Conservation writer Freeman Tilden described the region as "peaks and valleys of delicately banded colors — colors that shift in the sunshine — and a thousand tints that color charts do not show. In the early morning and evening, when shadows are cast upon the infinite peaks, or on a bright moonlit night when the whole region seems a part of another world, the Badlands will be an experience not easily forgotten."

Some 64,000 acres of the park are officially designated wilderness and are the site of the re-introduction of the black-footed ferret, the most endangered land mammal in North America. In addition to 56 different types of grasses, the Badlands produces a large variety of wildflowers, desert plants and shrubs that provide food and habitat for many species of birds, mammals, amphibians and insects.

President Franklin D. Roosevelt established Badlands National Monument January 25, 1939, to protect its abundant fossil resources and spectacular landscape. In the late 1960s, Congress added more than 130,000 acres of Oglala Sioux tribal land — used since World War II as a U.S. Air Force bombing and gunnery range — to the Badlands to be managed by the National Park Service. An agreement between the tribe and the National Park Service covering the management of these lands was signed in 1976, and two years later, on November 10, 1978, Congress redesignated the area as Badlands National Park.

The Design

Postal Service officials originally considered the Badlands a subject for a stamp in the Scenic American Landmarks series, and Ethel Kessler, art director for the series, created a stamp design using an aerial photograph of the region's bizarre geological formations. However, after the Citizens' Stamp Advisory Committee decided to make the Badlands the subject of a postal card, it was decided that the photo wouldn't work satisfactorily in that format, given that the screening and paper stock used to produce a card are of lower quality than those used in stamp printing.

The alternative photograph chosen by Kessler for the card "could have been exquisite as a stamp," she said. "But it's also one of the few images we found that we felt wouldn't get lost in the printing process as a postal card.

"Acadia, for example [the subject of a stamp in the series that also was issued in 2001] never would have worked well as a stamped card. The detail of the photograph is so important that the paper stock was crucial in making it work. If we tried to take that same image and make it a card, it would have looked fuzzier and a little less interesting. Even though we go a little larger in our postal card images, it would not have worked better. It would have worked a lot worse."

The photograph that ended up on the Badlands card was made by David Muench of Santa Barbara, California, a veteran free-lance photographer whose work has appeared in wilderness and conservation publications as well as other magazines, books and advertisements. Kessler displayed the photo in a long horizontal rectangle occupying much of the upper-right quadrant of the card's address side.

Muench's shot is an eye-level view of jagged and pyramidal formations with a field of grass in the foreground. Early-morning or late-afternoon sunlight casts a golden glow on the surfaces facing the sun and leaves the remaining areas of the rocks in deep shadow. The background is a dark, cloudless sky. The letters "USA," vertically arranged, and the denomination, "70," all in dropout white type, are in the upper-left and lower-right corners of the imprinted stamp, respectively. The small stylized silhouette of a jet plane next to the denomination — a part of all Scenic American Landmarks designs — is printed in gray. The words "Badlands National Park, South Dakota" are in tiny black letters just below the frameline on the right side.

First-Day Facts

The Badlands postal card, along with varieties of the 20¢ George Washington and 21¢ Bison stamps and the 55¢ Art Deco Eagle stamp, had their first-day sale February 22 in Wall, South Dakota, on the edge of the Badlands National Park. They were placed on nationwide sale the next day. No official USPS dedication ceremony was held. For information on the first-day event organized by local and district postal officials, see the chapter on the Bison stamp varieties.

20¢ YALE UNIVERSITY POSTAL CARD
HISTORIC PRESERVATION SERIES

Date of Issue: March 30, 2001

Catalog Number: Scott UX361

Colors: magenta, yellow, cyan, black

First-Day Cancel: New Haven, Connecticut

First-Day Cancellations: 11,588

Format: Cards printed in 80-subject sheet but available only as single-cut cards. Offset printing plates of 80 subjects (8 across, 10 down).

Size: 5.5 by 3.5 inches

Marking: "©2000 USPS." Recycled logo followed by "recycled."

Photographer: photo supplied by Yale University

Designer, Art Director and Typographer: Derry Noyes of Washington, D.C.

Card Manufacturing: Cards printed by the Government Printing Office in Washington, D.C., on a 5-color MAN Roland sheetfed offset press. Cards processed and shipped by GPO.

Quantity Ordered: 6,000,000

Paper Type: 22-pound bright white

Tagging: vertical bar to right of stamp

The Card

On March 30, the Postal Service issued a 20¢ postal card in its Historic Preservation series to commemorate the 300th anniversary of the founding of Yale University in New Haven, Connecticut, the third oldest institution of higher learning in the United States.

The two institutions that are older had been honored previously by USPS on significant anniversaries. The 350th anniversary of Harvard University's founding in 1636 was marked in 1986 with a 56¢ stamp in the Great Americans definitive series picturing John Harvard, for whom the school was named, and the tercentenary of the College of William and Mary was commemorated with a Historic Preservation postal card in 1993.

The Yale card sold for 21¢. USPS explains that the surcharge covers the cost of manufacturing what it now refers to as a "stamped card."

It was the first of four Historic Preservation cards issued in 2001 to have a short practical life. On July 1, four months after its issuance, the postcard rate rose to 21¢. After that, users of any 20¢ postal card would be required to affix a 1¢ stamp next to the card's stamped image.

Like other cards in the series in recent years, the Yale card was a regional issue. It was available March 30 at the first-day ceremony and at New Haven post offices. Beginning March 31, the card was sold at other post offices in Connecticut and at postal stores and philatelic counters around the country. Yale alumni living in other states had to buy it at those facilities or by mail from Stamp Fulfillment Services in Kansas City, Missouri.

Six million Yale cards were ordered, the same print quantity as for other regional cards except the card issued in 2000 for Middlebury College, Vermont, which had a printing of four million.

The imprinted stamp on the card depicts a contemporary photograph of Connecticut Hall on Yale's Old Campus. The first of Yale's brick buildings and the oldest remaining structure on the campus and in the city of New Haven, Connecticut Hall is a national historic landmark. It was listed on the National Register of Historic Places October 15. It was erected by Thomas Bills and Francis Letort between 1750 and 1753.

As described in the register's statement of significance, Connecticut Hall is "the lone survivor of 'Brick Row,' a group of Georgian-style buildings built before 1820 and razed after the Civil War." Originally a dormitory, Connecticut Hall now houses faculty offices and meeting rooms.

Yale was chartered as the Collegiate School of Connecticut on October 9, 1701, and was renamed Yale College in 1718 after benefactor Elihu Yale. Its final name change to Yale University was made in 1887.

Some 11,000 students from all 50 states and nearly 100 countries are enrolled in the undergraduate college and the 11 graduate and professional schools. Yale's graduates include five U.S. presidents, but only one, William Howard Taft (Yale College, 1878), has appeared on a U.S. stamp. The others, all still living as of this writing, are Gerald Ford (Law School, 1941), George Herbert Walker Bush (Yale College, 1948), William Jefferson Clinton (Law School, 1973) and George W. Bush (Yale College, 1968).

The Design

The nearly square imprinted stamp depicts a corner view of Connecticut Hall, with its gambrel roof, double chimneys and shuttered windows, framed by foliage from nearby trees. In the foreground are a lamppost and crossed walkways typical of a college campus. The color photograph was supplied by Yale University.

Designer Derry Noyes placed the words "Connecticut Hall Yale University," in dropout white Garamond type, on a panel of Yale blue beneath the image. "20 USA" is in two lines of dropout type in the upper-right corner.

"Originally, we went with an old engraving of the campus, in a black or sepia monotone," Noyes said. "Very elegant. But some of the buildings don't exist anymore. Yale didn't want to look backward; they wanted to be contemporary. That's why we used the photograph. Connecticut Hall was the obvious building to show, and it was just a matter of finding the right image of it."

Derry Noyes originally intended to depict this etching of the buildings of Yale College circa 1807, after an engraving by Amos Doolittle. But "Yale didn't want to look backward; they wanted to be contemporary," Noyes said.

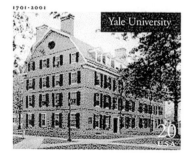

Noyes experimented with these two alternative type treatments for the Yale University postal card.

349

First-day Facts

John F. Walsh, a member of the USPS Board of Governors, dedicated the postal card in a ceremony in Connecticut Hall.

The United Nations Postal Administration offered a commemorative cancellation in honor of Yale's tercentenary. Joseph Verner Reed, undersecretary of the U.N., dedicated the cancellation.

Speakers at the ceremony were Richard C. Levin, president of Yale University; New Haven Mayor John DeStefano Jr.; and C. Douglas Lewis, curator of sculpture and decorative arts at the National Gallery of Art and vice chairman of CSAC.

Linda Koch Lorimer, vice president and secretary of Yale, gave the welcome. Alexander Lazaroff, lead executive and Connecticut District manager for USPS, presided. Honored guests included Anthony J. Fouracre, chief of the U.N. Postal Administration, and Denise D. Porter, postmaster of New Haven.

The earliest-known prerelease use of a Yale postal card was a card machine-canceled in Cincinnati, Ohio, March 29, one day before the official first-day sale.

20¢ UNIVERSITY OF SOUTH CAROLINA POSTAL CARD HISTORIC PRESERVATION SERIES

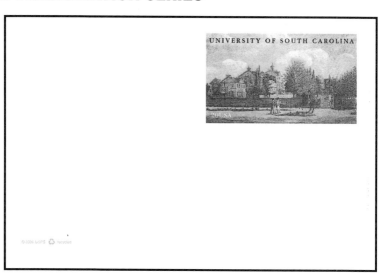

Date of Issue: April 26, 2001

Catalog Number: Scott UX362

Colors: magenta, yellow, cyan, black

First-Day Cancel: Columbia, South Carolina

First-Day Cancellations: 14,855

Format: Cards printed in 80-subject sheet but available only as single-cut cards. Offset printing plates of 80 subjects (8 across, 10 down).

Size: 5.5 by 3.5 inches

Marking: "©2000 USPS." Recycled logo followed by "recycled."

Designer, Art Director and Typographer: Ethel Kessler of Bethesda, Maryland

Card Manufacturing: Cards printed by the Government Printing Office in Washington, D.C., on a 5-color MAN Roland sheetfed offset press. Cards processed and shipped by GPO.

Quantity Ordered: 6,000,000

Paper Type: 22-pound bright white

Tagging: vertical bar to right of stamp

The Card

On April 26, the Postal Service commemorated the 200th anniversary of the founding of the University of South Carolina by issuing a postal card in the Historic Preservation series. The card, the 52nd in the series by the Postal Service's count, was dedicated on the university's main campus in Columbia.

Like other recent postal cards honoring institutions of higher education, its distribution was only regional. On its first day of issue, it was sold at the ceremony and at Columbia post offices. Beginning the next day, it was available for sale at other post offices in South Carolina, as well as postal stores and philatelic windows throughout the country and by mail from Stamp Fulfillment Services in Kansas City, Missouri.

The University of South Carolina card had its origin in 1997 when John M. Palms, the president of the university, appointed a "preplanning group" to make recommendations for the bicentennial celebration four years later. One of the first things the group decided, said Thomas L. Stepp, secretary of the board of trustees, was to ask the Postal Service for a stamp to commemorate the occasion. Like other colleges and universities before them, the group quickly learned that the criteria of the Citizens' Stamp Advisory Committee allow only postal cards for the anniversaries of institutions of higher education.

The university encouraged letters of support to CSAC from alumni and the state's congressional delegation. Richard Riley, then U.S. secretary of education and a University of South Carolina graduate, lent his endorsement. CSAC had no difficulty deciding that the 200th anniversary of one of the nation's major state universities was worthy of commemoration.

The institution was chartered as the South Carolina College December 19, 1801. It was the first state university to receive continuous support from annual state appropriations.

Offering a traditional classical curriculum, the college became one of the South's most influential educational institutions before 1861, earning a reputation as a training ground for the state's antebellum elite.

During the Civil War, it closed its doors for want of students. State leaders revived it in 1866, and under Reconstruction the university enrolled black students, the only Southern state university to admit and grant degrees to former slaves during this period.

When Reconstruction ended in 1877, the state's political leaders closed the institution, reopening it three years later as an all-white agricultural college. For the next quarter-century, the institution went through several reorganizations in which the curriculum frequently changed and its status shifted from college to university and back again. In 1906 the institution was rechartered for the final time as the University of South Carolina.

In 1917 it became the first state-supported college or university in

South Carolina to earn regional accreditation. After World War II, its enrollment more than doubled, and in the 1950s the university established campuses in communities across the state.

A federal court order in 1963 ended the institution's policy of racial segregation, and on September 11, three young men became the first of an increasing number of African-American students to enroll at the university in the 20th century. Today, the University of South Carolina offers more than 400 undergraduate and graduate degree programs and serves more than 38,000 students from all 50 states and more than 100 countries on its eight campuses throughout the state. Of these, more than 26,000 attend classes on the main campus in Columbia.

The original campus of the South Carolina College, known as the Horseshoe District, is listed on the National Register of Historic Places as the "Old Campus District."

The Design

From time to time in recent years, the Postal Service has chosen to use historic pieces of art for its commemorative postal cards rather than commission a new painting. This course was followed with the University of South Carolina postal card, with the full concurrence of university officials.

Ethel Kessler, a USPS art director, developed her design for the card's imprinted stamp from a large panoramic watercolor that hangs in a research room at the university's South Caroliniana Library. She had originally seen the painting reproduced in a book called *An Architectural History of South Carolina*, and "kind of zeroed in on it," she said.

The painting, signed "T. Ulor," was made circa 1827 and shows the Horseshoe District of South Carolina College from outside its surrounding wall. At least eight of the college buildings are visible. Several strollers, two men on horseback and another man driving a horse-drawn cart are seen in the foreground, while a guard stands at a gate opening onto the campus. A cloud-dappled sky is overhead.

The painting posed two problems. First, it was so large that roughly one-half of its panorama had to be cropped to allow the remainder to fit into even the generous-sized imprinted-stamp area of the postal card. Second, the passage of nearly two centuries had left it dark and dull in color — much too dark to make it acceptable for reproduction on a postal card.

Kessler tried three different croppings of the card. The one ultimately chosen shows the pedestrians and one horseman, but omits the second rider and the horse-drawn cart. However, it includes the gate in the wall, something that had been requested by the university's Thomas Stepp.

"I asked them if they could keep the gate, because we still use the gates to the Horseshoe as a symbol of the openness of the university to the world," Stepp said. "The gates look different now, but the concept of higher education as a gate is an important one, and they were very kind to be responsive to that suggestion."

Shown here is a reproduction of the painting by "T. Ulor" of the South Carolina College, circa 1827, that Ethel Kessler cropped to obtain the image for the postal card's imprinted stamp. The portion shown on the card is from the right-center of the panorama and includes the open gate, as requested by a university representative.

The darkness problem was solved by using a computer to lighten the color transparencies of the painting that were supplied by the university. The result is a cheerful-looking image with oranges and browns predominating. "We took it back to the university, and they said it looked great," said Terrence McCaffrey, manager of stamp development. "They were very happy with it."

"University of South Carolina" is in black Garamond capitals across the top of the imprinted stamp, and "20 USA" is dropped out of the lower-left corner. In keeping with CSAC's less-is-better approach to design, there is nothing on the card to indicate that the university was marking an anniversary.

First-Day Facts

Joyce Carrier, manager of public affairs and communications for USPS, dedicated the postal card in a ceremony in front of the Faculty House in the university's Horseshoe District.

John M. Palms, president of the university, gave the welcome. Speakers were Walter B. Edgar, Neuffer professor of Southern studies at the university and a member of its bicentennial commission; another commission member, John E. Courson, a state senator; and Robert D. Coble, mayor of Columbia. Lawrence Jordan, Columbia's postmaster, presided.

For this event, USPS unveiled a new "economy" first-day ceremony program that would be used for subsequent stamp dedications. In contrast with the sometimes elaborate, die-cut, full-color custom-designed programs of recent years, it consisted of a single sheet inserted into a generic folder of heavy, glossy stock. One side of the sheet contained the ceremony program itself, listing the participants, and the other side bore text describing the issue.

According to a USPS press release, "The ceremony programs will feature a more cost-effective standardized design noting the year of issuance, with an insert uniquely designed to correspond with each issuance. One or more stamps (or one stamped card or envelope), bearing a first-day postmark, will continue to be included in the programs."

20¢ NORTHWESTERN UNIVERSITY POSTAL CARD
HISTORIC PRESERVATION SERIES

Date of Issue: April 28, 2001

Catalog Number: Scott UX363

Colors: magenta, yellow, cyan, black

First-Day Cancel: Evanston, Illinois

First-Day Cancellations: 10,713

Format: Cards printed in 80-subject sheet but available only as single-cut cards. Offset printing plates of 80 subjects (8 across, 10 down).

Size: 5.5 by 3.5 inches

Marking: "©2000 USPS." Recycled logo followed by "recycled."

Illustrator: Arnold Holeywell of Warrenton, Virginia

Designer, Art Director and Typographer: Howard Paine of Delaplane, Virginia

Card Manufacturing: Cards printed by the Government Printing Office in Washington, D.C., on a 5-color MAN Roland sheetfed offset press. Cards processed and shipped by GPO.

Quantity Ordered: 6,000,000

Paper Type: 22-pound bright white

Tagging: vertical bar to right of stamp

The Card

On April 28, the Postal Service issued a 20¢ postal card in its Historic Preservation series to commemorate the 150th anniversary of the found-

356

ing of Northwestern University in Evanston, Illinois.

Like other current U.S. postal cards, it sold for 21¢, with the extra 1¢ explained by USPS as covering the cost of what it now refers to as the "stamped card."

The university's sesquicentennial planning committee originally had asked for a stamp for the event, following a suggestion by an alumnus in Portland, Oregon, Richard A. Carlson. Told that the criteria of the Citizens' Stamp Advisory Committee permitted only postal cards for the anniversaries of universities and colleges, the committee revised its request accordingly. CSAC voted approval, and USPS unveiled the design of the card October 20, 2000, in a ceremony at Deering Meadow on the Northwestern campus.

Most Historic Preservation cards depict buildings that are on the National Register of Historic Places. In fact, officials at one college — Middlebury, in Vermont — took steps to obtain a National Register listing for its "Old Stone Row" for the specific purpose of enhancing their chances of persuading CSAC to approve a postal card for the college's 200th anniversary. The strategy was successful, and the Middlebury card was issued in 2000.

But Northwestern's only site on the National Register is Shakespeare Garden, listed in 1988. The garden was established in 1915 as a gesture of unity with Great Britain, which was at war with Germany, and to commemorate the 300th anniversary of William Shakespeare's death. Designed by landscape architect Jens Jensen and hidden from view by a double wall of hawthorn hedges, it showcases plants that are mentioned in Shakespeare's plays.

Late in 1999, Howard Paine, the card's art director and designer, commissioned some color sketches of Shakespeare Garden from artist Arnold C. Holeywell. But after looking them over, Paine and CSAC concluded that the garden wouldn't work as a design subject, and settled for an alternative image suggested by the university: the main tower of University Hall, the oldest building on the campus.

The postal card was the 53rd in the Historic Preservation series, by the Postal Service's count, and the sixth to feature a site in Illinois, the most for any state. Previous cards with Illinois subjects were for Chicago's Hull House, Orchestra Hall and University of Chicago; Illinois College, in Jacksonville; and Abraham Lincoln's home in Springfield.

Under USPS policy, the Northwestern card was sold at post offices only in Illinois, although it was available at postal stores and philatelic centers throughout the country, as well as by mail from Stamp Fulfillment Services in Kansas City, Missouri.

In May 1850, nine Methodist men met above a hardware store in the burgeoning frontier town of Chicago to establish an institution "of the highest order of excellence" to serve the people of the Northwest Territory. The following year, Northwestern University was incorporated, and in 1853 the trustees bought and began to develop 379 acres of farmland on Lake Michigan, north of Chicago.

By 1855, the first building was up and a college of liberal arts was in operation with two faculty members and 10 male students. By 1869, Northwestern had admitted its first female students; four years later, it negotiated a merger with the Evanston College for Ladies, whose president, suffragette and temperance leader Frances E. Willard (depicted on a 5¢ Famous Americans stamp of 1940, Scott 872) became Northwestern's first dean of women.

The university was guided through its critical years by John Evans, a physician who founded the Illinois Republican Party and was a confidante of Abraham Lincoln. Evans chaired the board of trustees for almost half a century, until his death in 1897. The town that grew up around the university was named Evanston in his honor.

Today, Northwestern is a private research university of distinction, with 12 academic divisions located on two lakefront campuses in Evanston and Chicago. In 2002 it had 2,044 full-time faculty, 13,618 full-time students and an annual budget exceeding $803 million.

The setting for University Hall was a crescent-shaped oak grove, bounded on the west by a ridge and the east by the lake, and was known to local Indians as "the Eyebrow of Beauty." The building, with its pictur-

esque towers, turrets and mansards, was designed in Gothic Revival style by architect G.P. Randall of Chicago after a sketch by Professor Donald Bonbright and built of a dolomite marble known as "Athens limestone" from a quarry near Joliet. Its cornerstone was laid in 1868, and it was completed the following year; construction cost $125,000.

The steeple of University Hall is shown on the Northwestern University postal card. This photograph of the building, the oldest on the campus, was taken in the winter of 1988. (Northwestern University photo)

This is a preliminary color sketch in gouache by Arnold C. Holeywell of North-western University's Shakespeare Garden, featuring the garden's sundial and bronze and stone memorial fountain that bears a relief of Shakespeare's head and a panel with quotations from his writings. Although Shakespeare Garden is the only site on the campus that is listed on the National Register of Historic Places, CSAC felt it was unsuitable as a design subject for the postal card.

University Hall was the main university building until Fayerweather Hall's construction in 1887. It housed all Northwestern's classes, the library, a chemical laboratory, a chapel, a dining area, two society rooms and a fourth-floor natural history museum. The Seth Thomas clock in the highest tower was the gift of the Class of 1879; in 1966 a new electrified clock replaced the old works, which were sent to the Smithsonian Institution. The bells were the gift of the class of 1880. In 1993 the building was re-dedicated after a $5.2 million renovation.

The Design

Illustrator Arnold Holeywell is the retired art director of Time Life books and an old friend and neighbor of Howard Paine, the card's art director. Holeywell also had created the artwork for the Middlebury College card in 2000, another of Paine's projects.

For Northwestern, Holeywell made some gouache (opaque watercolor) sketches of Shakespeare Garden, featuring a bronze and stone memorial fountain installed in 1929 and a sundial added in 1990, along with the surrounding hedge. But CSAC and USPS officials were dissatisfied. "I think they felt the garden didn't have enough historic significance," Holeywell said. "It didn't have an academic or school look to it."

Holeywell then painted the replacement subject, the tower of University Hall, in a combination of blues, greens and grays. To fill in the horizontal rectangle that normally is used in postal card designs, he and Paine came up with the idea of a simplified map of the Evanston campus, without wording and with the buildings and thoroughfares indicated by shapes and lines. "It was subdued, subtle," Holeywell said. "It was like a ghosted

The Postal Service proposed this design in which a simplified map of a portion of the Evanston campus, showing the lagoon, Lake Michigan and the shapes of some of the prominent buildings, is a backdrop for the University Hall tower. The colors of the map are muted, with the land area in yellow, the lake in blue and the building shapes in lavender. However, Northwestern officials didn't like the map, and it was dropped from the final design.

image behind the strong image of the tower."

To make the map horizontal, however, Paine said, "We had to tip north over to the left," so that Lake Michigan, a lagoon and the area of land that defined it were along the top instead of on the right side as they normally would be shown. "I was quite happy with it," Paine said of the design. "The map made a nice abstract horizontal pattern, and the tower in front of it was a nice little cachet. Arnold traced the map in black ink on vellum, and we assigned PMS colors for the people at Dodge Color [the company that does the Postal Service's prepress work] and they produced some proofs."

However, university officials didn't like the map, for several reasons. They objected to its unconventional orientation, with the lake at the top instead of in its natural position on the right side. They noted that it showed only the university's main campus and omitted an auxiliary campus in Chicago, where the law school, medical school and a portion of the business school are located. Finally, they pointed out that a prominent area of the map, the lagoon and landfill, had been created as recently as the 1970s. "Anyone who graduated before 1972 would look at that portion and would not recognize it as their Northwestern campus, because it just doesn't look like anything they remembered," said Monica Metzler, director of the sesquicentennial celebration.

The USPS design team agreed to eliminate the map, keep the tower and

360

Howard Paine sketched more than a dozen different arrangements of tower and type. Terrence McCaffrey, manager of stamp development, chose a sketch similar to this one for its relative compactness, but suggested that horizontal rules be placed above and below the wording. Paine responded with this sketch, which he later modified at McCaffrey's suggestion by limiting the rules to the right of the tower rather than extending them behind it.

fill the remaining portion of the imprinted-stamp area with type. By now, time was growing short; it was mid-September 2000, and Northwestern wanted to unveil the finished design October 20. Paine dashed off a dozen pencil sketches, varying the wording and its arrangement, and faxed them to Terrence McCaffrey, manager of stamp development for USPS.

McCaffrey chose two of the sketches in which the type was in a compact area to the right of the tower. "The others look too 'strung out' and don't work well as a unit," he told Paine in a faxed reply. He suggested that a set of horizontal rules be added above and below the type. "Try playing with these, or spinoffs," he added. "But whatever we do, it needs to be fast. ... If we can't come up with an acceptable solution, I may have to cancel their unveiling."

Paine responded with a version in which the words "Northwestern University SESQUICENTENNIAL 1851-2001," in Galliard type, are sandwiched between Oxford rules (double lines, one thick, one thin) beside the tower. In slightly modified form, this became the final design. The typography is in Northwestern's school color, purple, which the Government Printing Office produced with a well-registered blend of process colors.

CSAC "wasn't enamored" of the result, "but the university said it was what they wanted," McCaffrey said. "It's one of our least favorite postal cards as far as designs go."

First-day Facts

Einar V. Dyhrkopp, a member of the USPS Board of Governors, dedicated the card in a ceremony in McCormick Auditorium at the Norris Center on the Evanston campus. Eugene Sunshine, Northwestern's senior vice president for business and finance, gave the welcome, and Mayor Lorraine H. Morton of Evanston was the principal speaker. Danny Jackson, USPS Great Lakes area vice president, presided.

Although the ceremony was held at 3:15 p.m., the Evanston post office began selling and canceling the postal cards at 7 a.m.

The first-day ceremony was Evanston's first in more than six decades. The only other stamp to have its initial sale in the city was the 5¢ Frances E. Willard Famous Americans stamp issued March 28, 1940.

20¢ UNIVERSITY OF PORTLAND POSTAL CARD
HISTORIC PRESERVATION SERIES

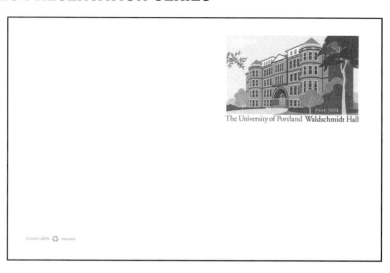

The University of Portland Waldschmidt Hall

Date of Issue: May 1, 2001

Catalog Number: Scott UX364

Colors: magenta, yellow, cyan, black

First-Day Cancel: Portland, Oregon

First-Day Cancellations: 11,905

Format: Cards printed in 80-subject sheet but available only as single-cut cards. Offset printing plates of 80 subjects (8 across, 10 down).

Size: 5.5 by 3.5 inches

Marking: "©2000 USPS." Recycled logo followed by "recycled."

Illustrator: John Pirman of New York, New York

Designer, Art Director and Typographer: Richard Sheaff of Scottsdale, Arizona

Card Manufacturing: Cards printed by the Government Printing Office in Washington, D.C., on a 5-color MAN Roland sheetfed offset press. Cards processed and shipped by GPO.

Quantity Ordered: 6,000,000

Paper Type: 22-pound bright white

Tagging: vertical bar to right of stamp

The Card

On May 1, the Postal Service issued a 20¢ postal card in the Historic Preservation series commemorating the 100th anniversary of the University of Portland, a Catholic institution of higher education in Portland, Oregon.

The card depicted Waldschmidt Hall, the oldest building on the campus. Like other recently issued U.S. postal cards, it sold for 21¢. USPS says the extra 1¢ covers the cost of what it now refers to as the "stamped card."

The University of Portland Waldschmidt Hall

The card was the 54th, by the Postal Service's count, in the Historic Preservation series, which began in 1977 with a 9¢ card depicting the Galveston, Texas, Court House. Twenty-eight of the cards — more than half — have marked the anniversaries of colleges or universities, including the four issued in 2001.

But it was the last to honor a college or university on its centennial or sesquicentennial, under revised criteria adopted by the Citizens' Stamp Advisory Committee and announced March 26, 2001.

CSAC's Article 11 previously had stated: "Requests for commemoration of significant anniversaries of universities and other institutions of higher education shall be considered only in regard to Historic Preservation series postal cards featuring an appropriate building on the campus."

The new Article 11 reads: "Requests for commemoration of universities and other institutions of higher education shall be considered only for [postal] cards and only in connection with the 200th anniversary of their founding."

"We found that we were going to have a large number of universities seeking cards for their 50th, 100th and 150th anniversaries," said Terrence McCaffrey, manager of stamp development for USPS. "We said, 'We can't just turn the [Historic Preservation] program over to colleges. If they survived 200 years, we'll put them on a card.' "

The University of Portland card was also the last U.S. postal card to be issued bearing a 20¢ denomination. Two months after its issuance, USPS increased the postcard rate to 21¢.

In 1901 Catholic Archbishop Alexander Christie purchased 28 acres on Wauds Bluff, including the red brick Waldschmidt Hall — then known as West Hall — for $20,000. Legend has it that Christie saw the building from the Columbia River and exclaimed: "That is the site of my university!" He named the institution he founded Columbia University and appointed the Reverend R.P. Murphy as its first president. Classes began September 5, 1901, with 52 boys enrolled and eight faculty members.

The following year, Christie persuaded the Congregation of Holy Cross to operate the university, and the Reverend Michael A. Quinlan, C.S.C., an English professor at the University of Notre Dame, succeeded Murphy as president. In 1911 construction work was completed on Christie Hall, Columbia's second building.

The university grew through the years, acquiring its present name in 1935. "There was a groundswell of support for the name Christie University, in honor of the founder," the university's Web site reports, "but those who wished to link the university more firmly with the City of Roses won the day." Today, the University of Portland enrolls more than 2,900 students in five undergraduate schools and one graduate school.

West Hall, the oldest building, was constructed in the early 1890s, and in 1992 was renamed Waldschmidt Hall in honor of the university's 15th president, Paul E. Waldschmidt, auxiliary bishop of Portland. The building was listed on the National Register of Historic Places in 1977.

Two other Oregon buildings were previously depicted on Historic Preservation series postal cards: Timberline Lodge on Mount Hood, in 1987, and Willamette University's Waller Hall in Salem, in 1992.

The Design

A few years ago, the Citizens' Stamp Advisory Committee became weary of "boring, literal pictures of buildings," as art director Richard Sheaff put it, and began exploring different illustration styles for its Historic Preservation series. In the process, it approved postal card designs incorporating photographs, antique paintings and engravings, architectural renderings and close-up structural details.

For the University of Portland card, Sheaff commissioned John Pirman of New York, New York, a computer illustrator, to create a contemporary view of Waldschmidt Hall. Sheaff sent the artist a selection of photographs and drawings furnished by the university, including one that incorporated the building angle he wanted. Using Adobe Illustrator software, Pirman made a simple, posterlike picture of the brick building with its arched entranceway and rounded corners surmounted by conical roofs. Green trees and shrubbery are on either side, and behind is a pale blue sky.

The typography consists of the words "The University of Portland," in lavender, and "Waldschmidt Hall," in green, below the rectangular vignette, and "20 USA" and "1901-2001" dropped out of the picture itself. The typeface is Garamond.

First-day Facts

Robert J. Sheehan, associate vice president for the Postal Service's Southeast Sales Region and a 1970 graduate of the University of Portland, dedicated the card in a ceremony at Waldschmidt Hall.

Also scheduled to participate were the university's president, the Reverend. David T. Tyson, C.S.C.; Dallas Keck, district manager for the Postal Service's Portland District; and James Covert, emeritus professor of history at the university.

20¢ BASEBALL'S LEGENDARY PLAYING FIELDS PICTURE POSTAL CARDS (10 DESIGNS)

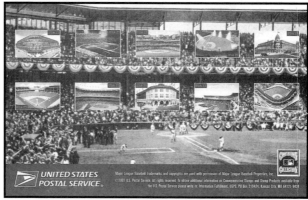

Date of Issue: June 27, 2001

Price: $6.95 for book of 10 cards

Catalog Numbers: Scott UX365-UX374, single cards; UX374a, book of 10 cards

Colors: black, cyan, magenta, yellow, postal cards and book cover outsides; red (PMS 485) and blue (PMS 302), book cover insides.

First-Day Cancels: New York, New York; Boston, Massachusetts; Chicago, Illinois; Detroit, Michigan

First-Day Cancellations: 1,219,195 (includes Baseball's Legendary Playing Fields stamps)

Format: Book of 10 stamped cards, with microperforations to permit removal of individual cards. Offset printing plates of 20 subjects.

Size of Card: 6.00 by 4.25 inches; 152.40 by 107.95mm

Size of Book: 6.75 by 4.25 inches; 171.45 by 107.95mm

Card Markings: On address side of each card: "© 2001 USPS/Major League Baseball trademarks and copyrights are used with permission of Major League Baseball Properties, Inc." Cooperstown Collection logo. On individual cards: "EBBETS FIELD, BROOKLYN/Home to the game's most colorful fans, this Brooklyn/park had quirks galore, including an angled right field/wall and a sign that when hit won the batter a new/suit. The Major League Baseball TV debut occurred at/Ebbets Field in 1939." "TIGER STADIUM, DETROIT/Opened in 1912 as Navin Field, Tiger Stadium was/home to the Detroit Tigers for 88 seasons. It put fans/very close to the field and featured a right field upper/deck that jutted out ten feet farther than the lower/deck." "CROSLEY FIELD, CINCINNATI/Major League Baseball night games debuted at this Cincinnati/park in 1935, with FDR switching on the/lights from the White House. One of the game's small-/est, most intimate stadiums, players had to run uphill/to the outfield fence." "YANKEE STADIUM, NEW YORK CITY/Yankee Stadium has hosted more World Series games/than any other ballpark. Deep to the power alleys but/short down the lines, beyond its left-center field fence/lie monuments and plaques honoring Yankee greats." "POLO GROUNDS, NEW YORK CITY/This storied ballpark — onetime home to the Giants, the/Yankees, and, briefly, the Mets — was the site of the/entire 1921 and 1922 World Series. The horseshoe-/shaped field hosted one of the most famous home runs:/the 1951 'Shot Heard 'Round the World.' " "FORBES FIELD, PITTSBURGH/With expansive foul territory and deep outfield dimen-/sions, this park was a pitcher's friend. Ironically, in the/61 years that the Pittsburgh Pirates called Forbes Field/home, no one ever pitched a no-hitter there." "FENWAY PARK, BOSTON/Boston's intimate Fenway Park has the Green Monster,/a 37-foot-high left field wall. Red Sox fielders who mas-/tered its unpredictable caroms became legends. The/home run that ended game six of the 1975 World Series/made history there." "COMISKEY PARK, CHICAGO/A symmetrical park that favored pitchers over hitters,/this South Side Chicago landmark featured graceful/arched windows. In 1933 it hosted the first All-Star/Game. A fan of gimmicks, the owner installed the first/exploding scoreboard in 1960." "SHIBE PARK, PHILADELPHIA/The first Major League Baseball concrete-and-steel/stadium, Philadelphia's Shibe Park featured a 34-foot-/high right field wall, as well as a facade with stately/columns and a French Renaissance cupola." "WRIGLEY FIELD, CHICAGO/Ivy-covered outfield walls, a hand-operated/scoreboard, and more day than night games are just/a few of the reasons fans everywhere love Chicago's/Wrigley Field. When the wind blows out, scores can/enter double digits; when it blows in, Wrigley is a/pitcher's delight."

Cover Markings: On outside front: "Baseball's Legendary Playing Fields/The U.S. Postal Service Ready-to-Mail Postal Stamped Cards." On outside back: "Major League Baseball trademarks and copyrights are used with permission of Major League Baseball Properties, Inc./© 2001 U.S. Postal Service. All rights reserved. To obtain additional information on Commemorative Stamps and Stamp products available from the U.S. Postal Service please write to: Information Fulfillment, USPS, PO Box 219424, Kansas City, MO 64121-9424." USPS logo and Cooperstown Collection logo. On inside front: no markings. On inside back: "Front and back covers/SPORTSMAN'S PARK, ST. LOUIS/This St. Louis landmark had joint occupants — the/Browns and the Cardinals — for 33 years. It hosted the/high jinks of the Cardinals' Gas House Gang. The/Browns' flamboyant owner once put a 65-pound, 3-foot-7-inch player up to bat."

Designer, Typographer and Art Director: Phil Jordan of Falls Church, Virginia

Stamp Manufacturing: Cards printed by Banknote Corporation of America, Browns Summit, North Carolina, on MAN Roland 300 offset press.

Quantity Ordered: 75,000 books (750,000 cards)

Paper Type: Temboard, 10 PT, Kallima Cover, C1S

Tagging: Vertical bar to right of stamp

The Cards

On June 27, the Postal Service issued a set of 10 picture postal cards as companion pieces to the 10 34¢ self-adhesive stamps depicting vintage major league baseball stadiums that were issued the same day.

The postal cards bear a 21¢ denomination and were the first to meet the new 21¢ postcard rate that would take effect four days later, July 1. They are bound in a book of 10 cards, one of each variety, with microperfing for easy removal. USPS sold the book for $6.95, or 69.5¢ per card.

Each card's imprinted stamp reproduces the design of one of the self-adhesive stamps. The same design, but without typography, fills the picture side of the card. Because the designs of the stamps themselves were taken from vintage picture postcards, the Postal Service's postal cards represented a process gone full circle.

Like the stamps, the postal card set is titled "Baseball's Legendary Playing Fields" and depicts Chicago's original Comiskey Park, Cincinnati's Crosley Field, Brooklyn's Ebbets Field, Boston's Fenway Park, Pittsburgh's Forbes Field, New York's Polo Grounds, Philadelphia's Shibe Park, Detroit's Tiger Stadium, Chicago's Wrigley Field and New York's Yankee Stadium. Two views of an 11th stadium, St. Louis' Sportsman's Park, appear on the front and back of the book cover. The same picture that is on the front of the cover, in a tightly cropped version, also illustrates the header of the pane of stamps.

The message side of each card contains a paragraph of text describing the stadium shown. It is the same text that is printed on the back of the liner paper of the corresponding stamp.

First-day ceremonies for both the stamps and postal cards were held at the four stadiums shown in the set that still are in existence: Tiger Stadi-

um, Fenway Park, Wrigley Field and Yankee Stadium. The last three continue to be used by their respective teams.

The cards were produced by offset lithography by Banknote Corporation of America, which is a major supplier of stamps for the Postal Service. The picture sides of the cards and the cover fronts were printed in

four-color process (black, cyan, magenta and yellow) plus what BCA termed an aqueous coating, using a relatively fine 200-line screen. The imprinted stamps on the address sides also were printed in four-color process, but with a 150-line screen, plus phosphor taggant. The insides of the covers were printed in blue and red, respectively, with no screening.

The Designs

The imprinted stamp on the address side of each postal card is identical to its postage-stamp counterpart except that the denomination is 21¢ instead of 34¢. There is a red frameline around the design that is not on the stamp, and the card design lacks a tiny "2001" year-of-issue date beneath it. These card images are less crisp than those on the stamps because of the coarser screening — 150 lines compared to 300 — and the difference in quality between postal card stock and stamp paper.

The aspect ratio of the picture sides is slightly different from that of the stamps. As a result, the picture-side images are cropped more tightly on one or both sides than the corresponding stamp images. Forbes Field, for example, loses the entire right side of its exterior facade on the postal card. On the other hand, the large size of the images reveals details, such as Wrigley Field's ivy-covered walls, much more clearly than do the stamps themselves.

A small portion of the picture side of each card overlaps the microperfs and remains on the stub when the card is removed from the book.

First-day Facts

For information on the first-day sale of the postal cards, see the chapter on the Baseball's Legendary Playing Fields stamps.

372

21¢ WHITE BARN POSTAL CARD
SCENIC AMERICA SERIES

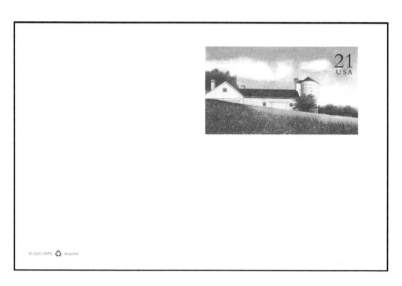

Date of Issue: September 20, 2001

Catalog Number: Scott UX375

Colors: yellow, magenta, cyan, black

First-Day Cancel: Washington, D.C.

First-Day Cancellations: 82,371 (includes 21¢ White Barn message-reply postal card and 21¢ Bison, 57¢ Art Deco Eagle and 23¢ George Washington stamps)

Format: Cards available as single cards or in 40-card uncut sheets.

Size: 5.5 by 3.5 inches

Marking: "©2000 USPS." Recycled logo followed by "recycled."

Illustrator: Wendell Minor of Washington Green, Connecticut

Designer, Art Director and Typographer: Derry Noyes of Washington, D.C.

Card Manufacturing: Cards printed by the Government Printing Office in Washington, D.C., on a 5-color MAN Roland sheetfed offset press. Cards processed and shipped by GPO.

Quantity Ordered: 42,000,000 (30,000,000 single cards, 10,000,000 cards in sheets of 40 and 2,000,000 cards in 5-card vending packs)

Paper Type: 22-pound bright white

Tagging: vertical bar to right of stamp

21¢ WHITE BARN MESSAGE-REPLY POSTAL CARD
SCENIC AMERICA SERIES

Date of Issue: September 20, 2001

Catalog Number: Scott UY43

Colors: yellow, magenta, cyan, black

First-Day Cancel: Washington, D.C.

First-Day Cancellations: 82,371 (includes 21¢ White Barn postal card and 21¢ Bison, 57¢ Art Deco Eagle and 23¢ George Washington stamps)

Format: Double message-reply cards, rouletted between cards.

Size: 5.5 by 3.5 inches

Marking: "©2000 USPS." Recycled logo followed by "recycled."

Illustrator: Wendell Minor of Washington Green, Connecticut

Designer, Art Director and Typographer: Derry Noyes of Washington, D.C.

Card Manufacturing: Cards printed by the Government Printing Office in Washington, D.C., on a 5-color MAN Roland sheetfed offset press. Cards processed and shipped by GPO.

Quantity Ordered: 2,000,000 cards

Paper Type: 22-pound bright white

Tagging: vertical bar to right of stamp

The Cards

On September 20, the Postal Service issued a 21¢ definitive postal card that was made necessary by the 1¢ increase in the postcard rate on the previous July 1.

The card came in two varieties: as a single and as detachable double cards for a message and reply. It was sold at a markup of 2¢ per card, which USPS says covers the cost of its manufacture.

The imprinted stamp on the address side bears the image of a white barn. It was the fourth in a series USPS calls Scenic America, which was launched with a 20¢ Red Barn card in 1995 and followed in 1996 by a 20¢ Winter Scene card and in 1999 by a 20¢ card depicting a lighthouse on Block Island, Rhode Island.

The art for the Red Barn, Block Island and White Barn cards was the work of Wendell Minor, of Washington, Connecticut. Minor was commissioned in 1990 to create seven paintings evoking different regions of the United States for use on Scenic America cards. The remaining subjects include Monument Valley, which straddles the Arizona-Utah border, and a South Atlantic coast scene featuring cabbage palms and laughing gulls. USPS plans to use them in the future as the need for new postal card designs arises.

The cards in the series carry no typography other than the denomination and "USA." Because their illustrations are meant to be generic, they aren't identified, even though the four issued so far depict specific locations. Officials originally intended to include the words "Scenic America" on each card, and an early mockup of the White Barn card contains that label. But the cards as issued have no inscription.

The White Barn single card also was sold in uncut 40-card sheets, measuring 22.5 by 35 inches. Such sheets are produced for the convenience of businesses or other mailers that want to print messages for large mailings.

The first double message-reply postal cards were issued in 1892, and for a few decades their message and reply units had different designs. Since 1956, however, they have had the same designs as the contemporary single cards, with no difference between the units. The cards are printed on opposite sides of the card stock, so that when they are folded along the rouletted line between them the reply card is on the inside.

The Design

Besides his two previous Scenic America postal cards, Wendell Minor's work for the Postal Service has included paintings for the 25¢ North Dakota Statehood commemorative stamp of 1989 and the 30¢ Niagara Falls postal card of 1991 in the old America the Beautiful series. A prolific illustrator, Minor has created the cover art for such well-known books as David McCullough's *Truman* and *The Path Between the Seas*, David Herbert Donald's *Lincoln* and Jean Craighead George's nature books for children. Scheduled for publication by Putnam in 2003 is a children's book depicting his personal vision of Katharine Lee Bates' anthem *America the Beautiful*.

The white barn with its attached silo shown on the postal card is in Minor's hometown of Washington, Connecticut. Part of the homestead of a family named Bryan, the barn dates to at least the 1920s, when a neighbor of the artist remembers milking cows there as a boy, and it probably is much older. It currently is unused, but is maintained in good condition.

"It's always been one of my favorite landmarks in town," Minor said. "I painted a portrait of that barn in the snow when I first came to town, perhaps 20 years ago, and used it as a personal Christmas card. The barn was gray then, and there was a stand of red pine off to the right that is no longer there.

"It sits up on a high knoll, kind of like a big old ship. I show only a portion of it in my painting [for the postal card]; it continues on to the left for another length.

"I come from a rural background in Illinois. Both my parents grew up on farms. The barn is a disappearing American icon, but it's part of our country's agrarian heritage, and any time I have a chance to document this

Wendell Minor painted this picture of the White Barn some 20 years earlier; it was gray then.

The White Barn card design carried a 19¢ denomination and the "Scenic America" series designation when then-Postmaster General Anthony M. Frank approved it January 31, 1991.

symbol of our past, I do it."

Minor worked from his own photographs of the white barn to make his gouache and watercolor painting on Bainbridge board. Art director and typographer Derry Noyes superimposed "21" and "USA" in two lines of black type on the blue sky in the upper-right corner of the stamped image.

First-day Facts

The White Barn cards had their first-day sale in Washington, D.C. There was no official ceremony.

21¢ PORKY PIG "THAT'S ALL FOLKS" PICTURE POSTAL CARD LOONEY TUNES SERIES

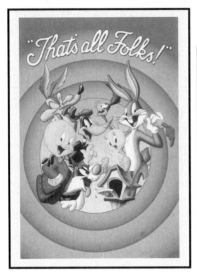

Date of Issue: October 1, 2001

Price: $7.25 for book of 10 cards

Catalog Number: Scott UX376, single card; UX376a, book of 10 cards

Colors: yellow, magenta, cyan, black

First-Day Cancel: Beverly Hills, California

First-Day Cancellations: 151,009 (includes "That's All Folks" stamp and special printing stamp)

Format: Book of 10 stamped cards, with microperforations to permit removal of individual cards. Offset printing plates of 20 subjects.

Size of Card: 6.00 by 4.25 inches; 152.40 by 107.95mm

Size of Book: 6.75 by 4.25 inches; 171.45 by 107.95mm

Card Markings: On address side of each card: "THE 2001 'THAT'S ALL FOLKS' STAMP." "©2001 USPS." "LOONEY TUNES, characters, names, and all related indicia are trademarks of Warner Bros. © 2001."

Cover Markings: On inside of front cover: "Bugs Bunny, who appeared on one of the most/popular stamps ever, is back to introduce one of/his old friends: Porky Pig. Cute, wide-eyed Porky/Pig has played the straight man in many silly/situations, ranging from hunting the uncatchable/Daffy Duck to traveling with him to outer space./Porky Pig's innocence and wry wit contrast with/Daffy Duck's zaniness./Porky Pig, already a famous star, was guaranteed/immortality when he was chosen to deliver his/famous phrase 'That's all Folks!' at the end of the/Looney Tunes cartoons. Even though Porky Pig/ends the Looney Tunes stamp series with this/trademark expression, that's no reason to stop/collecting stamps." On outside of back cover: USPS logo/"© 2001 U.S. Postal Service. All Rights Reserved. To obtain additional information/on Commemorative Stamps and Stamp Products available from the U.S. Postal Service/please write to Information Fulfillment, USPS, PO Box 219424, Kansas City, MO 64121-9424."/Warner Bros. and Looney Tunes logos. "LOONEY TUNES, characters, names and all related indicia are trademarks of Warner Bros. © 2001/WB SHIELD:™ & © 2001 Warner Bros."

Illustrator and Designer: Ed Wleczyk, Warner Bros., Los Angeles, California

Character Art: Frank Espinosa, Warner Bros.

Concept: Brenda Guttman, Warner Bros.

Art Director: Terrence McCaffrey, USPS

Card Manufacturing: Cards printed by Banknote Corporation of America (BCA), Browns Summit, North Carolina, on MAN Roland offset press.

Quantity Ordered: 100,000 books (1,000,000 cards)

Tagging: vertical bar to right of stamp

The Card

When the Postal Service issued its 34¢ "That's All Folks!" Porky Pig commemorative stamp October 1 in Beverly Hills, California, it also issued a picture postal card, as it had done with the four previous stamps in the Looney Tunes series. The card's denomination is 21¢, which covered the new postcard rate that had gone into effect July 1.

As before, the stamp design is reproduced in the card's imprinted stamp, with only the denomination changed. Unlike the other cards in the series, however, the picture side of this one isn't based on the stamp, which shows Porky Pig alone. Instead, it is a replica of the large image on the selvage of the stamp pane, which depicts Porky with the six Looney Tunes characters that appear on the earlier stamps and postal cards.

Like its predecessors in the series, the Porky Pig card was printed by the offset process and bound in books of 10 cards, with microperforations to facilitate their removal. The image on the front cover of the book is the same as that on the picture side of the card, but slightly deeper.

The Postal Service sold the book for $7.25, or 72.5¢ per card, by mail order and through self-service postal stores. The 51.5¢ premium over face value was the highest USPS had ever charged for a picture postal card.

The card and book was printed by Banknote Corporation of America on a MAN Roland offset press. The printing order was 1 million cards, the same as that of the Wile E. Coyote-Road Runner cards the year before.

The Design

The design of the card's imprinted stamp features the illustration devised by Warner Bros. artists Ed Wleczyk and Frank Espinosa for the postage stamp. It shows a beaming Porky in the center of a series of blue concentric circles. He is attired in a dark blue jacket and trousers and a red bow tie, with a "U.S. Mail" bag hanging at his side, the strap across his shoulder, and is standing by a mailbox. He holds up a letter in his left hand, on which the address, "ACME ACRES/U.S.A." can be made out. Across the top of the imprinted stamp, in a line of curved script, is "That's all Folks!" with quotation marks and a dropped shadow. At the bottom is "USA 21" in white block type.

On the picture side of the card, which duplicates the large selvage image on the stamp pane, Porky shares the center of the concentric circles with his predecessors in the series, Bugs Bunny, Daffy Duck, Sylvester, Tweety, Wile E. Coyote and Road Runner.

First-day Facts

The Postal Service called off a scheduled first-day ceremony for the stamp and postal card because the date of issue was too close in time to the events of September 11, 2001.

21¢ HOLIDAY SANTAS PICTURE POSTAL CARDS (4 DESIGNS)

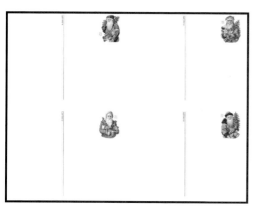 

Date of Issue: October 10, 2001

Price: $9.25 for set of 20

Catalog Numbers: Scott UX377-UX380, single cards; UX380a, sheet of 4 cards

Colors: yellow, magenta, cyan, black

First-Day Cancel: Santa Claus, Indiana

First-Day Cancellations: 376,615 (includes all versions of Holiday Santas stamps)

Format: Cards are in sheets of 4, with each card rouletted on 2 sides to permit separation. Cards are sold in shrink-wrapped sets of 5 sheets. Offset printing plates printing 5 sheets per impression.

Size of Cards: 5.50 by 4.25 inches (address side); 139.70 by 107.95mm

Size of Sheets: 11.0 inches by 8.5 inches; 215.9 by 279.4mm

Card Markings: On address side of each card, "©2000 USPS."

Designer, Typographer and Art Director: Richard Sheaff of Scottsdale, Arizona

Card Manufacturing: Cards printed by Banknote Corporation of America, Browns Summit, North Carolina, on MAN Roland 300 offset press. Cards processed by BCA.

Quantity Ordered and Distributed: 2,000,000 cards (100,000 sets of 5 sheets of 4)

Paper Type: Temboard, 10 Pt. Kallima Cover, C1S

Tagging: vertical block to left of stamped image

The Cards

On October 10, as part of a package of Christmas holiday postage items that included 12 collectible stamp varieties, the Postal Service issued four picture postal cards bearing Santa Claus images from the 19th and early 20th centuries. Each card reproduces on its imprinted stamp and its picture side one of the four Santa designs used on the postage stamps.

The cards were the second set of picture postal cards to be created specifically for the holiday season. In 2000, USPS had issued four cards reproducing the previous year's stamp designs that featured a stylized leaping deer in gold against four different background colors.

Banknote Corporation of America printed the Santa cards by the offset process. BCA cut the press sheets into distribution sheets containing four cards — one of each variety — and microperfed them for easy separation. USPS sold the sheets in shrink-wrapped packages of five (20 cards) for $9.25, making the individual card price slightly over 46¢, against a face value of 21¢.

Cards sold in sheet form can be used by quantity mailers, who are able to imprint messages and addresses on them using a laserprinter or photocopying machine.

The Designs

The four Santa images on the stamps and postal cards came from USPS art director Richard Sheaff's collection of ephemera, or antique printed paper. For information on the individual images, see the chapter on the

Holiday Santas stamps.

The postage stamps were produced by Avery Dennison (vending booklet of 20) and Sennett Security Printers (pane of 20 and convertible booklet of 20), and the two printers' products differ in size and coloration.

The imprinted stamps on the BCA-produced postal cards differ in some details from both of them. Their image areas are larger, measuring 1.125 by 1.375 inches, compared to 0.77 by 1.05 inches for the Sennett-printed images and 0.720 by 0.818 inches for the Avery Dennisons. The denomination and "USA" are in green and red, respectively, as they are on the Avery Dennison stamps, but are in varied locations on the postal cards, rather than being uniformly in the upper-left corner, which is where they appear on the stamps of both printers.

On most postal cards, the tagging is a vertical bar applied to the right of the imprinted stamp. On the Santas cards, however, the bar of taggant is to the left of the stamp.

The picture sides of the cards bear enlarged versions of the stamp images, but without typography. On these, the detail and color of the Santas, scanned from vintage Old World chromolithographs, can be fully appreciated.

First-day Facts

For details on the first-day ceremony at Santa Claus, Indiana, see the chapter on the Holiday Santas stamps.

Inverts Found in 1992 Stock Exchange Pane

The first bona fide United States invert stamp since the 1986 discovery of the $1 CIA Candleholder error was found in Texas. The full pane of 40 of the U.S. 29¢ New York Stock Exchange stamp of 1992 (Scott 2630) contains 28 inverted-vignette, or central-image, errors (2630c) and 12 errors in which the black color is missing (2630a).

According to stamp dealer and auctioneer Greg Manning, a Texas family purchased the pane at a post office shortly after the stamp was issued in 1992.

The Stock Exchange invert is one of the most subtle of the U.S. inverts, until now a group restricted to 12 different stamp issues going back to 1869. The Stock Exchange stamp was intended to look like a tiny stock certificate. The two black intaglio vignettes show the facade of the New York Stock Exchange at left and a view of the trading floor at right. They are so small and symmetrical that, at first glance, it is difficult to distinguish whether they are right-side up or upside down.

"There are no serious stamp collectors in the family," Manning explained, "so the inverted vignettes went unnoticed for almost a decade. It wasn't until this past December [2001] that the family realized what a

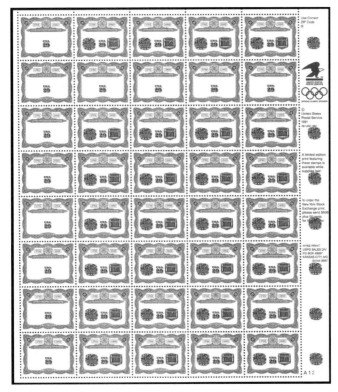

This pane of 40 29¢ New York Stock Exchange stamps includes 28 stamps that have vignettes inverted on either side of the "USA29" and 12 color-missing errors. The pane sold for $488,750 June 16, 2002, at the Greg Manning Rarities auction in New York City.

marvelous find they had. The family then searched the Internet for more information and learned that some inverts can be quite valuable."

The right four stamps in the first row and third through eighth rows — for a total of 28 — each bear an inverted black vignette on either side of the green "USA29." The remaining 12 stamps — in the first column and second row — are missing the black vignettes and are thus color-missing errors. The black-color-missing error was first listed in the 2002 Scott *Specialized Catalogue of United States Stamps and Covers.*

The unique intact pane of 29¢ New York Stock Exchange major-error stamps sold for $488,750 June 16, 2002, at the Greg Manning Rarities auction in New York City. According to associate editor Charles Snee, writing in the July 8, 2002, issue of *Linn's Stamp News*, to *Linn's* knowledge, this is the largest sum ever paid for a modern U.S. error pane.

Rare Perforation Error Found in Mission Mix

A spectacular find that languished for 36 years in a collector's stock book was authenticated in late 2000 by the American Philatelic Expertizing Service. News of the authentication was reported by senior editor Rob Haeseler in the January 22, 2001, issue of *Linn's Stamp News.*

The rare perforation error is the U.S. 2¢ carmine George Washington stamp of the 1922 regular series. Initially, stamps in the series were printed on flat-plate presses and given gauge 11 perforations.

But this stamp, identified as Scott 554d, is an anomaly. It was printed on a flat-plate press, but it has gauge 10 perforations on the bottom and gauge 11 on the other three sides.

According to Haeseler, Don Shehane, a Missouri collector, told *Linn's* he found the error in a mission mixture in 1964 and did nothing to verify his find until quite recently. The stamp was certified genuine by the APES in November 2001.

Haeseler explained that the error was created when a gauge 10 perforating wheel was added to a perforating machine equipped with gauge 11 wheels. Hence, only one row of each sheet perforated on the machine received the gauge 10 perforations.

Because of the wide margins and superior centering of Shehane's stamp, it may be the best example of the rare error. Sixteen examples of the error appear to have been authenticated, according to Haeseler.

A rare 2¢ perforation 10 at-one-side error from the 1922 U.S. regular series came to light in 2001, although it had been in a Missouri collection for 36 years. The stamp has gauge 11 perforations on all sides except for the bottom, which was perforated by an odd wheel set for gauge 10.

Six Color-Missing Error Stamps Reported

Six new color-missing error stamps were reported in 2001, all part of Stan Goldfarb's extensive collection of errors that he has painstakingly formed during the past 30 years. The six color-missing errors are the 8¢ Eisenhower of 1971 (Scott 1394), the 6¢ Douglas MacArthur of 1971 (1424), the 10¢ Veterans of Foreign Wars of 1974 (1525), the 22¢ Ameripex of 1986 (2145), the 22¢ World War I of 1985 (2154), and the 25¢ South Carolina of 1988 (2343).

Associate editor Charles Snee, writing in the September 3, 2001, issue of *Linn's*, said, "These stamps are coming to light only now because the hobby is beginning to fully understand or become aware of a change in catalog-listing policy that Scott Publishing made in late 1996, as published in *Scott Stamp Monthly* in January 1997, page 11. The new policy is to evaluate a stamp based on how it appears, not on how it was or might have been produced."

Another new dramatic error, a 5¢ Holly Christmas stamp of 1964 (1254) printed on the gum side of the paper (caused by a foldover), was reported in the same story.

Color-Missing Error Discovered

A color-missing error of one of the four U.S. Ameripex 86 show souvenir sheets was discovered by a collector from Wisconsin in late June 2001. The sheets (Scott 2216-19) were issued for the international stamp exhibition held May 22-June 1, 1986, in Chicago (Rosemont, Illinois).

Each of the nine 22¢ stamps on each sheet (except the middle stamp of Scott 2219, which shows the White House) depicts a U.S. president.

Associate editor Charles Snee reported in the September 3, 2001, issue of *Linn's* that close examination under 30X magnification reveals that the engraved (recess printed) gray-black ink of the presidential portraits is

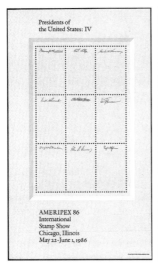 

Shown here, far left, is a 1986 Ameripex souvenir sheet (Scott 2219) that is completely missing the blackish-blue ink. A normal example of the sheet is illustrated at left.

386

missing from all nine stamps on the sheet. Only the offset red ink of the presidents' facsimile signatures is visible on each stamp. The rest of the sheet — the offset tan background and the offset black legends at top and bottom — appears normal.

A collector in Wisconsin found the sheet in an original USPS Commemorative Stamp Club album that was owned by his next-door neighbor. Each of the Ameripex sheets was still mounted on the stamp club pages supplied by the Postal Service.

The Wisconsin collector told *Linn's* that his neighbor had purchased the sheets, stamp club album and associated pages from the Philatelic Sales Division (now Stamp Fulfillment Services) in Kansas City, Mo.

The error is listed in the Scott U.S. specialized catalog as 2219 l.

Imperforate Error of 3¢ Bluebird Surfaces

A previously unreported imperforate error of the United States 3¢ Eastern Bluebird stamp of 1991 (Scott 2478) came to light in 2001. The item is a horizontally imperforate plate-number block of six Bluebird stamps. The block comprises three imperforate-between pairs.

John Stewart of Texas purchased the pane at a post office in his hometown about a year or so after the Bluebird stamp was issued.

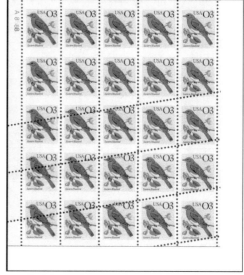

Above is a block of six 3¢ Eastern Bluebird stamps (Scott 2478) that is missing the horizontal perforations. At right is the top-left portion of a horizontally misperforated pane of 100 Bluebird stamps. The block shown above came from this portion of the pane.

Missing-Color Desert Plants

A full pane of 40 of the U.S. 1981 20¢ Desert Plants issue (Scott 1942-45b) was found with the dark brown offset color missing.

The error pane realized $25,760, including a 12-percent buyers premium, when it was auctioned July 27-28, 2001, by the Stamp Center.

The Desert Plants issue was printed by combination offset (surface) and intaglio (engraved) by the U.S. Bureau of Engraving and Printing, using three intaglio inks — brown, blue and green — and five offset inks — yellow, red, blue, green and dark brown.

With the dark brown omitted, the stamps most dramatically lack "USA 20¢" and shadows at the bottom of each stamp that define the letters for the name of the plant. The normal version has seven plate numbers; this one has only six plate numbers.

The pane received a certificate of authenticity April 5, 2001, from the expertizing service of the American Philatelic Society. The 2001 editions of the Scott *Specialized Catalogue of United States Stamps and Covers* and the *Datz Catalogue of Errors on U.S. Postage Stamps* list errors of the stamp with the brown intaglio missing but not with the brown offset color missing.

A full pane of 40 of the United States 1981 20¢ Desert Plants issue was found with the dark brown offset color missing, as shown in this graphically cropped image displaying the plate-number block.

Transitional Perforations Discovered

A new perforation variety of the U.S. 4¢ yellow-brown Martha Washington stamp of 1923 (Scott 556) was certified by the Philatelic Foundation July 30, 2001. According to associate editor Charles Snee, reporting in the August 27, 2001, issue of *Linn's*, the stamp was described on Foundation certificate No. 371869 as "genuine with transitional perforations at top, perforated 10 at left to perforated 11 at right."

"The statement can be confusing if one is not aware that the gauge of perforation changes mid-stamp from 10 to 11 along the top edge only — a phenomenon seldom if ever seen," Snee explained.

The stamp was originally part of Thurston Twigg-Smith's stellar collection of used U.S. stamps. It realized $10,500 in the sale of the Twigg-Smith collection by Robert A. Siegel Auction Galleries April 10, 2001 (lot 520).

Normal examples of the 4¢ Martha Washington, along with the other stamps of the 1922-25 definitive (regular-issue) series, were printed

This 4¢ Martha Washington stamp has transitional perforations across the top. The stamp was recently certified by the Philatelic Foundation.

from flat plates and given gauge 11 perforations on all four sides.

Scott 556 is the designation for a normal Martha Washington stamp. The new error stamp is a variety of Scott 556b, the perforation 10-at-one-side error.

Olympians Color-Missing Error Pane Found

A newly discovered color-missing error pane of 35 of the U.S. 25¢ Olympians stamps (Scott 2496-500) came to light more than 11 years after the stamps were issued in 1990.

The error pane is completely missing the cyan (blue), one of the four process inks used to print the stamps. The other three inks are black, magenta (red) and yellow.

The blue "1" is missing from the "A1111" plate number combination that appears in the right selvage of the top strip.

The missing blue is most striking on the 25¢ Helene Madison stamp — the water looks gray, instead of the normal blue on the stamp in the bottom strip. The backgrounds of the Ray Ewry and Hazel Wightman stamps also are discernibly different from their normal counterparts.

A New Jersey stamp dealer and his assistant discovered the error pane at a stamp show in Virginia in January 2001.

The error is listed in the Scott U.S. specialized catalog as 2500b.

Shown here are two strips of five 25¢ Olympians stamps, cropped from complete panes of 35. The top strip is missing the cyan (blue), while the bottom strip is normal. The missing color is most obvious on the Helene Madison stamp at far right on the top strip — the water appears gray, instead of blue.

Hologram Missing on Space Souvenir Sheet

An unusual and previously unreported hologram-missing error of the U.S. $11.75 Earth souvenir sheet came to light in August 2001.

The sheet is one of five in the Space Achievement and Exploration set of 2000: Earth (one $11.75 stamp), Landing on the Moon (one $11.75

stamp), Escaping the Gravity of Earth (two $3.20 stamps), Exploring the Solar System (five $1 stamps) and Probing the Vastness of Space (six 60¢ stamps).

If the hologram overlay were present, it would be centered within the perforations.

The error sheet was still housed in its distinctive U.S. Postal Service packaging when it was submitted to *Linn's* for inspection, reported associate editor Charles Snee in the October 1, 2001, issue of *Linn's*. Miroslav Vrzala of New York purchased it at a postal store.

The error is listed in the Scott U.S. specialized catalog as 3413d.

The hologram overlay is missing from this $11.75 Earth souvenir sheet. The sheet is still housed in its USPS packaging.

YEAR IN REVIEW

USPS Reacts To Anthrax Scare

On September 11, as the World Trade Center and the Pentagon came under terrorist attacks, the U.S. Postal Service board of governors approved higher postal rates, including a 37¢ first-class letter rate. The rate increase, which was scheduled to go into effect in late July 2002, was projected to raise $5.3 billion to offset $1.7 billion in losses from the fiscal year that had just ended, according to *Linn's* Washington correspondent Bill McAllister, writing in the December 31, 2001, issue of *Linn's Stamp News*.

About one week after the terrorist attacks, a letter containing anthrax spores was mailed to the office of a tabloid newspaper in Boca Raton, Florida, killing the editor who opened it. This was the first of a number of incidents around the country. A Trenton postal facility in New Jersey and the Brentwood postal facility in Washington, D.C., were massively contaminated with anthrax spores. Two postal workers died and a number of others became ill. The Stamp Fulfillment Services center located in the Hunt-Midwest Subtropolis caves under Kansas City, Missouri, was closed October 31, 2001, after swabs from two trash bags from the first-day-cancellation area tested positive for anthrax spores. The facility reopened for business a few weeks later, on November 14. Brentwood and Trenton remain closed in late 2002.

The anthrax scare dealt a serious blow to an already financially weakened United States Postal Service, which now was faced with escalating costs to try to make the mails safe.

In November, the Postal Service began irradiating mail that may have been exposed to anthrax. Eight truckloads of contaminated mail from the Postal Service's Brentwood facility were decontaminated in November by Titan Scan Technologies in Lima, Ohio, and returned to Washington, D.C., for distribution. At the time this *Yearbook* was written, all mail addressed to government offices in Washington, D.C., was still being irradiated prior to delivery by a contractor in New Jersey.

Mail from the Trenton, New Jersey, postal facility that was irradiated to sanitize it from anthrax contamination was delivered to individual addresses in plastic bags with a notice identifying it as having been sanitized.

USPS community relations specialist Don Smeraldi said that irradiation could cause some physical changes in mail processed for decontamination.

Stamp Fulfillment Services responded to the anthrax scare in another way. In early November, stamp shipments mailed out from the stamp cave contained a 3½-inch by 6½-inch card informing the recipient that the packing process for the stamps includes the use of food starch as a desiccant to inhibit moisture and prevent cracking and spotting. The advisory printed on white card stock read in part, "What's that powder? It's food starch. We use it to protect our products."

On November 14, the House of Representatives voted 418-to-0 for a resolution praising "the men and women of the U.S. Postal Service" for their "outstanding job of delivering the mail during this time of national emergency."

"Congress will work with the [USPS] to assure the safety and well-being of postal workers as they carry out their duties and responsibilities," the resolution said.

No More BEP Stamps After 2005?

The United States Bureau of Engraving and Printing could be out of the stamp printing business after 2005, a source close to the Bureau told *Linn's* in early June 2001.

However, the BEP is seeking legislative changes that would allow it to print postage stamps, currency and other security paper for foreign countries.

Federal law mandates that the BEP print stamps, currency and other security items only for the federal government.

The U.S. Postal Service contracted with the BEP to print roughly 15 billion stamps in 2001.

Stamped Envelopes Removed From Sale Temporarily

The USPS halted all sales of postal envelopes at its post offices October 31, 2001.

In response to questions about why the envelopes were taken off sale, the Postal Service prepared the following statement:

"Many customers and employees have expressed concern about our temporary suspension of the sale of prestamped envelopes.

"Some have heard rumors that they were suspended because of possible contamination. There is absolutely no truth to any of those rumors.

"We are studying the design and construction of the envelopes."

The Postal Service told *Linn's* November 2, 2001, that no further information was available at the time, including whether the withdrawal of the envelopes from sale had anything to do with anthrax investigations.

The 34¢ Federal Eagle envelope issued Jan. 7, 2001, was used to mail letters containing anthrax. The number 6¾-size envelopes were addressed to Senator Tom Daschle, Senator Patrick Leahy, NBC newsman Tom Brokaw, and an unnamed editor of *The New York Post*.

All four envelopes were canceled at a Trenton, New Jersey, mail facility.

The Daschle and Leahy envelopes were postmarked October 9, 2001, and the other two were postmarked September 18, 2001. The letters contained in the envelopes all were dated September 11, 2001.

Stamped envelopes were returned to sale at post office counters throughout the country on November 9, 2001.

Design Must Accompany Uncacheted FDC Requests

In mid-October 2001, USPS expanded a previous policy regarding offensive cachets added to envelopes or first-day covers in the wake of the September 11 terrorist attacks.

The USPS has had a long-standing policy that it will not service first-day covers submitted with offensive cachets, but the new policy stated that uncacheted envelopes would not be serviced unless a copy of the cachet design that eventually would be applied to them is submitted along with the envelopes.

Don Smeraldi, USPS community relations specialist, told *Linn's* that the policy is intended to prevent offensive material from being applied to a cover after it had been serviced by the USPS to avoid giving the impression that the USPS endorses offensive sentiments that might be expressed with a cachet.

"The USPS doesn't want to help people make a profit from offensive material," Smeraldi further explained.

The decision as to whether or not a cachet design is considered offensive is made at the department level in the Stamp Fulfillment Services in Kansas City, Missouri.

This policy applies to all first-day covers serviced by the USPS, not just to the 34¢ United We Stand definitive booklet and coil stamps.

Linn's associate editor Rick Miller pointed out that "carrying the war to the enemy on patriotic covers has a long and hoary history in stamp collecting. No doubt many of the patriotic covers of the Civil War and the two World Wars would not pass muster today because of their inflammatory nature and lack of ethnic, cultural or racial sensibilities."

Potter Named Postmaster General

John E. "Jack" Potter was named the nation's 72nd postmaster general on May 21, 2001. He replaced William J. Henderson, who resigned in May. A 23-year postal employee, Potter served as the Postal Service's chief operating officer and executive vice president.

Potter campaigned long and hard for postal reform during his first term as postmaster general. Top among the postal reform issues was loosening restrictions on setting postal rates.

Potter came under attack soon after he took office when he advocated giving senior postal executives bonuses of up to 25 percent in a year in which USPS has said it is facing a deficit of up to $2 billion.

CSAC Changes Stamp-Selection Guidelines

The Citizens' Stamp Advisory Committee revised three of its stamp criteria to reflect changes that had already taken place. One of the three revised guidelines, released March 21, 2001, restates the intention of the Postal Service to avoid releasing stamps that "promote or advertise commercial enterprises or products." But it adds: "Commercial products or enterprises might be used to illustrate more general concepts related to

American culture."

Many stamp collectors were surprised that the Celebrate the Century stamp series included illustrations of a number of commercial products, from Ford Mustang cars to Crayola crayons.

Another change in the guidelines calls for commemorations of universities and other institutions of higher education to be considered "only for stamped (postal) cards and only in connection with their 200th anniversaries of their founding." That is a shift away from the old guideline that called for colleges to be honored only with postal cards in the Historic Preservation series that would "feature an appropriate building on campus."

The third change in the 12 guidelines states that no stamp will be approved if a stamp on the same subject has been issued in the past 50 years. "The only exceptions to this rule are traditional symbols and holidays," the new guidelines state.

New Members Appointed To CSAC

Actress Liz Torres joined the Citizens' Stamp Advisory Committee in early January 2001. She was the last CSAC appointment for Postmaster General William J. Henderson, who left the post in May 2001.

Yale University design critic Sylvia Harris was the first appointee to CSAC to be named to the panel by Postmaster General John E. "Jack" Potter. Harris became the 13th member of the committee that advises the postmaster general on what subjects should be honored on U.S. postage stamps and how the stamps should be designed.

The founder of a New York graphic arts firm in 1980, she was a principal in the firm until 1993.

Television personality Larry King resigned from the panel in 2001 without ever attending a meeting. Scheduling conflicts were blamed.

American Illustrators Pane Tops *Linn's* Poll

The American Illustrators pane of 20 self-adhesive 34¢ stamps was the overall favorite in *Linn's* 2001 United States Stamp Popularity Poll. This was the third year in a row that *Linn's* readers chose a self-stick, se-tenant issue as their favorite U.S. stamp issue in the annual popularity poll. Selection of the Illustrators stamps as overall favorite marked the 18th consecutive year that readers picked a stamp issue with multiple se-tenant (attached) designs.

In the 1999 poll, the 33¢ Sonoran Desert stamps, the first issue in the Nature of America series, was their favorite U.S. stamp issue. In the 2000 poll, the Pacific Coast Rain Forest set of 10 33¢ self-adhesives, the second issue in the Nature of America series, was chosen for the top honor.

In the 2001 poll, the American Illustrators pane received 368 votes. Runners-up were the pane of 10 34¢ Great Plains Prairie stamps, 279 votes; Pan-American Inverts and 80¢ Buffalo, 256; 34¢ U.S. Veterans, 229; and 34¢ Baseball's Legendary Playing Fields, 207.

Other categories and the top three finishers were:

Commemoratives, best design: American Illustrators, Great Plains Prairie, Pan-American Inverts and Buffalo.

Commemoratives, worst design: Diabetes Awareness, Frida Kahlo, Year of the Snake.

Commemoratives, most important: U.S. Veterans, Diabetes Awareness, James Madison.

Commemoratives, least necessary: Frida Kahlo, Porky Pig That's All Folks!, Carnivorous Plants.

Definitives/specials, best design: Washington Monument, Mount McKinley, Capitol Dome.

Definitives/specials, worst design: Art Deco Eagle, Eid, Atlas Statue.

Definitives/specials, most important: United We Stand, We Give Thanks, Eid.

Definitives/specials, least necessary: Eid, Apple and Orange, Kwanzaa.

Postal stationery, best design: Badlands postal card, Lovebirds envelope, Baseball's Legendary Playing Fields cards.

Postal stationery, worst design: Federal Eagle envelope, Lovebirds envelope, Community Colleges envelope.

Postal stationery, most important: Community Colleges envelope, Baseball's Legendary Playing Fields cards, Federal Eagle envelope.

Postal stationery, least necessary: Porky Pig That's All Folks! card, Lovebirds envelope, Baseball's Legendary Playing Fields cards.

PLATE NUMBER COILS, SHEET, BOOKLET AND SELF-ADHESIVE STAMPS

Changes to the plate number listings that appeared in the 2000 *Linn's U.S. Stamp Year-book*, as well as all new listings, are shown in bold typeface.

Great Americans sheet stamps

Scott number	Stamp	Plate number	Perf type	Tagging type
1844	1¢ Dix	1 floating	bull's-eye	block
1844c	1¢ Dix	1, 2 floating	L perf	block
2168	1¢ Mitchell	1	bull's-eye	block
1845	2¢ Stravinsky	1, 2, 3, 4, 5, 6	electric-eye	overall
2169	2¢ Lyon	1, 2	bull's-eye	block
2169a	2¢ Lyon	3	bull's-eye	untagged
1846	3¢ Clay	1, 2	electric-eye	overall
2170	3¢ White	1, 2, 3	bull's-eye	block
2170a	3¢ White	4	bull's-eye	untagged[17]
1847	4¢ Schurz	1, 2, 3, 4	electric-eye	overall
2171	4¢ Flanagan	1	bull's-eye	block
2171a	4¢ Flanagan	1, 2	bull's-eye	untagged
1848	5¢ Buck	1, 2, 3, 4	electric-eye	overall
2172	5¢ Black	1, 2	bull's-eye	block
2173	5¢ Munoz	1	bull's-eye	overall
2173a	5¢ Munoz	2	bull's-eye	untagged
1849	6¢ Lippmann	1 floating	L perf	block
1850	7¢ Baldwin	1 floating	L perf	block
1851	8¢ Knox	3, 4, 5, 6	L perf	overall
1852	9¢ Thayer	1 floating	L perf	block
1853	10¢ Russell	1 floating	L perf	block
2175	10¢ Red Cloud	1	bull's-eye	block
2175a	10¢ Red Cloud	1, 2	bull's-eye	overall
2175c	10¢ Red Cloud	2	bull's-eye	prephosphored[17]
2175d	10¢ Red Cloud	2	bull's-eye	prephosphored[18]
1854	11¢ Partridge	2, 3, 4, 5	L perf	overall
1855	13¢ Crazy Horse	1, 2, 3, 4	electric-eye	overall
1856	14¢ Lewis	1 floating	L perf	block
2176	14¢ Howe	1, 2	bull's-eye	block
2177	15¢ Cody	1, 3	bull's-eye	block
2177a	15¢ Cody	2, 3	bull's-eye	overall
2177b	15¢ Cody	1	bull's-eye	prephosphored
1857	17¢ Carson	1, 2, 3, 4, 13, 14, 15, 16	electric-eye	overall

Scott number	Stamp	Plate number	Perf type	Tagging type
2178	17¢ Lockwood	1, 2	bull's-eye	block
1858	18¢ Mason	1, 2, 3, 4, 5, 6	electric-eye	overall
1859	19¢ Sequoyah	39529, 39530	electric-eye	overall
1860	20¢ Bunche	1, 2, 3, 4, 5, 6, 7, 8, 10, 11, 13	electric-eye	overall
1861	20¢ Gallaudet	1, 2, 5, 6, 8, 9	electric-eye	overall
1862	20¢ Truman	1 floating	L perf	block
1862a	20¢ Truman	2	bull's-eye	block
1862b	20¢ Truman	3	bull's-eye	overall
1862d	20¢ Truman	4	bull's-eye	prephosphored[18]
2179	20¢ Apgar	B1, B2, B3	bull's-eye	prephosphored
2180	21¢ Carlson	1	bull's-eye	block
1863	22¢ Audubon	1 floating	L perf	block
1863d	22¢ Audubon	3	bull's-eye	block
2181	23¢ Cassatt	1	bull's-eye	block
2181a	23¢ Cassatt	1, 2	bull's-eye	overall
2181b	23¢ Cassatt	2, 3	bull's-eye	prephosphored[19]
2182	25¢ London	1, 2	bull's-eye	block
2183	28¢ Sitting Bull	1	bull's-eye	block
2184	29¢ Warren	S1, S2 (six positions)	bull's-eye	prephosphored
2185	29¢ Jefferson	S1, S2 (six positions)	bull's-eye	prephosphored
1864	30¢ Laubach	1 floating	L perf	block
1864a	30¢ Laubach	2	bull's-eye	block
1864b	30¢ Laubach	2	bull's-eye	overall
2933	32¢ Hershey	B1, B2	bull's-eye	prephosphored
2934	32¢ Farley	B1	bull's-eye	prephosphored
2935	32¢ Luce	B1	bull's-eye	prephosphored
2936	32¢ Wallaces	P1	bull's-eye	prephosphored
1865	35¢ Drew	1, 2, 3, 4	electric-eye	overall
2186	35¢ Chavez	S1, S2 (six positions)	L perf	prephosphored
1866	37¢ Millikan	1, 2, 3, 4	electric-eye	overall
1867	39¢ Clark	1 floating	L perf	block
1867c	39¢ Clark	2	bull's-eye	block
1868	40¢ Gilbreth	1 floating	L perf	block
1868a	40¢ Gilbreth	2	bull's-eye	block
2187	40¢ Chennault	1	bull's-eye	overall
2187a	40¢ Chennault	2	bull's-eye	prephosphored[17]
2188	45¢ Cushing	1	bull's-eye	block
2188a	45¢ Cushing	1	bull's-eye	overall
2938	46¢ Benedict	1	bull's-eye	prephosphored

Scott number	Stamp	Plate number	Perf type	Tagging type
1869	50¢ Nimitz	1, 2, 3, 4	L perf	overall[18]
1869a	50¢ Nimitz	1, 2	bull's-eye	block
1869d	50¢ Nimitz	2, 3	bull's-eye	overall
1869e	50¢ Nimitz	3	bull's-eye	prephosphored[17]
2189	52¢ Humphrey	1, 2	bull's-eye	prephosphored[20]
2940	55¢ Hamilton	B1, B2, B3	bull's-eye	prephosphored
2941	55¢ J. Morrill	B1, B2	die-cut	prephosphored
2190	56¢ Harvard	1	bull's-eye	block
2191	65¢ Arnold	1	bull's-eye	block
2192	75¢ Willkie	1	bull's-eye	prephosphored[17]
2942	77¢ Breckinridge	B1, B2	die-cut	prephosphored
2943	78¢ Paul	B1, B2	bull's-eye	prephosphored
2193	$1 Revel	1	bull's-eye	block
2194	$1 Hopkins	1	bull's-eye	block
2194b	$1 Hopkins	1	bull's-eye	overall
2194d	$1 Hopkins	2	bull's-eye	prephosphored[17]
2195	$2 Bryan	2	bull's-eye	block
2196	$5 Bret Harte	1	bull's-eye	block
2196b	$5 Bret Harte	2	bull's-eye	prephosphored

Great Americans sheet stamps notes
17 Shiny gum and dull gum
18 Shiny gum
19 Plate number 3 shiny gum
20 Plate number 1 shiny and dull gum, plate number 2 shiny gum

General notes
Plate positions: Floating plate number positions are left or right, either blocks of six or strips of 20 (number must be centered in selvage in a block of six). All other plate number positions consist of upper left, upper right, lower left and lower right, with the following exceptions: 29¢ Warren, 29¢ Jefferson and 35¢ Chavez, which have positions of upper left, center upper right, upper right, lower left, center lower right and lower right. (Traditional corners have plate numbers to the side of the stamps; center positions have plate numbers above or below stamps.)

Tagging types
Block: tagging block centered over design of stamp; no tagging in selvage.
Overall: tagging applied to entire pane, often leaving an untagged strip at outer edge of large margin selvage.
Prephosphored: paper that has phosphorescent taggant applied to the paper by the paper supplier prior to printing. On some stamps, under shortwave UV light, the appearance of the phosphorescent tagging is smooth and even (surface taggant), while on others, the taggant appears mottled (embedded taggant). Examples that exhibit both are the 10¢ Red Cloud, 23¢ Cassatt, 40¢ Chennault, 52¢ Humphrey, 75¢ Willkie and $1 Hopkins from the Great Americans and the 23¢ Lunch Wagon, 29¢ Flag Over Mount Rushmore and the variable-denomination coil (Scott 31, 31a, 31b and 31c) from the plate number coils.

Transportation coil stamps

Scott number	Stamp	Plate number	Tagging type
1897	1¢ Omnibus (1983)	1, 2, 3, ,5, 6	overall
2225	1¢ Omnibus (1986)	1, 2	block
2225a	1¢ Omnibus (1991)	2, 3	untagged[2]
2225a	1¢ Omnibus (1997)	3	untagged[19]
1897A	2¢ Locomotive (1982)	2, 3, 4, 6, 8, 10	overall
2226	2¢ Locomotive (1987)	1	block
2226a	2¢ Locomotive (1993)	2	untagged
2226a	2¢ Locomotive (1997)	2	untagged[20]
1898	3¢ Handcar (1983)	1, 2, 3, 4	overall
2252	3¢ Conestoga Wagon (1988)	1	block
2252a	3¢ Conestoga Wagon (1992)	2, 3, 5, 6	untagged[15]
2123	3.4¢ School Bus (1985)	1, 2	overall
2123a	3.4¢ School Bus (1985)	1, 2	untagged
1898A	4¢ Stagecoach (1982)	1, 2, 3, 4, 5, 6	overall
1898Ab	4¢ Stagecoach (1982)	3, 4, 5, 6	untagged
2228	4¢ Stagecoach (1986)	1	block
2228a	4¢ Stagecoach (1990)	1	overall
2451	4¢ Steam Carriage (1991)	1	overall
2451b	4¢ Steam Carriage (1991)	1	untagged
2124	4.9¢ Buckboard (1985)	3, 4	overall
2124a	4.9¢ Buckboard (1985)	1, 2, 3, 4, 5, 6	untagged
1899	5¢ Motorcycle (1983)	1, 2, 3, 4	overall
2253	5¢ Milk Wagon (1987)	1	block
2452	5¢ Circus Wagon (1990)	1	overall
2452a	5¢ Circus Wagon (1991)	1, 2	untagged[33]
2452B	5¢ Circus Wagon (gravure) (1992)	A1, A2, A3	untagged
2452Bf	**5¢ Circus Wagon (gravure) (1992) A3**		**untagged[32]**
2452D	5¢ Circus Wagon (gravure) (1995)	S1, S2	untagged[12]
2452Dg	**5¢ Circus Wagon (gravure) (1995) S2**		**untagged[32]**
2453	5¢ Canoe (1991)	1, 2, 3	untagged
2454	5¢ Canoe (gravure) (1991)	S11	untagged
1900	5.2¢ Sleigh (1983)	1, 2, 3, 5	overall
1900a	5.2¢ Sleigh (1983)	1, 2, 3, 4, 5, 6	untagged
2254	5.3¢ Elevator (1988)	1	untagged
2125	5.5¢ Star Route Truck (1986)	1	block
2125a	5.5¢ Star Route Truck (1986)	1, 2	untagged
1901	5.9¢ Bicycle (1982)	3, 4	overall
1901a	5.9¢ Bicycle (1982)	3, 4, 5, 6	untagged

Scott number	Stamp	Plate number	Tagging type
2126	6¢ Tricycle (1985)	1	block
2126a	6¢ Tricycle (1985)	1, 2	untagged
2127	7.1¢ Tractor (1987)	1	block
2127a	7.1¢ Tractor (1987)	1	untagged[3]
2127b	7.1¢ Tractor (1989)	1	untagged[4]
1902	7.4¢ Baby Buggy (1984)	2	block
1902a	7.4¢ Buggy (1984)	2	untagged
2255	7.6¢ Carreta (1988)	1, 2, 3	untagged
2128	8.3¢ Ambulance (1985)	1, 2	overall
2128a	8.3¢ Ambulance (1985)	1, 2, 3, 4	untagged
2231	8.3¢ Ambulance (1986)	1, 2	untagged
2256	8.4¢ Wheel Chair (1988)	1, 2, 3	untagged
2129a	8.5¢ Tow Truck (1987)	1, 2	untagged
1903a	9.3¢ Mail Wagon (1981)	1, 2, 3, 4, 5, 6, 8	untagged
2129	8.5¢ Tow Truck (1987)	1	block
1903	9.3¢ Mail Wagon (1981)	1, 2, 3, 4, 5, 6	overall
2906	(10¢) Auto (1996)	S111	untagged[12]
2257	10¢ Canal Boat (1987)	1	block
2257a	10¢ Canal Boat (1991)	1	overall
2257b	10¢ Canal Boat (1992)	1, 2, 3, 4	prephosphored[1]
2257c	10¢ Canal Boat (1999)	5	prephosphored[25]
2457	10¢ Tractor Trailer (1991)	1	untagged
2458	10¢ Tractor Trailer (gravure) (1994)	11, 22	untagged
2130	10.1¢ Oil Wagon (1985)	1	block
2130a	10.1¢ Oil Wagon (1985)	1, 2	untagged[5]
2130a	10.1¢ Oil Wagon (1988)	2, 3	untagged[6]
1904a	10.9¢ Hansom Cab (1982)	1, 2, 3, 4	untagged
1904	10.9¢ Hansom Cab (1982)	1, 2	overall
1905	11¢ Caboose (1984)	1	block
1905a	11¢ Caboose (1984)	1	untagged[7]
1905a	11¢ Caboose (1991)	2	untagged
2131	11¢ Stutz Bearcat (1985)	1, 2, 3, 4	overall
2132	12¢ Stanley Steamer (1985)	1, 2	overall
2132a	12¢ Stanley Steamer (1985)	1, 2	untagged
2132b	12¢ Stanley Steamer (1987)	1	untagged
2133a	12.5¢ Pushcart (1985)	1, 2	untagged
2133	12.5¢ Pushcart (1985)	1, 2	block
2258	13¢ Patrol Wagon (1988)	1	untagged
2259	13.2¢ Coal Car (1988)	1, 2	untagged

Scott number	Stamp	Plate number	Tagging type
2134	14¢ Iceboat (1985)	1, 2, 3, 4	overall
2134b	14¢ Iceboat (1986)	2	block
2260	15¢ Tugboat (1988)	1, 2	block
2260a	15¢ Tugboat (1988)	2	overall
2261	16.7¢ Popcorn Wagon (1988)	1, 2	untagged
1906	17¢ Electric Auto (1981)	1, 2, 3, 4, 5, 6, 7	overall
1906a	17¢ Electric Auto (1981)	1, 2, 3, 4, 5, 6, 7	untagged
2135	17¢ Dog Sled (1986)	2	block
2262	17.5¢ Racing Car (1987)	1	block
2262a	17.5¢ Racing Car (1987)	1	untagged
1907	18¢ Surrey (1981)	1, 2, 3, 4, 5, 6, 7, 8, 9, 10, 11, 12, 13, 14, 15, 16, 17, 18	overall
1908	20¢ Fire Pumper (1981)	1, 2, 3, 4, 5, 6, 7, 8, 9, 10, 11, 12, 13, 14, 15, 16	overall
2263	20¢ Cable Car (1988)	1, 2	block
2263b	20¢ Cable Car (1990)	2	overall
2463	20¢ Cog Railway (1995)	1, 2	prephosphored
2264	20.5¢ Fire Engine (1988)	1	untagged
2265	21¢ Railroad Mail Car (1988)	1, 2	untagged
2464	23¢ Lunch Wagon (1991)	2, 3, 4, 5	prephosphored[17]
2266	24.1¢ Tandem Bicycle (1988)	1	untagged
2136	25¢ Bread Wagon (1986)	1, 2, 3, 4, 5	block
2466	32¢ Ferryboat (1995)	2, 3, 4, 5	prephosphored[13]
2468	$1 Seaplane (1990)	1	overall[28]
2468b	$1 Seaplane (1993)	3	prephosphored[1]
2468c	$1 Seaplane (1998)	3	prephosphored[19]

American Transportation coil stamps

Scott number	Stamp	Plate number	Tagging type
2905	(10¢) Auto (1995)	S111, S222, S333	untagged[12]
3229	(10¢) Green Bicycle (1998)	S111	untagged[23, 25]
3228	(10¢) Green Bicycle (1998)	111, 221, 222, 333, 344, 444, 555, 666, 777, 888, 999	untagged[21, 23, 24]

Special services self-adhesive panes

Scott number	Stamp	Denomination	Total value	Number of subjects	Date of issue	Plate numbers	Notes
3261	Shuttle Landing	$3.20	$64.00	20	11/9/98	B1111, B2222, B3333	15
3262	Shuttle Piggyback	$11.75	$235.00	20	11/19/98	B11111, B22222, B33333	15

Scott number	Stamp	Denomi- nation	Total value	Number of subjects	Date of issue	Plate numbers	Notes
3472	Capitol Dome	$3.50	$70.00	20	1/29/01	B1111, B2222	
3473	Washington Monument	$12.25	$245.00	20	1/29/01	B1111	

Regular issue 1982-85

Scott number	Stamp	Plate number	Tagging type
2005	20¢ Consumer Education (1982)	1, 2, 3, 4	overall
2150	21.1¢ Letters (1985)	111111, 111121	block
2150a	21.1¢ Letters (1985)	111111, 111121	untagged

National Symbols coil stamps

Scott number	Stamp	Plate number	Tagging type
2602	(10¢) Eagle & Shield (1991) "Bulk Rate USA"	A11111, A11112, A12213, A21112, A21113, A22112, A22113, A32333, A33333, A33334, A33335, A34424, A34426, A43324, A43325, A43326, A43334, A43335, A43426, A53335, A54444, A54445, A77777, A88888, A88889, A89999, A99998, A99999, A1010101010, A1011101010, A1011101011, A1011101012, A1110101010, A1110101011, A1110111110, A1111101010, A1111111010, A1211101010, A1411101010, A1411101011, A1412111110, A1412111111	untagged
2603	(10¢) Eagle & Shield "USA Bulk Rate" (1993)	11111, 22221, 22222, 33333, 44444	untagged[9]
2603b	(10¢) Eagle & Shield "USA Bulk Rate" (1993)	11111, 22221, 22222	tagged error
2604	(10¢) Eagle & Shield (gold) "USA Bulk Rate" (1993)	S11111, S22222	untagged[16]
2907	(10¢) Eagle & Shield (1996)	S11111	untagged[12]
3270	(10¢) Eagle & Shield "USA Presorted Std" (1998)	11111	untagged
3270a	(10¢) Eagle & Shield "USA Presorted Std" (1998)	22222	untagged
3271	(10¢) Eagle & Shield "USA Presorted Std" (1998)	11111, 22222	untagged[21, 22, 24]
3271a	(10¢) Eagle & Shield "USA Presorted Std" (1998)	33333	untagged[21, 22, 24]
3271b	(10¢) Eagle & Shield "Presorted Std"	11111	tagged error[21, 22, 24]
2149	18¢ Washington (1985)	1112, 3333	block
2149a	18¢ Washington (1985)	11121, 33333, 43444	untagged[10]

Scott number	Stamp	Plate number	Tagging type
3475	**21¢ Bison (2001)**	**V1111, V2222**	**prephosphored**
3263	22¢ Uncle Sam (1998)	1111	prephosphored[21]
3353	22¢ Uncle Sam (1999)	1111	prephosphored[21]
2606	23¢ USA Presort (1992) (dark blue)	A1111, A2222, A2232, A2233, A3333, A4364, A4443, A4444, A4453	untagged
2607	23¢ USA Presort (1992) (light blue)	1111	untagged[2]
2608	23¢ USA Presort (1993) (violet blue)	S111	untagged
3475A	**23¢ George Washington (2001)**	**B11**	**prephosphored**
3452	(34¢) Statue of Liberty (2000)	1111	prephosphored
3453	(34¢) Statue of Liberty (2000)	1111	prephosphored
3466	**34¢ Statue of Liberty (2001)**	**1111, 2222**	
3476	**34¢ Statue of Liberty (2001)**	**1111**	**prephosphored**
3477	**34¢ Statue of Liberty (2001)**	**1111, 2222, 3333, 4444, 5555, 6666, 7777**	**prephosphored**
3550	**34¢ United We Stand (2001)**	**1111, 2222, 3333**	**prephosphored**
3550A	**34¢ United We Stand (2001)**	**1111**	**prephosphored**

National Symbols panes

Scott number	Stamp	Denomi-nation	Total value	Number of subjects	Date of issue	Plate numbers	Notes
3482a	George Washington	20¢	$2.00	10	2/22/01	P1, P2, P3	
3483c/f	George Washington	20¢	$2.00	10	2/22/01	P1, P2, P3	
3484d	Bison	21¢	$2.10	10	2/22/01	P111111, P222222, P333333	
3484Ag/j	Bison	21¢	$2.10	10	2/22/01	P111111, P222222, P333333	
3468	Bison	21¢	$4.20	20	2/22/01	V1111, V1112, V2222	
3259	Uncle Sam	22¢	$4.40	20	11/9/98	S1111	15
3468A	George Washington	23¢	$4.60	20	9/20/01	B111	
2431a	Eagle & Shield	25¢	$4.50	18	11/10/89	A1111	1, 2, 3
2595a	Eagle & Shield	29¢	$4.93	17	9/25/92	B1111-1, B1111-2, B2222-1, B2222-2, B3333-1, B3333-3, B3434-1, B3434-3, B4344-1, B4344-3, B4444-1, B4444-3	3, 6, 7
2596a	Eagle & Shield	29¢	$4.93	17	9/25/92	D11111, D21221, D22322, D32322, D32332, D32342,	3, 6, 7

Scott number	Stamp	Denomination	Total value	Number of subjects	Date of issue	Plate numbers	Notes
2596a	Eagle & Shield (continued)					D42342, D43352, D43452, D43453, D54561, D54563, D54571, D54573, D54673, D61384, D65784	
2597a	Eagle & Shield	29¢	$4.93	17	9/25/92	S1111	3, 6, 7
2598a	Eagle	29¢	$5.22	18	2/4/94	M111, M112	5
2599a	Statue of Liberty	29¢	$5.22	18	6/24/94	D1111, D1212	5
3122a	Statue of Liberty	32¢	$6.40	20	2/1/97	V1111, V1211, V1311, V2122, V2222, V2311, V2331, V3233, V3333, V3513, V4532	13, 14, 16
3122E	Statue of Liberty	32¢	$6.40	20	2/1/97	V1111, V1211, V2122, V2222	14, 16, 18
3451a	Statue of Liberty	(34¢)	$6.80	20	12/15/00	V1111, V2222	
3549a	**United We Stand**	**34¢**	**$6.80**	**20**	**10/24/01**	**B1111, B2222, B3333, B4444**	
3471	**Art Deco Eagle**	**55¢**	**$11.00**	**20**	**2/22/01**	**S11111**	
3471A	**Art Deco Eagle**	**57¢**	**$11.40**	**20**	**9/20/01**	**S11111**	

Flag coil stamps

Scott number	Stamp	Plate number	Tagging type
1891	18¢ Sea to Shining Sea (1981)	1, 2, 3, 4, 5, 6, 7	block
1895	20¢ Flag Over Supreme Court (1981)	1, 2, 3, 4, 5, 6, 8, 9, 10, 12, 13, 14	block
1895e	20¢ Flag Over Supreme Court precanceled (1984)	14	untagged
2115	22¢ Flag Over Capitol Dome (1985)	1, 2, 3, 4, 5, 6, 7, 8, 10, 11, 12, 13,14, 15, 16, 17, 18, 19, 20, 21, 22	block
2115a	22¢ Flag Over Capitol Dome (1987)	T1	prephosphored
2605	23¢ Flag Presort (1991)	A111, A112, A122, A212, A222, A333	untagged
2280	25¢ Flag Over Yosemite (1988)	1, 2, 3, 4, 5, 7, 8, 9	block
2280	25¢ Flag Over Yosemite (1989)	1, 2, 3, 5, 6, 7, 8, 9, 10, 11, 12, 13, 14, 15	prephosphored
2523	29¢ Flag Over Mount Rushmore (1991)	1, 2, 3, 4, 5, 6, 7, 8, 9	prephosphored
2523A	29¢ Flag Over Mount Rushmore (1991) (gravure)	A111111, A222211	prephosphored
2609	29¢ Flag Over White House (1992)	1, 2, 3, 4, 5, 6, 7, 8, 9, 10, 11, 12, 13, 14, 15, 16, 18	prephosphored

Scott number	Stamp	Plate number	Tagging type
2913	32¢ Flag Over Porch (1995)	11111, 22221, 22222, 22322, 33333, 34333, 44444, 45444, 66646, 66666, 77767, 78767, 91161, 99969	prephosphored[14]
2914	32¢ Flag Over Porch (1995)	S11111	prephosphored[12]
2915	32¢ Flag Over Porch (1995)	V11111	prephosphored
2915A	32¢ Flag Over Porch (1996)	11111, 22222, 23222, 33333, 44444, 45444, 55555, 66666, 78777, 87888, 87898, 88888, 88898, 89878, 89888, 89898, 89899, 97898, 99899, 99999, 11111A, 13211A, 13231A, 13311A, 22222A, 33333A, 44444A, 55555A, 66666A, 77777A, 78777A, 88888A	prephosphored[1, 2]
2915B	32¢ Flag Over Porch (1996)	S11111	prephosphored[12]
2915C	32¢ Flag Over Porch (1996)	55555, 66666	prephosphored
2915D	32¢ Flag Over Porch (1997)	11111	prephosphored
3133	32¢ Flag Over Porch (1997)	M11111	prephosphored
3280	33¢ Flag Over City (1999)	1111, 2222	prephosphored
3280a	33¢ Flag Over City (1999)	3333	prephosphored
3281	33¢ Flag Over City (1999) (large date)	6666, 7777, 8888, 9999, 1111A, 2222A, 3333A, 4444A, 5555A, 6666A, 7777A, 8888A, 1111B, 2222B	prephosphored
3281c	33¢ Flag Over City (1999) (small date)	1111, 2222, 3333, 3433, 4443, 4444, 5555, 9999A	prephosphored
3282	33¢ Flag Over City (1999)	1111, 2222	prephosphored

Flag panes

Scott number	Stamp	Denomination	Total value	Number of subjects	Date of issue	Plate numbers	Notes
2920a	Flag Over Porch	32¢	$6.40	20	4/18/95	V12211, V12212, V12312, V12321, V12322, V12331, V13322, V13831, V13834, V13836, V22211, V23322, V23422, V23432, V23522, V34743, V34745, V36743, V42556, V45554, V56663, V56665, V56763, V57663, V65976, V78989	5, 9, 10, 11, 16
2920c	Flag Over Porch	32¢	$6.40	20	4/18/95	V11111	16
2920De	Flag Over Porch	32¢	$3.20	10	1/20/96	V11111, V12111, V23222, V31121, V32111, V32121, V44322, V44333, V44444,	10

Scott number	Stamp	Denomination	Total value	Number of subjects	Date of issue	Plate numbers	Notes
2920De	Flag Over Porch (continued)					V55555, V66666, V66886, V67886, V68886, V68896, V76989, V77666, V77668, V77766, V77776, V78698, V78886, V78896, V78898, V78986, V78989, V89999	
3278	Flag Over City	33¢	$6.60	15	2/25/99	V1111, V1211, V2222	14, 15
3278d	Flag Over City	33¢	$3.30	10	2/25/99	V1111, V1112, V1113, V2222, V2322, V2324, V3433, V3434, V3545	14
3278e	Flag Over City	33¢	$6.60	20	2/25/99	V1111, V1211, V2122, V2222, V2223, V3333, V4444, V8789	14, 16
3278Fg	Flag Over City	33¢	$6.60	20	2/25/99	V1111, V1131, V2222, V2223, V2227, V2243, V2323, V2423, V2443, V3333, V4444, V5428, V5445, V5446, V5576, V5578, V6423, V6456, V6546, V6556, V6575, V6576, V7567, V7663, V7667, V7676, V8789	14, 16
3449	Flag Over Farm	33¢	$6.60	20	12/15/00	P1111, P2222, P3333	
3469	**Flag Over Farm**	**34¢**	**$34.00**	**100**	**2/7/01**	**P1111, P2222**	
3470	**Flag Over Farm**	**34¢**	**$6.80**	**20**	**3/6/01**	**P1111, P2222, P3333, P4444, P5555**	

Nondenominated rate-change coil stamps

Scott number	Stamp	Plate number	Tagging type
2112	D (22¢) Eagle (1985)	1, 2	block
O139	D (22¢) Official (1985)	1	block
2279	E (25¢) Earth (1988)	1111, 1211, 1222, 2222	block
2518	F (29¢) Flower (1991)	1111, 1211, 1222, 2211, 2222	prephosphored
2893	G (5¢) Old Glory (1995) nonprofit	A11111, A21111	untagged
2888	G (25¢) Old Glory (1994) presort	S11111	prephosphored
2886	G (32¢) Old Glory (1994)	V11111	prephosphored
2889	G (32¢) Old Glory (1994)	1111, 2222	prephosphored
2890	G (32¢) Old Glory (1994)	A1111, A1112, A1113, A1211, A1212, A1222, A1311, A1313, A1314, A1324, A1417, A1433, A2211, A2212,	prephosphored

Scott number	Stamp	Plate number	Tagging type
2890	G (32¢) Old Glory (1994) (continued)	A2213, A2214, A2223, A2313, A3113, A3114, A3314, A3315, A3323, A3324, A3423, A3426, A3433, A3435, A3436, A4426, A4427, A4435, A5327, A5417, A5427, A5437	
2891	G (32¢) Old Glory (1994)	S1111	prephosphored[11]
2892	G (32¢) Old Glory (1994)	S1111, S2222	prephosphored
3264	H (33¢) Hat (1998)	1111, 3333, 3343, 3344, 3444	prephosphored[25, 26]
3265	H (33¢) Hat (1998)	1111, 1131, 1141, 2222, 3333	prephosphored[21]
3266	H (33¢) Hat (1998)	1111	prephosphored[21, 22, 23, 27]

Nondenominated rate-change panes

Scott number	Stamp	Denomi- nation	Total value	Number of subjects	Date of issue	Plate numbers	Notes
2886a	G	(32¢)	$5.76	18	12/13/94	V11111, V22222	5
3268a	H (Hat)	(33¢)	$3.30	10	11/9/98	V1111, V1211, V2211, V2222	
3268b	H (Hat)	(33¢)	$6.60	20	11/9/98	V1111, V1112, V1113, V1122, V1213, V1222, V2113, V2122, V2213, V2222, V2223	16

American Scenes coil stamps

Scott number	Stamp	Plate number	Tagging type
2902	(5¢) Butte (1995)	S111, S222, S333	untagged[12]
2902B	(5¢) Butte (1996)	S111	untagged[12]
2903	(5¢) Mountains (1996)	11111	untagged
2904	(5¢) Mountains (1996)	S111	untagged
2904A	(5¢) Mountains (1996)	V222222, V333323, V333333, V333342, V333343	untagged[12]
2904B	(5¢) Mountains (1997)	1111	untagged[11, 21, 23, 24]
3207	**(5¢) Wetlands (1998)**	**S1111**	**untagged**
3207A	(5¢) Wetlands (1998)	1111, 2222, 3333, 4444, 5555, **6666**	untagged[11, 21, 22, 23]

American Culture coil stamps

Scott number	Stamp	Plate number	Tagging type
3447	(10¢) Lion Statue (2000)	S11111, S22222	untagged
3520	**(10¢) Atlas Statue (2001)**	**B1111**	**untagged**
2908	(15¢) Tail Fin (1995)	11111	untagged
2909	(15¢) Tail Fin (1995)	S11111	untagged[12]
2910	(15¢) Tail Fin (1996)	S11111	untagged[12]

Scott number	Stamp	Plate number	Tagging type
3522	**(15¢) Woody Wagon (2001)**	**S11111**	**untagged**
2911	(25¢) Jukebox (1995) "Presorted First-Class"	111111, 212222, 222222, 33222	untagged
2912	(25¢) Jukebox (1995) "Presorted First-Class"	S11111, S22222	untagged[12]
2912A	(25¢) Jukebox (1997) "Presorted First-Class"	S11111, S22222	untagged[21, 22, 23, 24, 27]
2912B	(25¢) Jukebox (1997) "Presorted First-Class"	**111111, 222222**	untagged[21, 22, 23, 24, 27]
3132	(25¢) Jukebox (1997)	M11111	untagged
3208	(25¢) Diner (1998) "Presorted First-Class"	S11111	untagged[23, 25]
3208A	(25¢) Diner (1998) "Presorted First-Class"	11111, 22211, 22222, 33333, 44444, **55555**	prephosphored untagged[21, 22, 23, 24, 27]

Flora and Fauna coil stamps

Scott number	Stamp	Plate number	Tagging type
3044	1¢ Kestrel (1996)	1111	untagged[29]
3044	1¢ Kestrel (1996-99)	1111	untagged[30]
3044a	1¢ Kestrel (1999)	1111, 2222, **3333, 4444**	untagged[31]
3045	2¢ Woodpecker	11111, 22222	untagged
3053	20¢ Blue Jay (1996)	S1111	prephosphored
3055	20¢ Pheasant (1998)	1111, 2222	prephosphored[21]
2281	25¢ Honey Bee (1988)	1, 2	block
2525	29¢ Flower (1991)	S1111, S2222	prephosphored
2526	29¢ Flower (1992)	S2222	prephosphored
2480	29¢ Pine Cone (1993)	B1	prephosphored
2598	29¢ Eagle (1994)	111	prephosphored
2599	29¢ Statue of Liberty (1994)	D1111	prephosphored
2492	32¢ Pink Rose (1995)	S111	prephosphored
2495-95A	32¢ Peach/Pear (1995)	V11111	prephosphored
3054	32¢ Yellow Rose (1997)	1111, 1112, 1122, 2222, 2223, 2233, 2333, 3344, 3444, 4455, 5455, 5555, 5556, 5566, 5666, 6666, 6677, 6777, 7777, 8888	prephosphored[1, 2]
3302-05	33¢ Four Fruit Berries (1999)	B1111, B1112, B2211, B2221, B2222	prephosphored[1, 2]
3404-07	33¢ Four Fruit Berries (2000) linerless	G1111	prephosphored
3462-65	(34¢) Four Flowers	B1111	prephosphored
3478-81	**34¢ Four Flowers**	**B1111, B2111, B2122, B2211, B2222**	**prephosphored**

Flora and Fauna panes

Scott number	Stamp	Denomination	Total value	Number of subjects	Date of issue	Plate numbers	Notes
3031	Kestrel	1¢	$0.50	50	11/19/99	1111, 2222, 2322, 4444, 5555, 5655, 6666, 6766, 7777, 8888, 9999, 1111A, 2222A, 3222A, 3322A, 4322A, 4333A, 4433A, 5433A, 5544A, 5644A, 6755A, 6766A, 7777A, 8888A, 9999A, 1111B, 2222B, 3333B, 4444B, 5555B	15
3031A	Kestrel	1¢	$0.50	50	10/2000	B111111, B222222, B333333, B444444, B555555	
3048a	Blue Jay	20¢	$2.00	10	8/2/96	S1111, S2222	10, 14
3050a	Pheasant	20¢	$2.00	10	7/31/98	V1111, V2222, V2232, V2332, V2333, V2342, V2343, V3232, V3233, V3243, V3333	14
2489a	Red Squirrel	29¢	$5.22	18	6/25/93	D11111, D22211, D22221, D22222, D23133	3
2490a	Red Rose	29¢	$5.22	18	8/19/93	S111	3, 4
2491a	Pine Cone	29¢	$5.22	18	11/5/93	B1, B2, B3, B4, B5, B6, B7, B8, B9, B10, B11, B12, B13, B14, B15, B16	5
2492a	Pink Rose	32¢	$6.40	20	6/2/95	S111, S112, S333, S444, S555	5, 9, 10
2494a	Peach/Pear	32¢	$6.40	20	7/8/95	V11111, V11122, V11131, V11132, V11232, V12131, V12132, V12211, V12221, V12232, V22212, V22221, V22222, V33142, V33143, V33243, V33323, V33333, V33343, V33353, V33363, V33453, V44424, V44434, V44454, V45434, V45464, V54365, V54565, V55365, V55565	5, 9, 10
3127a	Botanical Prints	32¢	$6.40	20	3/3/97	S11111, S22222, S33333	14, 16
3052d	Coral Rose	33¢	$6.60	20	8/13/99	S111, S222	14, 16
3052Ef	Pink Coral Rose	33¢	$6.60	20	4/7/00	S111, S222, S333	14, 16
3297b	Fruit Berries (single sided)	33¢	$6.60	20	4/10/99	B1111, B1112, B2211, B2222, B3331, B3332, B3333, B4444, B5555	14, 16

Scott number	Stamp	Denomination	Total value	Number of subjects	Date of issue	Plate numbers	Notes
3297d	Fruit Berries (two sided)	33¢	$6.60	20	3/15/00	B1111	
3457e	Four Flowers	(34¢)	$6.80	20	12/15/00	S1111	
3461b	Four Flowers	(34¢)	$6.80	20	12/15/00	S1111	
3461c	Four Flowers	(34¢)	$6.80	20	12/15/00	S1111	
3490e	**Four Flowers**	**34¢**	**$6.80**	**20**	**2/7/01**	**S1111, S2222**	
3492b	**Apple & Orange**	**34¢**	**$6.80**	**20**	**3/6/01**	**B1111, B2222, B3333, B4444, B5555, B6666, B7777**	
3036	Red Fox	$1	$20.00	20	8/14/98	B1111, B3333	15

Regular issue coil stamps, 1991-94

Scott number	Stamp	Plate number	Tagging type
2529	19¢ Fishing Boat (1991)	A1111, A1112, A1212, A2424	prephosphored
2529a	19¢ Fishing Boat (1993)	A5555, A5556, A6667, A7667, A7679, A7766, A7779	prephosphored
2529c	19¢ Fishing Boat (1994)	S11	prephosphored

Holiday coil stamps

Scott number	Stamp	Plate number	Tagging type
2799-2802	29¢ Christmas Contemp. (1993)	V1111111	prephosphored
2813	29¢ Sunrise Love (1994)	B1	prephosphored
2873	29¢ Christmas Santa (1994)	V1111	prephosphored
3014-17	32¢ Santa/Children with Toys (1995)	V1111	prephosphored
3018	32¢ Midnight Angel (1995)	B1111	prephosphored

Holiday panes

Scott number	Stamp	Denomination	Total value	Number of subjects	Date of issue	Plate numbers	Notes
2802a	Christmas	29¢	$3.48	12	10/28/93	V111-1111, V222-1222, V222-2112, V222-2122, V222-2221, V222-2222, V333-3333	5
2813a	Sunrise Love	29¢	$5.22	18	1/27/94	B111-1, B111-2, B111-3, B111-4, B111-5, B121-5, B221-5, B222-4, B222-5, B222-6, B333-5, B333-7, B333-8, B333-9, B333-10, B333-11, B333-12, B333-14, B333-17, B334-11, B344-11, B344-12, B344-13, B434-10, B444-7,	5

Scott number	Stamp	Denomi-nation	Total value	Number of subjects	Date of issue	Plate numbers	Notes
2813a	Sunrise Love (continued)					B444-8, B444-9, B444-10, B444-13, B444-14, B444-15, B444-16, B444-17, B444-18, B444-19, B555-20, B555-21	
2873a	Christmas	29¢	$3.48	12	10/20/94	V1111	5
2949a	Love Cherub	(32¢)	$6.40	20	2/1/95	B1111-1, B2222-1, B2222-2, B3333-2	16
3011a	Santa/Children with Toys	32¢	$6.40	20	9/30/95	V1111, V1211, V1212, V3233, V3333, V4444	5, 16
3012a	Midnight Angel	32¢	$6.40	20	10/19/95	B1111, B2222, B33333	5, 10, 16
3030a	Love Cherub	32¢	$6.40	20	1/20/96	B1111-1, B1111-2, B2222-1, B2222-2	16
3112a	Madonna and Child	32¢	$6.40	20	11/1/96	1111-1, 1211-1, 2212-1, 2222-1, 2323-1, 3323-1, 3333-1, 3334-1, 4444-1, 5544-1, 5555-1, 5556-1, 5556-2, 5656-2, 6656-2, 6666-1, 6666-2, 6766-1, 7887-1, 7887-2, 7888-2, 7988-2	16
3116a	Family Scenes	32¢	$6.40	20	10/8/96	B1111, B2222, B3333	16
3118	Hanukkah	32¢	$6.40	20	10/22/96	V11111	15, 17
3123a	Love Swans	32¢	$6.40	20	2/4/97	B1111, B2222, B3333, B4444, B5555, B6666, B7777	16
3175	Kwanzaa	32¢	$16.00	50	10/22/97	V1111	15
3176a	Madonna and Child	32¢	$6.40	20	10/27/97	1111, 2222, 3333	14, 16
3177a	American Holly	32¢	$6.40	20	10/30/97	B1111, B2222, B3333	14, 16
3203	Cinco de Mayo	32¢	$6.40	20	4/16/98	S11111	15
3244a	Madonna and Child	32¢	$6.40	20	10/15/98	11111, 22222, 33333	16
3252a	Wreaths	32¢	$6.40	20	10/15/98	B111111	
3252b	Wreaths	32¢	$6.40	20	10/15/98	B111111, B222222, B333333, B444444, B555555	14, 16
3274a	Victorian Love	33¢	$6.60	20	1/28/99	V1111, V1112, V1117, V1118, V1211, V1212, V1213, V1233, V1313, V1314, V1333, V1334, V1335, V2123, V2221, V2222, V2223, V2324, V2424,	15

Scott number	Stamp	Denomination	Total value	Number of subjects	Date of issue	Plate numbers	Notes
3274a	Victorian Love (continued)					V2425, V2426, V3123, V3124, V3125, V3133, V3134,V3323, V3327, V3333, V3334, V3336, V4529, V4549, V5650	
33309	Cinco de Mayo	33¢	$6.60	20	4/27/99	B111111	15
3352	Hanukkah	33¢	$6.60	20	10/8/99	V11111	15
3355	Madonna and Child	33¢	$6.60	20	10/20/99	B1111, B2222, B3333	19
3359a	Deer	33¢	$6.60	20	10/20/99	B111111	14, 15
3363a	Deer	33¢	$6.60	20	10/20/99	B111111, B222222, B333333, B444444, B555555, B666666, B777777, B888888, B999999, B000000, BAAAAAA, BBBBBBB	14
3368	Kwanzaa	33¢	$6.60	20	10/29/99	V1111	15
3496a	**Rose and Love Letter**	**(34¢)**	**$6.80**	**20**	**1/19/01**	**B1111, B2222**	
3497a	**Rose and Love Letter**	**34¢**	**$6.80**	**20**	**2/14/01**	**B1111, B2222, B3333, B4444, B5555**	
532	**Eid**	**34¢**	**$6.80**	**20**	**9/1/01**	**V111**	
3536a	**Madonna and Child**	**34¢**	**$6.80**	**20**	**10/10/01**	**B1111**	
3537-40	**Four Santas**	**34¢**	**$6.80**	**20**	**10/10/01**	**S1111**	
3540d	**Four Santas**	**34¢**	**$6.80**	**20**	**10/10/01**	**S1111, S3333, S4444**	
3546	**We Give Thanks**	**34¢**	**$6.80**	**20**	**10/19/01**	**P1111, P2222**	
3547	**Hanukkah**	**34¢**	**$6.80**	**20**	**10/21/01**	**V11111**	
3548	**Kwanzaa**	**34¢**	**$6.80**	**20**	**10/21/01**	**V1111**	
960a	Love Cherub	55¢	$11.00	20	5/12/95	B1111-1, B2222-1	9, 16
3124a	Love Swans	55¢	$11.00	20	2/4/97	B1111, B2222, B3333, B4444	16
3275	Victorian Love	55¢	$11.00	20	1/28/99	B1111111, B2222222, B3333333	15
3499	**Rose and Love Letter**	**55¢**	**$11.00**	**20**	**2/14/01**	**B1111**	
3551	**Rose and Love Letter**	**57¢**	**$11.40**	**20**	**11/19/01**	**B11111**	

Distinguished Americans stamps

Scott number	Stamp	Denomination	Total value	Number of subjects	Date of issue	Plate numbers	Notes
3420	Joseph W. Stilwell	10¢	$2.00	20	8/24/00	B11-1	
3426	Claude Pepper	33¢	$6.60	20	9/7/00	B11-1	

Scott number	Stamp	Denomi-nation	Total value	Number of subjects	Date of issue	Plate numbers	Notes
3330	Billy Mitchell	55¢	$11.00	20	7/30/99	B11111, B11211	15
3431	**Hattie Caraway**	**76¢**	**$15.20**	**20**	**2/21/01**	**B11-1**	

Scenic American Landmarks panes

Scott number	Stamp	Denomi-nation	Total value	Number of subjects	Date of issue	Plate numbers	Notes
C134	Rio Grande	40¢	$8.00	20	7/30/99	V11111	15
C133	Niagara Falls	48¢	$9.60	20	5/12/00	V11111, V22111, V22222	15
C135	Grand Canyon	60¢	$12.00	20	1/20/00	B1111	
C138	**Acadia National Park**	**60¢**	**$12.00**	**20**	**5/30/01**	**B1111**	
C136	**Nine Mile Prairie**	**70¢**	**$14.00**	**20**	**3/6/01**	**P11111, P22222**	
C137	**Mount McKinley**	**80¢**	**$16.00**	**20**	**4/17/01**	**V11111**	

Official coil stamp

Scott number	Stamp	Plate number	Tagging type
O135	20¢ Official (1983)	1	block

Variable-denomination coil stamps

Scott number	Stamp	Plate number	Tagging type
CVP31 and CVP31a	variable-denomination coil (1992)	1	prephosphored[8]
CVP31b and CVP31c	variable-denomination coil (1994) (new font)	1	prephosphored[8]
CVP32	variable-denomination (1994)	A11	prephosphored
CVP33	variable-denomination (1996)	11	prephosphored

Test coil stamps

Scott number	Stamp	Plate number	Tagging type
Unassigned	**For Testing Purposes Only self-adhesive coil (1996) black on blue printing paper**	**1111**	**untagged[12, 18]**
Unassigned	**For Testing Purposes Only self-adhesive coil (1996) black on white**	**V1**	**untagged**
Unassigned	For Testing Purposes Only self-adhesive ATM booklet straight-line die cut	V1	untagged
Unassigned	For Testing Purposes Only self-adhesive ATM booklet serpentine die cut gauge 7.8	V1	untagged

Scott number	Stamp	Plate number	Tagging type
Unassigned	**For ATM Testing (blue temple)** **self-adhesive ATM booklet**	V1	**untagged**
Unassigned	Eagle Over Forest sheet (World Stamp Expo 2000)	S1111	untagged
Unassigned	Eagle linerless coil (1997)	1111	untagged
Unassigned	**NCR For ATM Testing** **paper ATM booklet**	**V1**	**untagged**
Unassigned	**For Testing Purposes Only** **self-adhesive ATM booklet** **magenta stamps/blue back cover**	**V1**	**untagged**
Unassigned	**29¢ red-rose paper ATM booklet**	**V1**	**untagged**

Automated teller machine (ATM) panes

Scott number	Stamp	Denomination	Total value	Number of subjects	Date of issue	Plate numbers	Notes
2475a	Stylized Flag	25¢	$3.00	12	5/18/90	—	
2522a	F	(29¢)	$3.48	12	1/22/91	—	
2531Ab	Liberty Torch (revised back)	29¢ 29¢	$5.22 $5.22	18 18	6/25/91 10/??/92	— —	8
2719a	Locomotive	29¢	$5.22	18	1/28/92	V11111	
2803a	Snowman	29¢	$5.22	18	10/28/93	V1111, V2222	
2874a	Cardinal	29¢	$5.22	18	10/20/94	V1111, V2222	
2887a	G	(32¢)	$5.76	18	12/13/97	—	
2919a	Flag Over Field	32¢	$5.76	18	3/17/95	V1111, V1311, V1433, V2111, V2222, V2322	
3013a	Children Sledding	32¢	$5.76	18	10/19/95	V1111	
3117a	Skaters	32¢	$5.76	18	10/8/96	V1111, V2111	
3269a	H	(33¢)	$5.94	18	11/9/98	V1111	
3283a	Flag Over Chalkboard	33¢	$5.94	18	5/13/99	V1111	
3450a	Flag Over Farm	(34¢)	**$6.12**	**18**	12/15/00	V1111	
3495a	**Flag Over Farm**	**34¢**	**$6.12**	**18**	**12/17/01**	**V1111**	

Plate number coil notes

1 *Shiny gum*
2 *Plate number 3 shiny and dull gum*
3 *Service inscribed in black "Nonprofit Org."*
4 *Service inscribed in black "Nonprofit Org. 5-Digit ZIP+4"*
5 *Service inscribed in black "Bulk Rate" (between two lines)*
6 *Service inscribed in red "Bulk Rate Carrier Route Sort"*
7 *Has two black precancel lines*
8 *Shiny gum and dull gum*
9 *22222 shiny and dull gum, 33333 dull gum*
10 *11121 shiny gum, 33333 and 43444 dull gum*
11 *Rolls of 3,000 and 10,000 have back numbers*

12 Has back numbers
13 2 and 4 shiny gum, 3, 4 and 5 low gloss and shiny gum
14 22221 shiny only and 11111, 22222 shiny and low gloss gum; others low-gloss gum only
15 2 dull gum, 3 dull and shiny gum, 6 shiny gum
16 S22222 has back numbers
17 Plate number 2 dull gum, 3 shiny dull, 4 shiny
18 Tagged paper printed with three layers of opaque white
19 3 low-gloss gum
20 Shiny gum, new white paper on 2¢ Locomotive
21 Die cut, equivalent to perf 10
22 Stamps spaced on backing paper
23 Back numbers, can be both top and bottom
24 Self-adhesive
25 Water-activated gum
26 Roll of 100, has shinier gum, plate numbers (1111) nearly touch "st-Cl" of "First-Class" on roll of 100, 1998 is ½mm farther to right of perforations as compared to roll of 3,000
27 Rounded corners (all four) are found only on spaced self-adhesive stamps
28 New white paper and shinier gum on $1 Seaplane with plate number 3
29 Process-color plate number digits ordered black, yellow, cyan and magenta
30 Process-color plate number digits ordered black, cyan, yellow and magenta
31 Process-color plate number digits ordered yellow, magenta, cyan and black
32 Luminescent ink
33 Plate number 1 dull gum, plate number 2 low-gloss gum

Notes for self-adhesive panes

1 Selling price was $5, which included a 50¢ surcharge. On September 7, 1990, the USPS announced it was sending 400,000 Eagle & Shield stamps to the U.S. Forces in the Persian Gulf Area. The selling price would be $4.50, thus eliminating the surcharge.
2 Plate numbers are in two positions, upper left and lower right.
3 Also available in coil format.
4 There are two different UPC bar codes on the back of the liner. The correct one is 16694. The other one, 16691, is the number for the African Violets booklet.
5 Also available in coil format with plate number.
6 When originally issued, the selling price was $5 (7¢ surcharge). The Postal Bulletin dated February 18, 1993, announced that beginning March 1, 1993, the new selling price would be $4.93, thus removing the surcharge.
7 The pane contains 17 stamps and one label the same size as the stamps.
8 Originally printed on prephosphored paper with and without a lacquer coating. When reissued with the revised back in October 1992, the panes were tagged on press (overall tagged). See Linn's Stamp News December 7, 1992, issue.
9 The Peach/Pear, Flag Over Porch, and the Pink Rose all have reorder labels in the lower right corner of the pane. To discourage the use of these labels as postage, later printings had a target and x die cut into the label. The Peach/Pear V12131, V33323 and V33333 exist both plain & die cut, while V33353 and higher numbers exist die cut only. The Flag Over Porch V23322 and V23422 exist both plain and die cut, while V12331, V13831, V13834, V13836, V23522, V34743, V34745, V36743, V42556, V45554, V56663, V56665, V56763, V57663, V65976 and V78989 exist die cut only. The Pink Rose S444 exists both plain and die cut while S555 exists die cut only. The 55¢ Love Cherub B2222-1 exists die cut only.
10 In 1996, to lower costs, USPS instructed printers that printing on the inside of the liners was no longer required. Several sheetlets that were originally issued with printed liners had unprinted liners on later releases. The following issues can be found with both printed and unprinted liners: 20¢ Blue Jay (S1111 and S2222 both ways); 32¢ Love Cherub (B2222-1 and B2222-2 both ways); 32¢ Pink Rose (S555 both ways); 32¢ Flag Over Porch (V23322, V23422, V42556 and V45554 both ways; V13831, V13834, V13836, V23522, V34745, V36743, V56663, V56763, V57663, V65976 and V78989 with unprinted liners only). The Flag Over Porch panes of 10 have unprinted liners on any panes with plate number V44322 or higher. The original Midnight Angel (B1111 and B2222) have printed liners while the reissue (B3333) has an unprinted liner.

11 *In 1997 the printing on the back of the pane was changed to "NATIONAL DOMESTIC VIOLENCE HOTLINE." The original inscription was "Stamps etc." Plate V34745 exists with both backings, while 36743, V56663, V56763, V57663 and V78989 exist only with the new backing. All other plates were printed with the original "Stamps etc." inscription.*

12 *There are three different back printings: "108th Tournament of Roses Parade," "Kids! Start Stampin!" and "Delivering the Gift of Life The National Marrow Donor Program." Both S1111 and S2222 are available with all three printings.*

13 *There are two different back printings: "Stamps etc." and "NATIONAL DOMESTIC VIOLENCE HOTLINE." Plate number V3333 exists with "Stamps etc." only; V1311, V2222, V2311, V2331, V3233, V3513 and V4532 are found with "NATIONAL DOMESTIC VIOLENCE HOTLINE" only. Plate numbers V1111, V1211 and V2122 can be found with both.*

14 *Also available in a folded version for vending-machine use: Blue Jay ($2.00), Ring-Necked Pheasant ($2.00), Yellow Rose ($4.80 and $9.60), Statue of Liberty ($4.80 and $9.60), Botanical Prints ($4.80) and American Holly ($4.80 and $9.60), Wreaths ($4.80), Flag Over City ($4.95), Fruit Berries ($4.95), Coral Rose ($4.95) and Deer ($4.95).*

15 *Each pane contains four plate numbers, in selvage adjacent to corner position stamps.*

16 *The pane contains 20 stamps and one label the same size as the stamps.*

17 *The reissue has a different style die cut in the backing paper than the original.*

18 *There are two different back printings: "Stamps etc." and "National Domestic Violence Hotline." Plate numbers V1111 and V2222 exist with "National Domestic Violence Hotline" only. Plate numbers V1211 and V2122 can be found with both.*

19 *Stamps are printed on both sides of the pane (single liner between them). Plate number is only present on one of two sides. Also includes a label identifying issue and the price of the pane.*

20 *Initially, the Breast Cancer semipostal stamp was valued at 32¢ for postage and 8¢ for cancer research. Effective with the 1999 rate change, this changed to 33¢ for postage and 7¢ for cancer research.*

21 *Exists with and without a special die cut for philatelic purposes.*

Booklets with plate numbers

Scott booklet number	Booklet	Scott pane number	Denomination	Plate numbers	Notes
137	$3.60 Animals	2 panes 1889a	18¢	1-16	1, 2
138	$1.20 Flag	1 pane 1893a	two 6¢ & six 18¢	1	
139	$1.20 Flag	1 pane 1896a	20¢	1	3, 4
140	$2 Flag	1 pane 1896b	20¢	1, 4	3, 4
140A	$4 Flag	2 panes 1896b	20¢	2, 3, 4	3, 4
140B	$28.05 Eagle	1 pane 1900a	$9.35	1111	2
142	$4 Sheep	2 panes 1949a	20¢	1-6, 9-12, 14-26, 28, 29	1, 2, 5
142a	$4 Sheep	2 panes 1949d	20¢	34	5
143	$4.40 D	2 panes 2113a	D (22¢)	1-4	5
144	$1.10 Flag	1 pane 2116a	22¢	1, 3	3
145	$2.20 Flag	2 panes 2116a	22¢	1, 3	
146	$4.40 Seashells	2 panes 2121a	22¢	1-3	
147	$4.40 Seashells	2 panes 2121a	22¢	1, 3, 5-8, 10	
148	$32.25 Eagle	1 pane 2122a	$10.75	11111	3
149	$32.25 Eagle	1 pane 2122a	$10.75	22222	
150	$5 London	2 panes 2182a	25¢	1, 2	6

Scott booklet number	Booklet	Scott pane number	Denomination	Plate numbers	Notes
151	$1.50 London	1 pane 2197a	25¢	1	
152	$3 London	1 pane 2197a	25¢	1	
153	$1.76 Stamp Collecting	1 pane 2201a	22¢	1	
154	$2.20 Fish	2 panes 2209a	22¢	11111, 22222	
155	$2.20 Special Occasions	1 pane 2274a	22¢	11111, 22222	
156	$4.40 Flag	1 pane 2276a	22¢	1111, 2122, 2222	6
157	$5 E	2 panes 2282a	E (25¢)	1111, 2122, 2222	
158	$5 Pheasant	2 panes 2283a	25¢	A1111	
159	$5 Pheasant	2 panes 2283c	25¢	A3111, A3222	
160	$5 Owl/Grosbeak	2 panes 2285b	25¢	1111, 1112, 1133, 1211, 1414, 1433, 1434, 1634, 1734, 2111, 2121, 2122, 2221, 2222, 2321, 2822, 3133, 3233, 3333, 3412, 3413, 3422, 3512, 3521, 4642, 4644, 4911, 4941, 5453, 5955	3
161	$3 Flag	2 panes 2285c	25¢	1111	
162	$4.40 Constitution	4 panes 2359a	22¢	1111, 1112	3
163	$4.40 Locomotive	4 panes 2366a	22¢	1, 2	6
164	$5 Classic Cars	4 panes 2385a	25¢	1	6
165	$3 Special Occasions 2396a/2398a	1 pane each	25¢	A1111	3, 6, 7
166	$5 Steamboat	4 panes 2409a	25¢	1, 2	7
167	$5 Madonna	2 panes 2427a	25¢	1	6, 7
168	$5 Sleigh	2 panes 2429a	25¢	1111, 2111	6, 7
169	$5 Love	2 panes 2441a	25¢	1211, 2111, 2211, 2222	6, 7
170	$3 Beach Umbrella	2 panes 2443a	15¢	111111, 221111	6, 7
171	$5 Lighthouse	4 panes 2474a	25¢	1, 2, 3, 4, 5	6, 7
172	$2 Bluejay	1 pane 2483a	20¢	S1111	7
173	$2.90 Wood Duck	1 pane 2484a	29¢	4444	7
174	$5.80 Wood Duck	2 panes 2484a	29¢	1111, 1211, 2222, 3221, 3222, 3331, 3333, 4444	7, 8
175	$5.80 Wood Duck	2 panes 2485a	29¢	K11111	7, 9
176	$2.95 African Violet	1 pane 2486a	29¢	K1111	7
177	$5.80 African Violet	2 panes 2486a	29¢	K1111	7
178	$6.40 Peach/Pear	2 panes 2488a	32¢	11111	6, 7
179	$5 Indian Headdress	2 panes 2505a	25¢	1, 2	7

Scott booklet number	Booklet	Scott pane number	Denomination	Plate numbers	Notes
180	$5 Madonna	2 panes 2514a	25¢	1	6, 7
181	$5 Christmas Tree	2 panes 2516a	25¢	1211	6, 7
182	$2.90 F	1 pane 2519a	F (29¢)	2222	6
183	$5.80 F	2 panes 2519a	F (29¢)	1111, 1222, 2111, 2121, 2212, 2222	6
184	$2.90 F	1 pane 2520a	F (29¢)	K1111	9
185	$5.80 Tulip	2 panes 2527a	29¢	K1111, K2222, K3333	7, 9
186	$2.90 Flag	1 pane 2528a	29¢	K11111	7, 9
186A	$2.90 Flag	1 pane 2528a	29¢	K11111	3, 9
187	$3.80 Balloon	1 pane 2530a	19¢	1111, 2222	7
188	$5.80 Love	1 pane 2536a	29¢	1111, 1112, 1212, 1113, 1123, 2223	6, 7
189	$5.80 Fishing Flies	4 panes 2549a	29¢	A11111, A22122, A22132, A22133, A23123, A23124, A23133, A23213, A31224, A32224, A32225, A33233, A33235, A44446, A45546, A45547	6, 7, 10
190	$5.80 Desert Storm/Shield	4 panes 2552a	29¢	A11111111, A11121111	7
191	$5.80 Comedians	2 panes 2566a	29¢	1, 2	7
192	$5.80 Space Explorations	2 panes 2577a	29¢	111111, 111112	7
193	$5.80 Madonna	2 panes 2578a	(29¢)	1	6, 7
194	$5.80 Santa Claus	4 panes 2581b-2585a	(29¢)	A11111, A12111	7
195	$2.90 Pledge	1 pane 2593a	29¢	1111, 2222	7
196	$5.80 Pledge	2 panes 2593a	29¢	1111, 1211, 2122, 2222	
197	$5.80 Pledge	2 panes 2593c	29¢	1111, 1211, 2122, 2222, 2232, 2333, 3333, 4444	6, 11
198	$2.90 Pledge	1 pane 2594a	29¢	K1111	7
199	$5.80 Pledge	2 panes 2594a	29¢	K1111	
201	$5.80 Hummingbirds	4 panes 2646a	29¢	A1111111, A2212112, A2212122, A2212222, A2222222	3, 7
202	$5.80 Animals	4 panes 2709a	29¢	K1111	7, 9
202A	$5.80 Madonna	2 panes 2710a	29¢	1	6, 7
203	$5.80 Christmas Contemporary	5 panes 2718a	29¢	A111111, A112211, A222222	7
204	$5.50 Rock 'n' Roll	2 panes 2737a & 1 pane 2737b	29¢	A11111, A13113, A22222, A44444	7
207	$5.80 Space Fantasy	4 panes 2745a	29¢	1111, 1211, 2222	7
208	$5.80 Flowers	4 panes 2746a	29¢	1, 2	6, 7

Scott booklet number	Booklet	Scott pane number	Denomination	Plate numbers	Notes
209	$5.80 Broadway Musicals	4 panes 2770a	29¢	A11111, A11121, A22222, A23232, A23233	7
210	$5.80 Country & Western	4 panes 2778a	29¢	A111111, A222222, A333323, A333333, A422222	7
211	$5.80 Madonna	5 panes 2790a	29¢	K1-11111, K1-33333, K1-44444, K2-22222, K2-55555, K2-66666	7, 10
212	$5.80 Christmas Contemporary	1 pane each 2798a, 2798b	29¢	111111, 222222	6, 7
213	$5.80 AIDS	4 panes 2806b	29¢	K111	7, 9
214	$5.80 Love	2 panes 2814a	29¢	A11111, A11311, A12111, A12112, A12211, A12212, A21222, A21311, A22122, A22222, A22322	7
215	$5.80 Flowers	4 panes 2833a	29¢	1, 2	6, 7
216	$5.80 Locomotives	4 panes 2847a	29¢	S11111	7
217	$5.80 Madonna	2 panes 2871b	29¢	1, 2	6, 7
218	$5.80 Stocking	1 pane 2872a	29¢	P11111, P22222, P33333, P44444	7
219	$3.20 G	1 pane 2881a	G (32¢)	1111	6
220	$3.20 G	1 pane 2883a	G (32¢)	1111, 2222	
221	$6.40 G	2 panes 2883a	G (32¢)	1111, 2222	
222	$6.40 G	2 panes 2884a	G (32¢)	A1111, A1211, A2222, A3333, A4444	3, 10
223	$6.40 G	2 panes 2885a	G (32¢)	K1111	9
225	$3.20 Flag Over Porch	1 pane 2916a	32¢	11111, 22222, 23222, 33332, 44444	6, 7
226	$6.40 Flag Over Porch	2 panes 2916a	32¢	11111, 22222, 23222, 33332, 44444	
227A	$4.80 Flag Over Porch	1 pane each 2921a, 2921b	32¢	11111	6, 7, 12
228	$6.40 Flag Over Porch	2 panes 2921a	32¢	11111, 13111, 21221, 22221, 22222, 44434, 44444, 55555, 55556, 66666, 77777, 88788, 88888, 99999	3, 6, 7
228A	$9.60 Flag Over Porch	3 panes 2921a	32¢	11111	6, 7, 12
229	$6.40 Love	2 panes 2959a	32¢	1	6, 7
230	$6.40 Lighthouses	4 panes 2973a	32¢	S11111	7
231	$6.40 Garden Flowers	4 panes 2997a	32¢	2	6, 7
232	$6.40 Madonna	2 panes 3003b	32¢	1	6, 7
233	$6.40 Santa/ Children with Toys	1 pane each 3007b & 3007c	32¢	P1111, P2222	7, 10

Scott booklet number	Booklet	Scott pane number	Denomination	Plate numbers	Notes
234	$6.40 Flowers	4 panes, 3029a	32¢	1	6, 7
237	$2.00 Blue Jay	1 pane each 3048b, 3048c	20¢	S1111	
241	$4.80 Yellow Rose	1 pane each 3049b-3049d	32¢	S1111	
242	$9.60 Yellow Rose	5 panes 3049d	32¢	S1111	
242A	$2.00 Ringed-Neck Pheasant	1 pane each 3051b, 3051c	20¢	V1111	
242B	$4.95 Coral Pink Rose	1 pane each 3052a-3052c	33¢	S111	
259	$4.80 Statue of Liberty	1 pane each 3122b-3122d	32¢	V1111	
260	$9.60 Statue of Liberty	5 panes of 3122d	32¢	V1111	
260A	$4.80 Statue of Liberty	5 panes of 3122Eg	32¢	V1111	
261	$4.80 Merian Botanical Plants	2 panes 3128b, 1 pane 3129b	32¢	S11111	
264	$4.80 American Holly	1 pane each 3177b-3177d	32¢	B1111	
265	$9.60 American Holly	5 panes of 3177d	32¢	B1111	
270	$4.80 Wreaths	1 pane each 3248a-3248c	32¢	B111111	
271	($6.60) H Hat	2 panes of 3267a	(33¢)	1111, 2222, 3333	
275	$4.95 Flag Over City	1 pane each 3278a-3278c	33¢	V1111, V1112, V1121, V1122, V1212, V2212	
276	$6.60 Flag Over City	2 panes of 3279a	33¢	1111, 1121	
276A	$4.95 Fruit Berries	1 pane each 3301a-3301c	33¢	B1111, B1112, B2212, B2221, B2222	
276B	$4.95 Deer	1 pane each 3367a-3367c	33¢	B111111, B222222	
280	($6.80) Statue of Liberty	2 panes each 3451b, 3451c	(34¢)	V1111	
281	($6.80) Four Flowers	1 pane each 3457c, 3457d, 2 panes of 3457b	(34¢)	S1111	
281A	**$2.00 George Washington**	**1 pane each 3482b, 3482c**	**20¢**	**P1, P2, P3**	
282	**$2.00 George Washington**	**1 pane each 3483a, 3483b**	**20¢**	**P1, P2, P3**	

Scott booklet number	Booklet	Scott pane number	Denom- ination	Plate numbers	Notes
282A	$2.00 George Washington	1 pane each 3483d, 3483e	20¢	P1, P2, P3	
282B	$2.10 Bison	1 pane each 3484b, 3484c	21¢	P11111, P33333	
282C	$2.10 Bison	1 pane each 3484Ae, 3484Af	21¢	P11111, P33333	
282D	$2.10 Bison	1 pane each 3484Ah, 3484Ai	21¢	P11111, P33333	
283	$6.80 Statue of Liberty	2 panes each 3485c, 3485d	34¢	V1111, V2212, V2222	
284	$6.80 Four Flowers	1pane each 2490c, 3490d, two panes 3490b	34¢	S1111	
284A	$6.80 Apple and Orange	1 pane each 3494c, 3494d, two 3494b	34¢	B1111	
285	$6.80 Rose and Love Letter	2 panes each 3498a, 3498b	34¢	B1111	
286	$6.80 Four Santas	1 pane each 3544c, 3544d, 2 panes 3544b	34¢	V1111	
287	$6.80 United We Stand	2 panes each 3549Bc, 3549Bd	34¢	S1111	

Notes for booklets with plate numbers.

1 Joint lines on some panes.
2 Electric-eye (EE) marks on tabs.
3 Cover varieties.
4 Panes available scored or unscored.
5 Plate number either on top or bottom pane.
6 Various markings on either the selvage or the panes themselves allow these panes to be plated by position.
7 Available as never-folded or never-bound panes.
8 Panes issued either overall tagged or on prephosphored paper.
9 Panes can be found with cutting lines on either stamp number 5 or 6 (vertically oriented panes) or stamp number 3 or 8 (horizontally oriented panes).
10 Each of the panes in these booklets can have different plate numbers on them.
11 Shiny and dull gum.
12 Pane 2921a has a 1997 year date.

No-hole panes

The following is a list of those panes that were officially issued by the U.S. Post Office Department and/or U.S. Postal Service as loose panes, i.e., not bound into a booklet and thus not having staple holes. Panes without staple holes can be found that aren't listed below. They aren't listed because they weren't officially issued without staple holes. The lack of staple holes can be caused by the following:

      1. Staples passing through the perf holes.
      2. Booklets assembled with one staple missing and the other passing through the perf holes or both staples missing.
      3. Staple holes at the top of a wide tab that have been trimmed off.

Scott number	Pane	Notes
1035a	3¢ Statue of Liberty (6)	
1036a	4¢ Lincoln (6)	
1213a	5¢ Washington (5 + Slogan 1)	
1278a	1¢ Jefferson (8)	
1278b	1¢ Jefferson (4+2 Labels)	
1280a	2¢ Wright (5+1 Slogan 4 or 5)	
1280c	2¢ Wright (6)	1
1284b	6¢ Roosevelt (8)	
1393a	6¢ Eisenhower (8)	2
1393b	6¢ Eisenhower (5+1 Slogan 4 or 5)	
1395a	8¢ Eisenhower (8)	2
1395b	8¢ Eisenhower (6)	
1395c	8¢ Eisenhower (4 + 1 each Slogans 6 & 7)	2
1395d	8¢ Eisenhower (7 + 1 Slogan 4 or 5)	2
1510b	10¢ Jefferson Memorial (5 + 1 Slogan 8)	
1510c	10¢ Jefferson Memorial (8)	2
1510d	10¢ Jefferson Memorial (6)	
C39a	6¢ Plane (6)	
C51a	7¢ Jet, blue (6)	
C60a	7¢ Jet, carmine (6)	
C64b	8¢ Jet over Capitol (5 + 1 Slogan 1)	
C72b	10¢ Stars (8)	
C78a	11¢ Jet (4 + 1 each Slogans 5 & 4)	
C79a	13¢ Letters (5 + 1 Slogan 8)	

Never-bound panes

By definition, a never-bound pane is one that was never assembled into a booklet. Loose panes such as Scott 1595a-d that were in booklets have small V-notches in the edge of the tab and traces of adhesive. The other panes in this category that were in booklets will have disturbed gum in the tabs showing that they were attached to either the booklet cover or each other.

Scott number	Pane	Plate number	Notes
1595a	13¢ Liberty Bell (6)		
1595b	13¢ Liberty Bell (7 + 1 Slogan 8)		2
1595c	13¢ Liberty Bell (8)		2
1595d	13¢ Liberty Bell (5 + 1 Slogan 9)		
2581b	(29¢) Santa Claus (4)	A11111	
2582a	(29¢) Santa Claus (4)	A11111	
2583a	(29¢) Santa Claus (4)	A11111	
2584a	(29¢) Santa Claus (4)	A11111	
2585a	(29¢) Santa Claus (4)	A11111	

Scott number	Pane	Plate number	Notes
2718a	29¢ Christmas Toys (4)	A111111, A112211, A222222	
2790a	29¢ Madonna (4)	K1-11111, K1-33333, K1-44444, K2-55555	

Never-folded panes

Scott number	Pane	Plate number	Notes
2398a	25¢ Special Occasions (6)	A1111	4
2409a	25¢ Steamboats (5)	1, 2	
2427a	25¢ Madonna (10)	1	4
2429a	25¢ Sleigh (10)	1	4
2441a	25¢ Love (10)	1211	4
2443a	15¢ Beach Umbrella (10)	111111	
2474a	25¢ Lighthouses (5)	1, 2, 3, 4, 5	3, 4
2483a	20¢ Bluejay	S1111	
2484a	29¢ Wood Duck (10)	1111	
2485a	29¢ Wood Duck (10)	K1111	5
2486a	29¢ African Violets (10)	K1111	
2488a	32¢ Fruits (10)	11111	4
2505a	25¢ Indian Headdress (10)	1, 2	
2514a	25¢ Madonna (10)	1	4
2516a	25¢ Christmas Tree (10)	1211	4
2527a	29¢ Tulip (10)	K1111	5
2528a	29¢ Flag w/Olympic Rings (10)	K11111	5
2530a	19¢ Balloons (10)	1111	
2536a	29¢ Love (10)	1111, 1112	4
2549a	29¢ Fishing Flies (5)	A11111, A22122, A23124, A23133, A23213, A32225, A33213, A33233	4
2552a	29¢ Desert Shield/Storm (5)	A11121111	
2566a	29¢ Comedians (10)	1	
2577a	29¢ Space Exploration (10)	111111	
2578a	(29¢) Madonna (10)	1	4
2593a	29¢ Pledge of Allegiance (10)	1111	
2594a	29¢ Pledge of Allegiance (10)	K1111	
2646a	29¢ Hummingbirds (5)	A1111111, A2212112, A2212122, A2212222, A2222222	
2709a	29¢ Animals (5)	K1111	5
2710a	29¢ Madonna (10)	1	4
2737a	29¢ Rock 'n' Roll (8)	A11111, A13113, A22222	6
2737b	29¢ Rock 'n' Roll (4)	A13113, A22222	
2745a	29¢ Space Fantasy (5)	1111, 1211, 2222	
2764a	29¢ Spring Garden Flowers (5)	1	4

Scott number	Pane	Plate number	Notes
2770a	29¢ Broadway Musicals (4)	A11111, A11121, A22222	
2778a	29¢ Country Music (4)	A222222	
2798a	29¢ Christmas Contemporary (10)	111111	4
2798b	29¢ Christmas Contemporary (10)	111111	4
2806b	29¢ AIDS (5)	K111	5
2814a	29¢ Love (10)	A11111	
2833a	29¢ Summer Garden Flowers (5)	2	4
2847a	29¢ Locomotives (5)	S11111	
2871b	29¢ Madonna (10)	1, 2	4
2872a	29¢ Stocking (20)	P11111, P22222, P33333, P44444	
2916a	32¢ Flag Over Porch (10)	11111	4
2921a	32¢ Flag Over Porch (10)	21221, 22221, 22222	4
2921a	32¢ Flag Over Porch (10)	11111	4, 7
2921b	32¢ Flag Over Porch (5 + 1 label)	11111	4
2949a	32¢ Love (10)	1	4
2973a	32¢ Lighthouses (5)	S11111	
2997a	32¢ Fall Garden Flowers (5)	2	4
3003b	32¢ Madonna (10)	1	4
3007b	32¢ Santa and Children (10)	P1111	
3007c	32¢ Santa and Children (10)	P1111	
3029a	32¢ Garden Flowers (5)	1	4

Notes for no-hole, never-bound and never-folded panes

1 **Shiny and dull gum.**
2 **Electric-eye (EE) marks on tabs.**
3 **Plate 1 panes available with and without scoring.**
4 **Various markings on either the selvage or the panes themselves allow these panes to be plated by position.**
5 **Panes can be found with cutting lines on either stamp 5 or 6 (vertically oriented panes) or stamp 3 or 8 (horizontally oriented panes).**
6 **Panes from A11111 have been found in 1993 Year sets only. They all had the bottom stamp removed and thus are panes of seven, not eight.**
7 **Has year date 1997.**